AMELIORATION AND EMPIRE

JEFFERSONIAN AMERICA

Jan Ellen Lewis, Peter S. Onuf, and

Andrew O'Shaughnessy, Editors

Amelioration and Empire

Progress and Slavery in the

Plantation Americas

CHRISTA DIERKSHEIDE

UNIVERSITY OF

VIRGINIA PRESS

CHARLOTTESVILLE

AND LONDON

University of Virginia Press

© 2014 by the Rector and Visitors of the University of Virginia

All rights reserved

Printed in the United States of America on acid-free paper

First published 2014

ISBN 978-0-8139-3621-5

9 8 7 6 5 4 3 2 1

Library of Congress Cataloging-in-Publication Data
is available from the Library of Congress.

Map following acknowledgments: Fernando Selma,
Carta general del Oceano Atlantico, 1804.
(Courtesy of the John Carter Brown Library, Brown University)

Cover art: Samuel Jennings, *Liberty Displaying the Arts and Sciences*, 1792.
(Courtesy of the Winterthur Museum)

MONTICELLO

Publication of this volume has been supported
by the Thomas Jefferson Foundation.

To M,
from C

CONTENTS

ACKNOWLEDGMENTS

Without question, this book must be dedicated to Peter Onuf. Without his patience, his uncanny skill as a "conceptualizer," or his genuine belief in my ideas and abilities, this project would have been half as good, if completed at all. I am deeply grateful for his continuing support and friendship; his scholarship and mentoring ability are the standard to which I will always aspire.

Financial support from a number of institutions gave me much needed space and time to research and write. The University of Virginia offered me a generous array of fellowships, allowing me to conduct research in distant archives. The John and Amy Griffin Foundation gave me the opportunity to implement several exciting transatlantic initiatives between UVa and Oxford. The Ruth and Lincoln Ekstrom Fellowship at the John Carter Brown Library allowed me to mine an unbelievable archive and meet a wonderful crew of fellow Atlanticists. And the Robert H. Smith International Center for Jefferson Studies offered me both a dissertation writing fellowship and the Gilder Lehrman Postdoctoral Fellowship, the latter of which enabled me to revise this project for publication.

I conducted research for this book in the United States, the United Kingdom, and the Caribbean, and benefited from the kind assistance of librarians and archivists in all of these places. I would like to extend my thanks to the helpful and knowledgeable staff members at the Special Collections Library at the University of Virginia, the Manuscript Division of the Library of Congress, the John Carter Brown Library at Brown University, the South Carolina Historical Society, the South Caroliniana Library at the University of South Carolina, the Southern Historical Collection at the University of North Carolina–Chapel Hill, the Perkins Library at Duke University, the Manuscript and Map divisions of the British Library, the National Archives at Kew, the Flintshire Record Office, the Gloucester Record Office, the National Library of Scotland, the Scottish Record Office, the National Library of Jamaica, and the Barbados Department of Archives and History.

A number of teachers and colleagues inspired and supported this project. My interest in comparative history and the Atlantic world began in a college class that I took with Richard Drayton about fifteen years ago; I am grateful for the guidance and encouragement that he and Dylan Penningroth gave me throughout my undergraduate years. As a graduate student at UVa, Louis Nelson, Maurie McInnis, Paul Halliday, Maya Jasanoff, and Ed Ayers always challenged me to sharpen my thinking and writing. Fellow students in Virginia's Early American Seminar always impressed and educated me, including Brian Murphy, Kate Pierce, Johann Neem, Brian Schoen, Leonard Sadosky, Rob Parkinson, Adam Jortner, Lawrence Hatter, Martin Öhman, Whitney Martinko, and Taylor Stoermer. I would also like to thank Jack P. Greene, Annette Gordon-Reed, Alan Taylor, David Konig, Max Edelson, Hannah Spahn, Frank Cogliano, Nicholas Onuf, Brian Steele, Simon Newman, and the late Naomi Wulf for enlightening conversations, sage advice, and moral support.

At Monticello, Susan Stein believed in me from the outset, hiring me for screenwriting and exhibition projects (despite my lack of experience) that challenged me to present "big ideas" to a lay audience. The Thomas Jefferson Foundation, headed by President Leslie Greene Bowman, graciously supported this book and its ideas. Andrew O'Shaughnessy has been an unwavering supporter and friend who gave me needed time to rethink and rewrite much of this book. He also gave me the job I love. I have benefited from the remarkable research and published work of Cinder Stanton and Bill Beiswanger, as well as the warm support and valuable perspective of Gaye Wilson. In the archaeology department, Fraser Neiman, Derek Wheeler, Beth Sawyer, and Jillian Galle have been invaluable resources and tremendous colleagues. My colleagues at Kenwood, including Mary Scott-Fleming, Aurelia Crawford, Mary Mason Williams, Tasha Stanton, and Kate Macdonald, have been patient and kind throughout this process.

Without the assistance and advice that I received from the University of Virginia Press, this book would have been a much weaker product. My editor, Dick Holway, has been a wonderful supporter for many years, and I appreciated his patience and guidance. Two anonymous editors for the press helped to transform this book and drastically improve its arguments. Ellen Satrom, Raennah Mitchell, Margaret Hogan, and other members of the press's team helped me to navigate the editorial process. Katie McKinney provided excellent copyediting assistance throughout this book; I am grateful for her keen eye and good humor. Wayne Dell gave expert assistance with permissions, for which I am deeply grateful. Any errors are entirely my own.

Anyone who spends a long time alone, researching and writing innumerable drafts, leans heavily on the support of family and friends. I am no different. Bryan Maxwell, Catherine Dunn, Todd and Janet Bertucci-

Lynch, Shawn and Michael Lipinski, Leah Stearns, Joey Tombs, James Covert, JD Ho, Elizabeth Chew, Jennifer Bedrosian, Kristin Onuf, Rachel and Zee Onuf, and Gabriele Rausse have all sustained me with their friendship, laughter, and generosity. I am also grateful to my family, especially my mother, who has always encouraged and supported my interest in writing history.

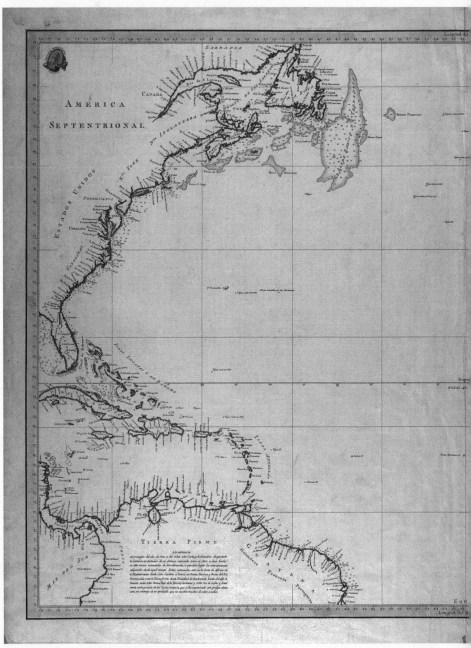

Fernando Selma, Carta general del Oceano Atlantico, 1804.
(Courtesy of the John Carter Brown Library, Brown University)

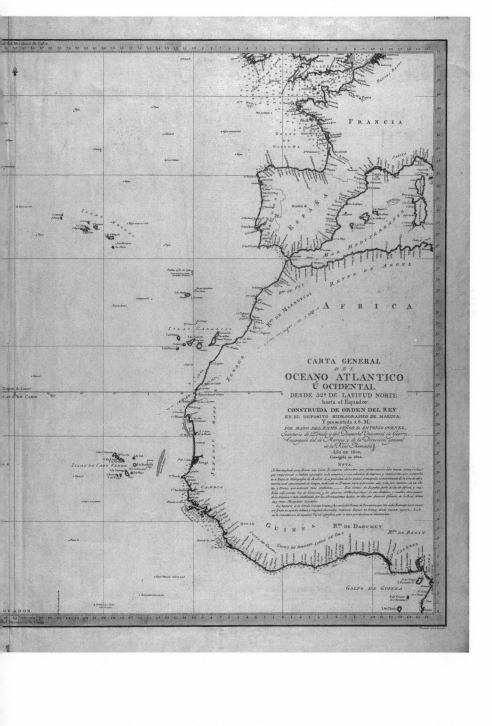

CARTA GENERAL
DEL
OCEANO ATLANTICO
Ú OCIDENTAL
DESDE 52º DE LATITUD NORTE
hasta el Equador.
CONSTRUIDA DE ORDEN DEL REY
EN EL DEPOSITO HIDROGRAFICO DE MARINA:
Y presentada á S. M.
POR MANO DEL EXMO. SEÑOR D. ANTONIO CORNEL,
Secretario de Estado y del Despacho Universal de Guerra,
Encargado del de Marina, y de la Direccion general
de la Real Armada,
AÑO DE 1800,
Corregida en 1804.

NOTA.

AMELIORATION AND EMPIRE

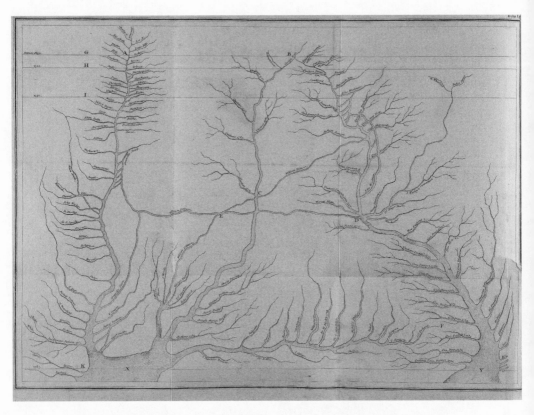

Thomas Clarkson, abolition map, from *The History of the Rise, Progress, and Accomplishment of the Abolition of the African Slave-Trade, by the British Parliament* (London: R. Taylor and Company, 1808). (Courtesy of Special Collections, University of Virginia, Charlottesville)

INTRODUCTION

From the bottom of the map flow two great rivers, and from those run dozens of tributaries next to which are written the names of Wilberforce, Franklin, Rush, Pinckney, and Jefferson. And two tributaries—those of Granville Sharp and the Pennsylvania Quaker William Dillwyn—connect the two great rivers. Sketched in 1808, this was Thomas Clarkson's map of the Anglo-American antislavery crusade, his teleological chronicle of the transatlantic movement that ended the slave trade.[1]

Clarkson's map, which stretched back hundreds of years and culminated in 1808, drew a literal connection between seemingly pro- and antislavery proponents of all stripes. The map linked enlightened slave owners, such as Thomas Jefferson and Thomas Pinckney, with avowed opponents of slavery like Sharp. So too were clergymen, from John Wesley to James Ramsay, connected to prominent political economists like Malachy Postlethwayt and Adam Smith. Clarkson wanted his readers to believe that, whether or not these figures had traded or owned slaves, they had each critically influenced the antislavery narrative that culminated in British abolition. For Clarkson's political purposes, abolition could be viewed as a much more powerful and important achievement if oppositional viewpoints—from Elizabeth I's slave-trade investments to the Pennsylvania Quakers' antislavery petition campaigns—were included in his history.[2] But even if Clarkson wanted his readers to think that the all-encompassing abolition movement had drawn even binary opposites into its vortex, the reality was that the luminaries identified on the map shared more likenesses than he was able to admit. Indeed, as the historian Philip D. Morgan has observed, "planters and abolitionists had more in common than is commonly assumed."[3]

What the Anglo-American planters, abolitionists, clergymen, and literary figures on Clarkson's map did share was a broad goal of gradual improvement, often known more specifically as "amelioration," in the eighteenth-century Atlantic world. Sometimes termed "gradualism" in the literature,[4] amelioration lay at the core of anti- and proslavery thought during the age of revolutions.[5] Often called "melioration" or "meliorism" before the later 1700s, the term, derived from the Latin "meliorare" and Old French "ameillorer," was defined as "to improve" or "to mitigate" suffering or ill will.[6] The process of—and capacity for—progress comprised the core of amelioration, a concept whose opposite was "degeneration." For Enlightenment thinkers who believed that all peoples shared a common nature and destiny, "amelioration" and "degeneration" represented opposite poles of the human condition. Abolitionists, American revolutionary patriots, and European *philosophes* believed that "God, who made the world, hath made of one blood all nations of men, and animated them with minds equally rational." This theory of the common origin of mankind suggested that the great task of the revolutionary age was to free man from the tyrannical forces—slavery, monarchy, and despotism—that had caused his degeneracy in order to effect his amelioration.[7]

How to ensure amelioration, particularly among slaves who had "degenerated" for centuries as a result of enslavement, posed a major question for both sides of the slave debate. Political alliances and interests tended to obscure this commonality, however. Abolitionists like Clarkson and others who opposed slavery defined their positions in opposition to those of planters and slave traders. But opponents and defenders were not the binary opposites that historians have so long supposed. Indeed, "by their commitment to improvement," planters "paradoxically found some compatibility with abolitionist aims." This compatibility meant that both sides endorsed gradual improvement schemes to mitigate and reform the slave trade and slavery. Those who opposed the trade believed that such amelioration would lead to the end of "inhumane" traffic and plantation slavery, while slavery's defenders thought that amelioration would lead to the entrenchment and perpetuation of the system. Thus, proslavery and antislavery thinking shared the same genesis but ultimately expected different outcomes.[8]

It is significant that most of the figures listed on Clarkson's map for the period of the later eighteenth century believed that slavery was incompatible with human progress. To them, the slave trade and the plantation slavery it spawned constituted an archaic system that retarded moral, economic, and political development in the Atlantic world. They imagined a world without slaves, a world in which legitimate commerce and free labor encouraged the perfection of mankind. To realize such a lofty goal, however, most religious and political thinkers believed that the transformation should be gradual rather than immediate. A sudden end to slavery was widely viewed as radical and dangerous, and gained little traction among many of the men who comprised Clarkson's narrative. Instead, believing the slave trade and slavery to be entirely codependent, many calculated that an end to the trade would gradually and naturally dislodge slavery's iron grip on New World plantation society and eventually end it. The premodern plantation world founded on slave trading and chattel slavery would be relinquished in favor of a more modern, expansive plantation world grounded in freedom. But despite the stark difference between these two worlds, it remained plausible that amelioration could undergird either one.[9]

Two seemingly opposite British political economists help to illustrate this point. Malachy Postlethwayt, the spokesman for the Royal African Company as a member of its Court of Assistants in the 1740s and 1750s, was no abolitionist.[10] He had published a number of pamphlets endorsing the African slave trade as the commercial bulwark that supported and sustained the British Empire. Abolish the trade, he feared, and other European nations, most notably France, would take over British commerce in Africa.[11] But despite the apparent necessity of perpetuating the trade, Postlethwayt did not so much endorse the commerce in human beings as commerce with Africa. To Postlethwayt, Africa was no marginal trading post; it was "one of the four principal parts of the world." Africa "stands . . . in the center, and has thereby much nearer communication with Europe, Asia, and America, than any other quarter has with the rest." He believed that "the country . . . is, and must be, capable of improvement, in all the nicest and most estimable productions, which the well cultivated world supplies us with, from other places in the same latitude." In other words, Africa was the gateway to global commerce; it was "capable" of civilized trade. What held Africa back from attaining this "improvement," Postlethwayt realized, was the African slave trade. The slave merchants traded in Africans, rather than in textiles, precious minerals, or agricultural products.[12] "What it affords in its present rude, unimproved state, is . . . merely for the use and benefit for the rest of the world, and not at all their own," he wrote. Thus, the "whole country was captive," which impeded expansion and connection to Atlantic markets.[13]

Adam Smith, often viewed as the darling of the antislavery cohort, criticized the artificial and baneful system of slave trading and slave owning in the British Atlantic world. At root, slavery inhibited commercial progress because the ownership of other human beings prevented slaves from exercising free will, which was, for Smith, the foundation of all free and independent economic activity. Labor for him was the primary means to ensure social progress; free labor, according to his calculations, was the only option that made economic sense, since slave labor was the "dearest of any" because slaves had "no other interest but to eat as much and to labour as little as possible." For the first time, Smith's thesis added an economic aspect to what had been abolitionists' purely moral arguments. In his discussion of the "culture of the sugar-cane," however, Smith unintentionally undercut the power of his assertions when he advocated the "improvement" of slaves on West Indian plantations. "The profit and success of that which is carried on by slaves," Smith wrote, "must depend equally upon the good management of those slaves." Through a policy of amelioration, humane masters might elevate their bondsmen to a status that rendered them almost equal to free laborers: "Gentle usage renders the slave not only more faithful, but more intelligent, and therefore, upon a double account, more useful. He approaches more to the condition of a free servant, and may possess some degree of integrity and attachment to his master's interest, virtues which frequently belong to free servants." Thus Smith, whose economic rationale for the universal superiority of free trade and free labor appeared to give grist to the abolitionists' mill, also inadvertently suggested that improvement might be wrought through slavery's continuation. And while Smith's free-trade principles differed from Postlethwayt's mercantilist tendencies, both political economists suggested that amelioration might better connect Africans and Africa to the market economy.[14]

Four years after Smith wrote his widely heralded masterpiece on laissez-faire ideology, the politician Edmund Burke, another luminary who claimed a tributary on Clarkson's map, drafted a plan to end the transatlantic slave trade and West Indian slavery. Although he did not circulate "Sketch of a Negro Code" until 1792, Burke's scheme astutely differentiated between "absolute and immediate abolition" and a "*gradual* abolition." In his view, immediate abolition would do little good; the "people like short methods" and the "consequences of which they sometimes have reason to repent of," he quipped. Viewing the slave trade and slavery as a single system, Burke argued in favor of ameliorating both, with the goal of ending them at a future time. "It is not that my plan does not lead to an extinction of the slave trade," he noted, but "it is through a very slow process." Burke's end goal, like Postlethwayt's, was to replace the slave trade with a more legitimate, civilizing commercial system. But what exactly would constitute the force that would ensure the "civilization and gradual manumission of

Negroes in the two hemispheres"? Burke trusted "infinitely more (according to the sound principles of those, who ever have at any time meliorated the state of mankind) to the effect and influence of religion" than he did in all of the British government's "regulations put together." Thus, for Burke, as for so many Anglicans and Quakers, religion would be the most effective ameliorator of slavery and the slave trade.[15]

Like Burke, many clergymen in Clarkson's own cohort advocated religion as the best means to ensure a gradual reform of slavery. James Ramsay, an Anglican clergyman who had served in the West Indies, was one of the most credible voices among the antislavery proponents. He saw Christianity as the ultimate ameliorator in the British West Indies, capable of ensuring the "humane treatment" of slaves. Christian principles, embraced by both masters and slaves, would help to assure the "gradual improvement of society" in the West Indies, and ensure a transition from "personal slavery" to a "voluntary compact of service and fidelity on one side, of wages and protection on the other." According to Ramsay, there could be no radical, immediate change; he could not "speak of the change of a bull into an horse, or of a swine into an elephant." Indeed, as he pointed out in an important passage, social change must always be gradual since the "annihilation of one is included in the transmutation of the other." Ramsay's emphasis on pragmatism and gradual change thus obscured the seemingly stark division between antislavery and proslavery forces.[16]

Although not listed on Clarkson's map, the former slave Olaudah Equiano, whose African name was Gustavus Vassa, lent significant authenticity to the British abolitionist movement with his bestselling autobiography. But his narrative, which was intended to trace his "conversion" from hapless slave to industrious Christian, also underscored his support of gradual improvement. In 1777, Equiano accompanied Dr. Charles Irving to the "Musquito shore"—present day Nicaragua—to establish an experimental plantation. They stopped first in Jamaica, where Equiano "went with the Doctor to board a Guinea-man" to "purchase some slaves to carry with us, and cultivate a plantation." Of the slaves that Equiano and Dr. Irving inspected, he "chose them all my own countrymen." Equiano then served as plantation manager of the slaves, trying to mitigate their condition as best he could. "I had always treated them with care and affection," Equiano declared, "and did every thing I could to comfort the poor creatures and render their condition easy."[17] Within the system of slavery, Equiano sought to ameliorate Irving's slaves, but he never once considered freeing them. And when he threw his support behind the Sierra Leone repatriation project of the late 1780s, Equiano echoed the goal of "improvement" that Postlethwayt had emphasized decades before: "A commercial intercourse with Africa, opens an inexhaustible Source of Wealth to the manufacturing interest of Great Britain: and to all which the Slave trade is a physical obstruction." For Equiano, the process of improvement and outcome of civilization ultimately eclipsed abolition.[18]

Clarkson made it clear from his map that the abolition of the transatlantic slave trade was a joint effort between Britain and America. Many of the American political leaders etched onto his "history" were slave owners, but they were nevertheless eager to rid the young United States of a system that they believed to be antithetical to human progress and inimical to nationhood. Antislavery amelioration was one way that revolutionary patriots attempted to elevate themselves from the depths of provincial semi-barbarism in a bid to join the civilized European states system.[19] Benjamin Franklin, who owned at least seven slaves in his lifetime, decried slavery as "an atrocious debasement of human nature" but nonetheless cautioned that "its very extirpation, if not performed with solicitous care, may sometimes open a source of serious evils." Franklin, described as a "cautious abolitionist," freed only one slave in his will but remained committed to improving the conditions of blacks in Philadelphia, which contained the largest concentration of urban slaves in the era of the American Revolution. He endorsed the opening of an Anglican school in 1758 to educate the slaves of Philadelphia masters. Franklin saw black education, which "imbued the minds of their [owners'] young slaves with good principles," as a way of improving slavery with an eye toward ending it. He even thought that the new school could serve as an "example" in the "other colonies, and encouraged by the inhabitants in general."[20]

John Jay, another revolutionary patriot and slaveholder listed on Clarkson's map, not only avidly supported an end to the slave trade and slavery in New York, but also endorsed education as the means to erode Americans' reliance on slavery. Jay advocated a gradualist scheme to end the practice of enslavement and elevate blacks' position in society. For instance, while he manumitted several of his own slaves, he did so on a conditional basis, and only after he deemed that they had been "improved" under his paternalistic supervision. "I purchase slaves and manumit them at proper ages and when their faithful services shall have afforded a reasonable retribution," he wrote in 1780. As governor of New York in 1799, Jay signed into law the Act for the Gradual Abolition of Slavery, which prohibited slave exports and granted freedom to all children born to slave parents after a period of indentured servitude. Freedom would only be bestowed after girls had served their mothers' owner for twenty-five years; the period of apprenticeship for boys would be twenty-eight years.[21]

Benjamin Rush, the prolific pamphleteer and widely renowned physician who also earned a place on Clarkson's map, advocated a similarly gradualist solution. He proposed to first "leave off importing slaves" and criminalize slave trading. Those slaves who were too old, disabled, or well-schooled in "all the low vices of slavery" and "unfit to be set at liberty" would live out their lives under the watchful eyes of their current masters. But for the younger slaves, Rush urged that they be "educated in the principles of virtue and religion—let them be taught to read, and write—and afterwards instructed in some business, whereby they may be able to maintain themselves." After some finite period of improvement, enslavement would end, entitling bondsmen "to all the privileges of free-born British subjects."[22]

The gradual abolition schemes mapped out by Franklin, Jay, and Rush provided moderate, pragmatic solutions to slavery and dovetailed with those of metropolitan British abolitionists. What was radical about these gradualist plans, however, was that they foresaw blacks remaining in American society after their eventual manumission; precious few American slave owners envisioned a biracial nation. In Virginia and the Carolinas, where enslaved blacks constituted a substantial portion (or majority) of the population, planters like Thomas Jefferson—who was listed alongside his distinguished northern colleagues on Clarkson's map—believed that mitigated slavery and emancipation *must* be followed by colonization to Africa or the West Indies.[23]

There were also those outside of Clarkson's narrative of Anglo-American abolition who profoundly influenced these men's antislavery views. Jefferson's ideas about slavery in the new American nation, for example, were guided by those of the Marquis de Condorcet, whose antislavery scheme Jefferson translated and integrated into his own ameliorative plan to end slavery. Clarkson sought to forge antislavery alliances in France during the 1780s and early 1790s, and ameliorative measures formed the backbone of many plans circulated within the Amis des Noirs, particularly by Condorcet, Jacques-Pierre Brissot de Warville, the Baron Lescallier, and the Abbé de Gregoire. Condorcet argued that slavery was both immoral and criminal since it was an act of theft in which a slave's right to ownership of his person was denied. But he reasoned that immediate emancipation would provoke a deadly slave rebellion and be viewed by slave owners as the nonconsensual removal of their valuable human property. Condorcet instead proposed an end to slavery "par degres"— an immediate suspension of the transatlantic slave trade, the immediate emancipation of all plantation-born mulatto children and plantation-born African slaves over the age of thirty-five, and an interim period of gradual "improvement" that would culminate in total abolition. He proposed laws "most certain to destroy slavery gradually, and ameliorate it while it lasts." As such, "laws like these might be capable, not of legitimizing slavery, but of making it less barbarous, and more compatible, if not with justice, at least with humanity." Not all French opponents of slavery agreed with the details of Condorcet's plan, but his ability to marry Enlightenment principles of human freedom and perfectibility with a pragmatic approach to the "problem" of slavery resonated with many of Clarkson's figures.[24]

Although Spanish officials were famously silent on the question of abolition in the late eighteenth century, many of the ameliorative slave codes in the Spanish colonies influenced the gradualist schemes of British critics of slavery. The colonial practice of *coartación*, which meant that a slave who was hired out or farmed a small plot of land might be able to purchase his own freedom, was of particular interest to early British opponents of slavery. Granville Sharp and Beilby Porteus, two of the most radical early reformers, lauded it as a "considerable step towards abolishing absolute slavery."[25] Of course, the Spanish slave code allowing for slaves' gradual self-purchase was in reality a plan to perpetuate and strengthen the colonial slave system, not abolish it.

A minority of Spanish antislavery reformers, including Isidoro Antillón and José Blanco White, however, attempted to direct Spanish amelioration toward a new goal: the end of the slave trade and slavery. Antillón, who was influenced by Clarkson's works, argued that Spanish colonial planters should "make the yoke of slavery more gentle" in a gradualist approach to the end of slavery. To help end the institution, Antillón suggested that Spanish planters turn to Native Americans as a source of labor and that they import goods, not slaves, from Africa.[26] Another Spanish pamphleteer and journalist, José Blanco White, translated William Wilberforce's treatises on the slave trade and offered his own analysis to a Spanish audience. White was convinced that the end of the slave trade would promote ameliorated conditions for slaves in colonial Spanish possessions, and thus pave the way for the end of slavery.[27] Although the institution was not abolished in the Spanish empire until 1886, the fact that both proslavery Spanish officials and antislavery critics embraced ameliorative strategies underscored the power and pervasiveness of a concept that went far beyond the Anglo-American confines of Clarkson's map.[28]

Thus, even though the map was intended to trace the trajectory of the abolition of the slave trade, it would be more accurate to view his diagram as the rise of ameliorative strategies to end slavery. The majority of figures he highlighted believed that the abolition of the slave trade was the most expedient way of ensuring a gradual end to New World slavery. Likely influenced by the incremental abolition of European serfdom, a process that took nearly three centuries, leading figures in Clarkson's "history" agreed that immediate social change would prove disastrous. Believing that plantation slavery was an archaic system sustained only through the transatlantic slave trade, opponents of the commerce reasoned that ending the trade would initiate the mitigation of slavery and its gradual end in the Americas. In 1804, Henry Brougham predicted that the abolition of the slave trade would put an end to "further interference" in the "concerns" of West Indian planters. "Few will continue so insane as to maltreat their stock [slaves]," he wrote, "when they can no longer fill up the blanks occasioned by their cruelty." Brougham prophesized that "in a very few years all the Negroes in the West Indies will be Creoles, and all the masters will treat them with kind indulgence." Brougham, like Clarkson and many of the figures on the map, assumed that New World slavery was a premodern system antithetical to human progress and artificially supported by the transatlantic slave trade.[29]

Few of Clarkson's luminaries predicted that amelioration could achieve an opposite goal—the perpetuation of the slave trade and plantation slavery. They assumed that the path to modernity in the revolutionary age was singular—it would result in the free and equal status of all nations in the Atlantic littoral committed to the improvement of mankind. And yet, the admission that both the slave trade and slavery were capable of being ameliorated dealt an enormous blow to such an idealized and prescriptive vision. If many planters, slave traders, and conservative politicians were able to argue that the slave trade and slavery were "improvable" systems, then radical calls for abolition and emancipation appeared moot. These traders and planters, of course, held a much different view of the path to modernity, one in which universal freedom posed a significant threat to human progress.[30]

Still, both supporters and opponents of slavery and the slave trade held remarkably similar visions for future colonization projects in the unsettled temperate zones of the Atlantic world. Both cohorts imagined a plantation empire that expanded across the Americas and Africa. For critics of slavery, it would be an empire without slaves; only with abolition would "amelioration" be unleashed to ensure the progress of humankind through free trade and free labor. In Africa, for instance, critics of the slave trade imagined a free labor plantation network "centered on agricultural exports" such as cotton. But for defenders of slavery, there would be an empire of slaves, with the crucial institution of slavery ensuring settlement and progress in new areas. Amelioration thus undergirded both pro- and antislavery colonization projects: the creation and expansion of new plantation empires and the "improvement" of provincial societies from barbarism to successive levels of refinement.[31]

AMELIORATION
Planters' Vision of the Modern World

This book is a cultural history of the concept of amelioration in Anglo-American slave societies during the age of revolutions. Scholars often depict provincial slave owners in plantation America as either backward reactionaries or freedom-loving hypocrites who reluctantly and belatedly came to embrace democracy's promise with the abolition of slavery. Instead, my book argues that "enlightened" planters in the British Caribbean and the American South were modern and cosmopolitan men who believed that gradual progress and mitigated slavery, rather than radical revolution and liberty, fueled the social and political development of the new American nation and the British Empire. These thinkers argued for a powerful alternative vision of progress in the Atlantic world—that "amelioration" and "happiness" constituted modernity and would prove the best means of driving the advancement and expansion of slave societies. Using a transnational approach that focuses on provincial planters rather than metropolitan abolitionists, this book recasts our understanding of slavery in the Anglophone Atlantic world in several ways. First, amelioration undergirded the seemingly binary opposites of proslavery and antislavery thought; planters could ameliorate slavery with the future goal of ending it *or* they could ameliorate slavery in order to strengthen and perpetuate the institution. Second, this book dispenses with the usual teleological genealogy of proslavery thinking from a so-called "necessary evil" to a "positive good." Instead, I show that proslavery and antislavery ideas were not simply confined to questions of morality or the master-slave relationship; rather, these two strains of thought provided the foundation for nation-building and colonization efforts in the Anglophone world. This book—which takes as a given that slavery was an inherently violent and coercive system—seeks to answer not why slave owners were too backward or corrupt to embrace abolition and natural rights, but rather how the gradual improvement of the slave trade and slavery could recast these institutions as modern, "natural," and civilizing systems, which allowed them to be perpetuated in the Americas well into the nineteenth century.[32]

At its heart, amelioration enabled provincial slave owners to reconcile the Enlightenment ideals of the era—equal nations, human rights, and the end of barbarism—with the realities of how social change could, and could not, be accomplished. It was meant to be a pragmatic approach to the intractable problem of slavery. A key idea of this book is that amelioration was a pervasive and legitimate form of intellectual thought predicated on a view of social development that began in the perfectionist tone of the Enlightenment but changed after the age of revolutions in order to accommodate newer, less idealized visions of the modern world in the nineteenth century. The great appeal and logic of amelioration was as an alternative to the jarring, disruptive social change of the French and Haitian revolutions; these revolutionary movements, especially to Anglo-American slave owners, demonstrated how the obliteration of racial and social hierarchies could also potentially obliterate entire societies. This hazardous "immediatism" seemed to be a relic of Old World despotic regimes; the New World plantation societies, with their emphasis on "newness" and exceptionalism, embraced amelioration as a more enlightened alternative. Gradual improvement thus became a practical solution that garnered wide appeal as members of slave societies began to argue that they should try to contend with the populations they had, not the ones they might wish, and shape the social order in terms of such demographic realities.[33]

As adherents to metropolitan Enlightenment doctrine, U.S. revolutionaries, British moral reformers, and French *philosophes* believed that man could be perfected in idealized, homogenous societies. As Condorcet famously stated in his treatise on human perfectibility, "Our hopes, as to the future condition of the human species" were the "destruction of inequality between nations," the "progress of equality in one and the same nation," and the "real improvement of man."[34] Slavery became a problem for these idealists, not least because enslavement, as the denial of personhood, prevented individuals from having the freedom and the capacity to perfect themselves. Slavery, which they defined in Lockean terms as a "state of war," was an inherently unnatural and inimical relationship that impeded advancement, both for the master and the slave. Furthermore, the presence of "foreign" African slaves prevented the development of "natural" and homogenous societies that were both progressive and modern. Thus, many of these thinkers proposed ending the slave trade and slavery, and "repatriating" enslaved blacks back to their own "country" in Africa. In their "natural" society, newly freed Africans would likely be able to pursue their own improvement project. These idealists did recognize that the cards were stacked against them: provincial whites conditioned to accept and embrace slavery as normative, and blacks "degraded" morally and physically by centuries of enslavement, did not bode well for the success of the plan. Still, the experiment in nationhood that was unfolding throughout the Atlantic world depended upon the equality of "races" and "nations"—two terms that were interchangeable in the eighteenth century. As a result, enlightened thinkers came to believe that amelioration would help to realize their goal of perfectible, homogenous, and equal societies.[35]

This formulation was turned on its head in the nineteenth century, when a pragmatic approach to social change trumped an idealistic one. A series of slave rebellions in the Caribbean, most notably in Saint Domingue, as well as the violence that erupted during the French Terror, convinced many Anglo-American provincials that the expansion of individual rights, which eighteenth-century enlightened thinkers had thought possible and necessary, seemed dangerous and inexpedient. But while the end goal of freeing and relocating entire populations appeared more like a dangerous fantasy, the means to achieving such a goal—amelioration—presented a much more realistic way to contend with the "problem" of slavery in the plantation Americas. Amelioration thus became both the means and end for many Anglo-American slave owners in the nineteenth century.[36]

Slave owners throughout the Anglophone Atlantic world embraced the concept of amelioration as a way to deal with multiracial societies and envision one in which broadening rights and privileges for whites could continue to coexist with racial subjugation. Planters sought to maintain the equality of slaveholders—white property owners—but did not wish to extend individual so-called natural rights to dependents, including women and slaves. In the revolutionary age, the equality principle gained traction only at the corporate level; natural-rights arguments threatened to destroy the social order rather than "ameliorate" it. An emphasis on the equality of property owners was based on the legitimate, early modern view of society as a hierarchical order composed of "independent" property owners and their propertyless "dependents." But although property owners could claim it was their "right" to own slaves—just as it was their "right" to own land—such an exercise of power did not come without attendant moral obligations and social sanctions. Slave owners had a moral duty to ensure that slaves were well treated, but this was done with an eye toward preserving their subordination. The end goal of amelioration was to broaden and protect the "rights" and equality of slaveholding patriarchs. Whites functioned as the "agents" of improvement, while blacks' own agency and individuality was ignored and marginalized; they were the coerced subjects of whites' amelioration schemes. Anglo-American slave owners thus embraced amelioration as the means to guarantee the success of their vision of a progressive society: an ever-expanding network of plantation households governed by equal planter-patriarchs who exerted mastery over dependent slaves. This network of plantation "households" constituted the basis of a profitable and expansive empire that stretched across the American South and Caribbean.[37]

INTERPRETATIONS OF AMELIORATION

In his landmark study of early America, Edmund Morgan first suggested that "freedom" and "slavery" were not the polar opposites that many historians had previously imagined. Morgan's work identified the unique "paradox" in American history—that the "rise of liberty and equality in America had been accompanied by the rise of slavery." By the end of the eighteenth century, Virginians had established the "conditions for the mixture of slavery and racism that was to prevail for at least another century"—a society in which "most of the poor were enslaved," and white slaveholders and nonslaveholders shared a mutual interest in maintaining and safeguarding private property "rights," especially the ownership of slaves. Although Morgan's example was confined to America, his most important contribution was to demonstrate that freedom and slavery were inextricably linked at America's founding, and that these two concepts ultimately shared the same genesis. This book's goal, like Morgan's, is to show how New World freedom and slavery could emerge and evolve in tandem under the rubric of amelioration.[38]

Few scholars have bucked Morgan's exceptionalist paradigm in an effort to demonstrate why freedom and slavery were so closely aligned in New World slave societies. But David Brion Davis has pointed out that gradual improvement, or amelioration, was the lynchpin of the Anglo-American debate over slavery and the slave trade during the age of revolutions.

Davis notes that the "theory of incremental social progress" was widely embraced by contemporaries; the precedent for slave emancipation in Europe was the gradual liberation of white slaves and serfs. Any reform of the system of slavery ultimately "depended on a process of progressive amelioration carried out by the slaveholders themselves," since planters alone could "improve" their private property in slaves.[39] This book is the provincial counterpart to Davis's metropolitan study. While he concentrates primarily on British politicians, abolitionists, and political economists, this study's focus centers on slaveholders in the American South and the British Caribbean, many of whom believed that they were carrying out the "progressive amelioration" of their slaves. Moreover, this book shows that while these slaveholders shared a common commitment to amelioration, they deployed it toward radically different ends—the end of slavery or its entrenchment and expansion.

Davis may have highlighted the importance of amelioration to metropolitan debates over slavery, but it is Winthrop Jordan who insightfully notes that amelioration had profound implications for the continuation or cessation of slavery in the Americas. He observes the "supreme irony" in the early American South that while "punishments were indeed becoming less harsh and familial relations less subject to arbitrary disruption," these "humanitarian victories" left slavery "more firmly entrenched than ever." Indeed, by eliminating "inhumane treatment, the humanitarian impulse helped make slavery more benevolent and paternal and hence more tolerable for the slaveowner and even for the abolitionist." But in the British West Indies, where slavery was never mitigated, the system "helped doom itself by its notorious cruelty." Jordan's observation is central to this book, which shows that the success of antebellum southern planters' amelioration projects reversed the founders' prescriptive plans to end slavery while also undermining and marginalizing abolitionism in America. But in the West Indies, where slavery was never adequately "improved" and mortality remained high, abolitionism was a much stronger and pervasive movement that culminated in full emancipation in 1838.[40]

Jordan's observations highlight a crucial point: as slave owners emphasized "familial relations"—both for themselves and their slaves—slavery became more firmly entrenched. This was a process that the historian Willie Lee Rose has referred to as the "domestication of domestic slavery." Slaves' amelioration resulted in their inclusion within the plantation household, the cultivation of their morals and manners, and the proliferation of slave families.[41] In Peter Onuf's useful metaphor, the "domestication" of the "captive nation" of "foreign" slaves transformed the "wolf by the ear" into a harmless and domesticated "lap dog." Although slaves could not be "incorporated"—a term that implied race-mixing—within the domestic household, they could be made "happy" through amelioration. Far from being archaic, the domestic household was a modern unit of society that emphasized individuality, improvement, privacy, and sympathetic ties. Thus, as slave "families" were ameliorated and included within the plantation family, the system of "domestic slavery" became a more modern—and resilient—system. The main criticism that British metropolitan critics leveled at West Indian slaveholders was that planters had failed to establish themselves as patriarchs of an extended plantation family who sought to ameliorate their slaves and include them within the domestic sphere. What Jordan initially observed was the modernization of slavery through its domestication or inclusion within the household.[42]

Still, even as other historians have touched on the centrality of amelioration to the slavery question, Seymour Drescher has demonstrated why the concept took on increased importance by the end of the eighteenth century. Drescher, who "traces the intrusion of social science into the politics of slavery," points out that, with the rise of statistics and demography studies in the late eighteenth century, amelioration could be quantified: "improvement" could be measured for the first time. In the mid-1700s, the challenge to slavery and the slave trade was first made on moral and political grounds in terms that were inherently unquantifiable. Consequently, for decades, the polemics written and delivered by those for and against the slave trade were locked in an inconclusive draw. But with the injection of statistics and expert knowledge into the slavery debate by the late 1780s, the landscape of the arguments shifted radically. Testimonials from former slaves, slave traders, West Indian planters, and other individuals who had firsthand experience with slavery were privileged over pamphlets written by those clergymen and members of Parliament who lived in Britain. Even more importantly, statistics allowed defenders and opponents to refashion the slave debate. "Improvement" could now be measured and calculated, especially through national censuses. As such, "the quest for a scientific understanding of slavery and its alternatives was a quest for the minimization of irrationality and the maximization of orderly discussion of social change." The question of amelioration lay at the heart of these new rational and scientific debates about slavery.[43]

Historians who have viewed the Anglo-American slave debate through a modern-day moral lens have overlooked the centrality of these eighteenth-century scientific calculations of social progress. The concentration on morality has led to historians' overwhelming preoccupation with abolitionism and antislavery in both the British and American contexts. By today's standards, the abolitionists appear to have espoused a morality that most closely resembles our own, and, therefore, must have been the most enlightened and modern of the revolutionary age. Alternatively, seen from the perspective of the U.S. Emancipation Proclamation in 1863 or the British Emancipation Bill of 1838, early abolitionists often appear as the stewards of the universal rights and liberties that were belatedly realized.[44] Consequently, studies of slavery have, more often than not, focused on abolitionists rather than on seemingly backward proslavery defenders. While several historians of the American South have argued that slavery was a modern enterprise, few have concentrated on proslavery ideology as a dominant and modern worldview.[45] Scholars have often overlooked the fact that proslavery thinkers' use of amelioration to strengthen and perpetuate slavery dealt a significant blow to their abolitionist foes. Indeed, "from the very outset, abolitionists discovered that their most dangerous opponents were not forthright defenders of black slavery" but rather those enlightened planters who sought to "'improve' the institution."[46]

Of course, the emphasis on antislavery and abolitionism has stemmed from our present-day view of modernity. This view stipulates that civilization is utterly incompatible with slavery because slavery connotes oppressive authority and the division of human beings according to race and rank. But for people in the revolutionary age, universal rights and freedoms were not necessarily the only guiding principles of the modern world. The Enlightenment may have introduced and circulated the possibility of equality and liberty for all mankind, but this did not mean that such notions would be universally embraced or applied in the nineteenth century. As it happened, many contemporaries, including Anglo-American planters, rejected these so-called universal truths—especially those laid down in the Declaration of Independence—and instead trumpeted the "exceptional" nature of national slave systems and embraced the corporate equality of white property holders rather than the individual rights of people, including women and blacks.[47]

Those scholars who have privileged the study of the plantation Americas over metropolitan abolitionism have traditionally viewed amelioration as an "on the ground" policy of British colonial governance or as a method of plantation management. Social historians have tended to emphasize how agricultural improvements dovetailed with the amelioration of slavery, especially in the West Indies.[48] Other historians have linked West Indian colonial policy to plantation management in an effort to determine whether amelioration actually improved or worsened slaves' conditions in the Caribbean. In other words, studies of amelioration that interpret the concept as slaves' treatment have also tended to reduce and deflate it. In reality, violence and the treatment of slaves simply provided the departure point for amelioration—mitigating violence and improving material conditions was a primary way to refashion slavery as a progressive tool that would ensure broader social development for entire "peoples." Amelioration was certainly applicable to conditions within the plantation household, but since such households served as the basis for the new American nation as well as the British Empire in the West Indies, amelioration also lay at the heart of colonization and nation-building efforts during the age of revolutions.[49]

This book demonstrates that amelioration—a term widely embraced and deployed by Anglo-American slaveholders—offers a lens through which to study the expansion of plantation societies. On a localized level, the amelioration of slavery resulted in the domestication of slavery on plantations. The household was the dominant unit of governance in the Anglo-American plantation world; under the federative systems of the United States and the British Empire, each planter patriarch was responsible for governing an extended household of dependents, both white and black.[50] Amelioration helped to transform the master-slave relationship from an unnatural "state of war" that impeded economic efficiency and production into a more natural and sympathetic relationship that became a source of social and economic progress. But the goal of amelioration on plantations was not simply to render slave owners more moral and benevolent masters, and slaves more industrious and domesticated workers. Rather, amelioration helped to forge a model plantation household—one in which a planter patriarch governed his white and black "family"—that could be replicated across space. Viewed against more violent plantations wherein oppressive masters brutalized their slaves, ameliorated plantation households appeared to be much more productive and progressive spaces.[51] Such "dynamic instrument[s] of colonization and economic development" could expand across the North American continent or the Caribbean in order to maximize economic output of staple crops like cotton, wheat, indigo, and sugar. Thus, the real goal of amelioration was not the "improvement" of race relations but rather the expansion of plantation empires—the accumulation of property, connection to markets, exploitation of the land, democratization of slave holding, and the civilization of society.[52]

Still, Anglo-American planters understood that when and where amelioration was deployed depended upon land and market conditions. In frontier plantation settlements, amelioration was almost always absent; planters sought to extract labor from slaves and crops from the soil with brutal and unrelenting force in order to increase production and maximize profits. Planters only turned to amelioration when soil became exhausted and crop prices dropped, or when slaves became too valuable to destroy quickly through hard labor. As Simon Newman has recently argued, "improved business and management practices, in the face of deteriorating environmental conditions and lower profit margins, help account for the improved conditions of enslaved plantation laborers."[53] This helps to explain why amelioration was more widespread in established but economically challenged polities like Virginia and Barbados, and why amelioration was almost always absent from frontier plantations in the Mississippi River Valley or newly settled sugar colonies in the Caribbean.[54]

Where and how planters embraced or deployed amelioration also depended upon the redefinition of the concept of civilized society during the long eighteenth century. The revolutionary age demolished Enlightenment hopes for the continuing progress of European civilization. No longer the gatekeepers of civilization and modernity, European states had apparently languished under the despotism and corruption of tyrannical kings who exploited their people and waged bloody wars.[55] With the dissolution of the mythic unity of Europe and its attendant claim to civility, contemporaries began to question whether the international states system produced civilization or whether nations were providentially destined to do so. In a reverse formulation, civilization did not bring about nationhood—nationhood instead ensured civilization.[56] Amelioration was viewed as the process that led to modernity, but when civilization cleaved along national lines, amelioration also came to be viewed in national terms. Understanding that the concept was first tied to a Euro-Atlantic conception of civilization, and only later linked to conceptions of "domestic" civilizations, helps to explain why planters in the sugar islands and southern states conceived of amelioration's goals in starkly different terms by the mid-nineteenth century. And the rise of censuses and demography studies dovetailed with the emergence of national civilizations; they allowed contemporaries to use statistics to define the modernity of particular, or national, slave systems in the Atlantic littoral.[57]

The geographic and temporal focus of this study is crucial to understanding the scope and evolution of the concept of amelioration in the Anglo-Atlantic world. This book examines how ideas of amelioration were inflected differently by enlightened planters across what scholars now refer to as the "greater Caribbean" during the revolutionary age. Both before and after the American Revolution, the West Indies and the American South remained deeply connected through ties of commerce, culture, and religion. Both areas were colonial outposts of the British Empire and shared identities as British subjects, participants in a wider mercantilist system, and followers of the Protestant faith.[58] Perhaps most importantly, as Jack Greene and others have shown, both the British Empire and the American union were federal systems in which the animating principles were divided sovereignty and, especially, the sanctity of property rights—including slaves.[59]

In the era preceding the American Revolution, the sugar plantations of the West Indies were some of the most profitable units of production in the New World. Because of this specialization, the southern colonies developed deep commercial ties with their Caribbean cousins, supplying timber, livestock, and grain to the monocultural islands. In turn, the mainland colonies consumed vast amounts of rum and molasses. South Carolina, settled by Barbadian colonists in 1670 and eventually emerging as a major rice exporter, maintained especially close ties to the West Indies. Moreover, the slave trade and slave labor followed the contours of the commercial and labor networks that connected the two regions. African slave traders usually moored in the West Indies with their human cargo before proceeding to port cities in the mainland colonies. And although sugar monoculture in the West Indies, intensive rice production in South Carolina, and tobacco and grain production in Virginia resulted in different work patterns, mortality rates, and demographic realities, these disparities did not overshadow the fact that slavery was central to the making of all of these societies.[60]

Even though commercial ties between the two regions remained strong after the American Revolution, the experiment in nationhood on the mainland peeled apart some of the shared ideas regarding the role of slavery and the definition of progress. Many revolutionary patriots in Virginia and the South Carolina Lowcountry began to see the slave trade and slavery as antithetical to nationhood and social progress, while their British West Indian colleagues continued to view the transatlantic slave trade and slavery as a civilizing system. In other words, Caribbean planters continued to frame progress in imperial terms, wherein provincial slaveholding posed no challenge to the civility of the metropole. But "enlightened" planters in the American South began to view progress within a national framework. Ending slavery and the slave trade—two systems reminiscent of "tyrannical" British rule—was central to their ability to make treaties and forge diplomatic alliances on the world stage.[61]

This book centers on a small group of enlightened planters in Virginia, South Carolina, and several West Indian sugar colonies between the 1770s and the 1840s. These slave owners, deeply enmeshed in their particular slave societies, were not just prominent intellectuals or proslavery reactionaries. Instead, in this study, these planters serve as representatives of their distinct provincial cultures. All of the figures highlighted in this book embraced amelioration as a path to modernization for plantation societies, but they also deployed the concept to different ends: either the abolition of slavery or its continuation. Examining these planters and their cultures side by side, rather than in isolated national contexts, helps us to understand how and why the question of slavery in the revolutionary age spawned such varying conceptions of modernity in the revolutionary Atlantic World.[62]

The first section begins in late eighteenth-century Virginia, at Thomas Jefferson's Monticello. The patriotic Jefferson was an opponent of slavery and the transatlantic slave trade, believing that both were archaic, Old World systems foisted on Americans without their consent. He advocated amelioration, believing that he, and other Virginians, could improve slavery in order to ultimately abolish it. Jefferson advocated amelioration as an interim period of "improvement" until slaves could be emancipated and "repatriated." But he inadvertently wrote the language for slavery's perpetuation—as soon as he conceded that slavery could be mitigated and "improved," abolition appeared to be unnecessary. Chapter 2, which focuses on Jefferson's grandson Thomas Jefferson Randolph, the agricultural improver John Hartwell Cocke, and the political economist Thomas Dew, shows that many Virginians, at least by the 1830s, believed that amelioration could lead to different goals. Whites did not agree about how slavery would be dealt with in Virginia, the state with the largest and fastest-growing slave population. Cocke and Randolph, as proponents of the "improvement" of slaves on plantations and their subsequent emancipation and "repatriation" to Africa, specifically Liberia, were ardent supporters of colonization. Dew, however, found colonization to be little short of a fantasy, and worked to show that mitigated slavery actually helped to civilize Virginia, rather than retard its development. Still, Dew did not envision slavery as a permanent fixture of society in the Old Dominion; the market would diffuse the "peculiar institution" westward until it disappeared.

Part 2 begins in eighteenth-century South Carolina with the merchant and planter Henry Laurens. Laurens amassed incredible wealth as a slave trader in the British Empire, fashioning himself as a civilized provincial gentleman. But his view of slave trading and slave owning was much altered by the American Revolution. Laurens believed that slavery and the slave trade impeded South Carolina's—and America's—progress in the world, thus jeopardizing the survival of the new federal union. Laurens advocated the abolition of the trade and the improvement of slaves on plantations, which, in future time, might also result in an end to slavery. In the 1780s and 1790s, before the invention of the cotton gin, some elites shared Laurens's view—they imagined South Carolina as a state-republic without slaves. But Laurens's antislavery amelioration was turned on its head in the early nineteenth century. The fourth chapter focuses on the jurist William Harper and a number of other South Carolina intellectuals who came to believe that an ameliorated slave regime would secure the state's wealth and power in the antebellum era. Harper denounced African colonization, arguing that an improved and domesticated slave regime would create a cohesive, exceptional, and progressive South Carolina society within the federal union.

Part 3 opens in Jamaica, the British Empire's leading sugar producer at the end of the eighteenth century. Bryan Edwards was a successful sugar and coffee planter there; he also became a prominent politician in the Jamaica House of Assembly and an MP in Britain. When the British abolition movement gained momentum in the latter 1780s, Edwards was one of its most creative opponents. His sophisticated formulation of the transatlantic slave trade as a civilizing system, albeit in need of improvement, helped to deflect many of the calls for immediate abolition. Throughout the 1790s, Parliament passed more than a dozen acts aimed at regulating the slave trade, thus rendering abolition unnecessary. Edwards also argued that the slave trade rescued hapless Africans from barbarism and tribal war; in the West Indies, and on his own Jamaican plantations, he advocated slaves' moral and physical improvement. Even after the abolition of the slave trade, many West Indian planters, an increasing number of them absentee, continued to view plantation slavery as a civilizing system that should only gradually end. The final chapter, which focuses on the absentee planter John Gladstone, shows how he advocated evangelical Christianity and more rigid plantation discipline to ameliorate his slave labor force in Demerara. Despite criticism from abolitionists in the 1820s that slavery was in decline and that free labor and free trade were more humane and modern policies, Gladstone believed that a reformed slave labor regime and a protectionist economy buoyed the sugar islands and brought wealth to the empire. Emancipation, he thought, would bring financial ruin to planters and devastation to the West Indies.

Taken together, the narratives of these Anglo-American planters offer a transnational perspective on a pervasive worldview during the revolutionary age. The usual reading of such provincial planters has suggested that they were simply hopeless provincials who remained stuck in an earlier era, when overseas expansion based on coerced labor and commerce yielded tremendous national wealth. While planters remained static figures on the margins, supposedly modern Enlightenment thinkers crafted a new narrative of human progress across Europe, a theory of human development that outlined man's advancement from unfree servitude to independence as laborer, trader, and consumer. It was within the context of the creation of this modern narrative of human progress that the slavery debate unfolded. This book's emphasis on enlightened planters in the American South and British West Indies, however, seeks to demonstrate that this was not the *only* narrative being created. Eschewing the metropolitan Enlightenment vision of progress, slave owners embraced amelioration as the path to modernization within their plantation slave societies and created their own "improved" vision of the modern world.[63]

I

Virginia

During the imperial crisis with Britain, many Virginia colonists resisted the perceived imposition of "tyrannical" British policies—including slavery and the transatlantic slave trade. Although nearly 40 percent of Virginia's population was enslaved when the American Revolution broke out, some whites supported the introduction of wage labor. Elite patriots believed that an ameliorative end to slavery, which would begin with the abolition of the slave trade and culminate in the "repatriation" of freed blacks, was the best plan to rid Virginia of slavery. Antislavery amelioration gained further traction in the wake of the revolution, when anxious revolutionaries were eager to prove their legitimacy on the world stage. The existence of slavery in the new nation impeded a "union" with civilized European states. But the democratization of slave owning, the increased practice of slave hiring, and the rise of the domestic slave trade only strengthened support for slavery in postrevolutionary Virginia. And in the absence of large-scale slave rebellions, white Virginians by the 1830s began to argue that slavery could be "improved" not toward abolition but in order to uphold the institution.

1

"THE GREAT IMPROVEMENT AND CIVILIZATION OF THAT RACE"

In the spring of 1801, Thomas Jefferson described the implications of the republican "revolution of 1800." He declared that "our revolution and its consequences," which had "excited" the "mass of mankind," would "ameliorate the condition of man over a great portion of the globe." After being "hood-winked from their principles" by the pseudo-monarchical Federalists, the "people," Jefferson believed, had finally "learned to see for themselves" by electing the Democratic-Republicans to political office. A Federalist-dominated regime, one that operated on the principle that "man cannot be governed except by the rod," would retard advancement in the union. The "tyranny" of consolidated power, of a resurgent aristocracy, had emerged to thwart the experiment in self-governance. But freed from the "bands" that deprived them of their liberties, the American people—and all peoples—could share in the "amelioration" of mankind under the auspices of a "just and solid republican government." In Jefferson's view, a people could only embark on a project of amelioration under the aegis of self-government and legitimate nationhood; despotism prevented progress wherever it manifested itself.[1]

Although it is debatable whether Jefferson's "revolution of 1800" was revolutionary at all, the logic that undergirded his imagined "revolution in principles" and "revolution in form" remain crucial to understanding Jefferson's political thought and his views on slavery. For him, slavery constituted the same despotism and imposed the same "bands" of oppression that he identified with the Federalists or George III. Hyper-vigilant about the preservation and progress of his cherished union, Jefferson believed that slavery threatened to stymie the development of the "spirit" of the people—their morals and manners—while also undermining the political advancement of the nation on the world's stage. His definition of slavery—

a "state of war"—and his definition of slaves—a "captive nation" living in bondage—suggest the despotic, regressive, and unnatural features that he believed to be inherent in the institution of slavery. The relationship between master and slave was an unnatural one—it was a selfish and wasteful "commerce" that represented a "perpetual exercise of the most boisterous passions." Jefferson wanted to remove the "blot" of slavery from America not merely for reasons of morality or benevolence, but because he viewed the excision of a despotic system as the necessary precondition of the amelioration of white citizens. Thus, Jefferson sought to facilitate the natural progress of a people—which he defined as amelioration—by removing the unnatural and adversarial "captive nation" of slaves from their midst.[2]

Of course, even though Jefferson understood slavery to be a form of tyranny, the process of removing the black population from American soil in the postrevolutionary period could not be tyrannical either. He knew full well that slaves constituted valuable private property; the sovereignty of the people also meant the sovereignty of their property. And under republicanism, the central government's jurisdiction was only over "foreign" concerns—treaties, war-making, and international commerce. Federal power could not constitutionally extend into the domestic realm and abolish slavery; it was antidemocratic and contrary to the principles of the revolution for the federal government to enact abolition. Thus, Jefferson proposed a gradual plan to end slavery that would, he thought, result in the "amelioration of the condition of mankind." First, the transatlantic slave trade would be abolished. Second, slaves and slavery would be ameliorated, that is, the violence of the institution mitigated and the material conditions of slaves improved. Third, slaves would be freed in a single, large-scale emancipation effort. Finally, slaves would be "repatriated" to an unspecified "country," such as Sierra Leone or an island in the West Indies.[3]

Jefferson was not alone in advocating for an ameliorative end to slavery in order to assure the progress of the American people. Many patriots opposed the continuation of the transatlantic slave trade and slavery, but these supporters of antislavery amelioration were almost always members of elite Virginia families rather than middling or poorer whites. The famous orator Patrick Henry, for example, believed that an interim period of "improvement" should take place between the abolition of the slave trade and emancipation. In a speech to the Virginia House of Burgesses, Henry declared that, though a "time will come . . . to abolish this lamentable Evil," the moment had not yet arrived. Still, in the interim, "every thing we can do is to improve it." Henry advised Virginians to "transmit to our descendants together with our Slaves, a pity for their unhappy Lot, & an abhorrence for Slavery." Indeed, he stipulated, "let us treat the unhappy victims with lenity, & it is the furthest advance we can make toward Justice."[4]

And when the time did arrive for emancipation, Jefferson and his contemporaries agreed, "repatriation" should follow. America would not survive if the "captive nation" of Africans was set loose on its soil. In 1791, Ferdinando Fairfax, a prominent Virginia landowner, suggested the "propriety, and even necessity of removing them [slaves] to a distance from this country." Fairfax believed that sending former slaves to Africa would, "from their industry, and by commercial intercourse, make us ample amends for our expenses, and be enabled to live without our protection." Moreover, he noted that "after some time," such colonized slaves would "become an independent nation."[5] The jurist St. George Tucker pinned his hopes on slaves' colonization beyond the "limits" of the union: "We might reasonably hope, that time would . . . remove from us a race of men, whom we do not wish to incorporate with us."[6] And in 1803, the Virginia slave owner and agriculturist John Taylor mused that, "if England and America would erect and foster a settlement of free negroes in some fertile part of Africa," slavery and the slave trade "might then be gradually re-exported, and philanthropy gratified by a slow re-animation of the virtue, religion, and liberty of the negroes." Abolishing the "foreign" slave trade and expelling "foreign" Africans from the union went hand in hand.[7]

With the slave trade and slavery eradicated from America, Jefferson believed that progress would ensue. One prong of this amelioration was the "enlightenment" and education of the people; through the improvement of their morals and manners, the people would become better guardians of their liberty. A second prong, however, implied America's political development. It was the process by which America would be transformed from a provincial slaveholding society into an independent and legitimate member of the Atlantic family of nations. For the young republic to join the civilized "confederacy" of European states—the wellspring of Atlantic civilization in Jefferson's mind—America needed to gain recognition as a legitimate "confederacy" of the New World by making treaties, forging alliances, and engaging access to new commercial markets. Thus the New World would have to purge itself of what Jefferson deemed to be an archaic system—the institution of slavery—in order to be closer to Europe and share in its civility.[8]

But if Jefferson wanted to eradicate slavery in order for Americans to embark on a project of improvement and move closer to Europe, his view was reversed by the time the Napoleonic Wars were drawing to a close. The failure of the French experiment in republicanism, and the "rivers of blood" that continued to flow as European monarchs slaughtered each other and their peoples, meant that Jefferson turned his back on Europe as the site of amity and civility. No longer did Europe provide the model of morals, manners, and political development for the federal union. "Our first and fundamental maxim should be, never to entangle ourselves in the broils of Europe," he declared, since "America, North and South, has a set of interests distinct from those of Europe, and particularly her own. She should therefore have a system of her own, separate and apart from that of Europe." Here Jefferson underscored the peculiarity of American nationhood—the young republic functioned as the only repository of liberty in the world because all others, including revolutionary France, had failed. Of course, the exceptionalism of American nationhood also legitimated exceptional institutions—a "system of her own." That system, even if Jefferson continued to resist it, included the "peculiar institution" of American slavery.[9]

Jefferson continued to define slavery as a vestige of the Old World even while he increasingly trumpeted the exceptional nature of the New World. The two definitions, however, were incompatible; he could not have it both ways. Jefferson's antislavery amelioration was predicated upon his stubborn view that slavery was an archaic system that had been born in the Old World. His gradualist plan to rid America of its slaves in successive stages suggested that slaveholders would chip away at the "blot" of slavery by mitigating the physical horrors and violence that defined bondage. But in admitting that slavery could be improved—that slaves could be "ameliorated" and domesticated—Jefferson made a fatal error. For if the institution could be reformed, then arguments to end it appeared moot. Why, planters would ask, should a system so widespread be abolished if it could simply be made better? Ultimately, the notion that slavery could be improved in America rendered the system both modern and exceptional—rather than an archaic figment of the Old World—which thus legitimized its expansion and perpetuation. As a result of their "exceptional" treatment, the "blot" of slaves increased. The self-regenerating power of the black population indicated the modernity and "newness" of American slavery. Thus, the system that had been antithetical to the amelioration of "mankind" in the postrevolutionary era had become entirely compatible with progress in America in the 1800s.[10]

Jefferson understood amelioration to be the social progress of the American people and the political development of their nation—slavery was at odds with both. Jefferson used his definition of slavery as an inimical "commerce" and of slaves as a separate "nation" as the crucial antecedent to the amelioration of the new American nation. Knowing that enlightened European *philosophes* believed slavery to be antithetical to human progress, Jefferson believed that the removal of the enslaved African "nation" from America was the only way to forge closer ties with civilized European states. In addition, he articulated two schemes, colonization and diffusion, that would "remove" an entire black population from the United States, leaving a homogenous American population of white citizens to improve and expand in its absence. And lastly, until slave owners would consent to diffusion or colonization plans, Jefferson argued for the amelioration of slavery on plantations. On his own properties, he implemented rational, enlightened plans of "government" to ameliorate his slaves with the goal of emancipating and "repatriating" them at some future time.[11]

AN OLD WORLD PROBLEM

Jefferson believed that slavery and the transatlantic slave trade were fundamentally Old World problems. These two systems, each dependent on the other, were manifestations of the tyranny, backwardness, and war-making that he thought characterized the Old World—especially monarchical Britain—on the eve of the American Revolution. In contrast, he imagined that after seceding from Britain, the New World would embrace republican principles, modernity, and perpetual peace. The binary of Old World and New animated Jefferson's thinking during the revolutionary era. But slavery in the recently formed state-republics could neither be "new" nor exceptional. Jefferson and many other patriots, seeking to rid themselves of slavery and the slave trade, reimagined their recent colonial past, claiming that it was George III and British merchants who imposed the oppressive and immoral practices of slave trading and slave owning on hapless colonists. In order to relegate slavery to the Old World, patriots had to gloss over their recent past as agents of empire—and proponents of the slave trade—in the New.[12]

Jefferson described British Americans as active participants in colonization, rather than passive bystanders. British settlers had civilized the land in the "wilds of America," where they "thought proper to adopt that system of laws which they had hitherto lived in the mother country." These enterprising colonists were conquerors and consumers; they "pacified" the land through bloody conflicts with native peoples and eagerly consumed British goods in order to civilize newly settled areas in British America. And while Jefferson did not say as much, one type of commodity that the colonists eagerly purchased was African slaves. Slaves were critical to the settlement of land and the connection of such lands to Atlantic markets. Jefferson believed that the experience of colonization was a formative one—it allowed colonists to forge a collective history, a collective identity, and a sense of themselves as a united people. But Jefferson conveniently forgot that the colonists' active role in the "empire thus newly multiplied"—from the rice plantations of the Carolinas to the tobacco estates of the Tidewater—was due in large part to the rapid importation of slave labor.[13]

Imagining the transatlantic slave trade and the slave labor system it spawned as archaic figments of the Old World allowed patriots to forget that their formative experience of colonization was made possible by slavery. During the imperial crisis in Virginia, colonists sought to overturn the oppressive policies of Parliament by abolishing the slave trade; revolutionaries believed that slavery was a direct result of the British transatlantic slave trade. Although Virginians in the 1770s had petitioned to end the trade, neither Parliament nor George III did anything to reform or curb the commerce in human beings. Residents of Prince George County, for example, petitioned in 1774 that "the African trade is injurious to this Colony, obstructs the population of it by freemen" and "prevents manufacturers and other useful emigrants from Europe from settling amongst us."[14] Indeed, when Jefferson addressed his grievances against the king in his political pamphlet *Summary View of the Rights of British America,* he insisted that the "abolition of domestic slavery is the great object of desire in those colonies where it was unhappily introduced in their infant state."[15]

The unanswered petitions helped to bolster colonists' arguments that the slave trade had been foisted on British America by a distant and despotic monarch. George III had "waged cruel war against human nature" by "captivating and carrying them [Africans] into slavery in another hemisphere" and by "keeping open a market where MEN should be bought & sold," Jefferson seethed in his draft of the Declaration of Independence. And what made George III a despot was "inciting those very people to rise in arms among us," so that he could pay "off former crimes committed against the LIBERTIES of one people, with crimes which he urges them to commit against the LIVES of another."[16] For Jefferson, not only was George III responsible for imposing the barbaric slave trade, which impeded colonists' moral development; he was also to blame for inciting devastating slave rebellions that would destroy his own subjects. The killing of the king, metaphorically speaking, was thus legitimized in 1776 by the seemingly brazen attempts to use slaves to kill his own subjects.

For colonists, this expression of the king's "tyranny" came to pass in 1775. John Murray, Lord Dunmore, the royal governor of Virginia, who raised troops to fight the colonists, decreed freedom to "all indented Servants, Negroes, or others . . . willing to bear arms." Less than a month later, Dunmore had organized his own "Ethiopian regiment," composed mainly of runaway slaves, to fight against their former masters. What the British did, however, was not simply lure slaves from their plantations; rather, the British forces sought a breadth of destruction beyond even Jefferson's comprehension.[17] Charles Cornwallis, Lord Cornwallis, whose troops had invaded Jefferson's Elkhill plantation during the war, Jefferson later wrote, had "destroyed all my growing crops of corn and tobacco" and those animals "too young for service he cut the throats." He had also "carried off about 30 slaves." Cornwallis "burnt all the fences of the plantation, so as to leave it in absolute waste," with "that spirit of total extermination with which he seemed to rage over my possessions." Jefferson proffered the hyperbolic estimate that Virginians had lost nearly thirty thousand slaves to Cornwallis's plunders in 1781, and "that of these about 27,000 died of the small pox and camp fever, and the rest were partly sent to the West Indies and exchanged for rum, sugar, coffee, and fruits, and partly sent to New York, from whence they went at the peace to Nova Scotia." Cassandra Pybus has shown that Jefferson's estimates were grossly inflated for effect; she argues that of the twenty thousand slaves who fled to British lines, only about two thousand gained freedom.[18] But even if Jefferson exaggerated the number of slaves who defected to British lines, it nonetheless highlighted the agency that he assigned enslaved men and women—he genuinely believed that tens of thousands of slaves would seek their freedom when given the chance. Thus, the combination of an emancipation on American soil and armed conflict was a scene of "whole devastations" that provided a real-life preview of the race war he had imagined. A tangible glimpse of such a potential conflict came again during the War of 1812, especially in the Tidewater regions of Virginia, when nearly five thousand slaves escaped to British lines in order to obtain their freedom.[19]

Just as the actions of Dunmore and Cornwallis exemplified Old World "tyranny" and war-making, so too was slave owning a tyrannical practice introduced by George III. In fact, Jefferson imagined a parallel between the despotic king oppressing and warring against his subjects, and a despotic master oppressing and warring against his slaves. "The whole commerce between master and slave," he wrote, was characterized by "the most boisterous passions, the most unremitting despotism on the one part, and degrading submissions on the other." Slaves were placed in a "miserable condition" through this violence and despotism, but so too were the despotic masters and the children of those masters made "miserable." Slavery created an "unhappy influence on the manners of our people" by destroying their morals and industry.[20]

But for Jefferson, the primary danger was that Old World despotism, manifested in slave owning, would be perpetuated *ad infinitum* since slaves were "entailed" to future generations; children of masters were schooled in the "unremitting despotism" of their parents. "Nursed, educated, and daily exercised in tyranny," a new generation of slave owners would also embrace the "lineaments of wrath." Jefferson hoped that the break with Britain and the usurpation of a despotic king would end the generational and tyrannical slave-owning practices that had been conceived, in his eyes, by Old World despots. In fact, Jefferson lauded the fact that the Virginia legislature had abolished entails in 1776 and primogeniture in 1785; he expected that this would increase equality among citizens, for it would guarantee that more men and women held property. This abolition instead, however, diffused slave ownership, thus broadening public support for slavery. Jefferson thus unintentionally supported legislation that democratized slaveholding in Virginia, rendering his antislavery amelioration more and more futile.[21]

Because Jefferson thought of the slave trade as an Old World system, he thought of it as inherently regressive. In this way, Jefferson embraced the same conclusion as many European *philosophes* of the era—slavery was antithetical to human progress. It was a static and despotic institution that lacked the main feature of modernity—self-regeneration. Throughout his life, Jefferson referred to slavery in the new states as a "blot" or "stain"—a bounded entity that presumably could be removed. This differed from a later generation of white observers in Virginia, most notably Thomas Dew, who not only identified slavery as a modern system but also as a "cancer" that had spread insidiously throughout the union by the 1830s. Although at one point Jefferson admitted that "this blot in our country increases as fast, or faster, than the whites," he could neither depart from his contained "blot" metaphor nor admit that the slave population's increase was due to the self-reproducing quality of a modern system. Jefferson would never concede that slavery was anything but an Old World "stain" that was designed to blemish the New World. Because he so fervently believed slavery to be archaic, he was keenly interested in abolishing the international slave trade as an unobtrusive and constitutional way to end slavery. Without the trade, Jefferson thought, slavery in America would wither and eventually perish. The federal government would enact legislation to end the slave trade, he surmised, making it unnecessary to interfere in slave owners' private property after the abolition of the trade. Without fresh supplies from Africa, the slave population would shrink and disappear; the invisible hand of the market would accomplish what the very visible hand of the federal government had no constitutional right to do.[22]

Jefferson's understanding of slavery as a contained entity dovetailed with his understanding of what he regarded as a separate "nation" of Africans living in bondage on American soil. Defining slavery in Lockean terms—as a state of war—Jefferson saw two nations, one black and the other white, occupying the same country and whose natural relationship was one of enmity and war. Slaves constituted a "captive nation" who had no "amor patriae," but at any moment, they might rise up against their white oppressors to vindicate their rights as well as unleash a race war that would destroy slave owners and the federal union. While in reality the majority of slaves in postrevolutionary Virginia had been in North America for generations, Jefferson imagined them as Africans, not as disconnected and disparate slaves. They were a bounded, coherent entity, an African blot in America. Even when describing blacks in the most derogatory terms, he consistently identified them as Africans, not as slaves. The first "difference" of blacks was of "colour," since the "immoveable veil of black" proved the "difference of race." From this racial distinction, all other differences emanated. For example, blacks "have less hair on the face and body" and "are more ardent after their female" than whites. These physical characteristics also pointed to blacks' mental capacities. "It appears," Jefferson wrote, "that in memory they are equal to the whites, in reason much inferior . . . and in imagination they are dull, tasteless, and anomalous." Yet Jefferson's descriptions articulated a definition of blacks as Africans, not as slaves. "African" denoted the identity of blacks in Virginia; enslavement was merely their condition.[23]

Jefferson's binary—which he refused to revise or relinquish in his lifetime—was the foundation for his understanding of American nationhood, African nationhood, and the colonization projects that had led, or would lead, to the providential fulfillment of each nation's destiny. A young Jefferson—a provincial lawyer in the British Empire—had already undercut this dualism, however; he had amended Locke's static and deterministic view of the state of war, arguing instead that the relationship between captives and captors was forever improving. The more humane treatment of prisoners in history, the young Jefferson noted, demonstrated a "remarkable instance of improvement in the moral sense." Indeed, captors "became more humanized"; they improved the treatment of prisoners from that "practice[d] by savage nations" to reflect a new "stage of refinement." It seemed possible to conclude that the relationship between captives and captors could become less inimical.[24] As a provincial lawyer, Jefferson seemed to have taken his prescriptions to heart. He attempted, as David Konig has argued, to ameliorate slaves' conditions, to recognize their entitlement to consideration as persons before the law, and even to liberate others; these actions constituted Jefferson's early antislavery initiatives. But his postrevolutionary and unswerving commitment to slaves as a separate nation and slavery as a tyrannical Old World system meant that he would later oppose the piecemeal measures that he had suggested in his notes and as a young British American jurist.[25]

Any private emancipation efforts within America would merely be piecemeal; they ignored the larger challenge of removing an entire African "nation," Jefferson argued. Thus he dismissed the emancipation plans of the Quaker tobacco planter Robert Pleasants, who gave 78 freed slaves 350 acres to farm, as well as the scheme of the Virginia slave owner Edward Coles, who emigrated to Illinois in 1819 to free his slaves. Jefferson also objected to the scheme of his protégé, William Short, which would transform slaves into serfs. Their plans would not solve the fundamental problem that blacks were a "foreign" people in a "foreign" country; Short's plan, in particular, promised a return to Old World manorialism. Moreover, because Africans had been so "degraded" by enslavement, they were ill-equipped to be successful freemen on American soil, in Jefferson's opinion. "To give liberty to" slaves, he wrote, is much "like abandoning children." Jefferson noted that several of his Quaker neighbors had "seated their slaves on their lands as tenants," only to find themselves "obliged to plant their crops for them, to direct all their operations during every season." But "what is more afflicting," Jefferson believed, was that the Quakers were "obliged to watch them daily and almost constantly to make them work, and even to whip them." These black tenants often "chose to steal from their neighbors rather than work," and became "public nuisances" who were "in most instances reduced to slavery again."[26] For Jefferson, black Africans could only embrace liberty in their homeland, not in America. Generations of enslavement had forced Africans to be "brought from their infancy without necessity for thought or forecast," their "habits rendered as incapable as children of taking care of themselves." And free blacks, lacking in morality and manners, "are pests in society by their idleness," he thought.[27]

Jefferson dismissed the plans of Pleasants, Coles, and Short and continued to believe that slavery was an Old World system throughout his life. Slaves could be nothing but a "blot," a "wolf by the ear," and the "captive nation"; redefining the master-slave relationship would undermine Jefferson's understanding of slavery in national terms. It would force him to revise many of his claims that slavery, as a vestige of European despotism, had no place in a New World regime. It would also force him to rethink his understanding of the abolition of slavery as the necessary precursor to the amelioration of American citizens. Jefferson clung stubbornly to his Old World definition after the American Revolution in order to imagine a New World without slaves.[28]

It was this understanding of slavery that helped Jefferson frame his solution to the problem in America. In defining slavery as a manifestation of Old World tyranny—a system of "boisterous passions" and "unremitting despotism"—he was also defining the New World as a place that could or would not be characterized by such tyranny. Trying to purge postrevolutionary America of vestiges of consolidated authority meant that only sovereign slave owners could end slavery throughout the union. In the 1770s, Virginians and Marylanders had sought to use provincial authority to end the slave trade. Still, George III's Privy Council vetoed the proposed legislation to abolish the "execrable commerce," preferring to patronize "a few British corsairs" in the trade, rather than defending the "lasting interests of the American states," Jefferson wrote in his *Summary View.* Provincials fought for their "right" to regulate or abolish the slave trade within their particular provinces and bucked against royal intervention. But after the revolution, with consolidated power purged from the union and the new U.S. Constitution protecting slave owners' rights in private (human) property, abolition could not be a top-down process. In the absence of a centralized nation-state that could compensate slave owners for their human property, the burden of emancipation was shifted to individual masters. To Jefferson, it was reminiscent of Old World power for the federal government to enact abolition and interfere in the sanctity of private property.[29]

Beginning in the 1780s, Jefferson's plans to abolish the slave trade and slavery operated on two premises. The first was that abolition must be accomplished in national terms: the entire African "nation" would have to be expelled from American soil through colonization. Attempts at piecemeal abolition or incorporating blacks into the state would jeopardize the American experiment in nationhood. The second premise was that only slave owners could initiate abolition; a centralized authority, such as Congress, could never emancipate private property. Thus, Jefferson formulated an ameliorative end to slavery. First, Congress would abolish the slave trade. Even those South Carolinians and Georgians who depended on the trade in Africans would soon withdraw in favor of new, "enlightened" commerce. Second, through enlightenment and improvement, American slave owners would ameliorate the material and moral conditions of their slaves. As white masters established ties of reciprocal obligation and sympathy with their slaves, they would prepare themselves—and their enslaved men and women—for emancipation and "repatriation." Only with slaves placed outside the union, Jefferson thought, could America ever progress and become a legitimate, civilized nation that could gain admission to the world of European states.[30]

Paradoxically, even though Jefferson identified slavery and the slave trade as having been imposed on Americans by despotic monarchs of the Old World, he sought to rid the federal union of these systems in large part to be closer to that world. In the decades following the American Revolution, Jefferson made blanket statements regarding Old World despotism, but, in reality, there were many European states that represented the progress and civility that he so desperately wanted the new nation to share in and emulate. As he intimated in a message to Congress in 1806, "citizens" would "withdraw ... from all further participation in those violations of human rights which have been so long continued on the unoffending inhabitants of Africa" with the abolition of the transatlantic slave trade. He tellingly also noted, however, that the true aims of abolition were to promote "the morality, the reputation, and the best interests of our country." In other words, he wanted European states to take America seriously, and the image of the federal union as a provincial slave-trading outpost impeded this goal. Patriots' aim was to demonstrate America's "treaty-worthiness" in order to assume a station "among the powers of the earth."[31]

THE POPULATION PROBLEM
Colonization and Diffusion

From the 1780s until his death, Jefferson advocated the colonization of blacks—which he referred to as "repatriation"—as the best solution
to the problem of slavery. Colonization was Jefferson's attempt to solve the
problem—and impending danger—posed by a heterogeneous population in America. As Jefferson intimated from his frequent use of "blot" and
"stain" metaphors to describe the "captive nation" of blacks, he thought of
nations as bounded, homogenous populations. He viewed the Malthusian
progress of populations through a national lens. Homogenous peoples, Jefferson thought, were "more peaceable" and "more durable" since "it is for
the happiness of those united in society to harmonize as much as possible
in matters" of governance by common consent. Homogeneity—which
Jefferson defined as the inclusion of domesticated citizens and the exclu-
sion of foreigners—was the basis for consensual government. Heterogeneity, such as in America, where two nations occupied the same country,
was dangerous and would provoke race war and disunion. A mix of "foreigners"—African slaves—and domesticated citizens—white Americans—would "infuse" the population with "warp and bias" and "render
it a heterogenous, incoherent, distracted mass." Such a "mixture" would
make America "more turbulent, less happy, less strong" than if it retained
its character as a homogenous nation. Such reasoning went to the heart
of Jefferson's understanding of slavery. He could not imagine race-mixing
since, to him, such "incorporation" would subvert the republic. For Jefferson, consensual government could never succeed in a heterogeneous population; a "mixed" nation would sound the death knell for the American
experiment in republican government. So dangerous was race-mixing, he
imagined, that his most "racist" condemnations of blacks in his *Notes on
the State of Virginia* functioned as a warning to planters—including himself—of the consequences of sexual liaisons with black women. This was
perhaps why Jefferson could never acknowledge his own mixed-race children with Sally Hemings.[32]

This danger spurred Jefferson to formulate his colonization schemes as
the solution to the slavery problem. He resisted any plans to emancipate
slaves on American soil: to "retain and incorporate" blacks would produce
the same heterogeneous nation that Jefferson feared would undermine the
experiment in nationhood. Instead, colonization would allow the entire
black population to be "removed beyond the reach of mixture."[33] The re-

sult, he believed, would be a homogenous American nation and a separate homogenous African people. For Jefferson, colonization was a formative experience; it allowed disparate individuals to make their own history and to forge a sense of themselves as a single people. In his view, colonization was the precursor to nationhood. In the case of British America, settlers had emigrated across the Atlantic, carved settlements from the wilderness, and established commercial connections with Atlantic markets. "America was conquered," he wrote, "and her settlements made, and firmly established, at the expence of individuals" rather than Britons. Settlers' "own blood was spilt in acquiring lands for their settlement, their own fortunes expended in making that settlement effectual." Indeed, for "themselves they fought, for themselves they conquered, and for themselves alone they have right to hold." The collective experience of the violence of conquest and the difficulty of settlement forged colonists' understanding of themselves as one people rather than disparate provincials.[34]

In the postrevolutionary era, Jefferson asserted that a colonization project of western settlement would school white settlers in the lessons of self-government, the essence of American identity. Land settlement would be the antecedent of new state formation and constitution writing. As Jefferson declared in his first Inaugural Address, there was "room enough for our descendants to the thousandth and thousandth generation." He believed the American West to be a blank space, a hinterland where white settlers would carry out colonization. They would conquer hostile native peoples and European rivals in their bid to claim the land and bring it under the auspices of the federal union. Western settlers would become the yeoman farmers he cherished; these "husbandmen" would expand the "empire of liberty" and preserve the republican experiment as the "strongest government on earth." This process of colonization forged the "manners and spirit of a people"—a nation of yeoman farmers—who would "preserve a republic in vigour."[35]

Jefferson applied the same logic of colonization to African slaves. The Middle Passage, he thought, had tragically forged a single "African" identity out of myriad tribal ones. As a separate nation, slaves retained this African identity while in bondage in America. In his mind, African colonization would be the crucial precursor to their establishment in Africa. Colonization was thus the solution to the problem of slavery in the postrevolutionary period—it "freed" white settlers to expand westward and fulfill their just claims to nationhood while removing blacks from America and allowing them to make similar legitimate claims to their own nation.[36]

Beginning in the 1780s, Jefferson outlined what he termed an "ex post nati" scheme to remove the "captive nation" of blacks from America. His plan stipulated that slave children "continue with their parents to a certain age, then be brought up, at the public expence, to tillage, arts or sciences, according to their geniuses, till the females should be eighteen, and the males twenty-one years of age." Young slaves would be ameliorated for an interim period before "they should be colonized to such place as the circumstance of the time should render most proper." They would then be sent to their new "country" with "arms, implements of household and of the handicraft arts, feeds, pairs of useful domestic animals, &c." This would allow Virginia to "declare them a free and independant people, and extend to them our alliance and protection, till they shall have acquired strength." And, after bringing former slaves to their new homeland, the ships would depart for ports in "other parts of the world for an equal number of white inhabitants." This steady stream of imported white laborers would replenish the loss of labor while also retaining the homogenous nature of the federal union.[37]

Jefferson believed that the colonization of slaves would result in a commercial exchange that would benefit both nations. "Going from a country possessing all the useful arts," slaves would "transplant" them and "thus carry back to the country of their origin, the seeds of civilization which might render their sojournment and sufferings here a blessing in the end to that country." As newly settled Africans established their own nation, they would export goods to America. For this reason, "exclusive of motives of humanity, the commercial advantages to be derived might repay all its expences." Commercial exchange would compensate the steep costs involved in sending newly emancipated slaves to what Jefferson considered their homeland as well as establish overseas markets for American goods.[38]

Jefferson's scheme was predicated on returning an African nation to its homeland—but few knew where that home lay. Whereas Jefferson asserted that the harrowing Middle Passage was a shared experience of horror that solidified Africans' sense of themselves as a single people, the reality was that the transatlantic slave trade created a diaspora that diffused Africans across the Atlantic world rather than uniting them as a coherent nation. This reality undercut Jefferson's understanding of slaves in America as a separate African "nation." And even if he conceived of American slaves as an African people, he vacillated over the location of their true place of origins. He waffled between the "island of St. Domingo," Africa as a "last resort," and the "western territory of the U.S." Yet Jefferson's suggestions were hypothetical and unrealistic. In fact, Jefferson's colonization ideas proved problematic since the legitimacy of the plan to "repatriate" slaves hinged on their return to an undetermined homeland. It also depended on slave owners' consent to emancipate their human property.[39]

But a slave conspiracy in Virginia forced Jefferson to depart from his idealized social vision; it compelled him to rethink whether colonization could realistically guide powerful demographic forces and establish America as a white, homogenous nation. In the summer of 1800, the enslaved blacksmith Gabriel Prosser conspired to stage a military-style invasion of Richmond. Prosser threatened to burn the capital and imprison or kill all of its white inhabitants. After one conspirator was captured, he evinced little regret, instead claiming, "I have nothing more to offer than what General Washington would have had to offer, had he been taken by the British and put on trial. I have adventured my life in endeavoring to obtain the liberty of my countrymen [blacks], and am willing to sacrifice in their cause."[40] In this conspirator's statement lay precisely what Jefferson and his contemporaries feared: a violent and united community of blacks—or an African "nation" as Jefferson imagined—who sought to overthrow and decimate whites. Yet, at the same time, the precise opposite of this insurrectionary conspirator was also present in Richmond. Two loyal slaves, Pharaoh and Tom, had disclosed Prosser's plot to their master, Mosby Sheppard, allowing violence to be averted and the conspirators to be captured.[41]

Whites in Richmond and the legislature of Virginia were in an uproar over the conspiracy. The threat of revolt had been so proximate that Governor James Monroe declared it to be "unquestionably the most serious and formidable . . . of its kind."[42] Yet in the wake of the alleged insurrection, after Prosser and twenty-six of his fellow coconspirators were publicly executed, members of the Virginia Assembly petitioned President Jefferson to acquire a site to which "persons obnoxious . . . or dangerous to the peace of society may be removed."[43] This deportation was not to encompass all Virginia slaves, however. Loyal slaves, like the ones who had unveiled Prosser's plot, did not deserve such an exile. Rather, only violent and rebellious blacks should be removed beyond the boundaries of Virginia, to a place from which they might never return.

Jefferson was unsure of where that place might be. Whether the "establishment of such a colony" for insurgent slaves should be "within our limits" or "beyond the limits of the US," Jefferson remained unclear. Yet he was convinced that those "persons who brought on us the alarm, and on themselves the tragedy, of 1800" should be exiled to a "receptacle" elsewhere in the Atlantic world. The "West Indies offer a more probable & practical retreat for them," since the sugar islands were already "inhabited . . . by a people of their own race & color." Indeed, Jefferson suggested, "nature seems to have formed these islands to become the receptacle of the blacks transplanted into this hemisphere." As nodes of chaos and violence, Jefferson imagined most of West Indian slave society to be on the verge of insurrection. Only in Saint Domingue had "blacks . . . established into a sovereignty" and "organized themselves under regular laws & government." Still, Jefferson feared that exiled American blacks "might stimulate & conduct vindicative or predatory descents on our coasts." What Jefferson wanted—and what many whites hoped—was to have these "exiles" banished from Virginia forever.[44]

In the summer of 1802, Jefferson could think of no better way to rid Virginia of these "exiles" than to deport them across the Atlantic. He proposed sending them to Africa, to "the English Sierra Leone Company." Begun as a fledgling settlement for black loyalists in 1787 by the British abolitionist Granville Sharp, the colony became the St. George's Bay Company in 1799 and finally the Sierra Leone Company in 1800. The company's mission, supported by abolitionist members of the Clapham sect in London including William Wilberforce and Zachary Macaulay, was, in Jefferson's mind, "the express purpose of colonizing blacks to that country." Jefferson asked his minister to London, Rufus King, to "enter into conference with persons private and public as would be necessary to give us permission to send thither" slaves "guilty of insurgency." Deporting slaves to Sierra Leone, Jefferson envisioned, would allow Virginians to "gradually" draw "off this part of our population," rebellious slaves. The "exile" of blacks to Africa might render their "sojournment and sufferings here a blessing in the end to that country."[45] King met with Henry Thornton, the president of the Court of Directors of the Sierra Leone Company, asking for permission to send to Sierra Leone those Virginia "Negroes that from time to time shall be emancipated in that State together with those whose residence in Virginia might prove injurious to the subordination of the slaves."[46]

Thornton balked at the prospect of his colony being flooded with rebellious American slaves. King tried to reassure a concerned Wilberforce, promising that the exiles "will include our most meritorious slaves and . . . will not be idle and vicious," as "they would not possess sufficient influence over their associates to become Leaders in the Scheme of Insurrection."[47] Of course, what neither Jefferson nor King realized was that Wilberforce and Macaulay did not see Sierra Leone as a "receptacle" for insurgent slaves. Rather, they saw it as a free labor experiment in Africa, as a counterpoint to the barbarity of the slave trade that plagued Africa's western coasts and an alternative to the slave-based sugar empire of the West Indies. Sierra Leone was for members of the Clapham sect a first foray into the wilds of Africa, an initial step in the civilizing process that might ameliorate Africa and include it in a global free market society.[48]

Jefferson's proposal for a "receptacle" for insurgent Virginia slaves differed from the broader colonization schemes he had articulated in his *Notes on the State of Virginia* several decades before. His desire to expatriate all blacks living on American soil continued to loom large in his imagination, even in the wake of the Prosser conspiracy. All blacks, he believed, especially those whose "degraded condition" had been ameliorated by benevolent masters, would one day be sent outside of the U.S. to form their own legitimate and civilized "people." But Jefferson's proposal for a repository for rebellious bondsmen and free blacks was markedly different. This scheme entailed sending a limited number of blacks, all of whom exhibited violent and barbaric tendencies, to a remote outpost, not to become a legitimate nation but to be severed from Virginia forever. In short, Jefferson maintained a firm commitment to the future emancipation and expatriation of all Virginia slaves, but in moments of exigency, such as after the discovery of the Prosser conspiracy in Richmond, Jefferson's first recourse was deportation and exile. The contrast and tension between the "receptacle" and the "nation" reveal the shortcomings of Jefferson's efforts to control and direct national populations. Although Jefferson's understanding of the "captive nation" of slaves necessitated that *all* blacks be "repatriated" to their own "country," the response to the Prosser conspiracy poked holes in that theory. He advocated not that all Virginia slaves be sent to form their own "people" in Sierra Leone, but that a fragment of the population— identified as so-called conspirators—should be exiled to a holding area, not a nation.[49]

Still, Jefferson refused to allow this idea to overshadow his commitment to his "ex post nati" scheme. To him, it remained the only proposal to guarantee a homogenous and "durable" American nation. In 1824, Jefferson suggested a plan similar to the one he had sketched in his *Notes* more than forty years before. As a "result of my reflections on the subject" under the "fourteenth query," Jefferson told Jared Sparks, "I have never yet been able to conceive any other practicable plan." Yet because "there are a million and a half of people of color in slavery" on American soil, to "send off the whole of these at once" would "not be practicable for us" or "expedient for them." Rather, Jefferson proposed "emancipating the after-born, leaving them, on due compensation, with their mothers, until their services are worth their maintenance," and then "putting them to industrious occupations, until a proper age for deportation." Jefferson allotted compensation for slave owners, the slow disappearance of older slaves from the continent, and the repatriation of younger, ameliorated slaves outside the boundaries of the United States. Although Jefferson conceded that "this subject involves some constitutional scruples" and that the "separation of infants from their mothers . . . would produce some scruples of humanity," he insisted that gradual colonization of black slaves was the only way to remove their presence from the union. The alternative, Jefferson imagined, was "six millions" slaves concentrated on the American continent, and "one million of these fighting men, will say, 'we will not go.'" In light of this horrific possibility, focusing on the "scruples" rather than on the broader goal of repatriation, "would be straining at a gnat, and swallowing a camel."[50]

The goal, Jefferson believed, was "most interesting to us" because it was the only recourse that guaranteed the improvement and subsequent "happiness" of two separate peoples. It was critical, he thought, to "our physical and moral characters, to our happiness and safety" to "provide an asylum" by "degrees" and "send the whole of that population from among us." Americans could then "establish them [Africans] under our patronage and protection, as a separate, free and independant people, in some country and climate friendly to human life and happiness." And "by doing this," Jefferson wrote, "we may make to them some retribution for the long course of injuries we have been committing on their population."[51]

Slaves' colonization was thus the avatar of Jefferson's idea of amelioration. On the one hand, the removal of black slaves from the American continent would secure their "happiness" as an ethnically homogenous people, and, in due time, secure their future as a viable political nation. Becoming a "people" would supplant the "injuries" done to Africans for centuries through the slave trade and slavery. Yet colonization would also guarantee the happiness of the American people. Uniting to remove a foreign population from domestic soil, Jefferson thought, would allow Americans to vindicate their rights to legitimate nationhood. No matter how much it was ameliorated, slavery remained a remnant of Old World tyranny, a "state of war," and an impediment to civilization. But with all slaves colonized, with the "blot" lifted from the American union, Jefferson saw no reason why it could not become the "strongest government on earth."[52]

Yet when Jefferson observed that no actual colonization plans were being implemented in America by the 1800s, he looked for new solutions to the problem of controlling an increasing black population. In Virginia, the slave population was 292,627 in 1790; a decade later, that number had climbed to 346,671. So quickly was the slave population reproducing itself in Virginia and other southern states that the heavily concentrated black population threatened to ink out the whites who lived among them. Indeed, the "burden" of slavery was not just the institution's moral depravity, but rather, the difficulty of subordinating—and ameliorating—an overwhelming population of slaves in a bounded area. With a concentrated number of slaves present in Virginia, Jefferson reasoned, the likelihood of a race war seemed more imminent. Slave owners would fear, rather than care for, their bondsmen.[53] Yet the increased population of slaves seemed to Jefferson a likely way to convince many of his neighbors to embrace large-scale emancipation and colonization. So much would they fear "the bloody process of St. Domingo," this time on Virginia soil, that masters would preemptively colonize their slaves to avoid their own death and torture.[54] It would be in the whites' interest, then, to save themselves and to consent to the ultimate act: the "repatriation" of all black slaves.

But as early as the turn of the century, Virginians attempted to alleviate the "burden" of slavery in their native state not through Jefferson's "ex post nati" plan but through diffusion. During congressional debates that sought to organize the territory ceded to the United States under the terms of the Treaty of San Lorenzo in 1798, several Virginians argued in favor of diffusing slaves over a wider geographic region as a precursor to emancipation. Spreading slaves across the new Mississippi territory would ease the burden of slavery in the old southeastern states. Congressman William Giles argued that "if slaves of the Southern States were permitted to go into the Western country, by lessening the number in those States, and spreading them over a large surface of country, there would be a great probability in ameliorating their condition, which could never be done whilst they were crowded together as they now are." Concentration of the slave population only exacerbated the tension between whites and blacks—their diffusion increased the likelihood of amelioration and future emancipation. "It would ... be doing a service not only to them [the slaves]," Virginian John Nicholas asserted, "but to the whole Union, to open this Western Country, and by that means spread the blacks over a large space, so that in time it might be safe to carry into effect the plan which certain philanthropists have so much at heart, and to which no objection could be effected, viz., the emancipation of this class of men."[55] Presumably, those slaves diffused across the continent would work alongside free laborers on farms, rather than on plantations, in the western territories. Over time, settlers would come to see bondage as an unnecessary system; with this logic, emancipation would soon follow.

The diffusion schemes advocated by men like Nicholas and Giles were augmented by the actual spread of slaves out of Virginia, this time through the internal slave trade. Indeed, Virginia was one of the first southeastern states to sell surplus slaves to new states in the southwest; the Old Dominion played a central role in the forced migration of about 1 million enslaved people through the domestic slave trade.[56] Selling first to Tennessee, Georgia, and Kentucky, slave traders in Virginia expanded their commercial networks as new states were carved from the Louisiana territory.[57]

Diffusion—and the question of slavery itself—assumed a new dimension in light of the Missouri crisis of 1819. On the one hand, many slave owners insisted upon their right to transport slave property westward without interference from the federal government. And since the Panic of 1819 had rendered land and currency virtually worthless because of the collapse of what Jefferson called "fictitious and doubtful capital," slave owners were all the more eager to maintain—and expand—property that continued to appreciate: slaves.[58] Jefferson saw the Missouri question as "a mere party trick." The "leaders of federalism, defeated in their schemes of obtaining power by rallying partisans to the principle of monarchism," he wrote to Charles Pinckney in 1820, "have changed their tack, and . . . are taking advantage of the virtuous feelings of the people to effect a division of parties by a geographical line." Because "they could never obtain" the "majority" on "principles of federalism," neo-Federalists substituted "Jeremiads on the miseries of slavery." Restrictionists, those politicians who sought to limit the spread of slavery, Jefferson believed, sought to use the slavery question to garner power, to pit supposedly proslavery forces against antislavery ones, to set section against section and divide the union. Yet restrictionists did not really care about slavery, or about slaves, Jefferson maintained. "Sincerity in their declamations should direct their efforts to the true point of difficulty, and unite their counsels with ours in devising some reasonable and practicable plan of getting rid of it." Of course, the "plan" Jefferson had in mind was the diffusion and subsequent eradication of slavery.[59]

During the height of the Missouri crisis, Jefferson advocated the diffusion of slaves westward not because he did not care about their welfare but because he believed he did care.[60] Insincere Federalists seemed to spin the limitation of slavery as having "a semblance of being Moral," arguing that the containment of slavery was the only way to halt the evil's progression. Yet for Jefferson, "moral the question certainly is not." Indeed, as he told Albert Gallatin, "if there were any morality in the question it is on the other side." Diffusion, in fact, was the only moral recourse, since spreading slaves across the continent ameliorated their condition. Through diffusion, slaves' "happiness will be increased, & the burthen of their future liberation lightened by bringing a greater number of shoulders under it."[61]

Jefferson's belief in the viability of diffusion rested on his assumption that slavery, especially after the abolition of the slave trade, was a regressive, Old World system that would not regenerate. In his eyes, diffusion of slaves would succeed because the institution of slavery was not growing and adapting—an assumption that seems ludicrous in hindsight. But Jefferson nonetheless reassured his friend the Marquis de Lafayette that "spreading" slaves "over a greater surface, will dilute the evil every where." Lafayette, who had purchased a plantation at Cayenne in French Guinea in 1786 to experiment with the gradual emancipation of slaves, remained skeptical of Jefferson's logic.[62] "Are you Sure, My dear Friend, that Extending the principle of Slavery to the New Raised States is a Method to facilitate the Means of Getting Rid of it? I would have thought that By Spreading the prejudices, Habits, and Calculations of planters over a larger Surface You Rather Encrease the difficulties of final liberation," the marquis wrote to his old friend. Unconvinced by Jefferson's "Argument in favor of dissemination," Lafayette made a point of adding that "one is I believe More Struck with the evil when Looking Upon it from without" than within.[63] Indeed, from within the southeastern states, "dissemination" seemed like the only way to ameliorate slaves and protect whites. Otherwise, as one Virginian wrote to James Monroe, whites might be "dammed up in a land of slaves."[64]

But of course, for Jefferson, advocating the diffusion of slavery westward did not signify the dawn of any new proslavery consciousness on his part. Such views would have had to rest on new assumptions about slavery— that it was modern, adaptable, and beneficial to the nation. But Jefferson never deviated from his prescriptive vision of slavery as an archaic, Old World system. Instead, Jefferson believed that the further amelioration of slavery through diffusion would pave the way for emancipation and colonization. Indeed, Jefferson's enthusiasm for "ex post nati" schemes remained undiminished in the 1820s—he emphasized the necessity of slaves' removal not just to preserve the union but also to serve as the basis for its cohesion. The Missouri crisis had threatened to pit states against other states, to inscribe a "geographical line" between north and south, rather than to sustain a union of states against a common foreign threat. Yet Jefferson believed that all states, whether slave or free, could unite to undertake the project of large-scale African repatriation. Amid the "prospect of evil" and disunion, Jefferson told Gallatin that he was reassured on at least one front. The Missouri question "has brought the necessity of some plan of general emancipation & deportation more home to the minds of our people than it has ever been before." And while a new scheme had been brought before the Virginia legislature, "it will probably not be acted on at this time" or "be effectual." Still, Jefferson's perception of an extended conversation was a critical first step in removing "this evil" that was "forced . . . on us." It would be such a discussion, replicated in every state in the union, that would bind the country together and prevent it from fracturing along artificial "Moral" or "Geographical" lines."[65]

AMELIORATION AND DOMESTICATION
The Plantation Household

Jefferson's ultimate goal in removing the "captive nation" from American soil was to fulfill American claims to nationhood. With the black population neatly excised from the white, Jefferson imagined that his "empire of liberty," and the western colonization project that undergirded it, would expand without limit. As he wrote in 1801, "it is impossible not to look forward to distant times, when our rapid multiplication will expand" and "cover the whole northern, if not the southern continent, with a people speaking the same language, governed in similar forms, & by similar laws." In this homogenous empire, Jefferson could not "contemplate with satisfaction either blot or mixture." The stain of slavery and "mixture" of the races would undermine Jefferson's vision of colonization for North and South America.[66]

Jefferson sought to create an expanding nation of farmers. Small-scale farms worked by "independent" men would replace large-scale plantations worked by enslaved laborers. "Those who labour in the earth are the chosen people of God" in "whose breasts he has made his peculiar deposit for substantial and genuine virtue," he wrote. Through their attachment to the land, farmers preserved—and invigorated—the "spirit" of the republic. Furthermore, the "moral and physical preference of the agricultural" would not simply expand the white population and the economy and pre-serve the union, Jefferson told the political economist Jean Baptiste Say. In a nation of agriculturists, "a double or treble portion of fertile lands would be brought into culture." As a result, "a double or treble portion of food" would be produced, "and its surplus go to nourish the now perishing births of Europe, who in return would manufacture and send us in exchange our clothes and other comforts." A homogenous population of farmers dif-fused across the New World could also alleviate the "misery" of popula-tions in the Old World, Jefferson thought.[67]

His "chosen people" would settle the land in separate family farms. Con-centrated populations were reminiscent of consolidated and illegitimate power—the "mobs of great cities" or "all the people gathered in villages" constituted the "1st step to[war]ds corrupt[io]n." But on family farms, Jef-ferson imagined, virtuous farmers were also virtuous heads of household who preserved the republic. The American republic was a great "family" of families; the basic unit of this larger family was the farm. Each household comprised the farmer patriarch and his dependents. But because Jefferson conceived of the "captive nation" as "foreign" and naturally hostile to their white masters, black slaves could never constitute a legitimate part of the domestic family farm. Thus, to preserve his homogenous population of farmers, Jefferson fervently believed that all blacks had to be emancipated and "repatriated" outside of the federal union.[68]

But until the day when slave owners would consent for their human property to be emancipated and repatriated, enabling white farmer-patriarchs to expand unimpeded, Jefferson crafted a "rational and humane plan" to ameliorate his slaves and his plantations.[69] He sought to construct an idealized domestic space that would serve as the wellspring of morality and "happiness." As he noted during his first retirement from public office in 1793, "I have my house to build, my feilds to form, and to watch for the happiness of those who labor for mine." In this sense, Jefferson's domestic sphere included not only his white family but also his black one; he used "family" as an inclusive term that encompassed the hundreds of members of his "household." But it was crucial that his black dependents could not, as perpetual enemies of the state (and their masters), remain permanent fixtures of Jefferson's land. His goal of "improving" enslaved men and women was done with an eye toward their eventual removal.[70]

Still, it was no accident that Jefferson embarked upon his "rational" plan of amelioration when Virginia's economy was facing disaster. Years of ero-sion and tobacco planting had slashed profits and depleted harvests. Compounding these conditions was the widespread indebtedness of most elite Virginia planters to British creditors after the revolution. The decades of extracting crops from the soil and labor from slaves without any thought of preserving either the land or labor force for future generations had detrimental consequences. This new difficulty in making money from the land forced planters to make agriculture and labor more efficient, profitable systems. In other words, hard times forced planters to "husband" and "ameliorate" both their lands and their slaves if they were going to survive in the postrevolutionary period. Planters like Jefferson, for the first time after the revolution, began rotating and manuring croplands and replacing brute force with a system of rewards and punishments for slaves.[71]

After the revolution, Jefferson imagined his landholdings not as tobacco plantations but as farms characterized by both reformed agriculture and domestic industry. His primary aim was to relinquish tobacco cultivation, not least because it "rapidly impoverished" the land and the farmers who tilled it.[72] Tobacco had been a crop cultivated by Virginians under the imperial regime, its produce destined for English (and Scottish) ports and buyers. Since tobacco required slave labor and exhausted the soil, it seemed artificial and baneful to a domestic economy. He insisted that "the more we can lay it [tobacco] aside, the happier I shall be."[73] When consulting George Washington about agricultural practices, Jefferson wrote, "Good husbandry with us, consists in abandoning Indian corn, and tobacco."[74] It was no accident that both these crops had been eagerly sought after by metropolitan Britons and West Indian planters throughout the eighteenth century.[75] Jefferson sought to improve his own lands and those of his fellow Virginians, to reclaim the landscape from "the barbarous state in which the slovenly business of tobacco had left them."[76]

In the end, Jefferson replaced most of his tobacco crop with wheat at Monticello in the 1790s. With poor harvests and impending war in Europe, grain was fetching high prices at overseas markets. "There will be war enough to give us high prices for wheat for years to come; and this single commodity will make us a great and happy nation," he wrote in 1790. While the introduction of wheat on Jefferson's plantations did not render slave labor superfluous, it did require only about one-fifth the labor of tobacco, allowing Jefferson to diversify and improve his plantation holdings. Still, Jefferson's efforts to create an ideal farm with his transition from tobacco to wheat were often marred by his own incompetence as a farmer. Although he successfully designed a new plow—"the Mouldboard of *least resistance*"—to save labor with its precise furrow-cutting capacity, his vertical plowing technique meant that the topsoil and manure washed off his fields. And while he zealously embraced wheat planting in the place of corn production, the fact that corn was a staple of the diet of his slaves and livestock meant that he had to purchase expensive barrels of corn from his neighbors. A poor speculator, Jefferson often generated marginal profits from his wheat crops at Monticello and tobacco crops at his Poplar Forest plantation. His limitations as a farmer were brought to light when his grandson, Thomas Jefferson Randolph, assumed the management of his Monticello lands in 1815 and tripled the yield of wheat.[77]

More successful than Jefferson's efforts to reform agriculture on his plantation was his domestication of manufacturing, especially on Mulberry Row, the main plantation street at Monticello. Jefferson, always the foe of large-scale urban industry, sought to create "household manufactures" on the scale of his idealized family farm. He tried to domesticate the industrial revolution on his lands.[78] The cottage industry that he promoted at Monticello would make his plantation self-sufficient and even provide supplies to his neighbors, Jefferson reasoned. His slaves were implicated and included in this project. Enslaved boys aged ten to sixteen worked in the Mulberry Row nailery, producing thousands of nails each day in seven different sizes. In 1795, he wrote that the "nailery which I have established with my own negro boys now provides completely for the maintenance of my family, as we make from 8. to 10,000 nails a day and it is on the increase." Jefferson weighed the nailrod—the iron rod from which the nails were produced—and nails daily to calculate the loss of iron and assess the efficiency of his young workers; he sold the nails to local markets and neighbors. By 1815, Jefferson had opened a textile "factory" on Mulberry Row; he first introduced mechanized cloth production to his plantation when trade embargoes and war with Britain cut off the supply of British cloth. Using spinning jennies, hand looms, and a hand-cranked carding machine, enslaved women and girls produced coarse cloth from wool, cotton, hemp, and flax in order to clothe as many as 140 slaves. In 1815, he boasted, "I make in my family 2000. yds. of cloth a year, which I formerly bought from England, and it only employs a few women, children and invalids who could do little in the farm."[79]

Jefferson's plantation at Monticello became not only a laboratory experiment in putting household manufacturing and agriculture in "equilibrio," but also an experiment in how to "husband" slave labor and make it more efficient. As such, Jefferson sought to improve labor and maximize

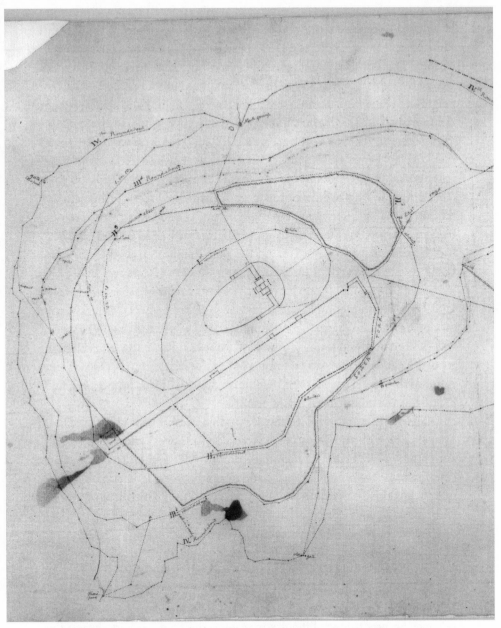

Thomas Jefferson, Monticello: Mountaintop, 1809. In this plat, Mulberry Row is the primary plantation street that runs perpendicular to the main house. It was the location of many dwellings for enslaved house servants and artisans as well as of several "shops," including the textile shop, joinery, and nailery. (Original manuscript from the Coolidge Collection of Thomas Jefferson Manuscripts. Courtesy of the Massachusetts Historical Society)

returns by reforming the "government" of his enslaved men and women. He sought to replace corporal punishment with incentives. Writing from Philadelphia in 1792, Jefferson's "first wish is that the labourers may be well treated." Even though Jefferson sold eighty-four slaves in an effort to discharge his debts in the 1780s and 1790s, and hired out most of his slaves to neighbors while he was minister to France, he sought to reform his plantation management schemes during his first retirement.[80] To that end, in 1793, Jefferson tried to acquire a new overseer from Maryland, believing that "the husbandry about the head of Elk is in wheat & grazing: little corn, & less pork." He told his son-in-law Thomas Mann Randolph that "this I think is what would suit us best, for which reason I turned my attention to that quarter." Jefferson thought the "labour there [in Maryland] being performed by slaves with some mixture of free labourers" allowed the "farmers there [to] understand the management of negroes on a rational & humane plan." Still, the tenure of these overseers was brief; Jefferson employed many other overseers who brutalized slaves. In 1804, a white house joiner complained of overseer Gabriel Lilly's "Barbarity" in disciplining a young slave. James Hemings, who was ill and unable to work, was "whip'd . . . three times in one day," James Oldham, the house joiner, reported, "and the boy was raly not able to raise his hand to his Head." Because of this "severe treatment," Hemings ran away from Monticello, taking up life as a boatman on the James River.[81]

Jefferson sought to replace the "degrading motive of fear" of corporal punishment with the "stimulus of character"—slaves' desire to emulate and improve—in order to encourage productivity and efficiency. Rather than use force to compel his enslaved artisans to work, Jefferson offered financial incentives—gratuities or percentages of workshop profits to those who maximized efficiency and output.[82] He stipulated that the whip "must not be resorted to except in extremities," but his instructions were often ignored during his long absences. In the Mulberry Row nailery, for example, the "small ones" could be whipped for "truancy."[83] Other times, it appeared that the whip was the only way to manage enslaved workers. In 1798, Jefferson's son-in-law reported that the African American overseer George Granger Sr. was having difficulty managing the field workers during the summer corn harvest. Since Granger could not "command his force," then "in some instances of disobedience so gross," Randolph was "obliged to interfere and have them punished myself."[84]

Jefferson sought to ameliorate and domesticate his slaves by dividing them into families. In the 1790s, when he embarked on a plan of "improvement" at Monticello and transitioned from tobacco to wheat, Jefferson also altered his slaves' housing. Rather than the multifamily barracks-style housing constructed at Monticello in the 1770s and the 1780s, single-family wooden dwellings were built on the plantation from the 1790s. In the 1800s, Jefferson even made plans to further improve these houses by building them out of stone rather than wood.[85] But his apparently humanitarian shift from group to family housing glossed over the fact that Jefferson's plan of "domesticating" his slaves in family units was also a plan for the "increase" of his human property. In Virginia, enslaved women achieved fertility rates that allowed for a self-reproducing slave population. Many slave owners, including Jefferson, understood that female slaves—and their future children—represented the best means to increase the value of his holdings, what he called "capital." "I consider a woman who brings a child every two years as more profitable than the best man of the farm," Jefferson remarked in 1820. "What she produces is an addition to the capital, while his labors disappear in mere consumption." The fact that Jefferson acquired many of the 607 slaves he owned in his lifetime through natural "increase" undercut his understanding of slavery as a static and regressive "blot" that would eventually be expelled from the union.[86]

Although Jefferson imagined his plantation as an improving and progressively domesticated realm, he drew a line between his idealized enslaved domestics and "foreign" and rebellious slaves who resisted his efforts through violence and misbehavior. Jefferson's imagined ideal of the domestic farm, governed by a patriarch and peopled by his dependents, was the image that allowed him to romanticize slaves. This exemplar for Jefferson was an improving, productive, and loyal domestic worker. Loyalty, or trustworthiness, was often the gauge for a slave's domestication or inclusion within the plantation household. During the American Revolution, when British troops approached Charlottesville, it was Jefferson's slave, Martin Hemings, who alerted him to the troops' approach; it was Hemings who hid the valuables from the British when they arrived at Monticello.[87] In 1790, Jefferson seemed convinced enough that Robert Hemings would not run away from his service; he allowed the slave to hire himself out to George Carter in Williamsburg.[88] While Jefferson was living in Washington, the slave Burwell became the "keeper of the keys" at Monticello and chief waiter. By 1811, Jefferson began offering express rewards for such loyalty—he paid both Burwell and the cabinetmaker John Hemmings an "annual gratuity" of twenty dollars each.[89]

These seemingly loyal and trustworthy slaves were not important because they were an indicator of Jefferson's benevolence or humanity. Rather, they demonstrated that the relationship between citizen and slave did not have to be a "commerce of the most boisterous passions." Instead, the relationship could be ameliorated and shorn of enmity, a notion Jefferson had first suggested as a young lawyer but refused to embrace in the postrevolutionary years. A relationship that was wasteful and selfish seemed capable of being reformed into a source for social improvement. Instead of the cart whip and violence, there were incentives and "rational" plantation management schemes. Instead of an "unnatural" relationship between two warring nations, slavery was transformed—through amelioration—into a "natural" connection between benevolent patriarchs and their enslaved "children." With this relationship recast, the model for slave owning became not absentee plantership but small-scale yeoman farms. As Thomas Mann Randolph told his father-in-law, large-scale planting "cannot be successfully pursued by means of Slaves (who tho admirable for labor are little worth for care & judgement,) unless upon a very small scale and where the person feeling the first interest joins in the daily business of the farm." Jefferson, as an absentee planter from the late 1790s until his retirement from the presidency in 1809, could never fit this model. His absence from his farms and slaves left his amelioration projects unfulfilled. For as many times that Jefferson lauded the seeming domestication and loyalty of his slaves, he was also pointing out the "foreign" and incendiary traits of runaways and rebels.[90]

Instances of slave violence and disloyalty reminded Jefferson that some of his slaves resisted being gathered into the affections of his "family." In 1803, one of the slaves working at the Monticello nailery, Cary, cracked the skull of another nailboy named Brown Colbert. "It will be necessary for me to make an example" of Cary "in terrorem to others," Jefferson wrote to Randolph. It was critical for Jefferson to "maintain the police so rigorously necessary among the nailboys." Certainly all the slaves employed at the nailery were, to varying extents, domestic workers. But these workers were still enslaved—Jefferson realized that even outwardly "happy" domestic slaves could be prone to violence. Yet Jefferson could not keep such slaves—exemplified by the dangerous figure of Cary—on any of his plantations. Slaves like Cary would impede Jefferson's amelioration efforts. "I would rather he should be sold in any other quarter so distant as never to be heard of among us, it would to the others be as if he were put out of the way by death," Jefferson wrote. Thus, being sold away to slave traders was a fate equal to execution, for Jefferson surmised that Cary's history, his very identity, all of which centered upon Monticello, would be erased when he was sold south. Jefferson regarded "price but little in comparison with so distant an exile of him as to cut him off compleatly from ever again being heard of."[91] A critical dimension of Jefferson's amelioration efforts was to grant deserving, loyal slaves identities, whether "keeper of the keys," "cabinetmaker," or "cook," as well as a history that was wholly domestic. But when slaves became violent, when they assumed the characteristics of barbarous insurgents, Jefferson could think of no worse punishment than "exile" from that history and "family."

Ultimately, Jefferson's efforts to "improve" and domesticate his slaves as the precursor to their eventual emancipation and "repatriation" undercut his definition of slavery as an archaic, Old World system and his understanding of slaves as a "captive nation." Despite being punctuated by incidents of violence—Cary's attack or overseers' brutality—Jefferson's plantation "family" by the 1820s seemed wholly domesticated according to his standards. The slaves on his plantations constituted families, including the Hemingses, Herns, Gillettes, Grangers, and Fossetts. The reproduction rate was high, indicating to Jefferson the "happiness" of his enslaved laborers. Several enslaved women were domestic servants in the main house or on Mulberry Row; dozens of enslaved men were highly skilled tradesmen. Still, Jefferson would not be swayed from his position that slavery should end despite his slaves' seeming amelioration and inclusion within his domestic household.[92]

Jefferson's understanding of slavery as a regressive and corrupting system was the result of his adherence to the European Enlightenment understanding of the institution as antithetical to progress. Like many other members of the revolutionary generation, he could no sooner contemplate the "amelioration of the condition of man" in the continued presence of slavery as he could comprehend race-mixing and blacks' "incorporation" into the state. A homogenous citizenry of independent farmers embracing the "empire of liberty" as they expanded across the continent epitomized his vision of amelioration in the federal union. The presence of the "captive nation" could have no place in this vision. The enslaved population in his mind would always remain a separate nation that was "the wolf by the ear," ready to incite a bloody race war that would tear the federal union apart. And slave owning—the relationship between master and slave—could never really be improved and reformed, he thought, despite his own experiments at Monticello that seemed to prove the contrary. The relationship was inherently violent and unproductive in his mind; coercing enslaved blacks marred his vision of a nation of yeoman agriculturists and their family farms. In a letter to William Short, Jefferson conceded the apparent success of the amelioration of slavery—"our only blot is becoming less offensive by the great improvement and civilization of that race." But a more benevolent slave regime did not reassure Jefferson. "Still," he declared, "it is a hideous blot." Despite the system's expansion and apparent improvement, Jefferson remained convinced of the necessity of "removing the evil" from American soil.[93]

By Jefferson's death, it appeared clear to many slave owners that American slavery defied Jefferson's Old World definitions. With the institution seemingly mitigated and domesticated, there was little need to fear the race war and tyranny about which Jefferson had warned his peers. The primary evidence of this amelioration was the self-reproducing slave population. In 1790, the U.S. slave population stood at 654,121. By 1830, four years after Jefferson died, it had swelled to 1,983,860. No longer did the black population look to pose a serious threat to the white—instead, it facilitated the progress and expansion of the American union as well as the equality of white property owners. Thus, Jefferson, through his plans to ameliorate slavery with an eye toward ending it, inadvertently crafted the language for the institution's perpetuation. As we see in the next chapter, amelioration became both a means and an end for slave owners. An expanding slave population in the southern states and a flourishing cotton economy offered proof that American slavery was a unique, modern, and improving system. There seemed little need to abolish a system that appeared to "improve"—rather than threaten to destroy—the new American nation. This proslavery amelioration represented a new understanding of progress in an "exceptional" nation. It was a critical reversal from previous Enlightenment conceptions of the sociopolitical advancement of equal nations within a single Atlantic system. Whereas the American patriots and European *philosophes* had believed that progress rested on the absence of slavery, successive generations of southerners argued that slavery, albeit in a mitigated form, was the very reason for national progress.[94]

2

"THE DESIDERATUM IS TO DIMINISH THE BLACKS AND INCREASE THE WHITES"

At age eighty-one, Thomas Jefferson was convinced that progress was spreading westward. "I have observed this march of civilization advancing from the sea-coast, passing over us like a cloud of light, increasing our knowledge and improving our condition," he wrote to William Ludlow in 1824. In the meantime, he assured, "barbarism has . . . been receding before the steady step of amelioration" and will soon "disappear from the earth." The Rockies he imagined as the least refined; the eastern coast, with its access to Atlantic markets, the most advanced. In surveying what he considered to be an ever-expanding and improving American civilization, Jefferson never imagined its limits. "Where this progress will stop," he wrote, "no one can say." This was Jefferson's vision of expansion, his rubric for the colonization of a continent. In his formulation, amelioration was the agent of progress; it peeled back barbarism in the western outposts and culminated in their civilization.[1]

Less than a decade after Jefferson sketched out his vision for the "march of civilization," in the 1830s, two Virginians who appeared to claim oppositional views on slavery confronted the question of how civilization would "spread" across Virginia and the union. The issue was whether slavery facilitated or impeded this civilization. The political economist and College of William and Mary professor Thomas Dew was the advocate of the so-called positive good thesis—the antebellum argument that slavery was a positive force in society. He observed that "every where you see the negro slave by the side of the white man," since slaves were "increasing and spreading" and had become "intertwined and intertwisted" in the population of Virginia. Preferring to yield to the market, Dew criticized the invasive—and potentially destructive—schemes of emancipation and colonization. Dew also dismissed Virginians' fear of race war and disunion, instead asserting that slaves were domesticated servants who only contributed to prosperity and security. If there was any impediment to progress, Dew quipped, it was the protective federal tariffs of 1828 and 1832 that stunted free trade. For Dew, slavery and whites' colonization westward went hand in hand. Conversely, the moral reformer and agricultural improver John Hartwell Cocke shared many of Jefferson's views. Cocke appeared to be an antislavery proponent; he adhered to the notion that emancipation and repatriation of blacks was critical to the survival of the union and its expansion across time and space. Slavery was, Cocke thought, inimical to progress, just as slave owning was the exertion of one man's "tyranny" over another. On his Bremo plantation in Virginia, and at his New Hope and Hopewell plantations in northern Alabama, Cocke set out to "improve" his slaves with the future goal of sending them to Liberia.[2]

Dew appeared to embrace an "empire of slavery" while Cocke seemed to adhere to Jefferson's "empire of liberty." But this chapter shows that the divisions were not as stark as contemporary observers or modern-day historians might have surmised. The parochial slave debates in the political arena obfuscated the larger issues at stake. Both men would have agreed with Jefferson's vision of the "steady step of amelioration" as outlined in 1824, a vision that would likely take centuries to fulfill. For both Cocke and Dew, eastern states in the federal union were the most civilized; white colonization of the West and the transformation of semi-barbarous outposts into civilized states depended on their connection to markets in more established and advanced states on the Atlantic coast. Cocke argued that slaves' colonization east to Africa had to be the critical antecedent of the union's expansion west. But Dew asserted that slavery should be left alone and governed by market forces; he thought that in the future, slavery would "diffuse" itself westward, thereby leaving Virginia as a progressively whiter state. Slavery was a primary *agent* of civilization, but it did not *represent* civilization, Dew thought. With the aid of internal improvements and commerce, he reasoned, Virginia would one day resemble nonslaveholding states in the Northeast. Virginia might "whiten" in the same manner as had Maryland. Thus, the apparent proslavery advocate and antislavery colonizationist actually shared the same vision: a future Virginia without slaves. The two men—like so many other elite white Virginians whose views they reflected—believed slavery could hold no permanent place in civilized society because it was not modern. Dew, despite believing that slavery was the crucial driving force behind man's progress from barbarism to enlightenment, ultimately believed that free labor would supersede slave labor in the proto-industrial future that he prophesied for Virginia. And Cocke thought that American citizens were prevented from advancing and that the union was prevented from expanding as long as the archaic and violent system of slavery continued to plague America's shores.[3]

In 1831, with the outbreak of the Nat Turner rebellion, Virginia's status as a civilized polity seemed to be in serious jeopardy. In August of that year, nearly sixty whites were killed by a band of armed slaves in Southampton County led by the slave Nat Turner. The resulting scene, as one cavalry officer described it, was of "whole families, father, mother, daughters, sons, sucking babes, and school children, butchered, thrown into heaps, and left to be devoured by hogs and dogs, or to putrefy on the spot."[4] In the days following the insurrection, at least ninety blacks were slaughtered by armed troops, their severed heads mounted on posts along the public roads. Although contemporary Virginians questioned the possible exaggeration of the extent of the rebellion—as have modern-day historians—what remains clear is that much of white Virginia was paralyzed by the outbreak of violence. In the months after the massacre, these Virginians returned to the scene again and again; the image of the staked heads of blacks and the bloody piles of white families led many to speculate, despite Jefferson's earlier claim, about whether the state lay on the brink of a race war between whites and blacks.[5]

Thus, the question of whether Virginia could continue to maintain its civility in the wake of the Turner affair was a critical one. A strong contingent of Virginians remained committed to the colonization of slaves to Africa. They believed that slavery should be ameliorated and that slaves should then be gradually colonized outside of America. In this view, only slaves' removal from Virginia assured that the state would both survive and progress. The continued presence of slavery only prevented moral and political development, some believed. "Virginia cannot in the nature of things be prosperous with slavery," wrote the jurist and pamphleteer Jesse Burton Harrison. "*Virginia* was made by Providence with the necessity of a homogenous population of freemen if she ever means to prosper," he wrote.[6] Because many planters and politicians agreed that slavery in Virginia was "improving," however, many disputed that colonization was necessary. Instead, since slavery was being mitigated, and slaves were becoming "domesticated" servants rather than "foreign" instigators of revolt, then it seemed plausible that the presence of slavery enabled progress. Nat

Turner, colonization opponents argued, was simply an aberration in an otherwise "happy" slave population.[7]

In the 1830s, the Turner revolt and a growing black population polarized Virginians and seemingly divided them into oppositional cohorts. The proslavery and antislavery binary appears even more marked when studied through the lens of state politics. But when we relate the "problem" of slavery in Virginia to the larger colonization project of the federal union, the differences fade considerably. This chapter thus bridges the divide of proslavery and antislavery thinking in the 1830s by demonstrating that Cocke and Dew both embraced amelioration and shared similar plans for the expansion and "whitening" of Virginia and the union. Improvement was always the goal of the removal of the black population—through African colonization, as Cocke argued, or through the "drain" of the domestic slave trade, as Dew related. Those who would act as ameliorators would be slave owners on individual plantations as well as more abstract "agents"—God, in Cocke's eyes, and the "invisible hand" of the market, in Dew's mind. Schemes to end slavery—even over the course of a century or longer—however, would be marginalized by an expanding and increasingly profitable domestic slave trade in Virginia as well as the rise of the cotton kingdom in the southeastern states.[8]

THE POPULATION PROBLEM

"Virginia was the mother of slavery," declared the former slave Louis Hughes after the outbreak of the Civil War. Hughes's statement was telling. Even in 1830, Virginia claimed the largest slave population in the union, with just shy of 470,000 souls. Virginia was also the primary supplier of slaves to other states through the domestic slave trade. Yet the substantial slave population was not a worry in itself for white Virginians in the wake of the Turner revolt. "Mother" was the key term in Hughes's description; the danger of Virginia's slave population was its limitless potential for increase.[9]

Since 1820, the number of free blacks had grown by over 10,000 and, in the same time period, the slave population had risen by about 45,000.[10] If the black population ever exceeded the white one, many white Virginians thought, a war between the races was virtually guaranteed. The Turner rebellion appeared to demonstrate that too many blacks, especially free blacks, resided in Virginia. Thus, in the ensuing months, delegates in the House of Assembly sought to devise a scheme to expel free blacks and slaves from their state. The main goal was not the eradication of slavery but the "gradual diminution, or ultimate extermination, of the black population of Virginia."[11]

The issue of population—and of the growth of populations—lay at the heart of the slave debates of 1831–32 because it was the primary marker of social progress or degeneracy in the nineteenth century. There was a direct correlation between "happiness" and a rising population; according to the British political economist Thomas Malthus and his peers, a miserable population contracted while a comfortable one expanded. Famine, poverty, and disease constituted the "miseries" that led to the death knell of populations while a parallel increase in subsistence and in population made for a happy and self-reproducing society. The presence of a self-regenerating slave population in Virginia thus seemed to prove that slaves themselves were happy. Virginians on both sides of the slave debate used the slave population statistics as evidence that slavery was being ameliorated in the Old Dominion: material conditions were being improved and violence was being mitigated. The more unsavory fact was that masters were providing for the material wants of their slaves in order to fetch higher prices for them at auction. Still, for those Virginians who perceived the Turner uprising as a harbinger for race war, amelioration was little consolation in the face of a rapidly increasing slave population. For these anxious Virginians, slaves might have become happy and deprived of misery, but this did not change the basic fact that a "captive nation" would inevitably rise against its white oppressors in due course.[12]

For many white Virginians, including Jefferson's own grandchildren, the revolt in Southampton County seemed like an indicator of future racial conflict. Writing from Edgehill plantation in the winter of 1831, Jane Hollins Randolph was wracked by fear. She stayed in the house, yearned for the company of her husband, and refused to travel to town. "The horrors that have taken place in Southampton have aroused all my fears which had nearly become dormant," she wrote to her sister. Indeed, "my worst fears & most torturing imagination had never conjured anything so terrifick as this unpitying & horrible slaughter." With her perception of slaves as loyal, domestic servants called into question, Randolph did not want to remain in Virginia. She sought to convince her husband, Thomas Jefferson Randolph, to "quit at once" and head west. "I feel as if I could never be happy here again," she lamented.[13]

Randolph attempted to assuage his wife's doubts. "I see by your letter that you are again making yourself uneasy about the negroes," he chided.

He tried to assure Jane that, "when the country is upon the alert, there is certainly the least danger." Indeed, he wrote, the "danger is to our children's children 40 or 50 years hence" but "not to us."[14] Yet even if Jane, along with the other Randolph-Jefferson women living at Edgehill, remained fearful of the specter created by the rebellion, the greatest source of their angst was their own imaginations. Cornelia Jefferson Randolph feared the worst when she wrote to her sister Ellen in Boston. "It is horrible to think that this may be in miniature the war that may hereafter be carried on a large scale" when "our swamps & mountains may be taken possession of by armies of dreadful banditti," she warned. Cornelia believed the revolt to be a preview of insurrections to come, each one successively more deadly and violent, as blacks began to outnumber whites.[15]

The alarming population increase of blacks in Virginia seemed to validate Thomas Jefferson's earlier fears of race war.[16] His granddaughter Mary Jefferson Randolph believed that "it is impossible not to see to what all this tends," namely, "that the black population is rapidly gaining ground on the white." It was not when the "whites are in numbers three to one against the blacks" and "with the advantage of having arms in their hands that Virginia need fear the fate of St. Domingo," she concluded.[17] Also, areas where "whites & blacks are equal," as in the Piedmont and Valley districts, held little threat of large-scale rebellion. Because, as Martha Jefferson Randolph wrote, the "majority is in our favor either 2/3d or 3/5th" with "fire arms and the habits of using them," whites, at least in Albemarle County, were safe. It was only when blacks outnumbered whites in ratios of "10 to one," as in Saint Domingue, that decimation would result.[18] Of course, some regions in Virginia seemed to be approaching that point. Thomas Jefferson Randolph mused that the "danger" lay in the "situation south of the James" where "blacks are 2 to 1 & more in a whole district of country." In other words, a white majority meant a secure slave society, but a black majority, such as the one that existed in southern Virginia, meant an unstable society prone to slave rebellions. Still, the danger was that slave societies with white majorities could quickly be transformed into societies with black majorities because the slave and free black populations self-reproduced so quickly.[19]

This perception caused throngs of Virginians to send petitions to the House of Assembly in the winter of 1831. Thousands of men petitioned the legislature to take action on the "slave question," which, to them, translated into a solution for the population problem. Some Virginians wanted the house to both end slavery and remove all blacks from Virginia. Others wanted all slaves and free blacks—as the perceived source of idleness and vice—colonized beyond the state's borders. Still others clamored simply for the removal of free blacks. In all, nearly 2,000 petitioners—698 from the Tidewater, 770 from the Piedmont, and 466 from the Valley and Allegheny regions—implored the state delegates to somehow curb the rising black population. None of these petitioners asked for an existential debate about the morality of slavery in the legislature; rather, they sought a practical solution to a very real threat. Of course, pleas for the removal of blacks, whether slave or free, could work toward two ends. On the one hand, removal could be the precursor to emancipation and the abolition of slavery in Virginia. On the other, deportation of blacks would only reinvigorate the current slave system by removing "dangerous" blacks. Thus, colonization, and the amelioration it implied, could lead to entirely different conclusions—emancipation *or* the continuation of slavery.[20]

This is what delegates in the House of Assembly debated during the winter session of 1831–1832. Several legislators presented various plans as possible solutions to the perceived crisis, all of which entailed some kind of removal of blacks from Virginia. Thomas Jefferson Randolph proposed the most radical scheme early in the debates. He did so at the behest of Edward Coles, the former Virginia planter and friend of Jefferson, who implored Randolph to "bring forward & press on the consideration of the people & their representatives" of the "absolute necessity of commencing a course of measures for the riddance of . . . that unfortunate & pernicious population."[21]

Randolph suggested that all children born to female slaves after July 4, 1840, become the "property of the commonwealth" and be hired out until the "nett sum arising therefrom shall be sufficient to defray the expence of their removal beyond the limits of the United States." Under Randolph's plan, the first slaves would not be liberated and deported until 1858.[22] Most delegates vehemently objected to this scheme, since it seemed to deny slave owners just compensation for their chattel. William Brodnax, a delegate from the Southside region, proposed a more moderate plan— levying a tax of thirty cents on every white person in the state. The resulting sum would finance the annual deportation of six thousand blacks. At some future time, Brodnax believed the state could purchase slaves from their masters and also transport them outside of Virginia. By 1910, Brodnax calculated, Virginia would achieve a free labor, all-white society.[23] In these proposals, as in those revisions proposed by delegates Henry Berry and Charles Faulkner, the real issues were subsidizing slave owners and financing deportation, as well as devising a transitional, gradual scheme for transforming blacks into freedmen.[24] Such schemes demanded a robust and bureaucratic government, neither of which existed in postrevolutionary Virginia. But the very next year a powerful central government, the British Parliament, abolished West Indian slavery with the provision that slaves become "apprentices" for a set period of time before achieving full freedom. Parliament also won the "consent" of slave owners because it compensated them for their lost human property.[25]

The debate over the colonization schemes in the house addressed the perceived threat of a rising black population. While the assembly refused "to make any legislative enactments for the abolition of slavery," the task at hand was to control the population through the forced removal of free blacks and slaves from Virginia.[26] The house thus did pass a colonization bill "for the removal of free persons of colour from the commonwealth" in January of 1832, although the senate defeated the bill, seventeen to fourteen. At the conclusion of the winter session in Richmond, the legislation did not so much aim to solve the problem of slave population growth as to prevent the onset of future slave insurrections. A new law made it difficult for slaves to congregate in groups without written permission, prohibited slaves from preaching, made it illegal for masters to teach their slaves to read and write, and stipulated harsher punishments for rebellious slaves. In the end, a resolution to the issue of the growing slave population did not come until 1833, when the legislature approved a law that would appropriate $18,000 annually to fund the deportation of blacks.[27]

Yet even if no actual law was passed to colonize blacks outside of Virginia, the debate about the relationship between white Virginia and its fast-increasing black population continued. In private, many white Virginians continued to voice their concerns about the growing number of slaves and their effects on the stability and economic progress of the state. Most believed that deportation of at least some blacks, whether enslaved or free, was the only way to ensure stability. Yet whites were also keenly aware of the financial impediments to such a recourse. Martha Jefferson Randolph understood these limitations from her vantage point at Edgehill; she witnessed her own son and many of her neighbors struggle to produce profits on their plantations. The Piedmont soil was exhausted from generations of tobacco planting; the climate was too cold to grow cotton. Some planters transitioned to wheat and also grew corn.[28] Yet the surplus commodity of value that Virginia produced—a perversity that Louis Hughes described when he identified Virginia as the "mother of slavery"—was enslaved men, women, and children. "Our own safety requires that exportation must be the consequence of emancipation," Martha wrote to her son-in-law Joseph Coolidge, though "our poverty will render that a very slow business." But what kind of "exportation" would this be? Exportation to Africa in ships paid for by former white owners? Or exportation to the southwestern cotton states, sold to slave dealers for several hundred dollars each? The answer was by no means clear, yet it was critical to many Virginians. The "very slow business" was a "state too painful to be borne."[29]

"THE GREAT CAUSE OF ALL THE CHIEF EVILS OF OUR LAND"

Today, in southern Fluvanna County, Virginia, the chapel that John Hartwell Cocke built sits by the side of State Route 657. The chapel was once a slave chapel—the only one ever recorded in Virginia—and he oversaw its construction in 1835. It is a simple Gothic Revival church; ogee-arched windows cut into the whitewashed vertical planking of the chapel's sides. Cocke originally built the chapel at Upper Bremo, his Palladian estate that unfolded over a thousand acres along the James River, as a place for his slaves to worship. Every Sunday, dozens of his bondsmen rose at dawn, dressed in clean shirts and skirts, and made their way to Chapel Field. There, squeezed together on wooden pews, they heard a missionary preach, gave thanks to God, and, on some occasions, became baptized members of the church. Perhaps some of Cocke's slaves embraced the evangelical religion of their white master, although many did not.[30]

But regardless of how his slaves actually gauged Christianity, the little chapel was the focal point of Cocke's plan of amelioration at Bremo. He tabulated his slaves' attendance and their baptisms, and tried to measure a sincere commitment to Christianity. Slaves were capable of improvement, Cocke thought, beginning spiritually, with the soul. He believed in the "universal recognition of the christian belief that negroes have souls." This recognition pointed to Cocke's adherence to metropolitan Enlightenment thinking—that all of mankind, regardless of race, was capable of advancement and, ultimately, of freedom and equality within their own "nations." Believing that his enslaved people could only be liberated from bondage once they were reunited with their "home" in Africa, Cocke devised his ameliorative schemes—including slaves' conversion to Christian principles—at Bremo as a preparation for those future goals. After slaves pledged their souls to God, Cocke thought, progress in other areas would follow. Slaves would be more loyal, productive laborers, "happy" in their life station as they worked in the fields under the eyes of God. They would ask to be baptized and married, and then produce children who lived according to the Bible. Enslaved men and women would abstain from drink, gambling, dancing, fighting, and a slew of other immoral acts that whites so often associated with the black race. And after years of demonstrated commitment to this amelioration—which Cocke could presumably measure—he envisioned sending a slave and his family to Africa, to live freely in the new colony of Liberia.[31]

Cocke was just as eager to implement his experiment in the "government" of slaves as he was for his fellow Virginia planters to follow suit. Slavery, he thought, was the "the great Cause of all the Chief evils of our Land."[32] But, of course, such a "Cause" had existed in Virginia for centuries. Cocke himself was descended from generations of tobacco planters who made their home in Surry County in the Tidewater. The first of the family to arrive was the Englishman Richard Cocke, in the mid-seventeenth century, who promptly began cultivating tobacco at his Bremo and Malvern Hills estates. Cocke's father, John, served in the militia during the American Revolution and cast Surry County's vote to ratify the federal Constitution in 1788. At his death in 1791, Cocke's father possessed 1,377 acres and 43 slaves in Surry, 450 acres and 27 slaves in Buckingham County, 3,184 acres and 44 slaves in Fluvanna County, 400 acres in Halifax County, and an additional 1,100-acre tract in Kentucky. Born in 1780, Cocke inherited his father's lands, though it was not until the first decade of the nineteenth century that he left Surry for his new estates in Fluvanna.[33]

It was there that Cocke befriended other members of the Virginia political elite, many of whom harbored similar views about the necessity of ending slavery. He was an admirer of St. George Tucker, a professor he had met during his college days at William and Mary, and named his son Philip St. George after the distinguished jurist. Cocke's closest friend was Joseph Carrington Cabell, and together they collaborated on such endeavors as founding the University of Virginia and supporting the James River and Kanawha Canal project, which sought to link the Chesapeake watershed with the Mississippi River Valley. Having much in common with Thomas Jefferson, Cocke called upon the retired president for his architectural recommendations—Jefferson designed Cocke's Bremo Recess estate—horticultural samples, and advice on the "problem" of slavery in Virginia. Jefferson even tried to convince Cocke to serve as the executor of Tadeusz Kosciusko's will, which stipulated that a number of slaves be educated and emancipated. Cocke refused. Since adolescence, Cocke had questioned slavery, scribbling in his college notebook that the institution was "absurd." Still, Cocke was keenly aware of the impediments to emancipation; he did not condone the seemingly liberal gesture of his uncle Richard, who freed fifty slaves from his Goochland estate upon his death in 1800. He did not believe that blacks could form a part of the new American nation. Slaves could not be emancipated on American soil. Thus, in Cocke's mind, a critical dilemma—the necessity of freeing slaves and the impossibility of them being freed in Virginia—became more urgent in the wake of the Turner rebellion.[34]

Cocke believed, as he wrote in 1833, soon after the Southampton revolt, "that late events which have opened the door to discussion so long barred by our irrational fears" will "never again be closed, until justice & truth shall triumph." His definition of "justice & truth" was the abolition of slavery and the colonization of slaves. But this, he knew, would not come easily. He predicted that emancipation would be a long time coming in Virginia; it might, he mused, take a century or more. Still, slavery jeopardized Virginia's self-preservation and retarded its progress; it undercut the moral and political development for which he believed whites providentially destined. Yet as the owner of three thousand acres of property in the James River bottoms and a substantial enslaved work force, Cocke was viscerally aware of the many financial and logistical limitations of emancipation and colonization schemes. At Bremo, facing decreasing crop production and profits as well as falling land prices, Cocke could not afford to fund the colonization of all of his slaves to Africa. But Cocke believed that America would not be able to realize its "empire of liberty" until it had extinguished the threat of race war and expelled members of the "captive nation" of slaves.[35]

As an ardent supporter of colonization and a leading member of the American Colonization Society (ACS), Cocke endorsed William Brodnax's proposal to send six thousand free blacks out of Virginia annually after a tax of 30 cents was levied on every white person in the state. Slave owners, the delegate from Dinwiddie County had reasoned, would voluntarily send their chattel to Africa after they witnessed the benefits of the free black colonization effort. By the early 1900s, Brodnax calculated, Virginia might achieve its goal of a free labor, all-white society. For Cocke, this seemed like the most plausible plan for eradicating slavery in Virginia. "I am brought to the conclusion," he wrote, "that an immediate & universal emancipation would thus operate little short of a decree of extermination."

Although Cocke knew that far from a majority of Virginia slave owners supported colonization—the 1831 debates had demonstrated the breadth of their divisions over the issue—he nonetheless maintained that they might someday be persuaded that it was not just one possible solution to the issue of slavery but, rather, the only solution.[36]

To that end, Cocke endeavored to prepare his own slaves for future colonization to Africa. But he understood that the process on his plantation, as in the rest of Virginia, would be gradual so as not to provoke race war through a jarring, immediate change. Although emancipation and deportation was "already beginning to be hoped for by a majority of the enlightened christian patriots of the country," Cocke believed that the "process [must be] so slow as to preclude the men of any generation from the honor of its accomplishment." To be sure, the "evil has been two centuries growing up" and will "probably require the lapse of one to eradicate it." Enlightened "patriots" like James Madison, James Monroe, and himself, as members of the ACS, would voluntarily begin to colonize their enslaved men and women to Africa. They would set the example that less-enlightened Virginia slave owners would one day follow.[37]

Of course, Cocke readily admitted the impediments to colonization. Targeting "ultra" abolitionists from New England, Cocke held that, while such "Christian philanthropist[s]" might think that as soon as white masters "became convinced of the evils of holding slaves and the means were offered of removing them . . . they would as naturally be carried away," the true nature of slavery in Virginia conjured a more sobering reality. "Believe me," Cocke wrote, "even after every sordid consideration had been subdued by the full recognition of a more enlightened moral & political economy, there are still great obstacles to emancipation connected to deportation." Virginians might have understood, at least in the abstract, that slavery was a moral evil, that free labor was superior to slave labor, and that a racially homogenous society would bring peace to the Old Dominion. But these principles—many of them so conspicuous in the revolutionary era—were ultimately not as important to white Virginians as their self-preservation and "improvement," which they defined as the accumulation of wealth and property.[38]

Cocke noted that the economic stagnation in Virginia was due in large part to the contraction of tobacco production; most tobacco growing was confined to the Southside of Virginia in the antebellum period. In the Tidewater, once a primary exporter of the cash crop to British markets, tobacco had all but disappeared. "There can be no other reason assigned" as to "why this once profitable culture has been abandoned," Cocke wrote, but that "the land had become too poor to produce it" and global markets had driven down prices. Thus, while the "most profitable agricultural employment of slave labor has entirely departed from the tide water districts," the slave laborers remained. And "deluded masters," as descendants of the prerevolutionary tobacco elite, remained convinced that "all his profits consists in the increased number & value of his slaves." Former elite tobacco planters, encumbered by debt to British creditors, often mortgaged their slaves and used them as collateral, rendering slaves crucial to these planters' economic survival. To increase their collateral, some slave owners "make sale of their negroes as their necessities demand" by fashioning their plantations into a "breeding Farm of human stock." Thus, Tidewater planters, deprived of a profitable cash crop, increasingly looked to slaves themselves as a source of income. By breeding slaves and selling their offspring to "speculators for transportation to the South," planters could hope to remain solvent. Using slaves as primary collateral in an uncertain economy was a crucial obstacle to colonization and emancipation.[39]

In other areas of Virginia, Cocke identified a "middle class" of slaveholders particularly predisposed to the perpetuation of slavery. Such slave owners had emerged in the postrevolutionary period as a result of the abolition of entail and primogeniture. While Jefferson had intended that this abolition would diffuse rights among a greater number of white men, the tragic irony was that it actually diffused slave ownership and broadened public support for slavery, particularly among the new "class" of slave owners that Cocke described. These "successful overseers" or "enterprising cultivators who have accumulated their own Fortunes" remained committed to slavery because human chattel constituted their first attempt to accumulate wealth and establish themselves as property owners. With the value of slaves increasing, poorer and middling whites who sought to "improve" themselves and generate profits invested in slaves rather than land. Even without owning land, slave owners could "hire their negroes out in the towns or else where as they find employment, and live upon their wages." With the hiring out and selling of slaves serving as their primary income, these "middle class" slave owners subsequently developed a "tenacious" grip on slavery. Slaveholders such as these, Cocke postulated, would "be among the last to adopt any liberal scheme" to end slavery. In his eyes, the primary obstacle to emancipation and colonization was not due to the threat posed by New England abolitionists but rather to a growing population of new slaveholders who owned five or fewer slaves.[40]

There was another kind of impediment to emancipation and colonization, this one arising from the slaves themselves. Just as Cocke had defined different kinds of slave owners, so too did he suggest that there were different kinds of slaves: faithful domestics and the "common herd of slaves." His formulation pointed to a tension in white Virginians' perception of slaves: masters perceived them both as the foreign "internal enemy" and as the domesticated and "happy" enslaved servant. The "Faithful Domesticks," Cocke wrote, usually inherited by the descendants of the Virginia elite, had established their "claim to the character of humble Friend to the Family." These slaves were most often either house servants or filled the "most confidential stations in the out door work of the plantation" as artisans in the "plainest mechanic arts." This "class" of "confidential domesticks or mechanicks" was "sufficiently enlightened to make liberty either useful to themselves, or beneficial to any free community." Cocke implied that those slaves who had become integrated into his household as domesticated members of Bremo were the only ones eligible for repatriation to Africa. Yet Cocke's description of slaves' amelioration and domestication only undercut his argument for the necessity of colonization. If slaves had become "held to their masters by strong ties of personal attachment" and were contained within the private domain of the plantation household, then the "threat" of race war was already being mollified. And if the danger of a widespread slave rebellion was quelled, then colonization seemed unnecessary.[41]

Cocke believed that few bondsmen on his plantation met the required criteria for "return" to Africa. He suggested that the "vast majority" of plantation slaves lived in a "state of abject ignorance" and were not skilled artisans or domesticated servants. As evidence, he noted that several of the "grown working slaves" on his Bremo estate "cannot count as far as twenty." Such workers were, in his estimation, like the "lowest grade of menial servants" who could be no better than "hewers of wood & drawers of water" in any "community enlightened enough to live under a civil government." Only because the faithful domestics of his plantation were "sufficiently advanced in intellectual & moral improvement" could Cocke ever comprehend emancipating them and sending them to Africa.[42]

Still, Cocke had great plans to improve even the lowliest field hands at Bremo; he believed that amelioration would prepare his bondsmen for emancipation and subsequent colonization to Africa. This showed that Cocke did not see his slaves' characters as static or fixed—the lowliest field hand could improve just as the more advanced domestic servants could quickly backslide into vice and corruption. Soon after the Southampton insurrection, Cocke adopted a more stringent "plan of my design" at Bremo. He endeavored to "increase the intelligence and improve the moral character of my Negroes" through religious instruction and temperance, and by his own example. Following this, "they will be rendered more valuable to me as slaves while I am obliged to hold them in bondage" and "less dangerous to the community" while slavery continued in Virginia "for at least a century to come." His slaves would be "happier as the result of increased respectability in life" and able to "meet the desideratum in the conscience of a christian master." From a keen "sense of duty," Cocke was "always endeavoring to make them sensible" by appealing to them as "rational creatures."[43] Through a system of rewards and punishments rather than the brute force of the lash, Cocke believed he could convert his slaves into productive, moral laborers. He introduced a rigid code for the "government of slaves" on his plantations, a code that he followed and distributed to his overseers. Cocke stipulated that no slaves could leave the plantation or sell anything without a written pass or permit; slaves were prohibited from fighting, quarrelling, or using "vexatious & insulting language" toward each other; and every "working hand" was required to appear in clean clothes on Sunday. He also encouraged his slaves to work extra hours in order to earn money toward self-purchase—after manumission, these slaves would be sent to Liberia.[44]

In order for slaves to be ameliorated, Cocke sought to remove the barrier between the slave quarters—the site of ignorance—and the master's house—the site of domesticity. The first step to such "improvement" was ameliorating slaves' material conditions and providing a measure of "comfort." Cocke hoped to eradicate the "filth & demoralizing morale of our too much neglected Quarters." The effects of these quarters, Cocke surmised, were "brutal." So he began with the slave dwellings themselves. Rather than ramshackle wooden cabins, Cocke built multifamily dwellings—suited for four or five families—out of pise, or rammed earth, and laid on sandstone foundations. When Cocke was satisfied that his slaves were living in cleaner domestic spaces organized around the family unit, he hired missionaries to preach to them. His wife, Louisa, set up "infant schools" at Bremo to ensure that slaves "are kept out of the mischief & in comfort & cleanliness." Moreover, as president of the Fork Union Temperance Society, Cocke found the oath for sobriety a "most powerful auxiliary in ... regenerating their Characters," since their "moral improvement" was "already manifest."[45] And each year, Cocke noted the "improvement" of his slaves. He counted his slaves by families, and noted marriages and births among them. He tallied the number of his bondsmen who took the temperance oath at the Temperance Temple at Upper Bremo.[46]

Believing that the true ameliorator of his slaves was God, Cocke admitted to looking at the entire slavery question through the lens of "Christian Morality." For him, God, rather than the state legislature or federal government, acted as an agent of amelioration. While slave owners would chip away at the problem of slavery on earth, Cocke believed that it was God who must ultimately solve the issue of slavery in the same way that Jefferson had believed that "Time" would solve it. Cocke believed that God "entails upon no people the irreconcilable necessity" to "violate the principles of his Eternal justice." As a result, God would "provide the means . . . of removing the curse of slavery from Christendom." Slavery was so deeply "interwoven with the very texture of Society" that only a divine being could ensure its eradication. All that mere mortals like himself could do, Cocke thought, was to offer slaves the "preparatory means necessary to this blessed result." This, of course, meant improvement through Christianity. At Bremo, this usually entailed attending chapel or reading the Bible. Despite protests from other planters in the wake of the Southampton insurrection that Christianity "render[ed] slaves more dangerous & ungovernable," Cocke argued just the opposite. Anyone "who knows any thing of Christianity," he wrote, must admit that a "christian would be more valuable & safer than an infidel slave." In his view, slaves' adherence to Christian principles transformed them from idle or miscreant "foreigners" into productive and obedient domestic workers within the plantation household. Thus, Christianity helped govern slaves by domesticating them and including them within the household, thus assuaging the animosity between the races and preventing future slave rebellions. Cocke's strategy of slaves' conversion to Christianity and "improvement" appeared to point to their permanent coexistence with whites within domestic households. But he instead continued to argue that amelioration and domestication were merely the requisite precursors to African colonization.[47]

Beginning in the 1830s and 1840s, Cocke mobilized two colonization projects to further his emancipation goals, one in northern Alabama and one in Liberia. The two were dependent on each other. Realizing that he could not emancipate his slaves without being compensated for the loss of his valuable human property, he endeavored to make them "earn" their freedom. But because the wheat and corn that slaves grew at Bremo did not generate enough income to fund manumission, Cocke established several plantations in the "cotton belt" in Alabama, hoping that the fertile soil there would yield increased profits to pay for his slaves' freedom and passage to Liberia. Only those slaves who had demonstrated their "improvement" by taking the temperance oath and being baptized at Bremo were eligible to be sent to the new plantations in Alabama. While Cocke's expansion into Alabama may have seemed like his way to expand slavery, his goal in buying new property there was to generate enough income to fund the repatriation of his slaves to Africa.[48]

Cocke began his experiment in slave manumission and colonization to Africa in 1833, when he freed Peyton Skipwith and his family and sent them to Liberia. Skipwith was "prepared for the change, advantageously to himself & useful to the Colony," Cocke wrote. Having offered thirty-three years of "valuable services" at Bremo, Skipwith was "intelligent" and commanded a "cultivated mind." He was a "Mechanick," a mason and stone-cutter, who had taken the temperance oath and possessed a "Christian walk & conversation." These things, Cocke decided, qualified him for freedom in Liberia. He hoped that his former slave would, in the "spirit of Christian enterprize," journey to Africa to "carry civilization & the blessed Gospel" to the "benighted Land of their forefathers."[49] Skipwith did travel there with his family aboard the ship *Jupiter* in October 1833. But between his arrival in Liberia and his death there in 1849, Skipwith remained ambivalent about his new home. Cocke and other Virginia slave owners believed that Skipwith and other colonized slaves would feel at home in Africa and compelled to improve the land of their supposed brethren. But seven years after his arrival in Liberia, Skipwith told his former master that it was "strange to think . . . that those people of Africa are called our ancestors. In my present thinking if we have any ancestors they could not have been like these hostile tribes in this part of Africa."[50]

The whole notion of African colonization rested on the belief, shared by Cocke and others, that American slaves had constituted a separate "people" and an artificially diffuse African "nation." Even though the transatlantic slave trade had pulled this "nation" apart by transporting Africans to distant corners of the New World, colonization remained unjustified unless contemporaries like Cocke (and Jefferson before him) could prove that disparate and creolized slaves who had lived outside of Africa for generations nonetheless comprised a single "people." But the fault lines in this reasoning were exposed when American slaves like Skipwith landed in Liberia. Whether Cocke could admit it or not, Liberia was a "lonsum country" for resettled American blacks; only Virginia was home to those who had been born and "domesticated" in Virginia society, having no African "history" to speak of.[51]

While Cocke observed the progress of Peyton Skipwith and his family in Liberia, he bought two cotton plantations in Alabama, Hopewell and New Hope. Installing Peyton's brother George Skipwith as slave driver, Cocke sent forty-nine slaves from Bremo to Alabama in 1840. Cocke hoped that cotton profits would finance the private manumission and colonization of his slaves. "This enterprise," he wrote to his son Charles, "is to take 50, 75, or 100 of our negroes to the Cotton Country" and "after realizing their value there, with a surplus give them an outfit in Africa & pay their passage thither."[52]

In 1841, Cocke assembled the newly transplanted slaves to take an emancipation oath. After they had earned the equivalent of their value—roughly $1,400 each—and remained committed to honesty, obedience, and abstinence from alcohol, Cocke would free them and send them to Liberia. Cocke stipulated a code of government for those slaves on his absentee plantations who would only be supervised by George Skipwith, the black driver, and Elam Tanner, a white overseer. He required written passes and submission to the authority of Skipwith and Tanner; he prohibited fighting and cursing. Yet the experiments at Hopewell and New Hope did not fare well—cotton production was low; profits were shaky; and drunkenness, sexual promiscuity, and disobedience characterized the plantations. Rather than disciplined Christian laborers and well-ordered slave households, Cocke encountered "a Plantation Brothel" when he visited his properties in 1848. Of the more than fifty slaves living on Hopewell and New Hope by 1853, Cocke manumitted only six and sent them to Liberia. Ironically, Cocke's Alabama experiments meant the expansion of slavery into the cotton belt in order to try to abolish the institution in the Old Dominion. While this scheme appears ludicrous in hindsight, Cocke formulated his plan based on two important principles: that slavery was antithetical to progress and expansion in the federal union and that it was a premodern and static system that was artificially perpetuated. In light of these beliefs, Cocke's experiments on his plantations and his unswerving commitment to amelioration and colonization seem much more rational.[53]

Despite the relative failures of the enterprises in Liberia and Alabama, Cocke's belief in the necessity of colonization never waned. He was not alone. In 1833, an aging James Madison sent a $50 check to the American Colonization Society, commending the society in its "noble object of removing a great evil from its own country."[54] The "missionary character" of the ACS, its objective to "restore" blacks to the "land of their ancestors," seemed like the only way to reverse the effects of slavery.[55] The ACS was no "intrusive abolition society," wrote Jesse Burton Harrison, the son of a wealthy tobacco merchant and cousin of Henry Clay. Rather, it was "regarded as the wisest and safest agent of the benevolent *slaveholders* themselves."[56]

Of course, while Cocke decreed that "light is daily increasing on this interesting subject," there were others in Virginia who saw the issue differently, including Thomas Dew. Cocke dismissed the "sordid speculations" of the pragmatic Dew, as well as the "whole herd of heartless philosophers who look at the matter thro' all other media except that of Christian Morality."[57] In other words, he bucked against Dew's dismissal of those universalist, Enlightenment ideals that informed Cocke's views of slavery and of the necessity of its abolition. Cocke shared his view of Dew with other members of the ACS, including his friend Richard Randolph Gurley, who acted as the society's secretary and was the chaplain to the House of Representatives. "Amongst the moral phenomena of the day," Cocke seethed to Gurley, "one hardly more startling can be conceived, than an elaborate pamphlet of 133 pages, from a sage professor" who palliated the "slave trade, and defend[ed] slavery—unmitigated slavery for ever."[58] Gurley agreed that Dew seemed to want to "find something" that demonstrated the "necessity & utility of perpetual slavery." Indeed, Dew may have "forgotten both the age in which he lives & the spirit which animates his countrymen."[59]

Dew hardly advocated the lasting presence of slavery in Virginia, but it is significant that both Gurley and Cocke thought as much. Rather than a proslavery consensus pervading Virginia in the years following the Nat Turner insurrection, what persisted was a division over the issue of the progress of two populations in Virginia, one white and the other black. Cocke insisted that the amelioration of slavery on plantations would secure the safety and advancement of the white population; in future time, the black population would have to be expelled from the state. But Dew revised many of the assumptions on which colonization rested. He challenged Jefferson's and Cocke's understanding of slavery as a "state of war," arguing instead that ameliorated and domesticated slavery resulted in the "happiness" and "improvement" of both races. Dew asserted that slavery was a necessary force in the course of human development, since it "impelled" progress from barbarism to civility. Yet Dew's revisionism stopped short of equating slavery with civilization or of arguing that slavery was modern and therefore a permanent fixture of America. In short, the main contest between Dew and Cocke—supposedly a "fierce & severe conflict... between abolitionists & anti abolitionists"—was actually over the definition of slavery and the place of slaves in Virginia and the federal union.[60]

"AN IMPULSE TOWARD CIVILIZATION"

What was it, Thomas Roderick Dew thundered in the opening pages of his 1832 pamphlet, which can "communicate an impulse toward civilization"? Although it might seem strange to "modern ears," Dew confessed that the answer was "domestic slavery." Indeed, the Romans owned slaves, as had the Greeks and many modern European empires. In his view, slavery was the only system that propelled man out of the depths of barbarism and toward enlightened civility. Only domestic slavery "fells the forest," "gives rise to agricultural production," eliminates the "roving and unquiet life of the savage," and "furnishes a home" for the "man of business and agriculturist." Dew's definition of the path to civilization in Virginia—and slavery's centrality to that process—was the most important contribution of his influential pamphlet. But even if slavery was an ameliorator, Dew did not think that it was synonymous with civilization. Too close a disciple of Adam Smith, Dew believed that modernity and civilization were defined by free labor and a free market. Still, Dew's vision was a dynamic one—the civilization he imagined was also a scheme of colonization and expansion. In the 1830s, when much of western Virginia remained a veritable "frontier," Dew envisioned that the slave-owning agricultural households he lauded would shift westward, taming the land as they settled it, and linking the western hinterlands to the more civilized areas of "lower" Virginia.[61]

Like other political economists in the early nineteenth century, Dew was primarily concerned with the progress of populations. More specifically, he was concerned with the effect of slaves—or too many slaves—on the white population. In this way, Dew had much in common with other prominent southern thinkers—Thomas Cooper, a friend of Jefferson's who took a post at South Carolina College, and George Tucker, a cousin of St. George Tucker, who taught at the University of Virginia, as well as Dew's William and Mary colleague Beverley Tucker. And Dew, of course, had firsthand knowledge of slavery. Born in 1802, he had grown up with slaves at his parents' Dewsville plantation in King and Queen County, Virginia.

He also knew Virginia; the first Thomas Dew had arrived in the English colony in 1642, serving as both speaker of the Virginia House of Burgesses and as a member of the governor's council, while his father served in both the American Revolution and the War of 1812.[62]

Yet Dew's thinking about the effects of slavery—and slaves—on Virginia was catalyzed by the Southampton insurrection and the debates in the Virginia House of Assembly. In the summer of 1832, Dew began writing a response to the various delegates' proposals. Dew's pamphlet was of seminal importance because it revised the revolutionary generations' definition of slavery. The institution was not, as Cocke and Jefferson had thought, a "state of war"; slaves did not constitute a "captive nation" ready to overthrow their white oppressors in a bloody race war. Rather, the institution had been ameliorated and transformed—slaves had become domestic servants and owners benevolent masters. Dew continued to think of slaves and whites as separate populations, or "peoples," but he believed that the two had become so intertwined under the rubric of amelioration that removal of blacks through colonization would destroy Virginia. He offered the following metaphor: "The physician will not order the spreading cancer to be extirpated although it will eventually cause the death of his patient, because he would thereby hasten the final issue."[63]

Although many of his readers balked at Dew's conclusions, they did understand the gravity of his argument. One writer linked his almost "mathematical train of reasoning" to his ability to shake "our former faith . . . upon this point." Even though John Quincy Adams labeled Dew's work as a "monument of . . . intellectual perversion," he nonetheless admitted that "this pamphlet deserves grave meditation, and has in it the seeds of much profitable instruction."[64] Perhaps some of the most remarkable commentary on Dew's pamphlet came not from his colleagues, many of whom integrated it into their lectures, but from a Virginia statesman of a different sort. Dew sent his pamphlet to a feeble James Madison in the winter of 1833, hoping that the former president might "glance" at the "argument."[65] A leading proponent of the ACS's efforts to colonize Virginia blacks, Madison still concluded that Dew offered "ample proof of the numerous obstacles to a removal of slavery from our country." Madison, however, did not think that Dew had considered the correct obstacles. For Madison, the impediments to colonization were finding the "requisite asylums" for blacks, the free blacks' "consent to be removed," and the "labor . . . vacuum" that would be created should blacks be deported from Virginia. But Madison did concur with Dew about the "depraved state" of Virginia, and chided him for failing to contrast the effect of slavery in Virginia with slavery in the "rapid settlement of the W. & S.W. Country."[66]

Madison missed Dew's crucial point—his criticism of African colonization was ultimately shaped by his vision for the colonization of western Virginia and the "W. and S.W. Country" of the cotton belt. In an abstract sense, Dew embraced colonization to Liberia. He believed the twinned missions of deporting blacks and civilizing Africa to be a "splendid vision" and the result of "pure feelings of a philanthropic and generous heart." But this was all that colonization amounted to, Dew thought. "Every plan of emancipation and deportation" was "totally impracticable," in part because Virginia slaves were worth so much money: $100,000,000, by his calculations. This was a third of the state's wealth; Virginia would never be able to offer slaveholders compensation, the *sine qua non* of emancipation and colonization. And even if Virginia did manage to deport the average annual increase of its bondsmen—approximately six thousand souls—it would cost between $1.38 and $2.4 million per year for at least a half century. The only way to raise such a sum would be to involve the federal government; as a fierce critic of any extension of congressional powers, Dew cited the potential unconstitutionality and corruption if the ACS requested federal aid money to fund the Liberia experiment. And even if the logistical and financial hurdles to colonization were overcome, Dew questioned whether Africa was a genuine "home" for enslaved men and women or if the day would ever "arrive when he [a slave] can be liberated from his thraldom, and mount upwards in the scale of civilization and rights, to an equality with the white?" Dew dismissed the idea that Africans could one day become a free and equal "people" in future time. This dealt a critical blow to metropolitan Enlightenment thinking, which had maintained that the "races" of mankind, while unequal in heterogeneous or "mixed" populations, could become equal when homogenous "nations" emerged in the Atlantic world.[67]

Still, Dew understood that the issue that undergirded the colonization question was a fast-increasing slave and free black population in Virginia. "In looking at the Virginia population," he wrote, "the desideratum is to diminish the blacks and increase the whites." Dew saw the advancement of separate "peoples" as a powerful force. Drawing on Malthus, he thought nothing was as dangerous as "too much tampering with the elastic and powerful spring of population." For Dew, even if "desirable," colonization was impossible because it "cannot possibly effect this exchange of slave labor for free." Slaves and free blacks simply could not be deported all at once, leaving the "vacuum to be filled by free labor." It was "utterly impossible," Dew thought, to "send away . . . more than the annual increase . . . of our slaves." And if that were true, then free white labor would have to be imported as black slave labor continued. This Virginia could not have. For free labor, "by association with slave labor," would be "brought down to its level, and even below it." The result would be free white laborers and enslaved black laborers who shared the same "idle propensities." Dew evidently thought that labor systems had to be homogenous; "mixing" labor systems would undermine the natural progression from slave to free labor in Virginia as a result of market forces.[68]

Moreover, if Virginia slaves were sent to Africa, depriving slaveholders of their most valuable property, many whites would leave the state and jeopardize Virginia's "position." With the decline in profits from agricultural commodities, slave selling and slave hiring constituted a main source of income and collateral for those planters who remained in Virginia. Even so, Dew maintained, Virginia had become the "'fruitful mother of empires'" by "pouring forth emigrants more rapidly to the west than any other state in the union" due to the "cheap fertile and unoccupied lands of the west" and the "oppressive action" of new federal tariffs. In the case of the slaves, half of the population could be exported through the slave trade without detrimental effects, Dew thought. This was because emigration "was a powerful stimulus to the spring of black population" since it encouraged masters to "attend to his negroes" and "raise" the "greatest possible number" of them in Virginia. On the other hand, the "emigration of the white man," removes a "laborer" and "capital likewise." While the emigration of blacks through the slave trade encouraged whites' amelioration of their chattel and increased capital, the emigration of whites would result in Virginia being "impoverished" and advancing "more slowly in the acquisition" of wealth.[69]

Not only did the domestic slave trade stimulate profit; it also regulated the slave population increase, Dew argued. Virginia was, in his estimation, "a negro raising state for other states" that "produces enough for her own supply and six thousand for sale." The six thousand slaves were the estimated annual increase of the Virginia slave population that politicians and planters hoped to "drain" out of the state. But since Virginians "can raise cheaper than they can buy" slaves as "one of their greatest sources of profit," Dew suggested that the slave trade be used as a drain to assuage the perceived threat of an increasing black population. At the same time, Virginia would generate a profit rather than bear the onerous financial burden of colonization. Even Cocke saw the internal slave trade as a lucrative alternative to colonization. Still, Cocke was appalled at the thought of using the slave trade to ameliorate Virginia: "I thought it was hardly possible, that the Moral sense of Virginia could have retrograded to the deep depravity of the Slave trade." He worried that becoming a breeder of slaves would signal Virginia's permanent degeneracy.[70]

Dew dismissed colonization by showing that the domestic slave trade was a more profitable and feasible way to control the slave population in Virginia than sending blacks overseas. Unlike Cocke's plan of colonization, however, Dew's scheme stipulated that a sizable slave population remain within Virginia. To argue for this plan, Dew had to prove that the remaining slaves posed no significant threat to white Virginians. He set out to show that slavery could no longer be defined as a "state of war" and that slaves had become a domesticated population in Virginia. Because so many white Virginians believed that the Turner rebellion portended a race war and disunion, Dew's argument presented a crucial reinterpretation of the revolt and of whites' conception of the "peculiar institution."[71]

Despite the fears of so many whites, including Cocke and many of the delegates present at the Virginia slave debates, that a bloody war would be fought between the two races, Dew was skeptical. He dismissed the "appalling phantoms" or a potential "crisis in the vista of futurity, when the overwhelming numbers of blacks would rise superior to all restraint" and incite the "universal ruin and desolation" of whites. In fact, there was no real "enmity" between the races; it was a "monstrous error" to suppose that "every slave in the slave-holding country" was "actuated by the most deadly enmity" that would lead him to "murder and assassinate" whites. Rather than Nat Turner's revolt suggesting that a race war would inevitably envelop Virginia, Dew suggested that Turner was merely a "fanatical negro preacher" and an "aberration" in the larger slave community. Instead of plotting or executing violence against whites, Dew argued, "the slave . . . generally loves his master and his family." Through the process of amelioration, the enmity between the races had been permanently assuaged.[72]

But how did slaves transition from violence-inciting "foreigners" to domesticated servants? Dew asserted that it was because they had been "improved" and included within planters' households; insurrection was impossible "where the blacks are as much civilized as they are in the United States." American slaves had "imbibed the principles, the sentiments, and feelings of the white"—a process that had rendered them "civilized—at least, comparatively." The "education" that slaves had received under whites' supervision steeled them against "poisonous principles" that originated from aberrant slaves or the West Indies and that might spawn the "midnight murderer." The fact that the "houses are scarcely ever fastened at night" throughout Virginia was a "demonstration" of the "conscious security of our citizens, and their great confidence in the fidelity of the blacks." While a slave might plunder a henhouse or a corncrib, "he can never be induced to murder you," Dew declared.[73]

The conspicuous evidence that slavery was no longer a "state of war," Dew argued, was that the master-slave relationship was no longer a "constant exercise of the most odious tyranny" as Jefferson had suggested in his *Notes on the State of Virginia.* Instead, "Mr. Jefferson is not borne out by the fact." The moral responsibility that entailed protecting childlike, enslaved dependents, Dew explained, meant that white patriarchs could not exhibit "cold, contracted, calculating selfishness." In fact, those masters who did mistreat their slaves were those "who have been unaccustomed to slavery"—they were poor patriarchs and a poor example to society. The ownership of slaves, he suggested, gave a white man a "more exalted benevolence" and a "greater generosity and elevation of the soul." Likewise, the "slaves of a good master" were his "warmest, most constant, and most devoted friends." While Jefferson had suggested that slaves hated their masters because they were a "captive nation" deprived of their *amor patriae,* Dew responded that slaves loved their masters since "we are well convinced that there is nothing but the mere relations of husband and wife, parent and child, brother and sister, which produce a closer tie, than the relation of master and servant." Precisely because the "boisterous passions" that Jefferson had described had been muted and transformed into familial ties of sympathy, masters found themselves relinquishing "tyranny" and embracing domesticity.[74]

For Dew, the amelioration of slaves and their inclusion within the household constituted concrete evidence that man had progressed from the "hunting into the shepherd and agricultural states." The domestic household was the basic unit of modern civilized society, and Dew was interested in proving that it was slavery that enabled the creation of such a unit. To him, slavery was the institution that allowed whites to progress through the stages of human development. The establishment of the domestic sphere began with the mother; the existence of slavery transformed women from hunter-gatherers and a "beast of burden" into the "cheering and animated centre of the family circle" who was "surrounded by her domestics" as well as her husband and children. Slavery also relieved man from "endless disquietude about subsistence for the morrow" and the "toil of wandering over the forest" in search of provisions. Slave labor allowed the patriarch to install himself within the household, exchanging the savagery of the wanderer for the "kindness and benevolence" of the domestic realm. Slavery facilitated the "ameliorated condition" of men and women, which, in turn, allowed them to create the basic units of civilization, Dew argued. But slaves, as "dependents" in this domestic household, were also ameliorated. Because the master's temper had been moderated and his habits changed as a result of his "improvement," he lost the "savage and brutal feeling which he had before indulged towards all his unfortunate dependents." Instead, the patriarch improved the moral and physical condition of his slaves; then, Dew argued, "even the slave" in the agricultural state was "happier than the free man in the hunting state."[75]

For Dew, "happiness," not liberty, was the ultimate consequence of an ameliorated—and thus by implication, civilized—society. The definition of "happiness" in the early nineteenth century was "comfort," or the absence of pain. Liberty, which he interpreted as a privilege, was designated for educated and "independent" property owners, while happiness characterized entire populations. For Dew, "happiness is the great object of all animated creation," since it could be "comprehended" by women, uneducated whites, and even slaves. Dew believed slaves' self-reproducing population and "happiness" to be a direct outgrowth of their amelioration: because they were "treated kindly" and "abundantly fed," slaves "formed the happiest portion of our society." He suggested that "infusing" a "vain and indefinite desire for liberty" into the minds of slaves, would "dry up the very sources of happiness." Thus, the emancipation of bondsmen would destroy blacks' own "happiness" while also destroying the comforts and wealth of the white population.[76]

Slavery, Dew deduced, was the "principal means for impelling forward the civilization of mankind." Without the "agency" of slavery, "society must have remained sunk into that deplorable state of barbarism and wretchedness" that characterized the world when it was "first discovered by Columbus." The presence of slave labor allowed for man to progress from hunter-gatherer to shepherd to planter. This progress was the amelioration that allowed for the creation of domestic households composed of white patriarchs and their white and black dependents. Amelioration also unleashed the happiness and benevolence that accompanied the moral and physical "improvement" of individuals as they advanced through the stages of development. He envisioned the Old Dominion as a state-republic of households, wherein "planting" constituted a more civilized stage of development than the "grazing" one of western Virginia.[77]

Dew's main goal was the preservation and expansion of civilized society within Virginia. The extension of civility would serve as a model for other states in the union. While the Virginia slave debates and the constitutional convention in the early 1830s appeared to pit a nonslaveholding west with a slaveholding east, Dew did not conceive of the issue in such static terms. For him, the nonslaveholding west that maintained itself through "grazing" livestock would, in time, come to resemble the "planting" areas of "lower Virginia." Because of western Virginia's "great distance from the market" and the "wretched condition of the communications leading through the state," the region had remained a sparsely populated "grazing country." The lack of progress in the west meant that white landowners were emigrating out of the state in search of cheap, fertile planting lands in the cotton belt. Even though Virginia depended on extensive riverine networks to connect markets, few rivers extended above the fall line, thus leaving western counties without access to eastern markets. The lack of access to nodes of commerce had stunted western Virginia's progress, Dew thought, in addition to the federal government's protective tariffs of 1828 and 1832. It was not that western landowners were doomed to a future of grazing—which he equated with the pastoral stage of development—but that they lacked the requisite tools to advance to the planting stage of development, a stage that would require slave labor.[78]

Dew suggested that the solution to the problem of stunted development in Virginia was internal improvements. "We do indeed consider internal improvement in Virginia," he wrote, "the great panacea, by which most of the ills which now weigh down the state may be removed," and "health and activity communicated to every department of industry." Indeed, as soon as a "central internal improvement" was completed, the "grazing system" of the west would be immediately "converted into the grain growing." The consequence of "sticking the plough into the soil," Dew wrote, would be an increased demand for labor, including slaves, a rise in population, and increased profits. The main internal improvement that Dew endorsed, as did John Hartwell Cocke, was the extended navigation of the James River. It was not until 1835 that the state incorporated the James River and Kanawha Company, which sought to link the Chesapeake to the Kanawha River, a tributary of the Ohio River in far western Virginia. The company, headed by Joseph Carrington Cabell, eventually completed 147 miles by 1840, stretching all the way to Lynchburg.[79]

But even if new internal improvements would stave off the "drain" of white landowners and assure the transformation of western Virginia from a "grazing country" into a "planting" one, this did not mean that lower Virginia would remain in planting stasis forever. Rather, in the east, internal improvements would "speed her on more rapidly in wealth and numbers" while also defeating all of the "gloomy predictions about the blacks." With the extended navigation of the James, larger towns would "raise up" and "have a tendency to draw into them the capital and free laborers of the north," and "in this way destroy the proportion of the blacks." Baltimore, Dew surmised, was an "exemplification" of this process, for "its mighty agency is fast making Maryland a non-slaveholding state." In other words, internal improvements would serve to whiten the eastern region of Virginia. The "rise of cities," as well as increased population density, would "render the division of labor more complete." Large farms would be broken into small ones, and the "garden" would be substituted for "plantation cultivation." As a result, "less slave and more free labor will be requisite." The market's invisible hand would work to eradicate slavery in Virginia, rather than intermeddling abolitionists or colonization advocates whose schemes would have only "impoverishing effects." In future time, the expansion of internal improvements would transition western Virginia from non-slave-owning grazing to slave-owning planting, while also converting eastern Virginia from slave-owning planting into a proto-industrial free labor system. Ultimately, Dew believed, as did Adam Smith, that free trade and free labor exemplified modernity, whether in Europe or the New World provinces.[80]

For Dew, slavery was simply a critical agent in the civilization of populations. But he neither conflated it with civilization and modern society nor considered it a permanent fixture of Virginia. The planting and grazing features he described in Virginia were informed by how he saw civilization unfolding across the entire union. The proto-industrial free labor of the northeastern states would expand southward, toward Virginia, just as slave-based planting would shift westward. At the same time, hunter-gatherers in the far West would be supplanted by the introduction of a grazing culture. As such, the entire union of states would advance and gradually whiten, until, at some distant future time, the whole nation would be a densely populated, proto-industrial society of free laborers. The market would diffuse slavery westward and introduce free labor, thus rendering the acts of emancipation and colonization moot. "The time for emancipation has not yet arrived," Dew declared, "and perhaps it never will" if the invisible hand of the market was left to solve the issue of slavery.[81]

Both Dew and Cocke shared Jefferson's vision of "barbarism receding" before the "steady step of amelioration" and the civilization of a continent. For Jefferson and later Cocke, the "repatriation" of slaves to Africa was the critical prerequisite of the colonization of western lands and the formation of new states in the union. So long as slaves stayed in America, they remained an obstacle to expansion because of the impending threat of genocidal race war and disunion. Ironically, Cocke expanded slavery westward in order to try to end it; he attempted to exploit the profitable cotton culture in Alabama to overcome the financial burden of "repatriating" his slaves in Liberia. Dew, on the other hand, dismissed the impracticality of African colonization, favoring the profit-generating domestic slave trade to control the Virginia black population. He reversed the widespread understanding of slavery as a "state of war" and argued that race war was a mere chimera. Since slavery had been ameliorated and domesticated, slaves posed no threat to whites. The value of their labor and as commodities that could be bought and sold meant that slaves advanced Virginia's economic position rather than retarding it. But although Dew argued that slave-owning "planting" was the present stage of Virginia society below the fall line in 1832, he did not predict that slavery would remain a permanent labor system there. At some point, with the aid of internal improvements, Dew's Virginia would be as white as Cocke and Jefferson imagined it, and based on free labor. This was the effect of the "steady step" of amelioration guided by time and the market, Dew thought.[82]

Dew believed that the market would "whiten" Virginia in the future, a view that differed sharply from later proslavery advocates who never predicted that the market for slaves and slave-grown produce would be superseded by proto-industrialist free labor. Thus, Dew proved a poor prophet—the market dictated that Virginia remain a supplier of slaves to the cotton and sugar planters in the Mississippi River Valley as British consumption of slave-grown cotton increased throughout the antebellum period. As a major component of southern economies and the lifeblood of the slave system, the domestic slave trade transported around 1 million enslaved men, women, and children from the Upper South to the Lower South between 1790 and 1860. Virginia alone sent over 300,000 slaves to markets in the southwestern states between 1830 and 1860. Slave prices fol-

Lewis Miller, "Slave Trader, Sold to Tennessee," from Sketchbook of Landscapes in the State of Virginia, ca. 1853. This watercolor depicts two slave traders driving about twenty enslaved men, women, and children from Augusta County, Virginia, to Tennessee. (Courtesy of the Abby Aldrich Rockefeller Folk Art Museum, The Colonial Williamsburg Foundation, Gift of Mr. and Mrs. Richard M. Kain in memory of George Hay Kain)

lowed the contours of cotton prices, and, as such, reached incredible highs and lows. The inflated prices that could be fetched for "prime" slaves doubled or tripled in some newly settled states by the 1850s; prices for slaves at the Richmond slave market were not dependent upon the local economy, but on what desperate cotton and sugar planters in the new states were willing to pay for human chattel. Virginia, and Richmond in particular, became the hub for slave selling in the antebellum period. Without the trade, Virginia might have become a free labor state, but in the absence of a widely cultivated cash crop, slave dealing established Virginia as a "breeder" of slaves for the rest of the union. As Henry Clay told the Kentucky Colonization Society in 1829, nowhere in the Upper South "would slave labor be generally employed, if the proprietors were not tempted to raise slaves by the high price of the Southern markets, which keeps it up in their own." By 1860, slaves were considered the most valuable commodity in the federal union, besides land, worth approximately $3 billion. The cotton crop registered at only $250 million.[83]

Even though Dew labeled Virginia as a "negro raising state for other states," he never predicted that the slave market would become a pri-mary—and more permanent—source of profit and commercial expan-sion in the antebellum era. Dew incorrectly forecast the market, but his revisions of Virginians' definition of slavery had a widespread impact on southern planters and intellectuals. In showing that slavery was not a "state of war," that race war was not imminent, and that slaves' amelioration led to their domestication, Dew laid the foundation for subsequent proslav-ery thinkers, particularly, as we see in the next section, in South Carolina. Dew stopped short of equating slavery with civilization; for him slavery was only a principal cause of it. Even though he dismissed emancipation and colonization, he still favored the ultimate goal of Jefferson and Cocke. Slavery helped civilize 1830s Virginia, he thought, but decades into the fu-ture, he envisioned it being pushed westward, outside of the state.[84]

Cocke, for his part, continued his Virginia and Alabama plantations, as well as his colonization schemes to Liberia, well into the 1850s. Even while he expanded his slave-based cotton operation in northern Alabama, he refused to believe that slavery could be extended without dire moral and economic consequences for whites in America. And despite signifi-cant problems on the Alabama plantations, Cocke continued to send freed slaves to Liberia.[85] His belief that colonization to Africa must precede white expansion and progress made him an outlier in Virginia during the antebellum period, especially as support for colonization waned and the market for slaves and slave-produced goods increased. Still, his assertion that slavery could be ameliorated with the goal of ending it shared much with his ostensible opponent Dew, who also saw that the "peculiar institu-tion," at least in Virginia, would likely be ameliorated toward its end in fu-ture time.

As we see in the next section, however, white South Carolinians em-braced and deployed amelioration differently than their northern cousins. While some Lowcountry elites of the revolutionary generation favored an-tislavery amelioration, albeit in a less articulate form than Jefferson and his Virginia peers, the proliferation of cotton farming and the democratization of slaveholding encouraged the rise of new ideas of proslavery ameliora-tion. During the antebellum period, white South Carolinians began to ar-gue that "improving" slavery was both the means and the goal. That slavery was an "improvable system" meant that it was also modern, and a modern system, many slave owners argued, had no need to end.

II

South Carolina

As in Virginia, antislavery amelioration emerged in South Carolina during the imperial crisis. At the onset of the American Revolution, about 60 percent of the population was enslaved in South Carolina; most slaves worked under the aegis of the "task system" on large indigo and rice plantations. But after the war, many Lowcountry planters tottered on the brink of ruin—British troops had destroyed property, and debts owed to British creditors were often enormous. In addition, some elite Lowcountry planters believed that slavery was incompatible with nationhood. Before the advent of large-scale cotton cultivation, some white South Carolinians envisioned a new free labor economy taking shape; they hoped to produce crops for new European markets. Some planters argued for the abolition of the slave trade and a gradual end to plantation slavery. But while amelioration retained some traction in the 1780s and 1790s when the economy of South Carolina remained uncertain, the invention of the cotton gin and the settlement of the Upcountry turned antislavery amelioration on its head. The expansion of cotton culture, the diffusion of slaveholding across the state, and the rise of the internal slave trade convinced planters that slavery was a civilizing system entirely compatible with progress.

3

"RISING GRADATIONS TO UNLIMITED FREEDOM"

There are no reminders of the scores of slaves who once worked there, or of the endless acres of rice planted in alluvial fields. There is no evidence of a great house that once stood in Georgian splendor at the end of an avenue of oaks. And other than a terraced graveyard, there is little to suggest that a prominent South Carolina family once lived in this spot. Instead, there is a monastery and extensive formal gardens. Mepkin plantation has all but disappeared—Mepkin Abbey now stands in its place.[1]

Over two hundred years ago, this 3,143-acre tract of Cooper River land did not boast the same scenes of solitude and tranquility. Instead, Mepkin was a crucial component of a profitable and diversified plantation system created by Henry Laurens, the exorbitantly wealthy South Carolina merchant and slave trader. His wealth was the result of a shrewd partnership he formed in 1749 with George Austin's merchant house in London, later extending it to include George Appleby and others. Laurens and his partners traded in deerskins, indigo, rice, naval stores, and African slaves. In time, Laurens created an empire of his own: he owned hundreds of enslaved people, built a large townhouse in Charleston, and acquired several plantations.[2]

Yet, by the time of the outbreak of the American Revolution, Laurens penned a letter that seemed out of character for a slave merchant and slaveholder. "I abhor slavery," he wrote to his son in 1776. Laurens decried that he had always "disliked it," even when he found the institution foisted upon him by "British Kings & Parliaments" and other self-aggrandizing "English men." Instead, Laurens was determined to do something about slavery in South Carolina, to ameliorate it, with abolition as his eventual goal. "I am devising means for manumitting many of" his slaves, he continued, and "cutting off the entail of slavery." Laurens insisted that he was not "one of those who dare trust in Providence for defence & security of their own Liberty while they enslave & wish to continue in Slavery, thousands who are as well intitled freedom as themselves." In effect, the plan Laurens shared with his son just after the onset of the revolution implied the emancipation of hundreds of bondsmen and Laurens's permanent removal from the lucrative slave trade.[3]

Historians have puzzled over Laurens's seemingly implausible statement. Why, they ask, would a slave trader and slave owner who drew his extraordinary wealth from those shiploads of Africans that arrived in Charleston and the hundreds of bondsmen who worked on his six Lowcountry plantations, choose to castigate slavery? How could a proslavery advocate suddenly become an antislavery proponent? This chapter seeks to answer these questions; it argues that American independence constituted the reason for Laurens's shift in attitude toward slave trading and slave owning. In his mind, both the slave trade and slavery became antithetical to American nationhood in ways that were not problematic to a British provincial identity. According to his rationale, one that resonated with Thomas Jefferson and many other patriots, the transatlantic commerce and the institution of slavery had been foisted on colonists by a distant and despotic monarch. Continuing to engage in the slave trade and slavery after the revolution, then, would be tantamount to continuing to submit to the "tyranny" of George III. Thus, these patriots formulated a policy of antislavery amelioration in the wake of civil war with Britain. It would be a tragic irony that, decades later, with the expansion of cotton, Laurens's support of the amelioration of slavery with a goal of moving toward abolition would be turned on its head by enterprising planters who sought to settle and develop the Upcountry of South Carolina. This later generation of planters began to embrace amelioration not to end slavery but to perpetuate it.[4]

In the decades preceding the revolution, Laurens and many other wealthy planters used the slave trade to "improve" themselves. That this improvement occurred because of slavery did not trouble them in the least; their civility on the imperial margins was not jeopardized by their status as slave-trading and slave-owning British Americans. For Laurens and other traders, slave trading and slave owning were dynamic forces that facilitated the progress of societies through the different stages of human development. When Laurens was a merchant in colonial South Carolina, it was slave trading and the accumulation of capital that allowed him to establish an extensive land-holding empire in the hinterlands. Thus, such activities were the *forces* that civilized and refined the margins of the British Empire. Nowhere was this better epitomized than at Laurens's townhouse and domestic compound, Rattray Green, in Ansonborough. On this five-acre tract, Laurens built a "large, elegant brick house" with piazzas overlooking the Cooper River and an extensive botanical garden that boasted oranges, olives, capers, and other exotic plants. That the labor of hundreds of slaves working on "crude" plantations in the swampy hinterlands enabled this wealth and refinement posed no contradiction for Laurens in the 1750s and 1760s. This view of provincial progress based on colonial slavery and the transatlantic slave trade was also shared by sugar planters in the British West Indies.[5]

Yet Laurens's perception of slavery as the great facilitator of progress on the imperial margins was much altered by the American Revolution. His vision of improvement in colonial South Carolina in the 1750s and 1760s was premised upon his understanding of the British imperial world, a world in which slave trading and slave owning served as acceptable means to attain civility in the colonies. Provincials like Laurens who established themselves in the rice country took their cues from civilized metropolitans, but they relied heavily upon slavery to accomplish this improvement, unlike their brethren across the Atlantic. The revolutionary war, which transformed South Carolina from a dependent colony into an independent polity, broke this world apart and radically changed how South Carolinians perceived the relationship between progress and slavery. South Carolina became an independent corporate entity, a state-republic within a republic of states. And as a new state in the Atlantic world, South Carolina could not rely on slavery and still hope to achieve peace, security, and world recognition. Two things—debt to British creditors incurred through slave trading and the absence of slavery in civilized European nations—seemed to demonstrate that what had facilitated progress in a colonial province would only jeopardize the survival of an independent republic. Thus, many patriots embraced a new vision of modernity that they believed would help ensure the survival of the new American nation, a vision in which New World progress depended on the absence of Old World, archaic systems such as the transatlantic slave trade and colonial slavery. Laurens, for one, had high hopes for the new federal union on the world stage. "The States are young & greatly distressed by the Effects of the War," he explained in 1783, "but the time will come when they will stand high in the scale of nations."[6]

For Laurens and many wealthy Lowcountry contemporaries—including Edmund Rutledge, Pierce Butler, Ralph Izard, Christopher Gadsden, and Charles Pinckney—the most pressing task after the revolution was to build a postcolonial regime in South Carolina that bore little resemblance to what it had been under the British crown. They wanted to excise every trace of British "tyranny," including monarchy and slavery, two institutions widely recognized by patriots as inherently despotic. Merchants and planters in South Carolina, all of whom had been intimately tied to the British commercial world, wanted nothing more than to extricate themselves from dependence on Britain and fashion South Carolina as a legitimate polity in the eyes of their European counterparts—their potential allies and trading partners. But exactly *how* to secure progress and civility outside of the confines of the British Empire remained unclear to many in the postrevolutionary age.[7]

What remained clear to Laurens, however, was that progress in the postcolonial regime could not include slavery. He envisioned a plan of antislavery amelioration in independent South Carolina that would result in newly improved agricultural staples, a free labor force, and new European markets for Lowcountry goods. An antislavery agenda—or more precisely, the *end* of slavery—was part and parcel of his vision of modernity in postrevolutionary South Carolina. Thus, in the 1770s and the 1780s, Laurens became a staunch advocate for the abolition of the transatlantic slave trade and the gradual improvement—or amelioration—of slavery, with vague gestures toward future emancipation. To be sure, his antislavery amelioration was not as coherent and developed as that of Jefferson—Laurens did not, for example, have any real plan for emancipating slaves. What he advocated was an experiment in the "government" of slaves and their elevation to a level comparable to freemen; he hoped other planters might follow suit. In the wake of the revolution, many elite Lowcountry planters believed that the slave trade should be abolished. A number of white farmers in the backcountry also did not welcome the expansion of slavery. In the 1780s and 1790s, with the rice market in a depression and cotton not yet a viable crop, many small farmers and Lowcountry planters could not—and did not—foresee a rapidly expanding agricultural market based on slavery. It seemed plausible that slavery was instead contracting, and that smaller farms maintained by free workers would emerge in the postrevolutionary landscape. A world before cotton, in their view, necessitated a world without slaves.[8]

This chapter underscores a moment of contingency in the history of slavery and expansion in eighteenth-century South Carolina. Using Henry

Laurens's experience as a slave-trading merchant and slave-owning planter as a focus, this chapter demonstrates why he eschewed the slave trade and slavery in favor of new antislavery amelioration schemes, how he sought to deploy them, and why these beliefs were ultimately reversed by the pro-slavery amelioration devised by new cotton planters at the turn of the century.[9]

A MERCHANT AND A PLANTER

During his presidency, Thomas Jefferson focused on Sierra Leone as a possible "asylum" for newly freed American slaves. But half a century earlier, Sierra Leone had been a slave-trading entrepôt from whence thousands of slaves had come. Established as an English trading post in the 1670s by the Royal African Company, Sierra Leone, or more precisely, the slave fort at Bance Island, had become a strategic point of intersection for slave dealers by the eighteenth century. In the 1750s, the London merchant firm of Grant, Sargent & Oswald assumed control of the fort; they expanded the physical structure and African work force, and employed smaller schooners to search for potential slaves in the surrounding areas. Since rice growing was indigenous to the culture of those Africans who inhabited the lands near Bance Island, Richard Oswald and his partners focused on selling slaves to one particular market: the rice-producing South Carolina Lowcountry. By 1756, Oswald's main point of contact for slave selling in South Carolina was Henry Laurens.[10]

Laurens, who generated hefty profits through commissions on slave sales, was the agent for supplies of African captives to Lowcountry rice planters. Importing slaves through Bance Island, which constituted part of the "Rice Coast," suggested that newly arrived captives already familiar with rice production would be able to begin work on plantations without additional training. This eliminated the necessity of "seasoning," a process that introduced new slaves to the demands and tasks of rice cultivation. It also introduced them to the brutality of slavery on the unsettled frontier. Seasoning described the period during which slaves contracted communicable diseases—including malaria and enteric maladies—endemic to the Lowcountry and then developed enough immunity to survive future infections. Slaves imported to work in the new rice country of South Carolina worked under the aegis of the task system; building levees, sluices, or planting and weeding the crop constituted some of the arduous daily duties demanded of slaves. Planters snapped up newly arrived Africans at

Charleston to sustain a rapidly expanding rice economy in South Carolina; between 1700 and 1730, rice exports from the colony had skyrocketed from 270,000 to 17 million pounds. Similarly, the slave population had swelled to twenty thousand souls, twice that of the white population.[11]

While factors at Bance Island dispatched slave ships according to directives from London merchants, Laurens received them. But Laurens was not simply a passive recipient of Bance Island's goods and slaves; he often advised Oswald's firm about which African ethnic groups were most popular among South Carolina rice planters. "Gold Coast and Gambias are best" and "next to them the Winward coast are prefer'd to Angolas," Laurens advised. Rice planters liked to purchase "tall people best for our business and strong withall." An ideal slave ship would be a cargo of "very likely healthy People," two-thirds of which would be men aged eighteen to twenty-five, and one-third females aged fourteen to eighteen. When the ships from Bance Island arrived in the Charleston harbor, they were usually laden with upwards of 250 slaves as well as ivory and other goods from the African coast. Laurens, who advertised the ships' arrival in local newspapers, sold the slaves at auction to rice planters, skimming off a 10 percent commission on each sale. This commission financed the establishment of Laurens's plantation empire and enabled him to fashion himself as a provincial gentleman.[12]

Even if Laurens was profiting handsomely from slave sales, the African slave trade was still fraught with uncertainty and disaster. The story of the slave ship *Emperor* provides a case in point. The story of the *Emperor* began in Cork, on the southern coast of Ireland, in July 1754. Piloted by her captain, Charles Gwynn, the *Emperor* set its course around Europe toward its intended port in western Africa. The ship apparently enjoyed a "short Passage to Angola" where "she was calculated for the purchase of 570 Slaves." Then, she disappeared.[13] Laurens wrote frantically to his commercial contacts in the Caribbean, seeking news of the lost slaver. There had been talk of war breaking out between England and France. Or perhaps the *Emperor* had been raided or sunk, since the "African trade is more liable to such Accidents than any other we know of." Gwynn reportedly had left West Africa with 390 slaves on board, 180 fewer than Laurens's estimate. For his part, Laurens hoped the account was "eronious," and that it was "high time he [Gwynn] was arriv'd in some part of America" so that some semblance could be made of a "most tatter'd Voyage," which had cost Laurens and his partners £7,100 at the outset.[14]

But "an ill Fate" had attended the *Emperor* in the Atlantic. On April 8, a "Violent Gale of Wind off this Bar" forced the ship off the coast of the Carolinas. For nearly a week, Gwynn stalled in the deeper Gulf Stream waters, waiting for the winds to slacken. His human cargo, he knew, was at risk. Soon Gwynn abandoned Charleston for Kingston, the southern port of Jamaica. When the *Emperor* finally laid anchor in the West Indies, 120 Africans were dead. Presumably, they had died during the storm, locked in the bowels of the ship. Perhaps they did not have food or water, or perhaps they had drowned in the high seas. But whatever actually happened aboard the *Emperor* in April 1755, it was, at the very least, "destructive" to human life.[15]

Gwynn "buried" 120 Africans in Kingston, hoping to put up the remaining 270 for sale. And yet, these men and women appeared to be "a great many . . . disorder'd" when they were unloaded from the *Emperor.* Most likely they were emaciated, or ill with smallpox or scurvy, or crazed from being taken from their homes, packed into the hold of a ship, and taken, blindly, on various routes across the Atlantic. Still, Peter Furnell, Laurens's merchant colleague in Kingston, brought all 270 Africans to market. Only 77 of them sold, averaging about £28.5 each. Gwynn told Laurens that the unsold Africans were those "the People of Jamaica dont like." West Indian planters often discriminated against buying chattel from Malemba, part of the Congo region of western Africa from which Gwynn had acquired the slaves.[16]

Laurens had estimated that the *Emperor* would carry 570 slaves from Angola to Charleston. With South Carolina planters' penchant for slave buying, he guessed he could sell each slave for between £30 and £33 sterling. Instead, Gwynn loaded only 390 slaves when he moored at Malemba. Of those, only 270 survived the storm in the Atlantic. And when Peter Furnell put the *Emperor*'s slaves up at auction in June 1755, only 77 sold—at prices far below those Laurens had estimated for the Charleston market. Gwynn's decision would cost Laurens and his partners thousands of pounds sterling in losses.

Of course, as Laurens himself would admit, this was the nature of the African slave trade. Even without the disaster of the *Emperor,* Laurens was under pressure from all corners of the Atlantic. In Europe, war with France loomed; Laurens's contacts in Britain and the Caribbean seemed sure of it. In Africa, especially in Gambia, smallpox was reaching endemic proportions, making quarantines, delayed sales, and smaller cargoes a likely reality. And in the Lowcountry, business was booming. Laurens estimated that he would ship 80,000 barrels of rice and 600,000 pounds of indigo to London. Indeed, "Our People," Laurens wrote, "have become so fond of the indigo business" that "we shall render a good deal more than Britain consumes." Nonetheless, Laurens hoped that "Marketts can be found," as the "assiduous pursuit" of indigo only meant planters' eagerness to purchase more African slaves from Laurens's firm. His reference to potential new markets for slaves was telling—it reflected Laurens's belief that the slave trade was a civilizing system that allowed provincials to embrace commerce and accumulate wealth, the key marker of civility.[17]

Supply was a problem in the summer of 1755, with several ships in quarantine in Charleston, the *Emperor* still moored in Jamaica, and planters' demand for slaves rising. In spite of this, the *Pearl*, commanded by a Captain Jeffries, appeared to be the saving grace of Laurens's firm. The sloop was removed from the quarantine just in time; Jeffries had arrived from Angola in June with 243 slaves on board. Apparently, between 60 and 70 slaves had perished during the voyage, probably from smallpox. But at the Charleston sale, the *Pearl*'s Africans sold for an average of about £33 each; Jeffries's human cargo grossed £6,556. In contrast, the sale of the 77 slaves from the *Emperor* had totaled only a fraction of that amount. While Gwynn's ship represented the potential losses to be had in the transatlantic slave trade, the profits reaped from the *Pearl*'s sail demonstrated just how lucrative the trade could be. And Laurens only hoped for more—"six or seven sail from Gambia" arrived in Charleston before the hurricane season set in.[18]

Despite the significant risks inherent in slave trading, Laurens continued to ply the business well into the 1760s. He used the money he reaped from commissions to expand his plantation empire. After 1763, Laurens reduced his participation in the trade, but this was not due to humanitarian considerations—he still avidly supported the trade to ensure the expansion of wealth and settlement in South Carolina. But the dissolution of his merchant partnership in Charleston dissuaded Laurens from further full participation in the trade. Since demand was rising, he could no longer handle the clamor for slaves on his own. In 1764, he boasted that he had "had the most kind and friendly offers from my friends in London, Liverpool, & Bristol & do believe that I might have sold 1,000 or 1,500 [slaves] last Year & more the Year we are in." Still, Laurens had "in general declined the Affrican business," since he had "no partner" and could not "chuse to embarrass & perhaps involve myself in concerns too unweildy." He was still engaged in the trade, only on a much smaller scale. "A few now and then of a good sort I can Manage well enough," he noted, at least as long as the "prices keep up."[19]

As late as 1770, Laurens was still dabbling in slave trading. "If you send any Slaves to this plan consign'd to me," he wrote to merchant John Holman, "you may depend upon it, that I shall either sell them myself, or put them into such hands as will do you the most Service in the sale."[20] Although Laurens devoted much of his energy to the maintenance of his plantations in the latter 1760s, he remained connected to the slave-trading world. While some historians have implied that Laurens withdrew from the slave trade for moral reasons, his objections were to slavery, not the slave trade. In 1768, he explained that he had "quitted the Profits arising from that gainful branch" because of the "many acts" of masters "toward the wretched Negroes from the time of purchasing to that of selling them again." In Laurens's mind, the fault lay with the planters, not the slave traders.[21]

Laurens was a deliberate, calculating man who withdrew from slave trading not because he hoped to abandon the British commercial world but because he hoped to exploit it more fully as a landowner. Moreover, he was "weary of constant Application to a Counting-House," to "add Thousands to Thousands, by grasping at, or by retaining every profitable Branch of Commerce." He lacked a Charleston partner to help offset the cost and risk associated with the rising costs of the slave trade, nor did he wish to "engage one." Thus, Laurens "relinquished the Gainful Commissions arising from the Sale of Negroes," transferring them instead into the "Hands of Gentlemen who could transact it to the greatest Advantage." Laurens had grown tired of the debts contracted from each voyage made to Africa, the risks involved, and the uncertain outcomes. He had made his money in the slave trade as a merchant embedded in the interstices of the British commercial world; he would apply his mercantile knowledge to the development and management of his bourgeoning plantation network.[22]

Beginning in the early 1750s, Laurens began building his empire. In 1756, he bought a half-interest in the 1,500-acre Wambaw plantation along the Santee River. In 1762, he purchased Mepkin, a 3,100-acre estate along the Cooper River. He then bought Broughton Island plantation, "1,000 Acres of as good River Swamp as in the Universe," along Georgia's Altamaha River in 1763. Soon after, Laurens established Wright's Savannah, also in Georgia. A fifth plantation, New Hope, was added in 1768.[23] Other Lowcountry merchants had the same idea; prominent traders like Peter Manigault, James Habersham, and Richard Hutson sought to "turn Planter & . . . reside a great part of my time in the country." Even Laurens's slave-trading partner in London, Richard Oswald, wanted to establish a "Farm, plantation & Vineyard" in the "back settlements" of South Carolina. Thus, Laurens, like several of his merchant colleagues, saw plantations as an increasingly valuable investment.[24]

Becoming a rich slave-owning planter was as close as Laurens could come to the English gentry. He modeled his own provincial gentility on that claimed by his metropolitan counterparts. Laurens bought thousands of acres of rice lands and built a townhouse in Charleston. He had a botanical garden, was a member of the Royal Society of Arts, and became obsessed with improving his crops in the same way a landed English gentleman might. Of course, commerce—the consumption of British goods and ideas—enabled Laurens to cultivate himself on the margins. In 1769, Laurens entered to win a prize for his indigo crop from the Society of Arts in London, declaring that he entered the competition to "encourage more planters to attempt making the best kind of Indigo & especially those who live remote from Market." And in 1771, while visiting London, Laurens sought out more efficient means for producing indigo and rice. "I have contrived an Axle and Arms for beating Indigo, which will save a vast deal of Labour," he wrote. "I have had a Model made, and intend to send it to Carolina, for the benefit of the Public or the Indigo Planters." Furthermore, Laurens was "in great hopes of procuring a Machine for raising large Bodies of Water" and "an easy and effectual Machine for pounding Rice." In sum, Laurens believed that these innovations would tie South Carolina planters more closely to the British commercial world and encourage productivity and profit.[25]

Laurens elicited a concern for laborers on his plantations that he never evinced for newly arrived African captives on slave ships. In 1765, he displayed "tender concern" for the "division of Wambaw Negroes." "I don't know anything that could have been contrived to distress me & embarrass my plantation more," he wrote, "than this unnecessary division of Fathers, Mothers, Husbands, Wives, & Children who tho Slaves are still human Creatures & I cannot be deaf to their cries." Again and again during the colonial era, Laurens poised himself as attuned to the demands of his slaves—whether for food, clothing, or protection from sale and familial separation—despite being far removed from them while he was in Ansonborough or Europe. What he perceived as increased sympathy for his slaves was also the gauge for what he viewed as his increasingly refined sensibilities.[26]

And yet, even as he sought to humanize the institution of slavery, he did not seek to end it—at least not in the 1760s and early 1770s, when colonial slavery was an established, and necessary, imperial institution. Laurens's perception of the "long and comical Story" of *Somerset v. Stewart* (1772)— in which Chief Justice William Murray, Lord Mansfield, ruled that it was unlawful for a Virginia slave, James Somerset, to be forcibly removed from England by his master—illustrates the absence of any antislavery feelings on his part. Shortly after Lord Mansfield laid down the famous verdict described in the *London Chronicle* as "the man's [James Somerset] being a Negro slave, did not authorize his master to transport him out of the kingdom: whereupon the Black was immediately discharged," Laurens came to the rescue of a slave-trading partner in need. The partner, Joseph Clay, had transported a slave to England. Laurens suggested that Clay, in order to avoid having to free the slave, send him across the Atlantic "by first Vessel for Charles Town," and that "proper precautions may be taken immediately upon arrival . . . to prevent Elopement." Of course, Laurens believed that blacks, whether free or enslaved, had no place in Britain; he feared that blacks' presence in London might cause the "mongrelization of the English race and the further corruption of Parliament." Their place, he implied, was in the provinces. Thus, Laurens's provincial vision of his own improvement and the improvement of his slaves occurred *within* the system of colonial slavery, not outside of it.[27]

Laurens considered provincial slavery part of the imperial design. But slavery could not exist at the imperial center—it would be a degrading influence on the metropole, the font of civilization for the rest of the empire. Slavery was permissible in the margins where it facilitated colonization projects, the accumulation of wealth, and the expansion of the empire. Enslaved people in the colonies did not present a threat to the ruling elite in Britain because the entrenchment of the aristocracy guaranteed that society would be "properly ruled" by "those of superior birth, manners, education, and wealth."[28] Thus, Laurens's vision for improvement was shaped by the imperial world in which he revolved as a "Loyal and Faithful Subject" of the crown. In exchange for the protection of the king, Laurens acted as an imperial agent, reaping enormous profits from the transatlantic slave trade and transforming the low-lying Carolina swamps into profitable rice fields. The accumulation of private wealth enabled the colonization of the "wilderness" of South Carolina; all of this was made possible by the institution of slavery.[29]

If the British imperial world protected Laurens, allowed him access to extensive commercial markets, and enabled him to generate enormous personal wealth, then it seemed natural that he would remain loyal to the sovereign who granted these "liberties." In the 1760s, his loyalty was tested when three of his schooners were seized by customs officials for carrying nonenumerated articles on board. Part of Laurens's outrage was attributed to the fact that, before the arrival of new customs house collectors in the spring of 1767, it had been common practice among merchants to clear their coastal trade ships—and the articles on board—without approval from the customs house. But new officers just appointed from Britain began to enforce a law that had been routinely, and benignly, evaded. Much to the chagrin of local merchants and planters, the officers placed transatlantic commerce and local coastal commerce on the same footing. In Laurens's mind, this was an effort to stymie trade. "Such men as that one in Office," Laurens wrote to Richard Oswald in London, "are the greatest Enemies to Britain of any Man in America" for "so does one such Officer or Man in power do more prejudice to the Interest of Britain in America than twenty Mouthing Liberty Boys." While Laurens perceived the unjustness of the "tyranny" of the new customs officials, the incident nevertheless did not undermine his commitment to the British imperial world. But the ship seizures—which Laurens interpreted as an obstacle to plantation business—were a harbinger of the disputes to come between imperial officials and colonists during the heightened imperial crisis in the 1770s.[30]

Even as late as 1775, when nonimportation resolutions against the British were approved by the South Carolina provincial congress, Laurens did not seek to be free of a world that had granted him so many liberties. "'Reasonable liberty' is all we pray for—Independence is not the view of America not a Sober Sensible Man wishes for it," Laurens insisted. In fact, South Carolinians "pray for King George 3d." and "desire to continue in that State of Subordination in which His present Majesty found us at his accession to the Crown." Along with his loyalty to the British crown, Laurens also retained his fealty to British institutions, including the slave trade and slavery. Laurens lamented that the nonimportation "resolutions remain a Bar to the importation of Negroes," since the arrival of new slaves would undoubtedly "make not only a saving but a gainful Remittance if our Resolutions did not prohibit the importation." In other words, the tyranny of Parliament, the corrosive source that Laurens imagined to be tainting the empire, had forced South Carolinians to boycott British goods, including slaves, a move that was depriving them of the wealth and expansion that were the hallmarks of empire.[31]

By 1776, when it appeared that George III was unresponsive to colonial grievances and colluding with a despotic Parliament, Laurens no longer looked to the mother country for protection or to uphold the rule of law. His vision of the world was fundamentally changed. As Laurens advised George Nugent-Temple-Grenville, Lord Grenville, because of the "Oppressive Laws, Oppressive Informers, Oppressive and unjust Decrees and final Sentences" imposed upon American provincials, colonists would "be driven through despair to Acts destructive of their own happiness and detrimental to that of the Mother Country." In sum, colonists would dissolve the union with Britain in order to form a union of their own. Before the imperial crisis, the empire had offered Laurens and his peers corporate equality through provincial assemblies, as well as the extension of British liberties, which included the freedom to expand and accumulate property without limitation. In 1776, with this equality jettisoned by a despotic king and Parliament, and colonization projects jeopardized by a string of oppressive taxes, ambitious men like Laurens began to imagine a new empire, one that would boast all of the features of the British Empire but without a despotic monarch to restrain it. The rupture of the British Empire and the onset of civil war had significant consequences for Laurens and his counterparts: they would revise what had been their understanding of progress within the confines of a British world. In the independent state-republic of South Carolina, slave trading and slavery could have only a temporary place. For the federal union to survive and advance within the Atlantic states' system, patriots believed that they would have to share the same vision of modernity as enlightened Europeans—a world of equal nations, free trade, and free labor.[32]

BUILDING A NEW "HOUSE"

The widespread physical destruction wrought by the war with the British in South Carolina constituted a visceral break with the empire that amplified the ideological split of 1776. The 1780 siege of Charleston—when General Henry Clinton invaded the city with fourteen thousand British troops—and the subsequent British occupation that lasted until 1782, devastated the city and the surrounding areas. Laurens, who was in Holland drumming up Dutch support for the patriots' cause and later imprisoned in the Tower of London for treason, suffered heavy losses to his plantations during the British occupation. Not only did several of his slaves join British ranks or succumb to disease, but Hessian mercenaries also burned and pillaged his Ansonborough townhouse. "The stable & Kitchen is entirely down," James Custer told Laurens shortly after the siege of Charleston, "the House barely worths repairing, the Garden entirely destroyed" and "the Brick House" had become "a Barack for Hessian soldiers." The extensive destruction of Laurens's property, the fleeing of his slaves, and his imprisonment as a "traitor" in the Tower constituted the basis for his visceral break with the British imperial world. The complete destruction of the British "union" to which he had previously sworn allegiance allowed Laurens to imagine postrevolutionary South Carolina as a *tabula rasa,* where British institutions and "tyrannies" would be completely erased.[33]

It was no surprise that Laurens considered the transatlantic slave trade and slavery to be wholly British systems. Like Jefferson, Laurens blamed George III and a complicit Parliament for the existence of slavery in America. "Britain is the fountain from whence we have been supplied with slaves upwards" of a century, Laurens wrote to the moral reformer and antislavery proponent Richard Price. It was Britain, not the provincials in the colonies, who "Passed Acts of Parliament establishing & encouraging the Slave Trade, even for monopolizing it in her own provinces." While Price directed blame for the slave trade toward provincial consumers of the captives, Laurens quipped that "the inhumanity cruelty wickedness & devilishness which you impute to the Traffic applies in the first instance" to "your 'own Country.'" In Laurens's eyes, patriots were absolved of the sin of slave trading because British officials had initiated it. In this way, Laurens cast slave trading and slavery as a problem of the Old World, not the new one that had been created post-1776. The traffic in human flesh and the labor of human chattel were fixtures of a backward and monarchical world; the "tyranny" exerted by a master over his slave was a synecdoche for the tyranny that despotic monarchs exerted over their loyal people.[34]

The trope of "enslavement" was an important one for Laurens and his contemporaries, for it allowed white planters—along with those loyal slaves who did not run away to the British lines—to imagine themselves and their human property collectively as the victims of British enslavers. Just as patriots had been denied "equality" with Britons, oppressed by far-reaching tax policies, and made subject to the despotism of a distant king and Parliament, so too had African slaves been wrenched from their homelands and stuffed into the holds of slave ships bound for the New World and a lifetime of bondage. The Lowcountry merchant and politician Christopher Gadsden concluded that South Carolinians were "riveted in a Slavery beyond Redemption, and by far exceeding that of the subjects of any absolute Monarch in Europe."[35]

The identification of wealthy white planters with their human property may seem perverse today, but for Laurens and others, viewing slaves and masters collectively as objects of British enslavement enabled them to begin to construct a series of binaries that would help define the postcolonial world: Old World and New, slavery and freedom, mercantilism and free trade, America and Britain. Expansion, and the slavery that underpinned it, once seen as the business of empire, was recast in Laurens's eyes as the greedy and illegitimate pursuit of a despotic regime: "they [Britons] would enslave Asia, Africa, America & Europe too if they durst" merely to increase their "own Navigation & Commerce." The federative empire in which South Carolinians had previously had an "equal" stake before the imperial crisis was demolished; a centralized and despotic regime that sought to "enslave" subjects had replaced it. Laurens pinned the hypocrisy of slave trading and slave owning on Britain. Its example was "exactly similar to a pious, externally pious, Man's prohibiting fornication under his own roof and keeping a dozen Mistresses abroad."[36]

For Laurens and other white South Carolinians, the break with Britain demonstrated that the mother country was no longer the wellspring of civility. As Laurens told Price, patriots would "never be reformed while they imitate 'your country.'" Britain had at one time offered the benefits of civilization to South Carolina within an imperial system. But revolutionaries recognized that civilization took a different shape outside of the framework of the British Empire. Laurens was a case in point. Before the revolution, he had been a prosperous merchant, fashioning himself as a planter and provincial gentleman. He never intended to be independent of British institutions; he sought to "improve" his bondsmen but not to free them. As a member of an independent state-republic within a union of republics, however, Laurens began seeking cues for civility from Europe. South Carolinians sought to align their postcolonial view of progress and modernity with the "enlightened" doctrine embraced by European states. Laurens and other planter-politicians prioritized political independence, the establishment of commercial ties with Europe, agricultural and manufacturing improvements and expansion, and the future end of slavery and the slave trade. South Carolina, they hoped, would one day advance to the same level as Europe. "Britain" may, scoffed the Lowcountry planter Pierce Butler, "enjoy her opinion of our distress or barbarism," but "we see light enough, & feel ourselves advancing so in civilization as to be content." One day, even "enlightened Europe," with its "Philosophy & Letters," would have to "acknowledge that we are not so entirely in the dark" as not to "find the end of Govert. completely answered in the freedom & happiness of the People." America, Butler implied, would one day be considered on the same footing as European nation-states.[37]

With the British king defined as an illegitimate and despotic slave trader, Laurens sought to fashion America, or at least his own state, in oppositional terms. In the wake of the revolution, Laurens eschewed any further role in the slave trade: "Guarantee for African Consignments I never will be for any Man," he declared in 1785. Americans should follow his example and relinquish slave trading in order to avoid indebtedness and total ruin, he thought. Yet even after the revolution, planters and merchants continued to import African slaves and remained financially ensconced in British trading firms and credit systems. The slave trade, which was reopened from 1783 to 1785, only furthered Lowcountry planters' dependence on British credit and plunged them ever further into debt. As Laurens confided to Alexander Hamilton in 1785, the "present number of slaves," which constituted "precarious riches," served as "our greatest weakness."[38] Writing to another colleague, Laurens concluded that "Nothing in my Opinion can recover the credit of this Country or save it from total ruin, but a prohibition of the importation of Negroes." His use of "credit" had a double meaning. He believed that America could not establish commercial creditworthiness in the world because of indebtedness owing to the slave trade, and that the new nation would gain little credibility, or legitimacy, in the eyes of future treaty partners in Europe. In this way, the end of the African slave trade was the first step in expelling all vestiges of British tyranny from America and creating an independent and legitimate nation in its place.[39]

In the later 1770s and 1780s, Laurens and other prominent patriots took up diplomatic posts abroad, hoping to establish closer commercial and political relationships that would allow them better access to markets. Laurens sent his two sons to boarding school in Geneva, and, in 1780, traveled to the Netherlands to seek a $10 million loan and to negotiate commercial amity between the Dutch and Americans. At the Treaty of Paris in 1783, John Adams, together with Laurens, John Jay, and Benjamin Franklin, pressed for access to Newfoundland fishing grounds and to prevent Britain's confiscation of slave property in the Americas. The avid agriculturalist William Drayton wrote to the U.S. minister to France, Thomas Jefferson, hoping to convince him to push "towards opening a commercial intercourse directly with France." Ralph Izard, the wealthy Lowcountry planter who had lived in London and Paris, and who served as commissioner to the Court of Tuscany during the 1770s, shared Drayton's anxiety about the future of the Carolina rice market with Jefferson. He lamented the "total loss of the Portuguese Market," which "is now supplied from Brazil." Izard heard news that "Constantinople alone might take the whole of our Crop at a better price than is obtained at present." But since America had no "Treaty with the Grand Signor," the "Barbary Corsairs deter our Merchants from entering into the Mediterranean." Thus, for Laurens, Drayton, Izard, and many other patriot-planters, the prerequisite of commercial "intercourse" was the establishment of treaties and other diplomatic ties with individual European nations.[40]

Anxiety about securing European markets for South Carolina produce weighed heavily on the minds of even the wealthiest planters after the revolution. Laurens lost about £250,000 during the revolution but was able to maintain some holdings in British financial houses. Even Izard, a rice planter once so wealthy that he vowed to use his estate to pay for war ships needed during the revolution, found himself in an increasingly precarious financial position by the late 1780s. When he wrote to his friend Gabriel Manigault in 1789, he believed his lands to be in an improved state but nonetheless worried that "I shall be very unlucky if in a few years a considerable part of my debts will not be paid." "They are a continual source of uneasiness to me," Izard continued, "& for that reason I would sell my House if I could meet with a purchaser, & give a credit of five, six, or seven years." Jacob Read, Laurens's sometime lawyer and a planter who served in the Continental Congress, wrote to his cousin in London to request a loan in 1787. Although he had managed to maintain "myself and my family and fed my Slaves from the Labour of myself & Clerks," the war and a three-year blight of the rice crop combined to produce a "general Calamity." He was left "in want of about fifteen hundred pounds to repair my house in Charleston and rebuild my Barn & Two [rice] Machines in order to be ready for the next Crop." Read assured his cousin that "with the blessing of God I think I should never have the occasion to borrow anything" again. But Read's father, William, was less optimistic—he feared "that we are not to be fortunate Planters."[41]

Despite the overwhelming problem of debt and a looming recession, Laurens believed that one way to secure European markets for South Carolina rice and indigo was to improve them. This new policy of agricultural amelioration took hold only as the era of extracting enormous profits from the rice and indigo trade under the aegis of British mercantilism came to a halt. Lowcountry planters only modified their land and labor management practices when faced with deteriorating market and environmental conditions.[42]

Since South Carolinians could not compete with indigo production in South America and India after 1783, they began to experiment with soil remediation techniques and crop diversification. Planters began cultivating corn, wheat, and rice for overseas markets. War-torn Europe's demand for grain was only increasing in the later eighteenth century, and Laurens and his counterparts believed that they could offer the supply. But the new agricultural regime in South Carolina would also be a manufacturing one. A progressive commercial system, one that more closely resembled Europe, would both produce raw goods and manufacture them for exportation. Laurens and other enterprising Lowcountry planters believed that they would set the tone for the development of this new regime. In 1785, for example, the South Carolina Agricultural Society was formed in order to help foster a civilized commercial society by retaining closer agricultural ties with Europe, for a "civilized state" was far superior to "the savage." William Drayton presented "wild rice" to the society, seeking to determine whether it might not "prove an advantageous Article for Exportation" to Europe. Laurens, for his part, was determined to transform his plantations into proto-industrial sites of production, where rice was planted, harvested, and then hewn in mills for market. His visits to "great Looms and great Forges" in Britain's industrial midlands in the 1770s provided a model for his rice plantations in the 1780s. After inspecting a wind-driven water pump at Lymington in 1774, he tried to build three of the same to create a rice mill reservoir in 1786. This vision of commercial progress in South Carolina was meant to lift planters out of debt, create new markets, and encourage expansion.[43]

Just as Laurens and his colleagues looked east toward a legitimate commerce with Europe that bore no vestiges of the "British" slave trade, they also looked west, toward the South Carolina frontier. In the postrevolutionary era, when cotton was not yet a viable crop, many Lowcountry planters, joined by some non-slave-owning farmers, foresaw a land without slaves. Independent farmers would settle the Upcountry, transforming the "remotest depths of our western frontiers" that were "barren wilderness" into "hospitable abodes of peace and plenty." These frontier settlements would be linked with Charleston and included in "free trade with all the world." Essentially, independent farmers would civilize the unsettled Upcountry, but they would not do so as slave-owning planters, since they were no longer "sacrificed to the interests of a selfish European island." In some future time, Laurens thought, all of South Carolina might be populated by farms owned by free white men.[44]

Laurens was also anxious that slavery not be expanded into the western reaches of South Carolina. Concerned with the "vacant Lands in our State," Laurens knew that "much disputation" would characterize the future of such settlements, since "future Grants of Land will in a considerable degree depend upon future importation of Negroes in the southern states." Laurens believed that non-slave-owning whites could be persuaded to settle the region if the slave trade was prohibited. If the "further importation be prohibited or greatly restricted," then lands could be "parcel'd out to poor White Adventurers at easy Rents or moderate purchases." The extension of these poor but "independent" farmers would make the "Riches of the State" more "permanent" and serve as a contrast to dependent, opulent colonial planters who devoted themselves to the "glare of precarios Riches" through their involvement in the slave trade and British credit networks. These non-slave-owning whites would settle the backcountry and "make a happy Exchange" of commerce there; in a society without slaves, "Mechanics will find full employment & good wages" while "Husbandmen may obtain Land upon much better terms than they have been accustomed." Laurens even thought it might be possible that the state government would grant "indulgences & even premiums" to "Men & families who are likely to become valuable Citizens," thus ensuring that free whites, rather than enslaved blacks, occupied the Upcountry. All of this, though, depended on the British institution of slavery being abolished, an institution that Laurens described as an "Old House" that "Totters." The "want of wisdom in that House," meaning those South Carolinians who remained pro–slave trade in the postrevolutionary period, was still powerful enough to undermine Laurens's antislavery vision, "throw us again into a flame," and "retard the building of our own" house.[45]

Laurens's new "house"—the state-republic of South Carolina—rested on his vision of antislavery amelioration. In order to join the ranks of modern and independent states in the Atlantic world, South Carolina and other states would have to mitigate slavery in order to end it and transition to a free labor society. After the prohibition of the slave trade, Laurens reasoned, South Carolina slave owners would soon be persuaded to manumit their slaves. "The time however for general emancipation will come," Laurens noted confidently in 1785. "I foresee it as clearly, as in the Year 1776" when he "foresaw & predicted that Great Britain would lose her Colonies by attempts to enslave the Inhabitants." Laurens never specifically articulated how emancipation would be brought about, but he remained clear that he sought a gradual, ameliorative solution to the slave problem. "I see rising gradations to unlimited freedom," he wrote to Alexander Hamilton. A first "gradation" would be the end of the slave trade while later gradations would improve slavery with an eye toward ending it. "When We shall be wise enough to stop importation, such happy families will become more general and time will work manumission or a state equal to it." Laurens's statement shared much with Jefferson, who noted in 1826 that the slave problem would be solved by "time, which outlives all things," and which would "outlive this evil also." Knowing full well that slave owners' consent was the prerequisite of emancipation, the "revolution in public opinion which this cause requires" might take an "age" or more. Thus, in the absence of slave owners' assuming any agency in the emancipation of their bondsmen, time itself became the agent of abolition. Amelioration was wholly compatible with this notion of time as a primary agent; Laurens and Jefferson both believed that during the age it would take slave owners to realize the necessity of emancipation, slaves' material and moral conditions might be ameliorated in preparation for their freedom.[46]

Even if Laurens echoed some patriots in his calls for a gradual end to slavery in the new state-republics, his vision for a multiracial, postemancipation society set him far apart from his colleagues. At a time when many southern planters thought that emancipation and colonization must be inextricably linked in order to avoid the outbreak of race war, Laurens instead believed that blacks could remain in America. In his view, "blackness"—which constituted a permanent color and barrier to entering white society for many South Carolinians—was for Laurens a temporary condition. He cited the example of Gideon Gibson, a free mulatto carpenter who emigrated from Virginia to South Carolina with his white wife in 1731. Concerned that Gibson's marriage was an example of interracial mixing, the Commons House of Assembly investigated Gibson but in the end deemed him and his family "not Negroes nor Slaves but Free People" who owned two tracts of land and seven slaves. In Laurens's estimation, "by perseverance the black may be blanched & the 'stamp of Providence'"—or providentially determined "blackness"—could be "effectually effaced." In the end, Gibson escaped the "penalties of the Negro Law" by producing more "Red & White in his face" than most of the members of the House of Assembly. After having passed through several "stage[s] of Whitewash," blacks could effectively become whites, Laurens reasoned.[47]

But even if their skin could become white, Laurens suggested that their internal "blackness" could not be altered as easily. He thought it best to "confine" blacks to "their original clothing," or prevent them from "passing" as whites, as had Gideon Gibson and his son, who had been a leader in the Regulator Movement and the owner of 1,100 acres.[48] In Laurens's eyes, newly freed slaves "may & ought to continue a separate people" who would be "subjected by special Laws, kept harmless, made useful & freed from the Tyranny & arbitrary power of Individuals." In other words, emancipated slaves would continue to constitute a separate "people" or "nation," but such a people could be included peacefully within South Carolina white society and freed from the arbitrary power of slave owners. This was a reversal of Jefferson's reasoning that race war was the inevitable result of two "nations"—one white and the other black—who continued to occupy the same country. Jefferson thought that animosity between the races would culminate in an outright war if blacks were freed and allowed to remain on American soil. But Laurens foresaw emancipation as diffusing the "state of war," not exacerbating it; relinquishing the "Tyranny & arbitrary power" inherent in the master-slave relationship would soothe the enmity between the two races and allow blacks to continue living as a peaceful, "separate people" in America.[49]

Of course, slaves' amelioration would be the chief means of ensuring that emancipated slaves assumed a nonviolent and "useful" role in southern society. As Laurens suggested, the formation of "happy" slave families, therefore, would be the antidote to the transience and violence of slavery and the slave trade, a dynamic system that had broken apart families and shuffled slaves from plantation to plantation. The "happy families" of slaves would signal the "improvement" of the institution and reinforce the amelioration of South Carolina—"good Servants" and "good Soldiers" would be "our Strength in time of Need" by offering peace and security in a dangerous and uncertain world. But amelioration was not yet "present," as evidenced by the "Number of wretched Slaves" and "precarios Riches" incurred by slavery, which threatened to slide South Carolina backward, into a state of semi-barbarism. Emancipation, Laurens reasoned, would only come after slaves had been fully ameliorated. It was clear to him that because "these Southern States are not at this moment in a disposition to be persuaded" to emancipate their human property, then "time" would have to serve as the principal agent of emancipation, not South Carolinians. In the meantime, individual planters' amelioration schemes, including the division of slaves into families, would "improve" slavery and pave the way for future emancipation. Still, Laurens warned that "our conversion by too long a Delay" would cause "a direful Struggle"—failure to destroy the system of slavery and emancipate slaves could result in war.[50]

Laurens, who predicted that "'tis not improbable I shall stand almost alone" in his plan for the ameliorative end of slavery, saw the first "gradation" of his plan—the ban on the importation of slaves—defeated in March 1785. Laurens and other Lowcountry planters who sought to close the slave trade in order to mitigate the drain of specie from the state (South Carolina had banned the use of paper currency) also pushed for the diversification of crops, a strategy that might lessen planters' dependence on slave labor. Even though planters defeated the motion to close the slave trade, William Drayton successfully led another campaign to form a state agricultural society; its purpose was to encourage agricultural improvement through the introduction of new crops and markets. Despite resistance from proslavery planters, Laurens committed himself to "proceed in the Plan laid down" for the "government of my own Conduct." His individual amelioration plan would serve as a model, as a means to persuade other planters governed by "Interest" rather than "moral Justice."[51]

THE "GOVERNMENT OF MY OWN CONDUCT"

In colonial South Carolina, the plantation was not a static or idyllic space. It was a system of dynamic production linked to Atlantic markets through a robust commercial network. And it was also the means by which agents of a colonizing society, like Henry Laurens, transformed uninhabited swamps into tremendously productive agricultural lands in the name of empire. Using his sophisticated mercantile acumen, Laurens built a plantation complex in the rice country in the 1760s that by the eve of the American Revolution was generating returns upward of 20 percent. The plantations he created, however, did not function as individual, bounded units of production in the low-lying swamps, but rather as an interdependent system unified by commerce. In effect, Laurens used the British commercial world in the Atlantic that he had come to know intimately as a template for his plantation world in the Lowcountry. Composed of central and "out" plantations, Laurens's empire constituted a model for colonization of the undeveloped rice country; his vision rested not on the plantation itself but on its ability to be replicated in frontier areas and connected to older, established plantations outside Charleston. The replication of semi-autonomous jurisdictions—the ability to carve new plantations from the wilderness and improve them—was precisely what defined Britain as a colonizing society in the New World.[52]

Laurens's colonial plantation enterprise can also be read as a civilizing project. His townhouse at Ansonborough in Charleston functioned as the primary node of civility; this was the site of Laurens's household of white and black dependents. The "core" plantations of Wambaw and Mepkin were less civilized spaces, but their proximity to Ansonborough rendered them more refined than the "out" plantations of Wright's Savannah, New Hope, and Broughton Island. Those plantations were furthest from Ansonborough and, as such, were also the furthest from civilization. But by linking all six plantations with a series of schooners that plied tidal rivers and the Atlantic shoreline, Laurens used commerce—or the consumption of goods—as a means to civilize even those plantations that lay furthest beyond the pale of polite society. In Laurens's system, the replication of plantations was as crucial as yoking them together. This dynamic system meant that the estates were not static areas; commerce was constantly "improving" existing plantations while also facilitating the expansion of Laurens's "enterprise."[53]

Similarly, Laurens "played the role of master" not by being physically present on his plantations, but as a "merchant who circulated the goods that connected plantations" to each other, to Charleston, and to Atlantic markets. The market, made available by Laurens, became a proxy for onsite patriarchy. Black slaves and white overseers—Laurens's dependents in his plantation empire—were bound closer to their master by the food, drink, and clothing that they consumed, all delivered by schooners at Laurens's behest. Their dependence and their consumption thus allowed Laurens to "know" them—at least through clothing and shoe lists—as well as manipulate and control their actions. Providing goods for consumption allowed Laurens to ameliorate the material conditions of his overseers and slaves; their comfort constituted an improvement over the abject poverty and malnourishment that surely would have characterized those dependents deprived of a robust commercial connection, at least in the "out" plantations. It was this material improvement, and the productivity that accompanied it, that enabled Laurens to see himself as "Master as their Father, their Guardian, & Protector" without having even seen most of the hundreds of slaves he owned.[54]

If Laurens imagined himself as a benevolent patriarch, then he also imagined his plantations organized in a similarly domestic image: the household. After all, the household was the unit of governance in the early modern world; a patriarch governed his dependents much as the state governed its patriarchs. Laurens's townhouse in Ansonborough, Rattray Green, easily met the criteria for a domestic household: it housed his wife, children, highly skilled enslaved laborers, and domestics, and boasted the architecture, furniture, and grounds of a refined provincial estate. Mepkin plantation could also meet several of the criteria of a domestic household; Laurens was a sometime resident planter there, he organized the slaves into "families," and the buildings were more finished and specialized. At Wambaw, to the northeast, there was less sense of the plantation as a household, although slaves there, as at Mepkin and Rattray Green, were organized into "families." But at the out plantations of Wrights' Savannah, Broughton Island, and New Hope, crude material conditions and the constant threat of violence—Laurens armed the thousand-acre Broughton Island plantation with six swivel guns—rendered them semi-barbarous spaces, not domestic households. Slaves on these plantations, called "new Negroes," were usually single men rather than families, a feature that only further undermined the domesticity of the out plantations. The crucial point was that, through commerce and gradual improvement, these plantations could one day become like the "core" domestic plantations near Charleston. With Rattray Green as the wellspring of civility and the standard of domesticity, the more barbaric plantations, in time—and especially as even more undeveloped plantations were integrated into Laurens's system—could become sites that boasted refined architecture, stability, and households of white and black families.[55]

Of course, Laurens tried to fend off threats to the civility and domesticity of Rattray Green, Wambaw, and Mepkin, and to the progress of the frontier plantations. Sexual impropriety posed a significant problem in Laurens's network of households. One overseer kept "a Wench in the House in open Adultery" while another at Mepkin was fired for "familiarity with Hagar," an enslaved woman. These sexually illicit households challenged the legitimacy of Laurens's own household. Such relationships caused "jealousy & disquiet amongst the Negroes" and were "very hurtful to my Interest." Laurens's interest, of course, was building a network of productive and well-ordered households that reaped substantial profits. Similarly, stealing, running away, or violent acts also threatened Laurens's plantation enterprise. A critical part of domesticity was the containment—and concealment—of a patriarch's private property *within* the bounds of that property. Dependents breached the "containment" of the domestic household through illicit acts, exposing Laurens's private property to public view and public influence. Unfortunately, Laurens employed violence to correct the threats made to his peaceful, domestic sphere. He did not shy away from directing overseers to flog slaves severely when they violated the terms of his household. In some cases, at Wambaw and Mepkin plantations, Laurens threatened deportation to the out plantations as a punishment for slaves' misdeeds. Laurens sought to ameliorate slaves' material condition through their conspicuous consumption of goods he provided, but when this strategy failed, he responded by brutalizing slaves. While cruel, Laurens's punishment regimen can be interpreted as a policy of containment, to correct or exile offending slaves and overseers before they could "corrupt" other members of the domestic sphere.[56]

The American Revolution upended Laurens's vision of a plantation empire. With his crop fields and plantation buildings burned and looted, as well as one quarter of his enslaved labor force gone (they succumbed to disease or ran away to the British ranks), Laurens began to rethink his world. He told his son John that he had come to "abhor" slavery in 1776, and in 1783 informed William Drayton that "I am no longer at a 'stand'" concerning the abolition of slavery. He sought to put this new antislavery sentiment into practice in the postrevolutionary period. As such, he envisioned plantations without slaves. Viewing plantations—at least in the future—as sites of production that did not depend on slave labor called into question much of Laurens's plantation empire of the colonial era. It seemed questionable that a slave-driven plantation network would provide a model for expansion and settlement in South Carolina in the 1780s and 1790s. After the ruin wrought by the revolution, Laurens decided that a single plantation might afford more security than a multiplantation network, which was more "precarios." Similarly, he wondered whether commerce alone could serve as an ameliorator and proxy for paternal domesticity on distant plantations. Wanting to purge South Carolina of British institutions, including the slave trade and slavery, Laurens also sought to rid the new state-republic of the tyranny and arbitrary will—two features he associated with illegitimate British rule—inherent in the master-slave relationship. In this way, rather than envisioning "stasis" or "contracted enterprise," Laurens instituted his own progressive plan of "government" for the sole plantation still in his possession, Mepkin.[57]

In 1786, after putting his frontier plantations up for sale and deeding a newer plantation, Mount Tacitus, to his remaining son, Laurens settled on the Cooper River, living in an "Overseer's ordinary House" until his enslaved workmen could build a new dwelling house at Mepkin.[58] To create a civilized and domesticated household on a single plantation, Laurens fashioned himself as a resident planter who was committed to ameliorating slavery with an eye toward ending it. His quest to refashion himself as a benevolent patriarch in the postwar years dovetailed with his image as a revolutionary statesman. In a portrait painted by John Singleton Copley in 1782, Laurens, who had only recently been released from the Tower of London, was dressed simply in an elegant velvet suit and modest wig rather than in the opulent taste of an exorbitantly wealthy British merchant. As Laurens remade his appearance, so too did he work to refashion his plantations.[59]

Laurens outlined his plan for ameliorating his slaves to Richard Price in 1785. Viewing them as part and parcel of his domestic household, he noted that "at present," his slaves "are as happy & as contented as laboring people can be"—meaning that he had secured their happiness by providing for their material wants and organizing them into families. This mitigated slavery, Laurens reasoned, and was preferable to freedom and independence. Freed from the protection of the plantation household, blacks would be deprived of comfort and subjected to the prejudices of Laurens's fellow planters and the draconian "Negro Laws" of South Carolina. He boasted that those slaves to whom he "proffered absolute freedom, wisely rejected it." Rather than granting his slaves total freedom, he offered them semi-autonomy and protection. "I am endeavouring to prevent their ever being absolutely Slaves" by offering incentives, such as wages, and by providing "to the whole every reasonable indulgence," including food, clothing, adequate housing, and other goods. Laurens deemed his slaves to be "in more comfortable circumstances than any equal number of Peasantry in Europe." Because they fell under his protection, none of his slaves lacked for "food, raiment & good Lodging." To reinforce his role as protector of his slaves, Laurens ensured that the "Lash is forbidden." The new substitute for corporal punishment at Mepkin was Laurens's declaration to his slaves: "If you deserve whipping I shall conclude you don't love me & will sell you." This was a departure from his colonial enterprise, where whippings were meted out without hesitation for misbehavior. So too was Laurens's commitment not to sell another slave—unless they misbehaved—or "buy another Negro," unless it was to "gratify a good Man who may want a Wife," a departure from the frequent buying, selling, and relocating of slaves on his colonial plantations.[60]

By 1786, Laurens worked not only to improve material conditions for his slaves but also to reduce their work. He intended to use water power "for turning a Pounding Machine for cleaning Rice," in order to "exempt my poor black Servants from that Branch of hard Labour." He noted that he had already "excused them from hoeing, or weeding Indian Corn which is hard Work" by "introducing Ploughs and fine Teams of horses,"

John Singleton Copley, *Henry Laurens,* 1782. (Courtesy of the National Portrait Gallery, Smithsonian Institution / Art Resource, N.Y.)

even though it posed "a very great Expence to myself." The substitution of horses for his slaves constituted a "Work of Benevolence" in his estimation, and was another example of his efforts to ameliorate slavery at Mepkin. The postwar domestic household that Laurens sought to build differed in conspicuous ways from its prewar antecedent. His commitment to mitigating slavery at Mepkin was Laurens's plan of amelioration with the future goal of emancipation; he would deploy it on his plantation until his fellow planters also concluded that slavery should be abolished. But for now, "time is required for maturing my Plan" of abolition, since "a whole Country is opposed to me."[61]

Still, one of the greatest challenges to the amelioration of slavery was, as he confided to Richard Oswald, the death of the resident master and slaves' subsequent division and sale. When Oswald attempted to sell many of his plantations in East Florida, Laurens urged him to do everything in his power to prohibit the separation of slave families. "We feel for those poor Wretches the Negroes and wish to make them as happy as their condition will admit of." The primary way of making them happy, Laurens argued, was by "keeping them together in families." Laurens told Oswald that he would "rather lose a large annual profit by keeping my Negroes to= geth comfortably together in families" than allow "violent Seperations of Man & Wife, Parents & Children." But while "during our lives" slaves enjoyed mitigated bondage, that "pleasing prospect" was "destroyed" when a benevolent patriarch died and his slaves were "scattered." This, he noted, was the primary "curse in Slavery." To prevent the "Evils which will arise after my Death," Laurens wished to be a master who lived among his dependents. "I ardently wish to be once more among those who are committed to my charge," he had reported in 1783, so that he could "take measures for cutting off, in some Degree if not wholly, the Entail of Slavery." Ironically, of course, the abolition of entail and primogeniture only facilitated the division of slave families by allowing more whites to become slave owners.[62]

But as Laurens embarked on his project to ameliorate his slaves and domesticate them in families, his policies were shaped as much as by those slaves who became trusted domestics as by those who rejected his paternal control. Samuel Massey, who was "as good a bricklayer as any in the province," was Laurens's most important, and most domesticated, slave. Massey oversaw construction and improvements to his master's property, served as an intermediary in disputes between slaves and overseers, oversaw plantation inventories, and drafted reports on overseers' work for Laurens. Massey, in many ways, epitomized the ideal, enslaved domestic in Laurens's eyes. Massey was a highly skilled worker, trustworthy manager, and disciplined servant (with the exception of a few bouts of drunkenness in the 1770s) who did not require punishment. Laurens viewed him as nearly the equivalent of a free tradesman. Nothing proved Massey's loyalty and "domestication" as much as a letter he wrote to Laurens in 1780, however, which detailed the siege of Charleston and reported on the slaves who had run away to the British lines in search of their freedom.[63]

One slave, Frederic, who in many ways constituted Massey's opposite, was among those who "joined the temporary Conquerors." Frederic claimed that he had "carried arms & . . . acted in the Trenches" during the British invasion, though Laurens found out that his slave was at Mepkin. Frederic was eventually captured by an American vessel and jailed in Georgetown; he escaped northward but then found himself again in jail and subsequently in the hands of the New York Manumission Society, which sought to sell him. When Laurens heard of the whereabouts of his runaway slave, he lamented that Frederic was "always a very good Lad before the War" but had been "contaminated no doubt by bad Examples in that dreadful Scene" during the siege of Charleston. Laurens believed that Frederic had betrayed the master who had treated him well. Refusing to allow the Manumission Society to sell his "property," Laurens reclaimed Frederic, even though he felt "no kind of satisfaction" from the slave's return. Frederic was only "carrying a little dirt out of the Garden" but not "earning his Victuals," a bad example that threatened "his old fellow Servants" who constituted "a happy orderly family." Laurens soon resolved to sell Frederic because his "Behaviour" proved "a burthen upon me"; the former runaway resisted his ameliorative efforts at domestication, and as punishment for this resistance, Laurens sought to excise him from his household at Mepkin. Laurens's treatment and attitude toward both Frederic and Samuel Massey demonstrated how whites continued to think of slaves in two radically different ways in the postrevolutionary period—as baneful and dangerous "enemies" and as loyal "domestics."[64]

For most of his life, Laurens's mercantile connections helped him to develop a sophisticated and dynamic understanding of the British commercial world of which slave trading and slave owning were critical components. He applied this learned mercantile calculus to the development of his far-flung plantation empire in the rice country of South Carolina and Georgia in the 1760s and early 1770s. Like his West Indian counterparts, Laurens believed that slavery and the slave trade were civilizing systems that helped to secure provincials' "improvement." He used commerce as the means to solve the problems of authority and build an interconnected series of plantation households. But after the revolution, as he resolved to excise all remnants of British institutions and "tyranny" from the new state-republic of South Carolina, Laurens sought to reformulate his vision of a productive plantation household. This vision did not include slaves. Still, his understanding of the commercial world of slave trading and his firsthand experience with British despotism helped him to formulate his antislavery vision: "Will it be righteous just and virtuous to enslave hundreds of thousands of free born Men and Women to sell them under the most arbitrary power of their fellow Mortals and to entail such slavery upon their posterity to the latest generations in order to enhance the value of Mr. Laurens's Lands or to encourage the manufactures of Birmingham and Manchester?" he asked.[65]

Laurens's new definition of the plantation, which he attempted to implement at Mepkin in the later 1780s, was as a domestic household, one in which he served as the resident patriarch. Such a household represented his view of antislavery amelioration—slavery would be "improved" in order to end the institution. In order to encourage slaves' domestication into "families," Laurens abolished the use of the whip, reduced slaves' workloads, and tried to improve their material conditions. All of this, Laurens believed, would be accomplished with the goal of slaves' emancipation in the distant future. While Laurens confined his experiments to his own plantation at Mepkin, he still believed that his fellow planters would follow his example. Laurens's postwar vision of precotton South Carolina called for a planter to own and live on a single farm in order to better manage crops and ameliorate slaves. The creation of a domestic plantation household was the precursor to slaves' emancipation as well as a way to recover from the devastation wrought by dependence on British creditors and markets. While Laurens's postwar plan for Mepkin seemed like a contraction of his colonial enterprise, his belief that other planters would follow his model suggested that his efforts could be replicated throughout South Carolina.[66]

Several Lowcountry planters anxiously anticipated an end to the transatlantic slave trade and then an end to slavery. In 1805, Joseph Manigault believed that closing the "Ports against the importation of Negroes" would "contribute to the happiness of our country" South Carolina. Henry De-Saussure thought that the perpetuation of the transatlantic trade would only "immeasurably increase the number" of slaves and "enormous debts contracted." These Lowcountry planters believed that ending the slave trade would also prevent slavery from becoming entrenched in the Up-country, a region booming with settlers in the postwar years. John Drayton suggested that the Upcountry offered the best opportunity for white set-tlers; he encouraged white yeomen to bring with them their families and livestock but not their slaves. Governor Paul Hamilton asserted that im-porting slaves discouraged whites from settling in the state, for "it must be admitted that, in proportion as you add to the number of Slaves, you pre-vent the influx of those men who would increase the means of defense and security." Of course, unbeknownst to these men, the expansion of slaves into frontier areas was only facilitating the settlement of that region. In-deed, as DeSaussure noted, most slave purchases were being made by the "Upper Country People."[67]

Of course, the expansion of cotton culture—and the slavery on which it depended—dashed many of these Lowcountry planters' hopes for the contraction and eventual end of slavery in South Carolina. By 1810, the slave population in the Upcountry had trebled from what it had been in 1790. As long as there were lands to be developed and settled, many South Carolinians argued that slavery was necessary. While "there remained one acre of swamp-land uncleared" in the state, declared Charles Cotesworth Pinckney, then he would vote "against restricting the importation of ne-groes." In the fragile postwar economy, many planters came to believe that slaves were the state's greatest asset and their greatest hope for avoiding "degeneracy" while regaining a firm economic footing. With the prospect of a cotton boom on the horizon, planters were eager to buy slaves and transport them to the undeveloped Upcountry.[68]

Laurens's postwar vision for progress and modernity for South Caro-lina ultimately failed. But Laurens could not have predicted this; his an-tislavery amelioration undergirded his understanding of the American nation-building project. Patriots had seceded from the mother country not because they no longer wanted to be part of an empire, but because a des-potic king and Parliament threatened to stymie and prevent expansion, the *sine qua non* of the imperial project in America. The expansion of land and markets were perceived as "rights" of colonists that they justly claimed as freeborn Englishmen; when Britain threatened these rights, colonists went to war to preserve them. Thus, patriots sought to create an increasingly ro-bust and expansive empire after 1783. This empire was dependent on the replication of semi-autonomous jurisdictions; plantations were the small-est units, and states, the largest ones. But Laurens's antislavery ameliora-tion was premised upon the idea that a new and growing body of middling white property holders neither wanted nor needed slave labor in South Carolina. Laurens was wrong. In the 1800s, the advent of cotton cultivation and the increasing value of slaves as collateral in the market meant that the ownership of slaves and support for slavery became more widespread. As we see in the next chapter, antebellum South Carolinians turned Laurens's antislavery amelioration on its head. These planters committed themselves to amelioration *within* the institution of slavery, not *without* it. The seemingly progressive and expanding "peculiar institution" enabled antebellum South Carolinians to trumpet their own exceptional progress in the modern world.

4

"THE ENORMOUS EVIL THAT HAS HAUNTED THE IMAGINATIONS OF MEN"

In 1835, the jurist and politician William Harper spoke eloquently before a crowded hall at the South Carolina Society for the Advancement of Learning in Columbia. His oration, however, was as much about the citizenry's "duty" to effect "moral and intellectual cultivation" within their society as it was about slavery. Harper urged his audience to educate themselves about the system, to "understand its character." Since slavery was destined to continue, he advised, then "we should derive from it all the good of which it is capable." Harper called upon South Carolinians to "improve it [slavery] so far as it can be improved, remedy its evils and abuses where they can be remedied, and mitigate or guard against them where they cannot." His speech was a rubric for the amelioration of slaves and whites, and a vision for a domestic, civilized society.[1]

Harper did not deny that slavery came with attendant evils. Yet, as an admirer of Burkean gradualism, he maintained that "we will not overturn the fundamental institutions of society," as French revolutionaries, British abolitionists, rebels in Saint Domingue, and northern abolitionists had sought to do. Instead, Harper wanted "to improve them." Of course, these institutions included slavery. The supposedly humanitarian and moral cause of ending slavery, Harper suggested, was qualified by the fact that emancipation—or immediate freedom—was not necessarily a proven good in society. He posited that an "improved" slave society might be the more humane and progressive solution. Harper questioned whether slavery was really "the enormous evil that has haunted the imaginations of men," and suggested that, in an ameliorated form, slavery was the domestic system that "elevated the character of the master, and contributed to the happiness of both master and slave."[2]

The ideas that Harper sketched out in his speech and treatises in the

1830s—which reflected broader proslavery support while also refining that position—spelled out his understanding of South Carolina in the modern world. To him, ameliorated slavery offered solutions to many of the challenges posed by the revolutionary age: how to legitimize rule, how to develop a particularized and national "domestic" regime against the foil of "foreign" threats, and how to maintain socioeconomic progress. His proslavery amelioration was a vision of a world—or at least his world, in South Carolina—that could not exist without slaves. But it was also a dynamic, forward-looking vision of how to sustain and perpetuate an expansive civilization through the "improvement" of slavery. He anticipated that South Carolina's ameliorated, domestic slave regime could be a model that might be embraced and replicated by other, newer states in an expanding federal union. As such, his comprehension of an American "empire of slavery" appeared to be a reversal of Laurens's antislavery amelioration of the 1770s and 1780s. Laurens's view of modernity had stipulated that slaves and slavery could play no part in the advancement of South Carolina, or in any other new states brought into the union in some future time. Laurens, like other revolutionary patriots including Thomas Jefferson, had believed that slavery should be mitigated until slaves could be freed. But all this would be accomplished with an eye toward the future, and ultimate, extinction of slavery in America. By the 1830s, however, Harper and a number of other South Carolinians were suggesting that amelioration was both a means and an end. The amelioration of slavery—and its continuation and expansion—would result in an exceptional and modern system unlike any other in the world.[3]

Harper and others reached this conclusion as a result of their apparent adherence to "scientific racism." For Jefferson and Laurens, antislavery amelioration had been premised on the notion that blacks had the "capacity" to improve. While slave owners would ameliorate their bondsmen until the day of emancipation, newly freed blacks would then improve themselves and establish their independence in their own "country." Planters would serve as the agents of amelioration on American soil, but once "repatriated," blacks would ostensibly become the agents of their own improvement. Blacks, men like Jefferson and Laurens reasoned, might not be "naturally" inferior but rather were *made* inferior by centuries of enslavement. Harper's proslavery amelioration reversed this formulation. To him and other planters, it was not the experience of bondage that rendered blacks inferior to whites—the black race was simply "naturally" lesser to the white race. Thus, according to Harper's logic, slave owners had a duty to ameliorate slaves in perpetuity, since blacks were childlike beings who had no capacity for freedom. This shift in racial thinking—and in denying slaves any agency in their own lives—legitimized the proliferation of pro-slavery amelioration in South Carolina and other slaveholding states in the union.[4]

This chapter demonstrates that Harper and other South Carolinians began to see slavery as an improvable system that would be perpetuated and used as the means to create a progressive and profitable society. Although they continued to characterize slavery as an "evil" like the founders had done decades before, these antebellum South Carolinians were no longer interested in excising it from America, either through colonization or emancipation. But this conclusion was not arrived at overnight, and this chapter traces how intellectuals, politicians, planters, and religious leaders gradually came to embrace amelioration as the means to "domesticate" their slave regime and create a civilized society. First, they evaluated the outcome of revolutionary change wrought in Europe. The social upheavals and failed experiments in civic equality there convinced South Carolinians to adopt gradual, rather than radical, means of social change. Second, while a number of South Carolinians believed that colonization was a viable solution to the slave problem in the early nineteenth century, they also understood that a precondition for colonization was an absence of "foreign" threats—slaves could only be emancipated and repatriated under peaceful conditions. But the proliferation of "foreign" attacks in the 1820s—the Denmark Vesey conspiracy, the publication of David Walker's *Appeal,* and attacks from northern abolitionists—magnified the potential for insurrection and, as a result, tabled the question of colonization. Third, in the absence of a viable solution to the slavery problem, South Carolinians began to think of ways to contend with—and "improve"—the existing slave population. Consequently, South Carolinians began to conceive of a domestic, ameliorated slave regime that would be created through the widespread adoption of Christianity and more bureaucratized plantation management schemes.

THE LESSONS OF REVOLUTION
National Civilization and Exceptional Slavery

The decades of social upheaval in the Atlantic world had a visceral effect on William Harper and many of his contemporaries in South Carolina. The European and Caribbean revolutions provided a critical foil against which they could envision and fashion their own society. In reaction to the anarchical and tyrannical forces that he perceived as being unleashed in Europe and the Caribbean, Harper, along with many antebellum southern thinkers, believed that improving slavery, rather than abolishing it, offered a more peaceful, practical solution to the problems of the revolutionary age. In the minds of these southerners, radical change and the extension of civic rights produced more detrimental effects than revolutionaries had ever predicted. For Harper, freedom was not progressive but regressive, often rendering individuals and states more barbaric, not less so. As he cautioned, "Experience has shown that revolutions and political movements—unless they have been conducted with the most guarded caution and moderation—have generally terminated in results just the opposite of what was expected from them."[5]

Although there had been no revolution in England, what Harper observed from South Carolina resembled one. A widespread economic depression and Parliament's implementation of the Corn Laws, a new tax on foreign grain designed to buoy the home grain market, pushed working-class English men and women into the streets in protest. Many of them vied for parliamentary reform, seeking to eradicate the so-called rotten boroughs and introduce more legitimate representation into the House of Commons. But protests for suffrage and economic relief seemed to devolve into anarchy all too often. At the Peterloo Massacre of 1819, textile workers gathered in Manchester to agitate for parliamentary reform only to be charged by the local cavalry with sabers drawn; supposedly, over four hundred people were wounded. That same year, the British government passed the Six Acts, aimed at suppressing radical meetings and publications. Southerners like Harper saw Peterloo as the devolution of a society, and the government's response as something close to tyranny.[6]

France appeared to be faring no better. With Napoleon's defeat and exile to Elba, the Bourbon Restoration looked to be the exchange of one form of despotism for another. The White Terror, as well as the pro-aristocratic policies of both Louis XVIII and Charles X, seemed to be symptomatic of the oppressive reaction to the years of the French Revolution and Napoleon's rule. But even with the July Revolution of 1830, the rise of the July Monarchy, and the coronation of Louis-Philippe, the self-declared "king of the French," the new constitutional monarchy gave the impression that it was just as willing to suppress the rights of the middle-class electorate as its forbears had. Rather than seeing a progression toward peace and stability,

Harper and others were appalled by the patterns of violence and oppression that characterized France in the early nineteenth century.[7]

The Caribbean, however, provided perhaps the greatest example of what revolution could bring. Saint Domingue, which became the all-black republic of Haiti in 1804, loomed large in the imaginations of many southern planters, especially in light of efforts by Jean-Jacques Dessalines, the nation's leader, to exterminate whites on the island. Many planters agreed that the slaves' uprising had been the result of metropolitan agitation by the French abolitionist group Amis des Noirs; they insisted that such an event might be duplicated in America, particularly if "foreigners" sought to incite their slaves to revolt. And it appeared that the Emancipation Bill of 1833 had rendered the British West Indies an utter wasteland. Production was stymied, once-beautiful sugar plantations stood languishing, and planters and "apprentices" (full freedom was not granted until 1838) seemed to be moving backward rather than forward. Economic and social upheavals in the French and British sugar islands were most significant to southern intellectuals, both because of their geographic proximity and because they too were slave societies. In short, they were colonies whose progressive trajectory had been reversed by the liberation of the enslaved, southerners reasoned.[8]

It was these examples of revolution as well as their particularity within the Atlantic world that prompted South Carolinians to reevaluate their understanding of what a modern civilization would look like in the antebellum period. During the American Revolution, the goal had been to abolish the "tyranny" that impeded moral and political development so that Americans, as their own nation, might join the ranks of other civilized European states. Americans' desire to adhere to—and become part of—a European standard of civility underscored an important feature of the eighteenth-century Atlantic world: that Europe was the perceived seat of civilization. Commercial exchange, political amity, and "union" were features of an increasingly civilized and progressive network of states in the Atlantic world.[9]

But in light of the age of revolutions, Harper and many of his fellow South Carolinians began to question whether Europe was really the wellspring of civilization. Intellectuals doubted whether these revolutions had "improved" nations like France or Haiti. "From the portentous political movements which agitate the rest of the civilized world," Harper declared, it was becoming critically important "whether they will result in an improved condition of human affairs in relation to government, or whether, after running the usual course of turbulence and licentiousness, nations will not be subjected to a more arbitrary rule than before." Thus, Harper and other prominent South Carolinians, including Thomas Cooper, the transplanted Englishman and political economist, and Hugh Swinton Legaré, the intellectual who founded the *Southern Review,* undertook a measured approach to examining, in comparative world-historical terms, what civilization meant in European and Caribbean polities, and the implications of their conclusions for South Carolina. These thinkers rejected the revolutionary-era confidence in the strong teleological bent of history toward freedom and emancipation in the wake of revolutionary violence and the resurgence of antidemocratic governments in Europe. They began to argue that the course of history—at least for the southern states—should include exceptional and ameliorated slavery.[10]

After studying law in Edinburgh and French in Paris, Legaré served as the American chargé d'affaires in Brussels between 1833 and 1836. It was these experiences that served as a platform for his burgeoning criticism of Europe and its conceptions of freedom and civility. Legaré was particularly critical of France. He believed that the French supposed themselves a "free people" by misconstruing the meaning of "liberty" altogether. If "liberty consists," he seethed in 1833, in a "readiness to rush into scenes of blood & outrage," in "thirsting for plunder and conquest," in "violence of passion, & the most concentrated, impenetrable, concerted egoism in wearing mastachios & red pantaloons," then Legaré could not endorse "liberty" for South Carolina. Legaré doubted that France was the origin of civilized society when they "think of nothing but war & sensual pleasures" and are "more unfit to be free than they were in /93" during the French Revolution.[11]

Legaré leveled similar criticism at Britain. After a meeting with Philip Henry Stanhope, Lord Stanhope, the Tory critic of poor laws and Catholic emancipation, Legaré was convinced that England was going the way of France. Some "great political convulsion" seemed to be at hand in England, which would culminate in a "revolution . . . of the low English." Legaré imagined a "hell of the haughtiest minds in the world, exposed to the mortifications of comparative poverty in the midst of their absolute wealth and haunted with apprehensions for the future." Moreover, Parliament's recent approval of slave emancipation also seemed a harbinger of disaster. Legaré had heard reports of the "frightful" state of society into which the West Indies were fast devolving; he considered emancipation an "impracticable" plan that would soon be "abandoned or modified when it comes to be put into execution."[12]

Harper agreed that emancipation in the West Indies was a debacle. Those "beautiful islands," wrote the Antiguan-born Harper, "the fairest that the sun shines on or the sea reflects—once the seats of refinement, hospitality, industry, and happiness, may become, like St. Domingo, the abode of miserable semi-barbarians—more miserable, aye, and more *enslaved* than they were under the dominion of their masters." But emancipation was only one feature of Britain's decline. Harper suggested that nothing was so "harsh and barbarous" as the English Poor Laws, which he thought made the poor more "miserable" and impeded independent labor. For this reason, he doubted whether Britons understood labor systems better than Americans did. Those in Britain "who conceive themselves to be best informed and best qualified to instruct, and who have taken the greatest pains to enlighten others on the subject" of slavery versus free labor, were "grossly ignorant, not only of the facts but of the very principles upon which a judgment is to be formed."[13]

These indictments of European revolutions and social upheavals transformed the meaning of the revolutionary age for antebellum South Carolinians. The bloody and chaotic era that Harper and his contemporaries witnessed repudiated the widely heralded notion that the European states' system was the arbiter of civilization. With the erosion of Europe's position as the pinnacle of civility, Harper and his contemporaries began to question whether the international states system produced civilization, or whether nations—and national systems—did so. This new emphasis on the latter idea was a result of the particularity and equality that characterized the international state system: nations justified their existence by being "distinct" yet "equal" to European states. This new conflation of nationhood and civilization led Harper to conclude that the American union of states constituted its own "exceptional" civilization.[14]

By the mid-1830s, Harper had concluded that slavery was the "sole cause" of a unique American civilization. Without slavery, Harper wrote, "there can be no accumulation of property, no providence for the future, no tastes for comforts or elegancies," all of which "are the characteristics of civilization." Every society, he confirmed, "either of ancient or modern times" had attained civilization through "this process" of slaveholding.[15] Slavery was an ameliorator that lifted man out of semi-barbarism and propelled him toward civilization. The link between the accumulation of capital and slavery was clear; in a free labor system, Harper reasoned, there would be no individual wealth and, thus, no civilization. Harper's contention was buttressed by the arguments of a new generation of southern thinkers—Jacob Cardozo, Thomas Cooper, and John C. Calhoun. These men often concluded that free trade and domestic slavery would sustain the wealth and power of the southern states.[16]

Not only did Harper and his contemporaries embrace new notions of an exceptional American civilization; they also rejected the ideas that animated the revolutionary age: natural rights and equality. In France, Legaré observed that "equality is perfectly established among" the "parisians and the french generally." And yet, this equality did not matter, since the monarchy continued to oppress the people. "The govt. of Louis Phillippe is worse than any thing they have had," Legaré reported. Under the "king of the French," social problems continued, and French society remained vulnerable to famine and war. The pursuit of equality for all French citizens had backfired, Legaré thought, leading to the collective "misery" of the French people.[17]

Other South Carolinians rejected the idea of natural rights promoted by the American founders. Thomas Cooper questioned what the Declaration of Independence had actually declared in 1776. Did "Mr. Jefferson, the slave holder, mean to say that the blacks were born free and equal to the whites"? Cooper thought not. To him, individual rights, or the "rights of man," mattered little in comparison to the corporate equality of slaveholders and the natural hierarchy of society. "We talk a great deal of nonsense about the rights of man," Cooper declared. "Nothing can be more untrue" than that man was "born free" or that men were "born equal to each other." Rather, "nature" had "ordained" that some men were born inferior and others superior. For him, society was inherently hierarchical—it mirrored nature's order—and was composed of autonomous masters and their dependents.[18]

Harper, too, was skeptical of the universal freedoms supposedly guaranteed by natural rights. He dismissed the "well-sounding, but unmeaning verbiage of natural equality and inalienable rights" in the declaration, noting instead that the freedom of all Americans, black or white, would result in "our lives . . . put in jeopardy, our property destroyed, and our political institutions overturned and destroyed." The enslavement of blacks and their "forfeiture of rights" was not antithetical to natural law but rather coterminous to it, since slavery upheld nature's first and most important law of "self-preservation." In other words, for Harper, the laws of slavery preserved South Carolina society, the most important goal and "interest."

Jefferson and the other founders had trumpeted *natural* rights while criticizing *unnatural* slavery; the abolition of slavery would therefore allow the people to claim their just rights and uphold the rule of law. But antebellum South Carolinians argued that slavery *was* the law of nature, that the system survived without the transatlantic slave trade, and that abolition would require positive—or artificial—legislation. This was a reversal of the definition of slavery that had been handed down in the *Somerset* case in England in 1772. There, Chief Justice Lord Mansfield had argued that slavery had no basis in "natural law" or common law, and thus required the enactment of "positive laws" by legislatures to exist legitimately. But Harper believed that it was abolition, not slavery, that would introduce a "forced and artificial state of things," which might culminate in chaos and, perhaps most disastrously, disunion.[19]

It had been the assumption of Jefferson and other founders that the American Revolution was fought to defend colonists from the "tyranny" of Britain. Once they became independent of the mother country, Americans' newly claimed rights would then lead them toward the light of civilization in Europe. But antebellum South Carolinians rejected this idea. After observing that true equality could lead to society's obliteration, as in the case of the Atlantic revolutionary struggles, they dismissed broader civic rights for individuals in favor of the corporate rights of white slaveholders. The existence of slaves substituted class differences with racial differences, guaranteeing the liberty and equality of all white men. This idea was further buttressed by the fact that the abolition of entail and primogeniture had expanded property rights, especially property held in slaves, while also broadening support for slavery.[20] As Harper noted, the existence of a permanent and racially based "servile class" helped "hold together the free citizens in a bond of common interest." It was the diffusion of slaveholding and the creation of a sense of equality among the "body" of slaveholders, Harper believed, that offered an alternative to the comprehensive, universal conception of equality that emerged during the French Revolution. He and other South Carolinians conceived of their state-republic as an interconnected "family" of plantation families; each plantation family contained a white patriarch and his white dependents as well as enslaved dependents. This conception of society offered independence and freedom to white male property holders, and protection and "happiness" to dependents—women, children, and black slaves.[21]

In rejecting European Enlightenment conceptions of freedom and immediate, revolutionary change, slave owners embraced a more attractive alternative: gradual reform and the "happiness" of slaves. These conclusions forced South Carolinians to rethink the definition of their own society as well as the role that slavery played within it. The task became especially urgent in the 1820s and early 1830s, when "foreigners" threatened to upend South Carolina through conspiracy and insurrection.

"FOREIGN" THREATS, DOMESTIC SOCIETY, AND THE END OF COLONIZATION

In May 1822, Peter Prioleau disclosed the plans of a large-scale slave revolt to his master, John Prioleau. Peter had heard of the plot from one of the coconspirators, William Paul. The leader of the conspiracy was supposedly a man named Denmark Vesey, a black carpenter who had purchased his own freedom after winning $1,500 in the city lottery in 1799. Ostensibly, Vesey had masterminded the plan to lead a mass exodus of free and enslaved blacks from Charleston into the Lowcountry, liberating bondsmen and killing whites as they proceeded through the countryside. Yet Vesey's ultimate goal was to flee South Carolina for the free black republic of Haiti. President Jean-Pierre Boyer had begun placing advertisements in southern newspapers, urging blacks to exchange American shackles for Haitian liberty. When John Prioleau heard of Vesey's plan, he rushed to alert the authorities. What followed was two months of chaos—widespread white panic, arrests, a trial, and the questioning of conspirators. In the end, 131 people were charged as conspirators, 67 were convicted, and 35 were executed. Among those hanged was Vesey.[22]

Although in recent years historians have debated the extent and even the existence of Vesey's plot, it is clear from the outpouring of white anxiety in the media, private letters, and government circles at the time was that the conspiracy, or at least the idea of the conspiracy, struck a nerve in the South Carolina community. Historian Michael P. Johnson has suggested that the Vesey plot was not blacks' plan to kill whites, but rather whites' scheme to kill blacks. In fact, he shows that Charleston mayor James Hamilton Jr. used the plot to discredit his rival, Governor Thomas Bennett, and advance his own political career.[23] Still, the suspected revolt caused whites throughout the state to reconsider how to shield their society from "foreign" insurrectionary influences and those influences' potentially devastating consequences. The *Official Report* of the Vesey conspiracy, written by the Charleston Court of Magistrates and Freeholders, explained the details of the so-called plot. First, Vesey, as a free black who had worked in Haiti, was essentially a "foreigner" in Charleston society. Second, the newly formed African Methodist Episcopal Church had been the venue for the conspirators' planning sessions. Third, the report suggested that the writings of northern abolitionists James Tallmadge and Rufus King had deluded slaves into thinking emancipation had been enacted, thus inciting the revolt. Whether the plot was fabricated or not, it remains critical that the *Official Report* pointed to external influences as the cause of the alleged conspiracy, not domestic ones.[24]

The suspected Vesey plot forced whites to reevaluate whether slaves would always seek their freedom and try to decimate white society, or whether a system defined by coercion and violence could be reformed.[25] The former assumption had been embraced by revolutionary patriots, including Jefferson and Laurens, who believed that the slavery issue had to be resolved, since race war was ultimately inevitable. The most plausible solution was the colonization of blacks to Africa or the West Indies. Although state-supported colonization gained much more traction in North Carolina and Virginia, several contemporaries in South Carolina reconsidered it in the 1820s as a way to rid the state of slaves or free blacks and prevent a future conspiracy. One writer proposed that the "whole United States join in a Colonization Society" and "provide a place of emigration and means of transportation when necessary." Another proclaimed that expatriation "would strengthen our union, and secure our liberties." Edwin Clifford Holland, editor of the *Charleston Times*, maintained that South Carolina had always "uniformly exhibited a disposition to restrict the extension of the evil [slavery]," a disposition that was manifest in their efforts to "ameliorate it as those of the Northern and Eastern divisions of our Empire." He also endorsed large-scale colonization of free blacks, citing them as "the greatest and most deplorable evil with which we are unhappily affected." A Congregational minister who supported "African colonization" to Liberia dismissed the Vesey affair as "so absurd and puerile" that it "would not have caused me one moment's uneasiness." The "fiery and inflammatory feeling" was "in a great degree confined to Charleston and the lower country," while Upcountry South Carolina, North Carolina, and Georgia, unaffected by the Vesey revolt, remained committed to colonization.[26]

As these Lowcountry writers intimated, colonization had become a complicated issue in the wake of the Vesey affair. There were essentially three positions. First, there was a minority cohort, like the procolonization minister, who thought that slavery was an "evil" but who also believed that slaves' "liberation among us would be a greater evil than their present degraded condition." Thus, colonization would rid South Carolina of slavery while also avoiding a large-scale insurrection or race war. A second position was that colonization would "drain" free blacks such as Vesey out of South Carolina and send them to Liberia, thereby protecting and entrenching the institution of slavery. A third position, which represented the majority position in the Lowcountry by the late 1820s, was that colonization efforts directed by the American Colonization Society (ACS) were thinly disguised schemes to deprive slaveholders of their property with the aid of federal funds. In this way, the ACS, which had branches in several states, began to constitute yet another "foreign" threat to domestic society in South Carolina.[27]

When the ACS began seeking additional federal support in 1824, South Carolinians unleashed an onslaught of criticism. Senator Robert Y. Hayne charged that it was unconstitutional for the federal government to allot monies for ACS use. He asserted that colonization "not only relates to a subject with which the Federal Government can have nothing to do, but which will be extremely dangerous for them to meddle with." Hayne's Charleston colleague, Robert J. Turnbull, wrote a pamphlet that cast the ACS in the same light as high tariffs and internal improvements, calling the project a conspiracy to create a "consolidated national government." The cotton planter and Lowcountry politician Whitemarsh Seabrook believed that the ACS was hiding its abolitionist agenda behind the protection of the federal government to engender the "most malevolent and serious excitement" among slaves that would result in slave insurrections and the decimation of plantation society. Even the more moderate Lowcountry planter Charles Cotesworth Pinckney sought to discredit the ACS, noting the "absurdity and cruelty" of colonization to Africa. While the ACS maintained that it was creating an "asylum for free blacks," Pinckney wrote, colonization had instead resulted in high mortality rates, so that free blacks had simply landed in "another charnel house . . . under the appellation of Liberia."[28]

Henry Clay, a slaveholder and one of the founding members of the ACS, attempted to defuse southerners' animosity toward colonization and shore up support. In a speech to the U.S. House of Representatives in 1827, Clay stated that slavery was an evil, and that colonization would be "instrumental in eradicating this deepest stain upon the character of our country, and removing all cause of reproach on account of it by foreign nations." In an argument reminiscent of ones made by the American founders, Clay suggested that only by removing all blacks from American soil would the

United States escape European criticism and fulfill its destiny as the world's greatest experiment in freedom. And "why should they [blacks] not go?" Clay queried his audience. "Here they are the lowest state of social gradation—aliens—political—moral—social aliens, strangers, though natives." Clay suggested that American legitimacy still hinged on the slavery question; he considered slavery incompatible with nationhood. Moreover, slaves had to be colonized because they were "aliens" among the people of the United States.[29]

Clay's position, and the position of the ACS, met with outrage from many southerners, including the South Carolina intelligentsia. By 1828, Harper was sure that colonization was a disastrous proposition. While Clay had called colonization "not visionary, but rational and practicable," Harper disagreed. He feared that the ACS agenda would "likely prove dangerous to the peace and safety of the slave-holding states." It was frightening to think that the ACS could successfully persuade the "general government" to push beyond its constitutional jurisdiction and interfere in individuals' property concerns. Add to that, Harper charged, was the simple fact that colonization schemes were, despite Clay's claims, "useless or impracticable, or dangerous, and likely to do infinitely more harm than good." Harper believed that ACS members were using their cause as a ploy to win support from the federal government to end slavery and send blacks abroad. Or, Harper suggested, ACS members were seeking to agitate southern slaves to rebel: there was a parallel between the ACS and the Amis des Noirs, with the possible outcome another Saint Domingue. Lastly, Harper asserted that voluntary repatriation would never happen. Having been in the United States for generations, few blacks would want to return to Africa, he predicted. And slave owners would not consent to the deprivation of their valuable human property. Worse still, there was no evidence that colonization would be a successful endeavor once blacks settled in Africa. It seemed all too probable that expatriated blacks, "unprepared for freedom, ignorant, and half savage," might "relapse into the habits of the other tribes of Africa." Colonization was predicated on the idea of the establishment of a coherent and viable African "nation" overseas as well as the notion that American slaves constituted an "internal enemy" that had to be removed from the continent before the entire union was engulfed in race war. Harper rejected these two important premises. In doing so, he strengthened the case for proslavery amelioration; it seemed more plausible to gradually reform slavery than to end it.[30]

But even with the colonization movement essentially dead in the water in South Carolina by 1830, the external threats to "domestic servitude" intensified after the publication of David Walker's *Appeal to the Coloured Citizens of the World* in 1829. Walker, a free black man born in North Carolina who later emigrated to Boston, denounced the hypocrisy of the American founders, Christianity, the colonization movement, and the so-called paternalism of slaveholders in his widely circulated pamphlet. Historian Peter Hinks has argued that Walker spent his formative years in Vesey-era Charleston, an experience that left a powerful impression regarding the successful mobilization of the black community to incite revolutionary change. "America is more our country than it is the whites—we have enriched it with our blood and tears," Walker declared. But what inspired real terror throughout the South was his prediction that a black leader would lead a rebellion that would extend to all corners of the slaveholding states. Walker urged future insurgents to "kill or be killed," and assured other blacks that a well-armed black man could "kill and put flight to fifty whites." The incendiary pamphlet made its way into South Carolina in 1830, when a white ship steward on board the *Colombo,* which hailed from Boston, was charged with distributing the *Appeal* to Charleston blacks.[31]

The threat posed by Walker's *Appeal* was only magnified by those radical abolitionists who endorsed the pamphlet, circulated their literature in the South, and brought their antislavery petitions before Congress.[32] William Lloyd Garrison's pledge to defend the "great cause of human rights" did not disguise his desire to "let southern oppressors tremble—let their secret abettors tremble—let their northern apologists tremble—let all the enemies of the persecuted blacks tremble."[33] Even more discouraging to South Carolinians was that Garrison ranked emancipation above the interests of the federal union. It "is in the highest degree criminal for you to continue the present compact" of the union, Garrison thundered to his readers in 1832. "Let the pillars thereof fall—let the superstructure crumble into dust—if it must be upheld" by the "robbery and oppression" of southern slavery.[34] Garrison also endorsed Walker's pamphlet while pointing the finger at slaveholders, suggesting that it was southerners who called "upon their slaves to destroy them" by denying them their freedom. This was the dangerous doctrine of natural rights that could have devastating and "revolutionary" social consequences, as South Carolina intellectuals had observed in France and the Caribbean. Only now, the danger was in their own backyard.[35]

The barrage of what South Carolinians perceived to be "foreign threats" between 1822 and 1835 pushed contemporaries to develop ways to prevent such attacks from infiltrating domestic society. In the wake of the Denmark Vesey conspiracy, for example, Lowcountry politicians pushed for new legislation that would curb the autonomy of black artisans and limit the mobility of free blacks, the two groups seen as most liable to revolt. But the proposals met with resistance in the Upcountry, where the burgeoning cotton culture depended on lax regulation and porous state borders to facilitate a robust interstate slave trade. Still, in 1822, the legislature passed laws that banned slaves from hiring themselves out on their own time, levied an annual tax of $50 on each free black man, prevented free blacks from re-entering the state after they had left, and stipulated that all free blacks must have white guardians or face expulsion from the state. An even more draconian law aimed at free blacks was the Negro Seaman's Act, which allowed local authorities to imprison free black sailors while their ships remained docked at a South Carolina port. The bill met with international opposition, and the federal government balked at such a measure. South Carolinians insisted that the law was necessary for their "security."[36]

Restricting the autonomy of free blacks was one way that South Carolinians sought to prevent future insurrectionaries from "poisoning" their domestic society. Most of these measures stemmed from Lowcountry radicals who wanted to curtail the activities not only of free blacks but also slaves, especially in the wake of the Nat Turner rebellion in 1831. Slave literacy and religion, both of which were thought to play a role in the dissemination of fanatical doctrines, became the primary focus of these planter-politicians, who banded together under the aegis of the South Carolina Association and functioned as self-appointed enforcers of slave and free black laws. From the late 1820s until the mid-1830s, several bills aimed at preventing slaves' being taught to read and write or from receiving religious instruction were presented before the legislature, with Upcountry planters usually recoiling from any measures to regulate slavery. The expansion of cotton in the Upcountry fueled whites' desire to buy and lease slaves without limitations. It was not until 1834 that a bill passed making it unlawful to "teach any slave to read or write." Legislation that would have banned the preaching of black ministers or slaves' attendance at religious meetings was tabled. Thus, the law reinforced whites' belief that slave literacy was the conduit of "foreign" threats originating in the northern states or the Caribbean, and could potentially undermine domestic society.[37]

An emphasis on cordoning off South Carolina from outside and potentially baneful influences extended to slaveholders' perception of an increasingly consolidated and dangerous federal government. Usually viewed as the advent of South Carolina radicalism and states'-rights fanaticism, reactions to a federally funded ACS and new federal tariffs and internal improvements were, in reality, responses to a central government that was seemingly exercising "tyranny" over the states and casting their sovereignty aside.[38] Egalitarian South Carolinians feared the rise of a resurgent tyranny when they faced the threat of federal tariffs and colonization measures; they equated such consolidation with illegitimate rule and domination by a "foreign" power, even in the form of a northern-dominated federal government. The danger of consolidated power was a recurring trope in the history of the federal union. Challenges to the sovereignty of the states appeared at several moments—the Hartford Convention of 1814–1815, the Missouri Compromise of 1819, and the Nullification Crisis of 1831–1832—all of which threatened the union with collapse. South Carolina nullifiers, who viewed themselves as the genuine patriots during the conflict, sought to curtail the "consolidationist" tendencies of the federal government in order to preserve a union rooted in constitutional principles rather than illegitimate "domination."[39]

Feeling their domestic slave society under assault from "foreign" threats—ACS agents, free blacks, literate slaves, northern abolitionists—and from a consolidated federal regime, South Carolinians increasingly turned to projects that would further "domesticate" their society and shield it from these external dangers. Rather than turning to radical solutions to solve the slavery issue, such as colonization, South Carolinians looked to contend with the population they had—in 1830, the slave population was 315,401, more than any state save Virginia—and improve it. For them, the "improvement" of slavery encompassed pragmatic solutions: the introduction of standardized religious practices, the improvement of slaves' moral and material conditions, and the bureaucratization of plantation management schemes. And for whites, amelioration helped sustain civilization and domesticity while also securing a corporate ethos of equality among planter-patriarchs across the state.[40]

AMELIORATION
Theory and Practice

In 1835, William Harper envisioned not just any system of slavery but rather an ameliorated version, shorn of its "evils." He argued that amelioration—which he interpreted as slaves' "protection" and "happiness"—was crucial to achieve the goal of improvement. In Harper's view, a slave society must be improved and domesticated, deprived of its violence and semi-barbarism, in order to qualify as civilized. As one historian recently put it, the "captive nation" had to be domesticated in order to quell the threat to white "security" and become a fixture of progressive, expansive societies in the modern era. Harper's view of mitigated slavery within domestic households was a dynamic and modern worldview which served as a model that could be replicated within South Carolina and outside of it. It was his hope that other states in the union, whether the cotton states or states not yet carved out of the western territory, would embrace his vision of a civilized society based on domesticated slave-owning households.[41]

The preservation of domestic society was crucial for Harper, since the household, or family, was the building block of the republic. The preservation of these households was critical to the survival of South Carolina in a dangerous and uncertain world. "Self-preservation, as is truly said, is the first law of nature"; all other laws became secondary. In his view, the enslavement of blacks protected society from its potential devolution into war and anarchy. "If the possession of a black skin" proved dangerous to society, he argued, then that same society had the "right to protect itself" from danger through the "disenfranchisement of civil privileges." In other words, to prevent the outbreak of race war or the destruction of private property, white South Carolinians enslaved blacks. Slavery, then, allowed for the "security of the lives of its members" while also ensuring the "security of their property," which constituted the "great essential of civilization." The enslavement of blacks, he reasoned, protected and safeguarded white citizens; with this protection assured, citizens were free to accumulate wealth and claim the fruits of civilization.[42]

By this logic, if the state guaranteed the protection of citizens' private property, then it should also guarantee the protection of slaves, since they too constituted private property. While citizens were entitled to the protection of the state, however, slaves, as "disenfranchised" noncitizens, were not. Instead, masters supposedly acted as protectors of their human property. Although both state and federal laws existed to protect the institution of slavery, Harper argued that slaves had "less need for the protection of law" if they were "protected by their very situation" by masters. It was in a slave owner's "interest" to guarantee the "security" of his private property; slaves were also protected from the "revengeful passions of each other" as a result of the master's "superintendence and authority." Harper surmised that such paternalistic protection was a stark contrast with the condition of English free laborers who were "masterless slaves." They devolved into poverty and vice without the same "interest and attachment in his relation to his employer, which so often exists between the master and the slave."[43]

In Harper's view, slaves' civic rights were sacrificed in exchange for protection from so-called paternal masters. Critics had charged that "one of the great evils of Slavery" was that "it affords the slave no opportunity of raising himself to a higher rank in society" or the "cultivation of his faculties." For Harper, the "compensation" for this "disadvantage is his security." Protection from hunger, violence, and disease seemed a good substitute for the extension of rights to a "menial" class. Again, Harper compared slaves in South Carolina to free laborers in industrial centers where there was "no obstacle to raising their condition in society." But even with the "freedom" to "improve" themselves, these free laborers ironically experienced a decrease in their moral and physical condition. This Harper again attributed to the lack of security offered by a wage employer when compared with that afforded by a slave master. Thus, contrary to the views of abolitionists, natural rights did not result in improvement, since freedom deprived individuals of the protection that was the necessary precondition for advancement.[44]

If Harper reasoned that protection ameliorated slaves' condition, then it also made them "happy." Happiness, he believed, eclipsed "inalienable rights" as the animating concept of the revolutionary era. "The Creator has sufficiently revealed to us that *happiness* is the great end of existence, the sole object of all animated and sentient beings." Indeed, Harper wrote, "happiness" was the "only natural right of man." While abolitionists charged that slaves' happiness was "evidence of their degradation," Harper reasoned that slaves were happier than other "laboring classes" throughout the world. Of course, Harper defined happiness as the "absence of pain"; "misery" and "happiness" were thus the binary opposites that energized his conception of domestic society, not liberty and slavery. It followed, by his reasoning, that if a slave's condition had been ameliorated and was no longer one of "misery," then they must be "happy." And since, according to political economists' calculations, populations only grew in the absence of misery, Harper could make the perverse rationalization that slaves' "comfort" resulted in their self-reproducing numbers and in their being "the happiest three millions of human beings on whom the sun shines."[45]

The inextricably linked notions of slaves' "protection" and "happiness," Harper believed, was what enabled their amelioration. With security and the absence of misery, slaves formed families on plantations and forged sympathetic ties: the place of work was also the place of home life. In this way, plantations were transformed from potential sites of insurrection and violence between the races into domestic units where the commitment to family—and the attendant sympathetic ties—resulted in peace, security, and more efficient production. The evidence of slaves' amelioration, Harper thought, was that for "the last half century," bondsmen had been "continually exhorted to insurrection" by abolitionists and other "foreign" fanatics. Despite this, there had been no successful, large-scale rebellion, only "a few imbecile and uncombined plots" that were instantly quelled. If slaves did not revolt, despite prompting from abolitionists, then, Harper reasoned, they had become happy members of domestic society who had no interest in threatening the security of South Carolina. Even though Harper could not imagine that the "two races will be blended together so as to form a homogenous population," the mitigation of slavery allowed the two races to "remain in the same country" without the outbreak of violence.[46]

But Harper did not confine the defining concepts of amelioration—happiness and protection—to slaves only. Rather, they were just as salient for the free white population. The state's protection of private property, most notably in slaves, allowed for the accumulation of wealth. Of course, the accrual of capital was in the interest of the state, since wealth was the engine of expansion and civilization. Slaves were "employed in accumulating individual wealth" as "agricultural laborers," which was the "most useful purpose to which their labor can be applied." "Agriculturalists" who did not own slaves would "remain comparatively poor and rude," while the slave owner "who acquires wealth by the labor of his slaves" has the "means of improvement for himself and his children." As Harper knew, southern cotton planters often used slaves as collateral to gain access to credit and markets, primarily in New York and London. Thus, the state protection of the "peculiar institution" and the capital it yielded allowed for whites' improvement and the formation of a progressively more civilized society. Even more importantly for Harper, this was a model that could be replicated across the continent; the process of Americans' "planting" new territories across the "fertile" continent began with the "accumulation" of slave property and resulted in the creation of agricultural societies in the West. In time, these new states would improve themselves, fashioning themselves in the image of older, civilized states in the east.[47]

Just as the government preserved and protected the master's private property, so too would masters protect their slaves. Owners had a moral responsibility to preserve property that was sanctioned by both God and the state, Harper believed. As the "civilized and cultivated man," masters had a right to exert power over the "savage and ignorant." But they could not abuse this authority. A master was "morally responsible for the use of his power" and would be "guilty" in the eyes of God and his fellow slaveholders if he "failed to direct" his slaves "so as to promote their happiness as well as his own." For Harper, the "tendency" of slavery was to "elevate the character of the master," since "association with ignorant and servile beings of gross manners and morals" would push masters to promote their "improvement," with the master serving as the model of behavior and manners. Owners who treated their slaves cruelly and did not exemplify good morals would violate the "law of God and humanity" and cast "a shade upon the character of every one of his fellow-citizens." But more critically, mistreatment of slaves "endangers the institutions in his country" and the "safety of his countrymen." Slaveholders who abused rather than protected their slaves were thus guilty of exposing society to slave insurrections, which would, in turn, threaten to overturn the "general manners and civilized state of society."[48]

Only a "domesticated" master who privileged family and manners, Harper argued, could ameliorate his bondsmen. Using a familial metaphor, Harper reasoned that slaves would be protected just as "wives are protected from their husbands, and children from their parents," since "excesses of cruelty or rage" were not acceptable behavior in the domestic sphere. Because slaves were, in Harper's estimation, "perpetual children," then it was the moral duty of masters to assume a parental role in their supervision. He asserted that, with the "exception of the ties of close sanguinity," slavery "forms one of the most intimate relations in society." These close ties would only become closer the longer slavery continued. The "severest masters," by comparison, were those who were "strangers" to their slaves and who "supposed that it consisted in keeping savages in subjection by violence and terror." Such masters were usually to be found in newly settled areas, like the western territories. But as society became civilized and "settled," and the "habits of our countrymen altered," so too would a larger proportion of slaves be "reared by the owner" or "derived to him from his ancestors." As such, the progress of society and the amelioration of slavery went hand in hand. A "settled" or "domesticated" master would have a genuine interest in protecting a slave "intimately regarded, as forming a part of his family."[49]

Even if Harper decreed that it was a master's duty to elevate the morals and manners of his slaves and shape them in his paternal image, these same "perpetual children" could not be improved beyond their "station." Thus, slaves had no need of the "liberal education" and breadth of knowledge that whites required to attain the highest "level of intellectual power." "He who works during the day with his hands," Harper argued, "does not read in intervals of leisure for his amusement, or the improvement of his mind." In fact, Harper believed that slaves did not need to read at all. Instead, verbal religious instruction "adapted to their comprehension" could be "calculated to improve them." Biracial churches would offer sermons and lessons that were given "practically, without pretension" so as to be "intelligible" to black and white congregants. Harper believed that masters and slaves should attend church together, rather than slaves' receiving instruction "addressed specially to themselves," which might look like a "device of the master's." Attending church as a plantation family would show slaves that masters also obeyed the law of God; this would legitimize white authority and encourage black obedience. It was "certainly the master's *interest*" that slaves have "proper religious sentiments," sentiments that he defined as a basic moral sense and obedience to higher authority.[50]

Harper's treatise implied that there were pragmatic applications to his theory of amelioration, including the religious instruction of slaves. By being themselves good Christian masters and transforming their slaves into Christian servants, planters were only strengthening the familial bonds that Harper emphasized. The rise of missionary efforts in the slave quarters dovetailed with the proliferation of evangelicalism among southern whites in the 1830s and 1840s. Christianity, predicated on a kind of paternalistic order, seemed to strengthen slave society while also improving it.[51] And the rise of more bureaucratized plantation management techniques also strengthened the "contract" by instilling greater order on estates and extracting more work from slaves. Masters began experimenting with new ways of improving efficiency, guaranteeing obedience, and minimizing punishment. They formulated rigid hierarchies of slaves and overseers, all governed by white masters. Planters styled their plantations as experiments in the government of an enslaved labor force, subject to revision and reinterpretation, and published in agricultural journals and political tracts. Together, Christianity and new plantation management strategies helped improve slavery by domesticating it, many planters believed. Slave owners concluded that they "had a duty to rule their slaves with an iron fist within a velvet glove."[52]

In the wake of the Vesey conspiracy and the Turner revolt of 1831–1832, planters in South Carolina exhibited considerable apprehension about the impact of Christianity on their slave labor forces. Yet prominent planters like Charles Cotesworth Pinckney sought to prove that domestic slaves needed a domestic religion, not the "foreign" influences of abolitionists' religious invectives or *obeah,* the African religion so often associated with slave rebellion. Pinckney believed that slaves needed Christianity to become more obedient laborers, but they also needed *domestic* Christianity. If religious teaching had played any role in Denmark Vesey's revolt, it had been defective religious teaching. Pinckney was convincing to many; planters began to invite South Carolina clergyman, most of them Baptists and Methodists, to preach to their slaves. Such religious leaders envisioned an ordered and hierarchical slave society that effected the moral improvement of slaves and masters catalyzed through religion. "God is the moral governor of the universe," wrote the Episcopalian minister Frederick Dalcho, "and the rulers of nations and communities, the fathers of families, and the owners of slaves, are each in respective spheres, the head of a moral government, in subjection to God, for the good of society, the happiness of the people, and the glory and honour of God's name." The society that Dalcho outlined was entirely in keeping with planters' vision of a hierarchical slave regime.[53]

While apprehension over religion continued to circulate among some planters, especially in the Lowcountry, many ministers assuaged masters' fears by proclaiming their own proslavery leanings and outlining rational plans for the religious instruction of slaves. In 1833, the Presbyterian planter Thomas Clay presented his plan of slaves' religious instruction at a presbytery meeting in Georgia that was modeled on the instruction that his slaves received at his own plantation, Richmond-on-Ogeechee. Even in communities that claimed a black majority, such as Clay's own Bryan County, slaves' "moral improvement" acted as a safeguard against insurrection. He advocated daily instruction on his plantation, which included evening meetings and Sunday schools; the daily evening meetings comprised hymns, scripture readings, and a Bible lesson. Still, the emphasis was on aural rather than written instruction. Led by white Presbyterian ministers, this model was being replicated on neighboring plantations with conspicuous success: slaves were more obedient and productive. Clay argued that refusing to provide religious instruction was indicative of a master's own moral failing and irresponsibility. As their "protector," it was a planter's moral duty to feed, clothe, shelter, and care for slaves, but these were material interests. A Christian master must also husband the spiritual welfare of his bondsmen, since spiritual improvement and the adoption of Christianity resulted in more obedient, productive domestic laborers.[54]

In the Lowcountry, Episcopal bishop Nathaniel Bowen proposed a progressive approach to slaves' education at the behest of the South Carolina Episcopal Diocese. While he did not advocate slave literacy and the reading of the Bible, often a sore point for Lowcountry planters, Bowen nonetheless believed that aural religious instruction was necessary. Depriving slaves of religious teaching, Bowen argued, was tantamount to forcing them to live in savage misery. "Deny your slaves the privilege of access to the means of Christian knowledge, and you characterize their condition, by a moral hopelessness, to which not even the roamer in the wilderness, and the tenant of the forest, are consigned," he admonished. Moreover, religious instruction of slaves played a crucial part in the domesticity of the plantation. Not only did it make slaves more obedient "children," but it also made slave owners more benevolent "fathers." As Bowen wrote, it was the "indispensable duty of the father, the master" to "have his household" kept in the "fear and knowledge of the Lord." And this religiosity, Bowen suggested, had tangible results. "The best ordered, and most prosperous plantations, are those where true religion flourishes among the slaves." Thus, there was a real connection between religious instruction and increased profits.[55]

Bowen's proposal to the Episcopalian laity and clergy, which drew heavily from Clay's experiments on his own plantation, emphasized a concrete plan to extend religious education to slaves. In Episcopal churches, Bowen suggested that weekly sermons be heard in "unison" by masters and slaves; additional Sunday school sessions, particularly for blacks, would be complementary. Knowing that many masters would not allow their slaves to attend a white church or leave the plantation, Bowen advocated that Episcopal clergy preach to slaves on plantations in the evenings. But because the clergy would never be able to manage the task of catechizing thousands of slaves in the outlying areas of the Lowcountry, Bowen suggested that white missionaries supplement the work of clergymen. He also posited that slave owners could assist the clergy in their duty of catechizing slaves. The "experience of the ages proves, that he who labours for spiritual improvement . . . never labours altogether in vain." Bowen advised that the "slaves of every plantation should be assembled twice every day for family worship." Such "daily worship" would have a "beneficial influence" and contribute to the "promotion of sound and happy religion among the slaves." "Family" was the operative term for Bowen—the embrace of religious practice and tenets by the entire plantation household only further strengthened the ties between master and slave and domesticated what had been an institutionalized state of war.[56]

Bowen significantly bolstered the appeal of his argument for the religious instruction of slaves by asserting that their catechizing was a crucial part of a well-managed and profitable plantation. At Clay's plantation in Georgia, religious instruction resulted in slaves that "do more, and better work, with greater cheerfulness, and in less time than before he [Clay] introduced religious instruction among them." As Clay's profits demonstrated, "his income has rather increased than diminished." Similarly, at the plantation of a Reverend Blodget, also a Presbyterian slave owner, the "slaves are assembled regularly in family prayers, morning and evening" with the result being that his "plantation is one of the best conducted, and most productive in proportion to the number of hands employed, of any Parish." Listing slave religiosity under the rubric of rational plantation management was a relatively new development in the 1830s, and suggested that planters could increasingly link "domestic" religion with profit.[57]

In South Carolina, rational plantation management schemes began to circulate in earnest after the Panic of 1819, when the bottom fell out of the cotton market. The economic depression and diminished profits forced planters to reconsider traditional agricultural practices. Only when faced with these deteriorating conditions—of the soil and the markets—did planters elicit interest in "improving" their croplands as well as their slaves. In 1828, John D. Legaré began publishing the *Southern Agriculturist,* a journal that served as a forum for planters throughout the South. Legaré aimed to make planting a "science," and encouraged planters to experiment with production techniques and then report on their successes and failures. Published for eighteen years, the *Agriculturist* became a medium of communication as well as a force behind the bureaucratization of plantation management in the antebellum period.[58]

Unsurprisingly, new discussions about "improving" agricultural practices dovetailed with new ideas about ameliorating slaves through better management schemes. Transforming slaves into domestic laborers and mitigating their condition would allow masters to extract more work from bondsmen, slave owners thought. As one Lowcountry planter asserted, the "model government of slaves" should be like a "well-disciplined army." A "rigid obedience" should characterize the enslaved workforce, but the master must reciprocate by providing "every thing necessary to primary wants, and every comfort that his condition admits of." The notion of slaves' "comfort" indicated that their conditions were improving, planters thought. In characterizing the plantation as a "machine" that needed to be maintained by disciplined workers, the emphasis was on Enlightened rationality; violence and tyranny, two features of emotional, and thus irrational, rule had no place on antebellum plantations. Property owners therefore rethought slave punishments, particularly the efficacy of the whip. The "fear of the lash," could compel slaves to perform only "reluctant services." Long associated with the arbitrary power of masters and overseers, the whip increasingly became seen as a tool of pain and punishment, and as a prop that inspired fear and begrudging obedience. But in the 1820s and 1830s, planters began thinking about how to incentivize labor, rather than force it. Masters' rational benevolence seemed promising—humanity could be a "generous motive for obedience" and result in efficiency and speed. Indeed, treating a slave "as a bondsmen but still a man" through "kindness, humanity, and encouraging benevolence" would supposedly result in the "respect and faithful discharge of the duties" by slaves.[59]

In 1833, John D. Legaré went in search of the model of rational plantation management, to a place where profits were high, labor was efficient, and slaves had been ameliorated. He found his ideal in the form of Hopeton plantation along the Altamaha River in the Georgia Sea Islands. Hopeton was the "best plantation" because of the "extent of the crops," the "number of operatives who have to be directed and managed," the "regularity and precision" of operations, and the "systematic arrangement of the whole." Here was Legaré's rational machine, a model that had salience not just for planters but for northern and European industrialists as well.[60]

With almost a thousand acres in cultivation and a labor force of five hundred slaves, Hopeton ranked as one of the larger estates in the plantation South. It was owned and managed by James Hamilton Couper, who inherited it from his father in 1818. Hopeton was also one of the most profitable, owing to shrewd management and crop diversification. Sea Island cotton, sugar, and rice were all under cultivation when Legaré visited in 1833. As he noted, "all the valuable crops of the South are cultivated in rotation" and also "prepared for the market at the place." Couper both grew crops and manufactured them in the mills at Hopeton. But these crops shifted as a result of economic pressure; with the onset of a cotton depression in 1825, Couper began planting sugar cane in addition to Sea Island cotton and rice. And when the Tariff of 1828 affected sugar prices, Couper again responded by planting more rice, a crop that remained profitable for several decades.[61]

Legaré told his readers that much of Hopeton's success was owed to its policy of rational and humane management of slaves. In the rice, cotton, and sugar fields, the aim of labor management was to "reduce every thing to a system" and "introduce a daily accountability in every department." To that end, slaves were separated into field hands and "jobbers." The field hands were divided according to gender and organized into "classes," which were "rated agreeably to his or her efficiency." Each gang performed a full or fraction of a daily "task," the standard unit of measure of work. "Ditching," planting cane, and manuring fields were tasks that these field gangs completed; each gang's work was supervised by a regular driver, and all of the gangs were supervised by a head driver. The aim of this system of management was to encourage efficiency with incentives. If slaves could finish their "task" in five hours, they could have the remainder of the day to themselves. And the goal of the division of labor was to "apportion the gang to the character of the work to be performed." In other words, only "prime" male field hands could perform an onerous task like "ditching," while for "moting and sorting cotton," work that did not require great strength, the third gang of women could be employed.[62]

Outside of the field, the "jobbers" were divided according to "class." These classes were skilled laborers and included carpenters, blacksmiths, masons, gardeners, nurses, livestock minders, coopers, and carters; each group was supervised by a "head of class." One innovation at Hopeton was the introduction of accountability into its system of management. At the end of the day, the "heads of classes and drivers make a report to the overseer . . . of the employment of their respective hands." The drivers reported on the number of hands employed and their efficiency, as well as the nature and quantity of the work performed. Similarly, the heads of class reported on the work performed by the skilled laborers they supervised. All of these reports were then copied into a carefully annotated plantation journal, which "forms a minute and daily record of the occupation and quantity of work done by the different gangs." The result of this division of labor and system of accountability was a highly efficient plantation "machine."[63]

Still, scrupulous management did not necessarily compel slaves to work efficiently. Punishments, and the way they were meted out, helped to manage slaves' work habits. The "most efficacious as well as humane system" was "regular, firm, and mild discipline" for slaves. Extremes, which included "passion," "indulgence," and "severity," were "fatal" to a work gang of slaves. The "rules and regulations" that governed slaves were "few and simple" and included "obedience, attention, honesty, and orderly behavior." Departures from "correct conduct" were "promptly but moderately punished." Although punishment was usually the lash, whippings were limited—regular drivers could give no more than six lashes; the head driver, twelve; and the overseer, twenty-four. The maximum number of lashes permitted on Hopeton was half that of surrounding plantations. As a result, episodes of disobedience, running away, or "riotous conduct" were "scarcely known on the plantation."[64]

Couper paired a highly regulated labor system and punishment regimen with the added incentives of semi-autonomy and ameliorated conditions. The task system allowed slaves a greater measure of independence in the afternoons and evenings, which men and women used to tend gardens, raise poultry, go hunting and fishing, or care for their own families. A robust slaves' economy characterized the plantation; bondsmen often sold their produce and other goods to the manager and his family. Couper also encouraged his enslaved men and women to attend church services, believing that it would help his slaves become more disciplined individuals who devoted themselves to work and family. Couper devoted considerable effort to the improvement of the material conditions of his slaves, whom he termed "my people." Slaves were given allotments of plantation-made clothing, shoes, and blankets as well as higher than average weekly rations of cornmeal, pork, rice, beef, mutton, and molasses. A slave hospital, an "airy, and warm building 80 feet by 24," was divided into sick wards and a nursery for infants; the large building contained four sick wards, an entrance room, an examining room, a medicine room, a bathing room, and a kitchen. Couper contracted with local physicians to care for sick slaves; older enslaved women and girls usually staffed the hospital. Nearby, the "negro settlements" featured houses that appeared to be "very comfortable" and were arranged in two parallel rows that flanked a broad street near the main house. The houses echoed Couper's emphasis on the slave family; he ensured that the gender ratios were kept equal on the plantation as a means to encourage the formation of families. Each single-family dwelling contained two sleeping rooms, a main hall, a fireplace, and a loft for children. Although the early dwellings were made of wood, the later slave houses were more sophisticated constructions of tabby.[65] Couper insisted on the importance of slaves' relative autonomy, their organization into families, and their improved material conditions as the criteria for producing an efficient, obedient workforce. This was also Couper's experiment in ameliorating his slaves and including them within his household.[66]

Perhaps the best example of Couper's ability to "domesticate" his slaves was his head driver, "Africa Tom" or "Old Tom." Born "Suli-bul-Ali" to a "family of considerable property" in the western Sudan, he was seized by slave catchers and taken to the "slave corrals" at the "port of Anamamboo" at age twelve. From there, he endured the Middle Passage before arriving at the Bahamas Islands, when he was purchased by Couper's father in 1800. Described as "tall, thin, and well made," Suli-bul-Ali was a strict Muslim who observed religious holidays, abstained from liquor, and read the Koran, a copy of which he kept in his possession. By 1816, he was made "head driver" of 450 slaves; his "quickness of apprehension, strong powers of comprehension and calculation, sound judgment, tenacious memory and the faculty of foresight" rendered him qualified for such a position of authority at Hopeton. Couper marveled at the manner in which his head driver was "fully competent to manage with advantage." "I have several times left him for months," Couper noted, "in charge of the plantation, without an overseer," and "on each occasion, he has conducted the place to my entire satisfaction." Couper believed that he had transformed Suli-bul-Ali from a "foreign" Muslim African into an obedient and loyal slave. Of course, this assessment overlooked Suli-bul-Ali's considerable individual intelligence and continued adherence to Muslim cultural practices. But for Couper, his head driver's agency and individuality was of less importance than the notion that he had changed a foreign and potentially insurrectionary enslaved African into an efficient and trustworthy manager of his plantation. The key had been Couper's method of amelioration: reasonable punishment, highly disciplined work, and improved living conditions.[67]

If antebellum slave owners imagined their society as a "family" of plantation families, then Couper's plantation management scheme at Hopeton constituted the microcosm of Harper's vision of civilized, domestic society. Couper's improvement of slaves' conditions, his well-regulated plantation machine, and his paternal benevolence were not ends in themselves. As Legaré recognized, Hopeton was an ideal plantation, a profitable and humanitarian model that could be replicated throughout the southern and western states. Replication was also crucial for Harper, who recognized that "mutation and progress is the condition of human affairs." In envisioning a "domesticated" regime in South Carolina, Harper, like Legaré, was imagining a model or standard of civilized society that would be replicated as new states were carved out, settled, and developed. These states would ameliorate and domesticate slavery as part of their bid for civilization. Viewing South Carolina's slave regime in this way—as the building block of a federal empire for slavery—demonstrates the dynamic, forward-thinking proslavery amelioration pictured by Harper and his colleagues in the antebellum period. Not only was their vision of modernity conceived in opposition to failed revolutionary experiments and foreign threats of abolitionism, insurrections, and a northern-dominated federal government, but they also made their image compatible with expansion and the replication of jurisdictions, two defining features of the federal union. In thinking about how to improve, domesticate, and ultimately civilize their society, the question became, as Hugh Swinton Legaré (a distant cousin of John Legaré) aptly put it, "What is to be the destiny of this quarter of the world—what race is to inhabit and possess it? Shall it be given up to barbarism—its inevitable fate under the dominion of a black race—or shall it continue to be possessed by the most improving, enterprising, active and energetic breed of men that have ever founded empires and peopled waste places."[68] Rather than being a moral problem or confined to the master-slave relationship, slavery was inextricably tied to nation-building—the expansion of slave-owning households—and became an indicator of national progress and "happiness" in the antebellum era. Slave owners believed that ameliorated slavery was a modern system that offered a viable alternative to antislavery and freedom; proslavery amelioration enabled the expansion and civilization of an "exceptional" nation.

But as we see in the following section, the amelioration of slavery and the creation of "domestic" society followed a different trajectory in the British West Indies, where slaves' "improvement" and transformation from "foreign" rebels to "domestic" servants proved to be a less successful project. Declining slave populations, incidents of slave rebellions, and decreased sugar production all allowed metropolitan abolitionists to claim that colonial slavery could not be ameliorated since it was a regressive, premodern system.

III

The British West Indies

Unlike Virginia and South Carolina, the British West Indies did not break with the British Empire in 1776. Rather than embracing independent nationhood, many West Indian planters proclaimed their loyalty to Britain and continued to depend on imperial systems, including the transatlantic slave trade and plantation slavery. When metropolitan abolitionists launched their attack on the slave trade in the later 1780s, West Indian planters admitted that the trade was in need of reform but not abolition. This proslavery amelioration gave many planters and their allies the upper hand in debates over the slave trade in the 1780s and 1790s. But after abolition of the trade in 1807, planters' arguments for the perpetuation of slavery, albeit in an ameliorated form, were severely weakened. Declining sugar production and slave reproduction rates indicated that the Caribbean sugar regime was contracting. Metropolitan abolitionists charged that planters were not "improving" their slaves' moral and material conditions. Shrinking populations and production, combined with the examples of free labor in the East Indies and the outbreak of large-scale slave rebellions in the Caribbean, paved the way for provisional emancipation in 1833.

5

"WE MAY ALLEVIATE,
THOUGH WE CANNOT CURE"

Venus arrived in Jamaica by way of Angola. The "sable" goddess rode in a scallop-shell throne of "burnish'd gold" atop the "curling seas," holding the "azure rein" of the "winged fish." Encircled by plume-bearing cupids, her "scepter" commanded the attention of the "tropicks" of "either Ind." Yet locked around the neck and raised wrist of the "sable Venus" were iron bands. For this "gay goddess" was also a slave.[1]

This was how Thomas Stothard imagined the African slave trade when he drew the lithograph "Voyage of the Sable Venus" in London in 1794. This was how the Jamaican clergyman Isaac Teale wrote about it when he inscribed his "Ode" to Bryan Edwards in 1765. In an introduction to the transatlantic slave trade and Caribbean slavery in his vaunted history of the West Indies, Edwards included both the lithograph and an abridged version of his mentor's poem. He made no mistake in enclosing both depictions; to him, the arrival of Africans in the British West Indies was not the end of a harrowing journey across the Atlantic but rather the providential deliverance of a people from a continent plagued by barbarism and senseless wars. In the spirit of Botticelli, Edwards believed that civilization could be borne on the shores of the Indies; it could be instilled in the minds and bodies of African slaves.[2]

This chapter explores how, at the end of the eighteenth century, many merchants and planters, Edwards included, understood the African slave trade to be about much more than the coerced transportation of slaves across the Atlantic Ocean. He and his West Indian supporters believed that the slave trade was a commercial system with civilizing properties that benefited all corners of the Atlantic world. The trade was an ameliorator, improving the British imperial world and linking it together. It included Newfoundland fisheries; New England manufacturing centers; tobacco,

Thomas Stothard, *Voyage of the Sable Venus*, 1801.
(Courtesy of The Mariners' Museum, Newport News, Va.)

rice, and indigo in Virginia and the Carolinas; and the British port cities of Liverpool and Bristol. It encompassed the West African slave-dealing entrepôts—Whydah, Bight of Benin, Kongo, and the Gold and Windward coasts—from whence Edwards's slaves had come. It comprised West Indian plantations, such as those owned by Edwards in Jamaica, where enslaved African workforces were "improved" and portrayed as comparable to European peasants. As such, Edwards and his contemporaries viewed the slave trade not in static institutional terms but as an inherently dynamic, improvable system: a mode of commerce that strengthened amity among Britain, Africa, and the sugar islands, and stimulated the improvement of the morals and manners of those who lived there. Far from being barbaric and retrograde, the African slave trade was the purveyor of civilization in the Anglophone world: it stimulated New World plantation production on a massive scale that would bring enormous wealth to the nation and establish a tangible connection between provincial societies and the wellspring of civilization—Britain. While Edwards's assertion that the slave trade was a civilizing force seems perverse today, his argument was imperial in scope, and thus ultimately eclipsed the abolitionists' parochial—or nationalist—arguments of the 1780s and 1790s.[3]

Edwards advocated proslavery amelioration, a view of the modern world rooted in imperial terms. His worldview was ultimately grounded in empire-building, not nation-building, as was the case for metropolitan abolitionists and American patriots whose greatest concern was the establishment or reform of a nation. For antislavery ameliorationists, the slave trade was antithetical to legitimate nationhood, encouraged the indebtedness of merchants and planters, retarded moral development, and functioned as the artery that kept the institution of slavery alive. These anti–slave trade proponents wanted an end to the slave trade, asserting that abolition would force slavery to gradually wither and perish. The end of such a perverse and premodern system, which abolitionists and revolutionary patriots firmly believed would be hastened by abolition, was the key to the survival of nations in the modern world. As such, Edwards shared more in common with Henry Laurens, the slave-trading colonist and empire builder, than American patriots or British opponents of the traffic. Edwards, like Laurens, saw no problem with colonial slavery serving as the engine of imperial progress. Edwards considered himself an imperial agent on the margins, believing that a regulated slave trade was entirely compatible with advancement. For provincial planters in the West Indies, expansion through conquest and settlement lay at the heart of the British

Empire: it depended on land acquisition, the creation of plantations, institutional replication, and the extension of law, liberty, and civility. And, Edwards believed, colonization projects were entirely consonant with, and dependent upon, the exploitation of servile labor and the coerced importation of Africans.[4]

Metropolitan opponents of the "barbaric traffic" shared the anti–slave trade beliefs of many American patriots. They could not accept Edwards's seemingly ludicrous assertions that the African slave trade constituted an imperial colonization project which introduced hapless Africans to civilization. Members of the Society for Effecting the Abolition of the Slave Trade, which formed in 1787, charged that only total abolition would give slaves their liberty and expunge the "sin" of slave trading from Britain. Their vision of "amelioration" would be wrought solely by outright abolition, a task that would be accomplished immediately or gradually—critics of the trade were divided over the process. Using a one-size-fits-all moralistic approach, they sought to bring supposedly retrograde or barbaric peoples—primarily West Indian planters and hapless Africans—under their humanitarian colors. Indeed, the reformers' happiest stories were of those men who converted from heathenism into good Christian subjecthood, all affiliated with the abolition movement. Albert Gronniosaw, once an African prince, found happiness in Calvinism and denounced heathenism in his native country. John Newton, a slave trader who spent years buying and selling thousands of Africans, repented his sins and wrote the hymn "Amazing Grace." James Stephen, who held a government post for many years in the slave society of St. Kitts, witnessed the burning of slaves and subsequently vowed loyalty to the abolitionist cause back in Britain. And William Wilberforce became the primary spokesman for abolition in Parliament after experiencing an evangelical conversion in 1785. An end to the slave trade, these men believed, would only encourage the proliferation of moral reform and the broadening sphere of human rights: the keys to modernity in the revolutionary age. Abolitionists pronounced slave trading a national sin, a commerce that inhibited the civility of the nation, and a practice that united Britons with their "popish" enemies—most notably Spain and France. Abolitionists implied that the end of the slave trade would peel away the moral stain that impugned Britain's image; without the trade, the nation would continue its reign as the undisputed pinnacle of civilization. Thus, in the wake of the American Revolution, they envisioned a centralized, bureaucratic state that would export the nation's morals and manners in a grand missionary enterprise extending to all parts of the British world.[5]

On the face of it, the critics and supporters of the slave trade seemed to stand on opposite sides of the fence. Generations of historians have said as much: planters supported a continuation of the slave trade to maintain the status quo of the empire while abolitionists agitated for its end in a bid for the moral reform of the British nation. According to numerous scholars, abolitionists were the triumphant humanitarians, a more modern party of activists committed to alleviating the condition of suffering Africans. Pro–slave trade constituents, on the other hand, remained committed to the barbaric principles of buying and selling human beings to maintain their own wealth. Viewed in this presentist light, the two factions appear to be binary opposites without common ground. And yet, both camps employed amelioration as a point of departure; they embraced it as the process that would ensure progress and modernity. Abolitionists sought amelioration through the *end* of the trade, while planters and merchants vied for amelioration through a *reformed* slave trade that would also result in "improved" West Indian slave societies. In either case, the advancing civilization of the British nation and empire was at stake. Abolitionists envisioned modernity as an "empire without slaves," while enlightened planters could not imagine a modern world without them. The two factions sought to realize their disparate goals of modernity through remarkably similar plans of "improvement."[6]

Amelioration was a theory of gradual progress through the stages of human development, but it also implied a pragmatic approach to the problems spawned by the transatlantic slave trade and plantation slavery. For British exponents of abolition in the 1780s and 1790s, this pragmatism was not fully conceptualized; they had a vague idea that the end of the slave trade—whether realized immediately or incrementally—would lead to a gradual end to the practice of enslavement across the Atlantic. James Ramsay, an influential member of the anti–slave trade cohort and once an Anglican clergyman in St. Kitts, published one of the more coherent plans for the end of the slave trade and the transition to free labor. Gradual improvement was the lynchpin of his scheme. Not until the "minds of our slaves be more enlightened, till their situation be made more easy, till they have a refuge against the effects of the caprice, ignorance, cruelty, poverty of their masters, till they think themselves intitled to the protection of society" could slaves be liberated, he wrote. Essentially, he could not contemplate offering freedom to individuals whom he believed could not yet understand the tenets of liberty. Still, Ramsay's treatise was more exceptional than representative; this underscored that antislavery amelioration was more parochial than imperial, and that their pragmatic plans to mitigate slavery too closely resembled those of West Indian planters.[7]

In general, planters' theory of amelioration encompassed the whole empire rather than just sugar estates in the West Indies. Since the slave trade was an imperial system, then all parts of the empire, from Britain to Africa to the Caribbean, would assume responsibility for improving it, planters asserted. This made the "public concern" over the traffic imperial in scope, rather than a cause confined to the British nation, as abolitionists conceived. Planters' more sophisticated reading of the slave-trade issue enabled them to formulate a more practical solution: regulation of the trade and plantation management reforms. Their recommendations for diversification of the West Indian economy, changes in labor organization on estates, and agricultural innovation combined with increased regulation of the slave trade offered a much more comprehensive reform scheme than abolitionists could muster. As one historian has noted, opponents of the traffic "viewed the eradication of the slave trade as a vital building block in the creation of a new world order." But planters "anticipated the abolitionists" and sought to create their own new world order by regulating the slave trade and ameliorating plantation slavery.[8]

Even among critics of the slave trade, the tension between gradualist and immediatist plans to abolish the trade often undermined the movement. A treatise on the gradual end to the African slave trade appeared in the political arena in 1788, when the Liverpool poet and lawyer William Roscoe published an essay against the slave trade. Roscoe believed that the trade could not be banned outright since "an act merely declaratory will be insufficient to bring about so desirable a reform." Instead, he advocated "a gradual restriction of the slave trade" by limiting importation of slaves and placing increased import duties on human chattel. These two measures, Roscoe argued, would encourage West Indian planters to take better care of their current slave workforces, encourage the "propagation" of slaves, and therefore reduce the need for new slaves from Africa. This idea flew directly in the face of the immediate abolition that William Wilberforce articulated in his first speech against the slave trade in the House of Commons. Wilberforce insisted that the trade necessitated immediate eradication, lest it continue to carry "misery, devastation, and ruin wherever its baneful influence has extended."[9]

Wilberforce's call for immediate abolition was weakened by the gradualists, such as Roscoe. But immediatism was also weakened by enlightened planters like Bryan Edwards in Jamaica, and by shrewd parliamentarians, including Scottish Member of Parliament and Home Secretary Henry Dundas, whose speech against Wilberforce's motion relied on the ameliorative argument. Dundas declared that "the Abolition was to be gradual," for this was what he considered the "Center from which all Reasonings on the Subject must proceed." He emphasized that his main concern was the "Progress of Civilization" in the British imperial world and an improved "commercial intercourse" that linked disparate colonial outposts to Britain. He believed that gradualism was the "only practicable method of cultivating and improving the Dispositions, civilizing the Manners and rendering the actual situation of the Negroes comfortable." But most importantly, he considered amelioration the fulcrum that would connect "Masters with their interest." And their collective "interest" was improving themselves, improving slaves, and maximizing the production of goods that brought wealth and power to Britain.[10]

Interimperial rivalry in the Caribbean, particularly with the French islands, also spurred planters to embrace "improvement" on their plantations in the later 1700s. From afar, British colonies seemed to be less advanced, owing to their comparatively lower production levels and harsh slave codes. Edward Long, a planter and historian in Jamaica, worried about his island's "declining into [its] original wilderness." He charged that "France, like a skilful gardener, has been careful in the choice of plants, and treated her colonies as a favourite nursery," while "Britain, on the contrary, treats her plantations as a distant spot, upon which she may most conveniently discharge all her nuisances, weeds, and filth, leaving it entirely to chance, whether any valuable production shall ever spring up from it." In the later eighteenth century, Jamaica was emerging as the sugar giant in the British trading world, but still the French colony of Saint Domingue produced more sugar than all of the other British islands combined.[11]

The British colonies seemed to lack the "flourishing progression" that was so characteristic of the French islands. One prominent French planter and politician, Venault de Charmilly, in rebutting Edwards's critique of Saint Domingue, boasted that his fellow planters managed their plantations and slaves better than their British counterparts, thus resulting in greater sugar production and prosperity. The "French planters from national character, are more willing to communicate with their Negros," and slaves "belonging to the French colonies are more kindly treated by their masters, who more usually reside on their plantations, than they are by English masters, who are unacquainted with their Negros." Charmilly suggested that French masters used ameliorative measures and their paternalistic sensibilities to ensure the "happiness" and productivity of their bondsmen.[12]

But the slave insurrection in Saint Domingue in 1791 changed the French critic's tune. The revolt also bolstered the West Indian planters' arguments for amelioration instead of abolition. Until Haitian independence was secured in 1804, the insurrection morphed into a protracted revolutionary struggle led by the black leader Toussaint Louverture. For over a decade, former slaves clashed with Spanish, French, and British troops, all of whom sought to pacify the violence, reinstitute the slave system, and claim the valuable sugar island as their own. To provide an eyewitness account of the insurrectionary violence to the British government, Edwards traveled to Saint Domingue from his Jamaican plantations and later wrote an influential treatise about what he saw. In an argument that gained credence across the Caribbean and southern United States for generations, Edwards charged that the abolitionist agitation in France and Britain incited Saint Domingue slaves to rebel and murder their masters. This formulation—that abolitionists' messages of equality and freedom actually resulted in bloody insurrection—became a powerful rationale for the continuation of New World plantation slavery. It also significantly weakened the Anglo-French abolitionist movement in Europe.[13]

British West Indian planters protested the charges leveled against them by metropolitan critics. Led by Edwards, these planters insisted that they were implementing ameliorative measures to gradually improve the conditions of the slave trade and plantation slavery, albeit from the colonial periphery. Colonial legislatures, as semi-sovereign governing bodies that had claims to corporate equality within the empire, would regulate and reform colonial slavery, rather than Parliament. But metropolitans like Edmund Burke, who advocated gradual abolition of the slave trade and slavery, maintained that the West Indians were doing little in the way of amelioration. The West Indian assemblies, he complained to Henry Dundas, "have done little; what they have done is good for nothing." Nonetheless, West Indians who sought to protect their status in the empire saw it as their "right" to implement ameliorative measures independent of Britain. For these planters, since amelioration encompassed their private property, such "improvement" should be managed locally, by owners of that property, not Parliament. Edwards, who published his history of the West

Indies as a rebuttal to Wilberforce's abolition agitation, declared that the West Indians were doing everything in their power to ameliorate the slave trade and slavery—to revise brutal slave codes and encourage reproduction of the existing slave labor force. Still, Edwards was not an unabashed supporter of the trade. Instead, in speeches and pamphlets, Edwards took an "enlightened" stance, calling for the reform of the trade. Initially, the agent for Jamaica, Stephen Fuller, warned that Edwards's position would "cut up by the root" the West Indians' arguments in favor of the trade. But, far from it, Edwards's support for the amelioration of the slave trade only strengthened the West Indian position. He argued that abolition was unjustified if the slave trade could be improved; only a retrograde system would be beyond the pale of reform.[14]

Edwards's position, however, did not represent a consensus among West Indian planters. A number of resident West Indians contended that the slave trade could be abolished without posing a threat to the perpetuation of plantation slavery. In the later eighteenth century, planters on some sugar islands began to encourage female slaves to have children—they offered relief from work during the pre- and postpartum period, provided incentives for childrearing, and built hospitals on their estates that provided better medical care. It seemed plausible to planters in the older and smaller sugar islands, including Barbados, St. Kitts, and Grenada, that improved slave reproduction rates could render the slave trade unnecessary. But these planters did not deploy amelioration because they were humanitarians; rather, soil exhaustion, lack of new land for expansion, and falling sugar prices led slave owners in these colonies to "improve" their lands and slaves simply in order to survive. Nevertheless, these same planters also understood that abolition might stymie expansion and development in undeveloped colonies like Jamaica and Demerara. So even if the established colonies might be able to deploy amelioration policies and increase their already-existing slave populations, the absence of the trade would limit imperial expansion elsewhere in the Caribbean. And if expansion was the creed of empire, then abolition ran counter to it. West Indian planters, like their American cousins before them, bucked against any parliamentary effort to stem growth and development in the provinces.[15]

Edwards inserted himself into the heated debate on the slave trade, emerging as an authority on how amelioration was applied in Africa and the West Indies. A cosmopolitan provincial, Edwards was born in Westbury, Wiltshire, in 1743, but soon after his father's death in 1756, departed for Jamaica under the care of his wealthy maternal uncle Zachary Bayly.

There, Bayly taught his nephew the sugar-planting business and eventually left him two estates in Trelawny Parish—Brampton Bryan and Bryan Castle—in 1769. Along with the houses, Edwards also inherited over 1,400 acres of sugar, coffee, and pimento fields and hundreds of slaves. In 1765, Edwards was elected to the Jamaica House of Assembly and, during the American Revolution, became a fierce advocate for the corporate rights of the mainland thirteen colonies. He also supported the West Indian colonies' right to regulate the slave trade and continue commerce with America. Edwards, however, did not emerge as a "formidable opponent" of the anti–slave trade movement until he returned to Britain. He became an MP, was elected secretary of the African Association under Joseph Banks, and obtained memberships in the Royal Society and the American Philosophical Society. Edwards used his position at the imperial center to bolster support for the notion that the African slave trade was a modern, dynamic system that sustained the component parts of the British world and encouraged its expansion.[16]

Edwards drew on his own expertise to offer evidence that the slave trade unified disparate imperial provinces as much as it pushed them toward civilization. He looked to his plantations in Jamaica to prove that the effects of the slave trade were not as baneful as opponents of the traffic had charged. Conducting interviews with many of his own slaves about the Middle Passage and their lives in Africa, Edwards explained that his slaves found their lives much improved in the West Indies. He emphasized that his bondsmen escaped war, death, or a more violent strain of slavery in Africa. He believed that his Africans' arrival in the West Indies via the slave trade was the first stage in their moral development; in time, he surmised, his enslaved workforce might one day resemble a proto-peasantry. And as secretary of the African Association, Edwards found his slaves' depiction of conditions in Africa to be incontrovertible. When the association sent Mungo Park, the Scottish explorer, to chart the direction of the Niger River, Edwards and others were keenly interested not in geography but in the origins of the African slave trade. Park discovered on his tour of the West African jungle that slavery had been embedded there for centuries; Britons were merely capitalizing on an existing system. Thus, armed with evidence from Africa and the West Indies, Edwards proclaimed that the slave trade was a system that "we may alleviate, though we cannot cure." So far-reaching, adaptable, and lucrative was the trade, Edwards suggested, that eradicating it in the British Empire would bring more harm than good. Accordingly, he supported a wide swath of reforms—onboard slave ships, on the African coast, and on West Indian plantations—that would ameliorate the slave trade without ending it. The result would be a modern and progressive British imperial world that outpaced its French, Spanish, and American rivals.[17]

OUT OF AFRICA

In 1789, Thomas Clarkson published a diagram of the slave ship *Brookes,* which crammed 292 slaves below deck and a further 130 slaves in stowage. Soon afterward, his colleague, William Wilberforce, passed around a wooden model of the slave ship in the House of Commons. After viewing this horrific depiction, opponents of the trade believed that few would be able to dispute that the human traffic impugned the nation and caused the deaths of thousands of Africans every year.[18]

Still, there were many slave traders and West Indian slave owners who *did* dispute the claim. Prime Minister William Pitt organized a parliamentary inquiry into the nature of the African slave trade in 1788, with a report given in the House of Commons in April 1789. A substantial portion of this report was devoted to testimonials, particularly from merchants involved in the trade. John Mathews, a trader on the Sierra Leone coast, proclaimed that, of all the European slave-trading nations, Britain was by far the most humane. "No nation treats these slaves on the passage to the W. Indies so well," he argued, since "our ships are cleaner, & our provisions better than the French," and "our manner of treating slaves infinitely better than the Portuguese who never suffer them [slaves] to stay upon deck." Mathews maintained that, aboard British slavers, captured Africans were given every "advantage as circumstances can admit." And while Africans "lie on the bare board," the ship's "Captains & Officers frequently do the same."[19] Another trader, James Renny, believed that slaves "are comfortably lodged in Rooms fitted up for them which are washed and fumigated with Vinegar or Lime Juice every day" and "afterwards dried with fires in which we throw Frankincense and Tobacco."[20] Essentially, these traders used their evidence to dismiss abolitionists' claims that slave ships were unhealthy and that the ships' high mortality rates were a primary reason to effect abolition.

Slave captains and merchants also argued that there were sources of mortality other than British slave ships. Many blamed conditions in Africa for the loss of life. In 1788, the Jamaican Assembly reported that the alleged decrease of slaves brought from Africa was due to the "disproportion between the sexes" and the "loss of new negroes, on or soon after their arrival, from epidemic diseases brought from Africa."[21] Captain William Sherwood testified to this in the assembly, recounting the mortality rates in a recent voyage from Bonny, in the Bight of Benin, to Kingston. During the transatlantic journey, 63 of Sherwood's 455 captives died when apoplexy and the measles broke out on board. Sherwood, however, was convinced that if the "contagious distemper had not happened," then "I should have brought the Slaves with as little loss as is sustained by ships in general coming from that part of Africa."[22] And Alexander Lindo, a slave broker based in Kingston, accused abolitionists of using skewed statistics to make mortality rates look higher than they really were. As evidence, Lindo noted that many of the slaves imported by his firm were resold to buyers on other Caribbean islands or the American mainland. In February 1786, Lindo noted that the slave ship *Brooks* carried 620 slaves from Anamabahoe across the Atlantic. Of those, 183 were sold in Jamaica, while 425 were re-exported to other islands. And in March 1788, the *African Queen* moored in Kingston with 466 slaves from Calabar. Only 212 were sold in Jamaica, while 239 were destined for market elsewhere. Lindo charged that because these slaves were resold, they were counted as deceased by abolitionists.[23]

And yet, Bryan Edwards, from his vantage point in the Jamaica Assembly in 1788 and 1789, did not deny the immoral aspects of the slave trade. He admitted that slavers crammed too many captives on board. "Slave vessels have been frequently crowded with a greater number of negroes than they ought," he wrote, and conceded that mortality arose from "diseases occasioned by improper treatment in the voyage." Edwards acknowledged the often-deadly nature of the slave trade, but this did not mean that abolition was the logical answer. In fact, death rates might "diminish" if slaves were transported under "a better mode of conveyance." Edwards believed that improvement of conditions onboard slave ships would reform the commerce, while abolition would not. With increased regulation of slave ships, Edwards found the trade "justifiable in all other respects," and argued that "if regulation alone is sufficient to correct the grievance, abolition cannot be necessary."[24]

Edwards's argument almost proved to be the death-knell of the abolition movement in Parliament. Advocates of the slave trade, both in Britain and the West Indies, supported a wide range of reform measures aimed at improving conditions and decreasing mortality on board slave ships. They supported the installation of ventilation systems, inspection of ships by customs officials, captains' logs of transatlantic journeys, ship physicians who managed and treated disease, an equal sex ratio of transported slaves, and sufficient food and water supplies for crew and captives. In October 1793, for example, the captain of the slave ship *Express* docked in St. Vincent in the British West Indies. There, Andrew Chester's cargo was inspected. He had to certify where the *Express* had originated, how many slaves he took onboard in Africa, how many were children, as well as the sex ratio of the slaves. Chester testified that there had never been more than 147 slaves on the *Express* at any one time, and that during the voyage, only a single slave had died. Chester's testimony in St. Vincent was the result of a number of reforms of the slave trade passed in Parliament between 1788 and 1799. During that period, thirteen successive acts were passed to better regulate the trade and supposedly reform its evils.[25]

After the first parliamentary legislation, also called the Dolben Act, was passed in 1788 to "improve" the slave trade, the issue of mortality rates onboard slave ships fizzled. Instead, anti- and proslavery ameliorationists shifted their focus to a much larger issue—whether the transatlantic slave trade impeded or encouraged the civilization of Africans (and Africa). Wilberforce claimed that the slave trade was making Africans' "barbarous manners more barbarous."[26] Thomas Clarkson charged that complete and immediate abolition was the only way to bring civilization to Africa. Ending the slave trade, he thought, would extend the benefits of free trade to that continent. "If a commerce were once established with the natives of Africa in the productions of their own country," then "civilization would be the consequence of it" as the "natives" improved themselves through free trade.[27] Indeed, there was little question, Clarkson wrote, that the "introduction of new commerce" would replace the "execrable trade in men." Thus, the result of abolition would be to attain "a step in the scale of civilization."[28] Then, under the regime of free commerce and free labor, Africa would be included in the Atlantic world as it never had before.

Supporters of the slave trade, however, disagreed with Clarkson's formulation. Edwards described Africa as a "field of warfare and desolation," a "wilderness, in which the inhabitants are wolves toward each other." But still, Edwards thought that the "scene of oppression, fraud, treachery, and blood" was not caused by British involvement in the trade.[29] Rather, the slave trade had been going on for centuries within the African continent; British traders were only capitalizing on the system. The Council of Jamaica argued that British slave trading had little to do with African barbarism. The "Traffic among Men for their own Species, to the extent of Parents selling their Children, prevailed thro' the vast Regions of Africa, many Centuries before a foreign purchaser landed on that continent," the council maintained. Even if Britain abolished the trade, the "Oriental Marts [would] still open," and Africans would remain in the throes of "Efficient brutal principles."[30] Indeed, if Britons could not "be charged with being the cause of it," then they could not be held responsible for enacting the solution. Perhaps Africa could be civilized, the council reasoned, but the way to effect the process would be through the slave trade's regulation, not its abolition.[31]

Of course, in the debate over whether the slave trade prevented African civilization or encouraged it, the glass was perpetually half full or half empty. It was not until the mid-1790s that any substantial evidence could be offered to resolve the question. In 1795, an exploration of the African interior was sponsored by the African Institution in London. Pioneered by the botanist Joseph Banks, the association attracted Londoners of all stripes: aristocratic scientists like Edward Gibbon and Henry Cavendish, evangelical abolitionists who had founded the British colony at Sierra Leone, conservative MPs, and members of the West India lobby. Yet despite their diverse political affiliations, all of these men styled themselves British gentleman united around a common interest: the integration of Africa into the British commercial world. Unsurprisingly, though, the terms of the slave trade debates framed much of the association's interest in Africa. Men on both sides of the issue continued to bandy around the still unanswered question: was the British slave trade the cause of African barbarism? The association supported the exploration of the continent not simply for geographical purposes or to extend imperial influence but also to answer this critical question. The result, members understood, might determine the outcome of the abolition movement.[32]

The association sent the Scottish explorer Mungo Park to chart the geography of western Africa and to find the origin of the Niger River. Park spent nearly three years stumbling through the dense West Africa jungle; he was held captive and nearly killed, but did somehow manage to settle on the direction of the course of the Niger and followed its banks from Segu to Silla. If Park was an inefficient explorer, he was even less adept at writing. After returning to London in 1797, he promptly handed over his journals to the secretary of the African Association, Bryan Edwards. Edwards's task was to prepare "an epitome or abstract of his [Park's] principal discoveries" to lay before the association.[33] When the association resolved to publish Park's findings, the explorer again engaged the help of Edwards, who substantially edited and rewrote much of the manuscript. As Edwards lamented to Joseph Banks while working through Park's drafts in 1798, "previous to his captivity, there is such a sameness in the Negro manners and the occurrences which he relates are so unimportant that it requires some skill in composition and arrangement to make the reading supportable."[34] Although the extent to which Edwards rewrote Park's journal is debatable, it seems logical that his "first object must have been, to gain the services of Park in the direct support of the Slave Trade" or to secure Park's "neutrality, and prevent him from joining the ranks of his opponents."[35]

What concerned Edwards and those West Indian lobbyists and slave trade critics who took their dinners together at the St. Albans Tavern on Pall Mall was not the direction of the Niger. Rather, they were interested in the slave trade—its origins, its routes, and its impact on African society. Both pro- and anti–slave trade advocates wanted to know whether British involvement in the slave trade caused its perpetuation or whether African tribes trafficked in human flesh independent of British involvement. If Park discovered that British merchants' purchases of African bondsmen increased slavery, drained the population, or fomented tribal warfare, then critics would be correct in calling the slave trade a British "national sin." But if Park determined that the slave trade in Africa was not a direct result of British intervention and commerce, then slave trade supporters, most notably Edwards, could prove that the commerce did not jeopardize national civilization. In short, Park was not simply charting the Niger but also "what could be termed its *moral* geography."[36]

In the 1799 published version of Park's journals, the explorer devoted a section to "observations concerning the State and Sources of Slavery in Africa." But he included no information on the encounters between British slave dealers and African tribesmen. Instead, Park depicted a society where the "slaves in Africa" are in "proportion of three to one to the freemen." A "great body of the Negro inhabitants of Africa have continued" in "this condition" from the "most early period of their history." Describing a world of slavery wrought without European influence, Park outlined how slaves purchased by European traders were brought to sale by two means: "petty wars" or "large caravans from the inland countries, many of which are unknown, even by name to the Europeans." Park suggested that those slaves offered for sale on the coast were either born slaves or were enslaved by their tribesmen because of famine, insolvency, or crimes committed in the African interior. Although Park's descriptions are one-sided and have since been revised and fleshed out by modern historians, it is nevertheless significant that Park's conclusions played directly into the hands of slave-trade advocates.[37]

Edwards was particularly interested in Park's conclusion that African slavery "is a system of no modern date." Rather, the practice of enslavement "probably had its origin in the remote ages of antiquity, before the Mahomedans explored the path across the Desert." The only modern part of the African slave trade was the consumption of its captives by modern "nations of Europe." And yet this modern appendage, as Park suggested and Edwards emphasized, had little bearing on the condition of African society. Africans had purportedly enslaved each other and lived in a state of semi-barbarism for centuries. Thus, the effect of the "discontinuance of that commerce" on the "manners of the natives . . . in their present un-enlightened state" would "neither be so extensive or beneficial, as many wise and worthy persons fondly expect." In effect, Park and Edwards argued that the abolitionists' campaign to end the transatlantic slave trade would not reverse the barbarism that pervaded Africa. In fact, since the slave trade was so deeply ingrained in African culture and history, abolition might not have any effect at all. And, even if British slavers stopped transporting seventy thousand slaves annually across the Atlantic, slavers flying Portuguese, Dutch, or French colors would replace them.[38] Alternatively, Edwards suggested that the only way to civilize Africans was to transport them out of Africa, via the slave trade, to plantation society in the sugar islands.

AMELIORATION IN THE INDIES

In a prologue to two reports on Jamaicans' response to Wilberforce's proposed abolition bill, a London editor conveyed his hope that planters in Jamaica would soon overcome their backward tendencies and understand that abolition was the most moral policy. Jamaicans maintained that legislation had been passed in their provincial assembly to mitigate slavery. The editor was skeptical but hoped that the alleged "melioration of the state of slavery will be accompanied by a melioration of the tempers of the slave-holders." He thought that this "melioration" would result in a single "national and provincial" realization that "no substantial and durable interest can be derived from so polluted a source as slavery."[39] In other words, the editor anticipated that Jamaicans' own enlightenment would inevitably result in their discovery that slavery was a moral evil. But, ironically, planters' "enlightenment"—which included the local knowledge they had accrued on sugar estates—made it clear to them that regulation and reform, not abolition, would assure modernization in plantation society.

Jamaican planters admitted that the "laws respecting our slaves" were "not so good as they might be."[40] Still, the planters insisted that they were in the process of ameliorating their slave society. Metropolitan opponents remained skeptical. Many believed that planters were caught in the throes of their own backward provincialism and unable to share in the enlightened civility of Britain. When the Jamaican planter Edward Long published an influential history of his native island in 1774, many of the views he expressed reinforced metropolitans' preconceptions about West Indian slave society. For example, Long described slaves as "ourang-outangs" who were "void of genius" and existed in "the same rude situation in which they were found two thousand years ago." Long suggested that bondsmen were synonymous with primates and incapable of being civilized; they were beyond the pale of improvement. "We cannot pronounce them insusceptible to civilization, since even apes have been taught to eat, drink, repose, and dress, like men," Long wrote mockingly, but "of all the human species hitherto discovered, their natural baseness of mind seems to afford least hope of their being . . . so far refined as to *think*, as well as act like *perfect men*." Long's work reaffirmed metropolitans' perception of West Indian slave society as one of corrupt planters who legitimized their brutality by referring to slaves as the "vilest of the human kind."[41]

Decades later, Bryan Edwards tried to revise Long's assertions about Africans' capacity for improvement. Edwards believed that Long's characterization of enslaved blacks as "ourang-outangs" was a "gross mistake." By contrast, Edwards had seen many examples of Africans' advanced culture and intelligence. The "Cotton Cloths brought from *Akim*" were "in manufacture . . . equal and in Color far superior to those made at Manchester in imitation of them." He believed that the "Senegal negroes in particular are a Civilized people," since "I have met with several who could read and write in the Arabic Language with great facility & they are in general docile and Ingenious." Essentially, Edwards believed that Long had incorrectly conflated *Africans* and *slaves*, when it was most likely the state of slavery, not race, that had "sunk and degraded them"—a conclusion that Jefferson had also tentatively reached in the 1780s. Edwards asserted that, "with regard to the General Character of the Blacks our Knowledge is limited," and "such as it is, it inclines us I confess to think unfavorably of their Dispositions, for the Negroes in our Colonies are Commonly believed to be fierce and faithless ingrateful Roguish revengeful and Bloody." He sought to remind his audience that a "state of Abject Slavery" was not one of "Progressive improvement," a fact showing that it was slavery which retarded blacks' development. And yet, Edwards did believe in the improvement of Africans within the regime of colonial slavery.[42]

By the 1790s, Edwards had developed an ethnography of African slaves that stood at odds with the one detailed by Long in 1774. Edwards's source was interviews conducted with his own slaves. Only by relating what his slaves remembered of Africa, the Middle Passage, and their introduction to West Indian slavery could Edwards delineate how they had progressed from so-called barbaric savages in Africa to improved bondsmen in Jamaica. In Edwards's view, the constant warfare that pitted African tribes against one another interfered in their moral development. Although capable of improvement, Africans would never improve in a society that did not itself progress, Edwards suggested. He looked for evidence of his assumptions in the histories of his own African slaves, who hailed from the Mandingoes of the Windward Coast, the Gold Coast, Whidah and Fida, the Bight of Benin, and the Kongo. He sought to identify the tribal differences among his slaves, to understand their particular tribal cultures and how those cultures were transformed in the West Indies.[43]

Edwards consulted his "old and faithful Mandingo servant" for information about the Windward Coast. The slave recalled "being sent by his father to visit a distant relation" when a "fray happened in the village in which he resided." He "himself was seized and carried off in a skirmish" not "by a foreign enemy, but by some of the natives of the place," who sent him downriver and sold him to a ship captain who brought him to Jamaica. From the slave's testimony, Edwards concluded that such "Mahometans" of the Windward Coast, near Sierra Leone, were "perpetually at war with such of the surrounding nations as refuse to adopt their religious tenets." And "prisoners taken in these religious wars," such as Edwards's own slave, comprised a "great part of the slaves which are exported from the factories on the Windward Coast" to the West Indies.[44]

Still more violent than the Mandingo society, Edwards thought, were the Gold Coast societies. Edwards interviewed his "most faithful and well-disposed" slave Clara, who had been brought from the Gold Coast to Jamaica in 1784, for information about her native tribe. Clara's family was born slaves to "a great man, named Anamoa" on "whose death she . . . was sold to pay his debts," eventually ending up in Jamaica. When Edwards asked Clara "which country she liked best," she answered Jamaica, because "people were not killed there, as in Guiney, at the funeral of their masters." Another slave, Cudjoe, was sold into slavery in Africa after his brother had committed adultery. Cudjoe's brother sold him "as a compensation" because he had "an unquestionable right" to do so. Once in the West Indies, however, Edwards noted that the slaves' "contempt of death, or indifference about life" abated as they "acquire . . . other sentiments and notions" and "nature resumes her lawful influence over them." Edwards lamented that Africans on the Gold Coast should be "sunk in so deplorable a state of barbarity and superstition." Once in the West Indies, Edwards was "persuaded that they possess qualities which are capable of, and well deserve, cultivation and improvement."[45]

Edwards was careful to outline the "various African nations in the West Indies separately and distinct from one another," if only to show that, despite their tribal distinctiveness, warfare and enslavement were prominent features of each individual nation. Still, Edwards claimed that it was the Middle Passage and West Indian slavery that eradicated tribal differences. Leaving the shores of Africa effaced the "native original impression which distinguishes one nation from another" and created a "similitude of manners, and a uniformity of character throughout the whole body" of Africans on his plantations. Mandingoes, Eboes, and peoples from the Gold Coast may have been warring tribes in Africa, but the Middle Passage and West Indian slavery forged a common interest and history among the disparate tribes, thus uniting them together. The "latent virtues . . . of sympathy and compassion towards persons in the same condition of life" were forged when captives "came on the same ship . . . from Africa." As "shipmates," they "recall[ed] the time when the sufferers were cut off together from their common country and kindred," and this awakened "reciprocal sympathy, from the remembrance of mutual affliction." Removal from barbaric tribal society in Africa, combined with shared "remembrance" of their violent pasts, united Africans and cemented peace among them, Edwards surmised. The evidence, he charged, was on his own plantations and among his own slaves. Perversely, Edwards envisioned the transatlantic slave trade as a kind of colonization scheme that furnished Africans with a common experience and history that would render them conscious of themselves as a "people."[46]

Edwards thought that a homogenous and peaceful society of enslaved Africans was critical to their amelioration in the West Indies. Edwards also detailed his own strategy for "further meliorating the condition" of enslaved Africans. He sought to render slaves' "labour certain and determinate" so that "each Negro, according to his strength," would perform a "specific quantity of work . . . in a given time." This system was also known as task labor, and the incentive to complete the assigned task was thought to motivate slaves to work more efficiently. After finishing an appointed task, slaves would be allowed to work their own land or be paid wages for extra work done on estates. This was the advent of the so-called provision-ground system, in which the emergence of a distinctive slave economy allowed bondsmen greater autonomy while simultaneously intensifying their work. The provision-ground system and increasingly regulated and specialized task labor fell under the rubric of amelioration but ultimately resulted in slavery becoming a more demanding, less-negotiable system for slaves.[47]

Of course, Edwards was advocating amelioration *within* the system of slavery, not outside it. Detailing the "extended and liberal plan" of "immediate abolition," Edwards criticized his opponents' plan of amelioration. He dismissed their view that an end to the slave trade would transform barbaric Africa into a civilized country. He questioned the notion that "stopping the further influx of Negroes into our islands . . . [would] compel the planters to cherish and husband their present stock; and sustain it in future by natural increase." Critics of the trade proposed that under this "milder treatment, and the Christian institutes, the manners of the slaves shall become gradually softened, their vices corrected, and their dispositions gradually prepared for a total emancipation from that absolute slavery in which they are now held." While Wilberforce's proposals to abolish the slave trade made no mention of emancipation, it was no secret that opponents of the trade viewed abolition as one step toward ending plantation slavery entirely.[48]

But there were serious problems, Edwards maintained, with a plan of amelioration that resulted in abolition and then emancipation. Like most other West Indians in the 1790s, Edwards equated emancipation with violence and the obliteration of plantation society, as he had witnessed first-hand during his visit to Saint Domingue. Emancipation "would involve master and slave in one common destruction," thereby destroying dreams for freedom and improvement in the West Indies.[49] Moreover, metropolitan opponents had charged that emancipation was necessary to modernize West Indian society and improve the moral and material conditions of Africans. Instead, Edwards believed that amelioration was already evident within the regime of plantation slavery. In fact, slavery was improving at such a rate in the sugar islands, he pronounced, that "may the time soon arrive, when the name only of Slavery shall remain, without any of its attendant miseries." In other words, if slavery, like the slave trade, was an improvable institution, calls to end it were moot.[50]

Slaves' amelioration within the regime of West Indian slavery hinged on the civility and benevolence of planters and modern plantation management techniques. Edwards believed that these elements were present in the West Indies, particularly Jamaica. Despite criticism from European observers, Edwards thought that in the sugar islands, "Nature has distributed the gifts of genius more equally and generally than is commonly imagined," for "it is cultivation and favour that ripen and bring them to perfection."[51] He thought it a grave mistake for European "authors" to "describe the West Indies as a herd of criminals and convicts" and to "cite the stale crimes and violence of lawless men" when "these islands were the rendezvous of pirates and bucaniers." Perhaps, "more than a century ago," that would have been an accurate description of West Indian society, Edwards maintained. But the sugar islands had come a long way in a century. Planters had become intelligent, benevolent, and committed to the improvement of their plantation societies. Indeed, the "generosity to each other, and high degree of compassion and kindness towards their inferiors and dependents, distinguish the Creoles in a very honourable manner." Humane masters, he argued, could extract as much labor from slaves as possible while also expanding Britain's imperial ambitions in the Caribbean.[52]

Edwards offered proof of his description of West Indians as improving, benevolent masters. He cited the ameliorated slave laws in the sugar islands, particularly in Jamaica in recent years, as evidence that the West Indian islands were—of their own volition—mitigating slavery. The "Criminal Slave Laws of this island have been meliorated," Edwards noted. Citing this new and improved legislation, Edwards sought to distance planters from the "conduct of our ancestors towards their Slaves" and their "antient colonial Slave Laws." In December 1787, the Jamaican Assembly revised the slave code to ensure that the "Negroes in this Island are under the Protection of lenient and salutary laws" that exhibited "humanity, kindness, and mercy."[53] The new code stipulated measures for the further amelioration of slaves, and differed, as Edwards pointed out, from the more draconian Slave Code of 1696. Essentially, the new 1788 code increased "protection" of slaves—masters were bound by law to provide sufficient clothing, medical treatment, and food to slaves. Whites caught maiming, killing, or unwontedly beating slaves were punished. Slaves were also allotted provision grounds, and planters had to report the annual increase and decrease of their plantation labor forces to local authorities.[54] With these new laws in place—and under the problematic assumption that they were regularly enforced—Edwards found it unnecessary to accuse the "Planters of this island, of improper and inhuman treatment of our Slaves." As "civility and improvement" would become ever more conspicuous in West Indian slave society, then slaves would "receive greater indulgence" from their masters. Indeed, "that civility, and that improvement are now making a silent, but visible progress." He suggested that modern West Indian slavery hardly resembled its more archaic, and more barbaric, antecedents.[55]

There were many slave owners who fashioned themselves as enlightened paternalists. The Antiguan planter Samuel Martin styled himself as the "loved and revered father" to his slaves; he sought to induce "love" from his bondsmen by setting the example of "benevolence, justice, temperance, and chastity." When a Scottish visitor toured Martin's Greencastle estate in 1774, she declared her host to be a "kind and beneficient Master" whose main goal was "improvement." This humanitarianism was thought to a have tangible impact, specifically on slave reproduction rates. Slaves "fed plentifully, worked moderately, and treated kindly . . . will increase in most places" and "decrease in no place," asserted the author of one Barbadian plantation manual in 1786. Indeed, the correlation between benevolence and "increase," whether in the form of crop yields or reproduction rates, became a powerful argument for planters' adoption of ameliorative methods throughout the British West Indies.[56]

And if slavery was improving in the West Indies, then that was also due to an improving plantation system, planters thought. After all, a sugar plantation was like a "well-constructed machine, compounded of various wheels turning different ways, yet all contributing to the great end proposed." To achieve the "great end" of maximized production, many Jamaican planters introduced labor changes and agricultural reform on their estates. Planters embraced agricultural improvement methods that had emerged in metropolitan Britain, not because they had experienced a moral conversion but because they were responding to market pressures: deteriorating soil, lower prices, and decreased production. As a result, they began feeding their livestock new kinds of grasses, substituting the plow for the hoe, rotating and manuring crop fields, and diversifying their crops. At the same time, planters demanded that their slaves become more efficient workers. Managers hired outside gangs of slaves to accomplish the most difficult work to conserve the strength of their own workforces. They often divided gangs of slaves into smaller groups, thus encouraging specialization and efficiency. And, in an effort to curb the use of the whip, planters in some cases set production quotas or offered incentives. And yet, as enlightened planters paid more attention to the efficiency of their plantation "machine," work for slaves also became more rigorous.[57]

Edwards believed that much had been done to improve West Indian plantations since the American Revolution. This improvement directly resulted in expansion; the British state, with enlightened and enterprising planters as its agents, was expanding its influence in Jamaica. Although a spate of hurricanes in the Caribbean had forced many planters to sell their estates or surrender them to British mortgagers, Edwards believed that the economy was beginning to right itself during the 1790s.[58] Between 1791 and 1797, 47 new sugar and coffee estates were settled, causing "rapid improvement" in Jamaica. Coffee and sugar exports were up, and nearly 1,740,000 acres of land were devoted to livestock "pens," plantations, or slaves' cultivation grounds. While "upwards of two millions" acres in Jamaica remained "an unimproved, unproductive wilderness," this was not due to the supposed indolence of planters and their slaves. Rather, the "interior" of Jamaica, Edwards explained, was composed of nearly impassable mountain jungle, and the southern part of the island was often too dry to grow crops. Edwards hoped to demonstrate that the West Indian plantation system was neither stagnant nor retrograde, as so many opponents of the slave trade had suggested in the 1780s and 1790s. Planters hardly wanted to maintain the status quo—they desired expansion and maximum returns on their investments in land and slaves. Edwards cited planters' expanding enterprises and commitment to increasing their sugar and coffee output to Europe. He wanted to stifle claims that the West Indies were economically impotent or violent. Jamaica alone, he calculated, was worth £39 million and growing in 1797.[59]

EMPIRE AND NATION

John Newton was not unfamiliar with the slave trade. In 1748, he served as first mate aboard the slave-trading vessel *Brownlow*. He was then promoted to captain, piloting one voyage aboard the *Duke of Argyle* and two on the *African*. Then in 1754, Newton retired from the slave trade, returned to England, sought peace with God as an Anglican minister, and composed hymns, including the renowned "Amazing Grace." It was over thirty years before he wrote publicly against the slave trade, in 1787. But when he did, Newton framed his anti–slave trade sentiments in a very particular manner. "It is Righteousness that Exalteth a Nation; and Wickedness is the present reproach, and will, sooner or later, unless repentance intervene, prove the ruin of any people."[60] Abolition of the slave trade, Newton suggested, would allow Britons to repent their involvement in the buying and selling of Africans. But his focus was on Britain and on moral decay precipitated by the slave trade. The empire mattered little to Newton. Many other opponents of the trade adopted a similar approach. William Roscoe worried whether the "British nation should be branded in future times as procurers of slaves for all Europe," a possibility that was of "real concern to every person who feels himself interested in the honour of his country."[61] Similarly, Thomas Clarkson believed that an abolition bill, by destroying the "many-headed monster" of the slave trade, would "improve the system of morals . . . at home."[62] In short, all of these men framed their claims to abolition in national terms. This focus on the "nation," rather than on empire, resulted in an emphasis on the necessity of exonerating the British people from the immorality of slave trading and their "conversion" from sin. Like revolutionary patriots in America, the antislavery amelioration of British abolitionists was at heart a critical part of a nation-making—or nation remaking—project. Despite claims to secure the "natural rights" of Africans, the British abolition movement was in reality rooted in nationalism that emphasized reforms within the nation, not within the empire.

Opponents of the slave trade purported to rescue the British nation from sin, to act with humanity toward those Africans who had been bought and sold by British traders for centuries. Yet many slave trade supporters questioned whether abolition was really a humane remedy. "There's an end of the question of humanity" of abolition, noted one member of Parliament, and that was "that the argument goes the other way." Abolition, he warned, could end up doing more harm than good because its focus was national rather than imperial in scope, and could thus have unintended consequences.[63] By contrast, many supporters of the slave trade, including Bryan Edwards, were much more concerned with how abolition could affect the empire as a whole. Ending the trade would destroy West Indian plantation society, demolish the commercial trading networks that knit Britain's Atlantic empire so tightly together, and thrust Africa even further into barbarism, Edwards warned. He believed that it was pure "imagination" to think that abolition would foment the freedom and equality that slave trade critics promised. Instead, Edwards advocated the reform of the slave trade and the mitigation of plantation slavery. He believed that the "miseries we cannot wholly remove, we may in some cases mitigate."[64]

The regulatory legislation passed in the 1790s, all of which built on or amended the Dolben Act of 1788, was proof of how powerful Edwards's sophisticated vision of a progressive commercial system—the African slave trade—really was. The idea that the trade was a dynamic mechanism that could be improved, rather than abolished, carried much weight with conservative MPs, merchants, and planters. Those who clamored for immediate abolition, including Wilberforce, Clarkson, Newton, and so many others, supported a radical policy that found fewer political allies. Often contemporaries thought opponents of the trade might redeem a nation but destroy an empire. Abolition carried far too many risks to garner much parliamentary support in the 1780s and 1790s, when, by comparison, a reformed slave trade seemed to secure progress, maintain the balance of trade, and mitigate the trade's moral transgressions. Only in the first decade of the nineteenth century did the war with Napoleonic France give abolitionists' nationalism the upper hand. In 1806, the brilliant young lawyer James Stephen drafted what became known as the Foreign Slave Trade Act. The bill prohibited British subjects—including slave traders—from selling goods to anyone trading with the French colonies. Hobbling nearly two-thirds of Britain's slave trade to the New World, the act paved the way for the Abolition Bill in 1807. Nonetheless, arguments for amelioration endured beyond the abolition of the slave trade. As we see in the next chapter, West Indian planters continued to assert that an ameliorated imperial system—mitigated slavery and economic protectionism—was more likely to secure the progress of the British Empire than the untested and "revolutionary" changes of free trade and free labor suggested by abolitionists. In the 1810s and 1820s, planters maintained that ameliorating plantation slavery, not ending it, was the only means to bring wealth and power to the empire.[65]

6

"A MATTER OF PORTENTOUS MAGNITUDE, AND STILL MORE PORTENTOUS DIFFICULTY"

By 1828, John Gladstone owned over a thousand slaves as well as several sugar plantations in the British Caribbean colony of Demerara, on the northern coast of South America, and in the eastern portion of Jamaica. Yet Gladstone had never set foot on any of his profitable estates at Vreeden Hoop, Success, Hordley, Oxford, or Fair Prospect; indeed, he had crossed the Atlantic only once, in 1790, for a brief tour through the eastern states of America, and did not intend ever to leave the British Isles again. For it was in Britain that Gladstone could become exactly what would have eluded him in the West Indies: a central political figure in the burgeoning industrial center of Liverpool, a landed gentleman whose estate, Seaforth, was the pinnacle of order and civility, and the head of a devoutly evangelical Christian household. Gladstone was by all accounts one of the richest West Indian planters in the early nineteenth-century British Empire.[1]

This chapter considers the proslavery amelioration of John Gladstone, who in many ways found himself at the center of the British antislavery movement in the 1820s. While Bryan Edwards's proslavery ameliorative vision of the 1780s and 1790s was centered on the transatlantic slave trade and its reform, the focus by the 1820s had shifted to conditions on plantations. As one of the more progressive planters of the era, Gladstone instructed his managers to implement the very same ameliorative measures that abolitionists supported, including improved material conditions and religious instruction for slaves. Despite these measures—or because of them—one of Gladstone's Demerara plantations, Success, and several of his slaves played a central role in a massive slave rebellion in the colony in 1823. Later, Gladstone sparred with the antislavery free trader James Cropper in a debate over whether an "improved" system of protectionism or new free-trade principles would benefit the British Empire. This was a debate over which trajectory of modernization—proslavery or antislavery amelioration—would best facilitate expansion and the accumulation of wealth. While most studies have viewed Gladstone and his plantation empire through the lens of abolitionism, this chapter shows that Gladstone's arguments for the improvement of existing institutions—economic protectionism for West Indian sugar and mitigated slavery and religious instruction on estates—constituted a sophisticated worldview that dealt a blow to the antislavery movement even as the movement gained popular momentum in the 1820s. The reform of existing imperial systems rather than their abolition constituted a cosmopolitan understanding of the empire and its parts, a far cry from abolitionists' more parochial views of natural rights and moral reform.[2]

The son of a middling corn and wheat merchant, Gladstone was born in Leith, Scotland, in 1764. After several years of working for his father in the Baltic trade, Gladstone moved to Liverpool and in 1787 became a clerk in the house of the grain merchants Corrie & Company. Gladstone eventually became a partner in the firm, though it dissolved after sixteen years. He then established the John Gladstone & Company merchant house and brought his six brothers from Leith to work in the business. The firm became prosperous—the Gladstones traded with Russia and the West Indies, and when the East India Company monopoly was broken in 1813, they were the first to send a private ship to Calcutta. He was keenly interested in the West Indies trade, particularly in the new and unexploited British Caribbean colonies of Demerara, Essequibo, and Berbice. Gladstone began investing in West Indian estates in 1817, primarily purchasing plantations with mortgages in default. By the time of slave emancipation in 1833, Gladstone either owned or had invested in nine Caribbean estates and had served as president of both the British Guyana Association and the West India Association. The immense wealth Gladstone derived from his plantations also allowed him to be active in prominent political circles. A close friend of the provincial Tory politicians George Canning and William Huskisson, Gladstone served in Parliament between 1818 and 1827.[3]

Gladstone's slaveholding enterprises in the West Indies made him rich. In an 1833 valuation of Gladstone's property, his West Indian holdings were estimated at £336,000, of which the slaves were valued at £106,769. He eventually owned over 2,500 slaves. Yet Gladstone's plantations were also his biggest liability. After the prohibition of the slave trade, abolitionists began working toward the immediate emancipation of West Indian bondsmen, which would have cost Gladstone enormous sums. In response,

during the 1820s, Gladstone wrote letters, gave speeches, lobbied humanitarians, and published pamphlets on the slavery question. He articulated
a different vision of modernity for the West Indies and the commercial
world of the Atlantic: an "improved" plantation system predicated on an
ameliorated slave labor force and reformed agricultural techniques, as well
as a continued policy of protectionism for the sugar islands. Although opponents of slavery charged that as long as sugar bounties and preferential
duties continued, masters had no incentive to ameliorate slaves, Gladstone
disagreed.[4]

For Gladstone, provincial slavery, at least in an "improved" form, was
completely consonant with progress in the modern world. This view
shared much in common with Bryan Edwards and the colonial slave trader
Henry Laurens, but was the polar opposite belief of metropolitan abolitionists, who argued that slavery was incompatible with human progress.
No longer was overseas slave labor and enormous plantation wealth the
badge of advancement for a modern nation; instead, it was the sign of a
premodern one, opponents of colonial slavery asserted. Abolitionists who
adhered to the Enlightenment worldview that depended on the equality of
"peoples" and an ever-widening sphere of individual civic rights could not
accept Gladstone's argument that an ameliorated slave system constituted
modernity. To them, a free trade and free labor system, rooted in the ideologies of Adam Smith and David Ricardo, could be the only policy of a
liberal and modern nineteenth-century empire.[5]

Still, Gladstone's plan of amelioration *within* the institution of slavery
held appeal and logic as a model of reform that did not necessitate revolutionary changes to the existing social order. The example of the Haitian and
French revolutions, and the continued threat posed by a number of Caribbean slave revolts, warned planters away from radical experimentation.
Instead, amelioration reconciled the need to "improve" colonial society,
in a moral and material sense, with the realities of the nineteenth-century
world—a world in which pragmatic, rather than idealistic, solutions were
increasingly deployed. In other words, the amelioration of slavery and the
increase of protective duties represented plausible solutions to the seemingly intractable problem of slavery. On the other hand, abolitionists' plans
to revolutionize the sugar islands with the introduction of free labor and
free trade were untried and unknown "experiments."[6]

In fact, Gladstone's arguments were only strengthened by the entrance
of new political economic ideas into the slave debates. Even though popular revulsion of West Indian slavery deepened significantly in the 1820s,

universalist free trade dogma did not help the abolition movement. Abolitionist free traders, such as the East Indian sugar merchant James Cropper, argued that slavery was the most wasteful labor system in the world; at the same time, American slave-grown cotton and slave-grown sugar from Cuba and Brazil dominated Atlantic commerce. If free trade principles and West Indian emancipation were adopted, Britain might plausibly turn to markets that could produce sugar for less than half the price in South America. The notion that free trade would not direct Britain to consume free-grown sugar in the West Indies or India but rather encourage it to import cheaper "blood-stained" sugar rendered many abolitionist free-trade arguments highly problematic. Free traders overlooked that their ideology would only succeed in a world of free and equal nations—the idealistic world that Enlightenment thinkers had imagined. Yet, in reality, the Atlantic world was a place of inequality and slavery. Thus, Gladstone's more rational argument for reform within existing economic and labor systems appealed to Tory politicians and antislavery MPs alike.[7]

The convergence of the debates about West Indian slavery and imperial political economic policies in the 1810s and 1820s provided the backdrop for Gladstone's ameliorative plans. The end of the Napoleonic Wars, the ban on the transatlantic slave trade, the advent of free-trade ideology, and the cleavage of the international system along national lines all contributed to a change in the definition of what the British Empire was, and how it would maintain its future position in the world. The slavery question played a key role in these changing conceptions of empire in the early nineteenth century. In 1824, one imperial official warned that the "danger and difficulties of the present colonial system in our West India Islands," characterized by the "vicious" and "unprofitable" system of slave-grown sugar, "must at no distant time be abandoned."[8] Although some economic historians have posited that the abolition of the slave trade was the result of Britain's shift toward a capitalist economy and the other social changes that accompanied this development, the debates between planters and abolitionists of the 1820s seem to suggest that it was abolition of the transatlantic slave trade that launched Britain into a new political economic era. In an effort to counter the perceived and actual "decline" of the West Indies, Gladstone and other planters argued for the "amelioration" of the protectionist slave regime rather than its total abandonment.[9]

The West Indies came under greater scrutiny after an era of warfare with the Americans and French. Metropolitan Britons perceived the islands' regression in comparison to other national markets. Low output and de-

creasing populations were the most conspicuous signs that the sugar islands were either static or regressing. Proof of this lay in intra-imperial and
international comparisons. The mainland American South, also a slave society, was expanding and maintained a self-reproducing enslaved population. Furthermore, within the empire, the colonies in the Caribbean were
no longer the only islands producing sugar. Increasingly, the East Indies—
India, Ceylon, and Mauritius—began producing sugar for the British
home market. Their sugar output began to rival that of the West Indies by
the 1820s. Moreover, East Indian sugar was produced by free peasants—
not enslaved Africans.[10]

Production, whether in the form of a self-regenerating population or
commercial growth, defined civilization and modernity in the early nineteenth century. And increasing numbers seemed to translate into improving, well-ordered, and "happy" societies. Only semi-barbarous societies
did not experience growth, which appeared to be the root of the problem
in the West Indies. Measuring civilization was *en vogue* by the 1820s, influenced by the rise of the study of political economy and the demographic
statistics that buttressed it. The first British census was taken in 1801 in response to the Malthusian claim that population was the primary indicator
of a nation's wealth and power. In the years that followed, there was an increased emphasis on counting people and the goods they produced. And
the division of the Atlantic along national lines during the age of revolutions meant that it was easier to measure the progress of different "peoples."
The end of the transatlantic slave trade only facilitated the calculation of
enslaved populations as slavery became bounded and national. These statistical measurements—national populations, slave populations, and economic production—played a leading role in debates about imperial labor
systems and trade policies in the nineteenth century. They also formed an
important component of the British antislavery debates between 1815 and
1833.[11]

The issue of expansion—of peoples and markets—lay at the heart of
the British slave debates in the 1820s. Ostensibly, one side lobbied for
emancipation and free-trade principles while the other pushed for the
continuation of protectionism and colonial slavery. The two cohorts' differences were mitigated, however, by their shared commitment to amelioration, both for Britain and the provincial outposts. But even the notion
that British antislavery and proslavery camps both adhered to gradual improvement schemes does not fully explain the crux of the issue. At stake
in the heated slavery debates in Parliament and the pamphlet wars was the

future of British colonization. Without France to impede expansion, what would the new British Empire look like? Many abolitionists supported a reformed empire modeled on the East Indies: a prosperous provincial outpost whose native population was rapidly being converted to Christianity as a result of the efforts of evangelical missionaries. They believed that this model could be replicated in the Americas and Africa. These antislavery agitators also supported parliamentary supremacy and imperial bureaucratization; they thought that Parliament, not the colonial legislatures, should implement amelioration and emancipation measures in the West Indies. Although this proposal seemed to run counter to the idea of the British Empire as a confederated entity whose provincial legislatures maintained semi-sovereign status, antislavery supporters suggested that imperial governance was the business of the imperial center.[12]

On the other hand, proslavery exponents envisioned a British Empire that appeared to be less progressive. They wanted the British government to continue the existing protectionist policy, believing that lower sugar duties and legislation such as the Corn Laws worked to insulate and encourage a strong home market less vulnerable to global competition. These advocates were staunchly anti–free labor, arguing that East Indian peasant labor was nothing but a form of pseudoslavery and that cheap, slave-grown sugar in Cuba and Brazil showed that slave labor was the most profitable in the western hemisphere. Intervening in what appeared to be a successful labor regime would only bring devastation to the Caribbean and potentially cripple the entire imperial system. But planters and merchants like John Gladstone were open to reform within the existing regime. In the nineteenth century, many embraced agricultural improvement and new plantation labor discipline that would encourage an increase in the slave population and a rise in sugar output. It was critical, however, that these reforms be implemented by provincial legislatures; planters upheld their understanding of the empire as a federal union in which the sugar islands claimed sovereignty over their own affairs, including the amelioration of their lands and slaves.[13]

Still, both factions agreed that the plantation constituted the basic unit of British colonization, whether in the Americas, Africa, or Asia. Of course, critics of slavery believed that a new kind of plantation should be replicated across the world under the aegis of the British Empire—a plantation cultivated by free laborers who produced goods for a free market. But abolitionists had yet to prove that their free-labor plantations could create the same dynamic plantation network as slave owners in the Americas had; failed free-labor agricultural experiments in West Africa, especially in Sierra Leone, seemed to indicate that expansive plantation networks could not be created without coerced labor. Only plantations that relied on slave labor could settle the land and civilize it, linking new plantations to established ones in order to create a profitable and ever-expanding network linked to the market. It was this dynamic, slave-driven plantation system that dovetailed with amelioration; the stagnant and often disastrous free-labor plantations never "improved" as abolitionists had predicted.[14]

In the nineteenth century, Gladstone sought to create his own plantation enterprise in Demerara. He bought several estates, switched them from coffee cultivation to sugar, and planned to rotate laborers, improve agricultural practices, and mitigate the brutality of West Indian slavery. His proslavery amelioration appeared to be a plan of expansion with an eye toward increased profits; it could be a model for colonization in the undeveloped Caribbean, particularly the Guyanas, Jamaica, and Trinidad. But a significant obstacle impeded the success of Gladstone's project. If the plantation was the basic unit of colonization in the marchlands of the British Empire, then it was also a household: the primary unit of governance in the early modern world. Yet Gladstone, as an absentee owner living outside of Liverpool, could hardly be called a patriarch of an extended plantation "family." Abolitionists' most powerful criticism of West Indian slavery was aimed directly at this point: only resident planters could fashion themselves as patriarchs of a domestic realm where slaves were ameliorated and organized into families. Abolitionists protested that Caribbean plantations were not domesticated—they were "foreign," barbaric, and licentious spaces where interracial sex and polygamy were commonplace. Gladstone attempted to mollify this criticism by inviting evangelical missionaries to preach to his bondsmen and by improving material conditions in the quarters. But that he was not physically present to manage or care for his bondsmen undermined Gladstone's ameliorative plans. His vision of an improved slave regime buoyed by a protectionist market was a legitimate and powerful one, but this vision was severely crippled by his inability to "domesticate" and improve his overseas plantations as a resident patriarch.[15]

THE PROBLEM OF PARLIAMENTARY AMELIORATION

In 1814, abolitionists began their push for the implementation of parliamentary amelioration laws in the West Indies. Believing that metropolitan legislation was the only way to effect reform in the sugar islands, abolitionists set about drafting ideas that would make planters more accountable for their bondsmen. The first step, many believed, was to find out how many slaves really lived in the West Indies. Without empirical data about the slave population, the debates between abolitionists and West Indians would inevitably result in a draw. Abolitionists, particularly William Wilberforce, James Stephen, and Thomas Buxton, knew that if they were going to charge West Indian planters with not caring for their slaves, resulting in neglect, disease, or even death, then the abolitionists would need to prove it.[16]

The opportunity arrived when the Anglo-French Treaty of Paris allowed France to reopen the slave trade for five years. This triggered a flood of petitions against the trade from all over Britain; within two months of its passage, 800 petitions containing 1.5 million signatures were received by Parliament.[17] Using the outcry over the reopening of the trade to fuel their antislavery agenda, abolitionists passed the Registration Act in 1815. As the first law passed under the new imperial policy of amelioration, the bill required all planters, managers, overseers, or attorneys to submit an annual register of plantation slaves to the Colonial Office. Owners were required to list the age, sex, name, and class of laborer for each slave. In theory, Wilberforce believed, his bill would make managers and planters more accountable for their slaves, curtail the illegal Caribbean slave trade, and ensure the physical comfort of bondsmen.[18]

But Wilberforce faced more than a measure of hostility from colonial planters, even if his bill was accepted in Parliament. Because the British Empire was a federal entity, he needed provincial legislatures to accept the laws and implement them in the islands. Absentee proprietor George Home wrote from Scotland in 1816 that the "Colonists still seem to continue in considerable agitation on the subject of Mr. Wilberforce's bill, tho for my own part I am willing to hope it may do some good." Home believed that the "Just Complaints against them, will make the resident Proprietors more attentive to Inforce every Collonial regulation for the advantage of the slaves, and make every Species of Cruelty or Misconduct, disputable."[19] Forcing colonial proprietors to embrace parliamentary legislation was clearly a hurdle for abolitionists. Indeed, the Registry Bill was soon regarded as a failed metropolitan attempt to exert control over colonists and regulate treatment of slaves. In Demerara alone, for instance, planters illegally imported eight thousand slaves from elsewhere in the Caribbean between 1808 and 1821.[20]

Soon after the Registry Bill was passed, however, it became apparent that the antislavery movement encompassed not just a moral argument but a political economic one as well. After the end of the war with France, discussion about slaves' oppression became entwined with a political economic understanding of slavery as an unpredictable and deficient labor system. Abolitionists asserted that if the slave regime had reached a stasis, it was no longer facilitating the expansion of the British Empire. All parties interested in the issue—parliamentary officials, planters, and abolitionists—focused on the critical question: could slave labor and protectionism be reformed or did they need to be replaced? The issue seemed particularly pressing in the wake of the Napoleonic Wars, when a victorious Britain expanded its commercial and territorial holdings in Asia, where peasant free labor predominated. The British Empire produced the same items for consumption under two different labor regimes.[21]

While abolitionists and West Indian planters agreed that the system of slave labor had to be reformed, they disagreed on exactly who would ameliorate the slaves and how those measures would be implemented. West Indians feared metropolitan interference in their private property. Leave the planters to the improvement of their own slaves, proprietors charged, and bondsmen would become more efficient, civilized workers. West Indians wanted Parliament to increase the bounty on West Indian sugar, arguing that better profits from that crop would allow them to spend more money on slaves' clothing, housing, and medical care. And some planters even endorsed the Christianizing of their slaves, but only if certified preachers from the established Anglican religion lived and worked on their estates.[22]

Abolitionists, on the other hand, did not want to let planters have their way. Humanitarians believed that slavery had tainted the planters' moral sensibilities; their addiction to luxury and profit rendered them unable to recognize the true "interest" of their own slaves. Corrupted by their own physical environments, abolitionists argued, planters needed a more objective body to regulate the treatment of slaves. Only Parliament had the power to deprive planters of the artificial and corrupting supply of slave labor. As abolitionist Thomas Clarkson wrote to Wilberforce, "if the owners of the slaves, and the Colonial legislatures are deaf to Reason, they must be compelled to obey it. They must be over awed by the Public voice." Indeed, abolitionists thought planters must be "compelled" to abolish corporal punishment, to allow slaves to go to church, and to improve the morals of both whites and blacks in colonial society. Yet there was a crucial difference between planters' and abolitionists' views of amelioration. Planters envisioned the "improvement" of laborers within an expansive and dynamic system of slavery. In other words, slavery would remain a dominant labor system in the British Empire while the working conditions and moral sensibilities of slaves continued to improve. Abolitionists, however, saw amelioration as the transition from slave labor to free labor, a temporary bridge whereupon religious convictions, individual self-interest, and loyalty to the Crown might be instilled in slaves, with freedom as the end result. These disparate conceptions of amelioration, and of labor systems within the empire, would come to a head in 1823.[23]

That year, British Antislavery Society president Thomas Fowell Buxton proposed a new bill for slaves' amelioration in Parliament. What mattered more than the content of Buxton's bill, at least initially, was how it was perceived. It was circulated in London and then copied and published in newspapers and pamphlets throughout England and the West Indies. The goals of Buxton's motion, which was supported by most Whig abolitionist MPs, were clear: promote Christianity and monogamous marriage among the enslaved, and reduce physical punishment.[24] Yet for those outside Whitehall, and especially for illiterate slaves in the Caribbean, agitation for amelioration appeared to be synonymous with agitation for emancipation.[25] With this in mind, the standing committee of the Society of West India Merchants and Planters resolved to head off the antislavery agitation with their own detailed plan of slave amelioration. This became the tactic only after "the [Tory] Govt did every thing in its power to prevent Buxton's Motion altogether: and that Mr. Canning in particular exerted all his personal influence with Mr. Wilberforce and others for that purpose."[26] Instead, George Canning, foreign secretary and a strong ally of many absentee planters including John Gladstone, took the ameliorative measures proposed by the West India committee and used them as the basis for the Tory government's own amelioration resolutions.[27] Canning's strategy was to appease abolitionists like Buxton and James Stephen while also seemingly accommodating the interests of the West India Committee. The strategy worked. Colonial secretary Henry Bathurst sent circulars to all Caribbean colonies detailing the new measures in May 1823. The resolutions stipulated that the whip be abolished as a "badge of authority," that flogging of female slaves be outlawed, that slaves be registered annually, that each plantation keep a record of slave punishments, that planters provide religious instruction for their bondsmen, and that slaves be allowed to give evidence in colonial courts.[28]

But there was a hitch. While West Indian supporters in London had approved the bill, no provincial legislature wanted to endorse the 1823 amelioration measures. The colonial assemblies were convinced of the "dangerous impressions and universal alarm excited in the Colonies by the measures." Although colonists declared that they too wanted to ameliorate the condition of slaves, this was a duty and matter "strictly within the provinces of Colonial legislatures, and concerning which they are respectively more competent to judge."[29] In fact, most of the West Indian islands did not ratify the amelioration measures until between 1827 and 1830.[30] For many colonial proprietors, including the agent on John Gladstone's Demerara estates, implementing the amelioration measures could mean a breakdown of order and authority on the plantation. Without the whip, necessary as a symbol of authority, anarchy would break out on sugar estates where blacks maintained a sizable majority. "The Negroes in general behave so well here that punishment is seldom necessary," Frederick Cort, Gladstone's plantation manager, wrote to Gladstone, "tho' the fear of it is essential to subordination."[31]

The 1823 measures exacerbated tensions among different factions. Colonial planters eyed their "transatlantic brethren" and purported metropolitan allies with suspicion. Imperial officials worried that West Indians no longer sustained unfailing loyalty to the Crown. Planters of all stripes condemned the work of evangelical missionaries, or "fanatics," among their slaves. Absentee proprietors feared that sugar production was becoming less productive and less efficient on their estates across the Atlantic. Essentially, planters, politicians, and merchants believed that the parliamentary measures would curtail sugar production and expansion in sparsely settled colonies, two things that seemed to contradict the goals of British colonization.[32] It was within this tangled web of issues that Gladstone found himself enmeshed in 1823.

THE WHIP AND THE BIBLE

John Gladstone believed in the gradual improvement of his bondsmen, his estates, and the system of slave labor. In fact, he was one of the first planters to sign a petition endorsing the new amelioration measures in 1823. Gladstone agreed with his friend William Huskisson that slavery was a "matter of portentous magnitude, and still more portentous difficulty." Only through "gradual amelioration, by moral and religious improvement, by humanity and kindness, by imperceptibly creating better domestic habits and feelings among the Slaves" could West Indian society be improved.[33] Gladstone encouraged his slaves to attend church at a missionary chapel located near his Demerara estates of Success and Vreeden Hoop. He tried to ensure that his laborers worked no longer than sunup to sundown, and that they were furnished with adequate food and water. He demanded that his slaves be clothed properly and that the estate's slave hospital dispense the appropriate medical care. These ameliorative measures, he reasoned, would result in increased production and profit. Yet Gladstone's ability to cast himself as the quintessential paterfamilias posed a problem. He was in Liverpool. Gladstone's slaves were in Demerara.[34]

Demerara, like most of the Caribbean, was another world. As one British explorer noted, "in spite of . . . the plague of Pestilence, the Sun, and the Wave . . . a Population of 100,000 people cover that Sea with merchantmen laden with produce, in a proportion absolutely unequalled, by any other portion of the known World." Such a place, many observers agreed, would easily become the "Giant of the Sugar Market."[35] Situated on the northern coast of South America just below Trinidad and Tobago, the colonies of Demerara, Essequibo, and Berbice (unified as British Guyana in 1831) were first captured by the British during the Napoleonic Wars. Although the colonies had been Dutch holdings since 1627, they came under British rule at a convention between Britain and the Netherlands in August 1815. The settlements comprised the newest and largest British holdings in the Caribbean and also seemed destined to become the next sugar-producing hegemons in the Atlantic. Sparsely settled, they had large slave populations; the slave to white ratio could sometimes be as high as thirty-four to one.[36]

Still, Demerara looked nothing like the jeweled islands of Barbados, Antigua, or St. Kitts. The coast was mud-clogged and the seawater thick with silt. A narrow dirt road traced parallel to the ocean, linking estates to the capital city of Georgetown. The estates themselves were long and narrow, cutting inland from the coast for hundreds of acres, though the boundaries of each were permeable and indistinct. Each estate was divided into areas for cultivating sugar, coffee, and plantains. Canals running through estates connected croplands with the Georgetown market. Slave boatmen ferried hogsheads through the canals to waiting ships, while others weeded the cane fields in gangs. Still others, called coopers, hefted big wooden paddles and stirred copper pots of boiling sugar cane juices. This was the picture of nearly every Demerara plantation, from sunup to sundown, except during the rainy season. This was also the picture of John Gladstone's estate Success.[37]

But the image of productivity at Success was permanently marred in

August 1823. Slaves in Demerara had become anxious that their masters and the colonial government were withholding a "free paper" handed down by the Crown. What these slaves did not know was that the so-called free paper was actually the amelioration measures passed in Parliament but not yet approved by the Court of Policy, the colonial governing body in Demerara. On Sunday, August 13, Jack Gladstone, a cooper on Success, met with several other slaves from neighboring plantations. Described as "handsome" and "well made" with a "European nose," the "Cooper Jack cannot only read the Bible, but Mr. Stewart [manager of Success] says he can give an account of many passages." Jack, his friends, and his father, Quamina Gladstone, began to plan an uprising. But Quamina wanted to seek the advice of the Methodist missionary who preached to most of the slaves on Success and in whose Bethel Chapel Quamina was a deacon. Sent by the London Missionary Society to bring the gospel to the slaves, John Smith had baptized fifty-one Success slaves and had a "large roomy chapel for receiving as many others" at Sunday services.[38] Smith, fearing violent retribution from the planters, begged Quamina, Jack, and their followers not to revolt.

On Monday night, even after a slave had revealed the plot and the colonial governor, John Murray, had proclaimed martial law, slaves seized and locked up white managers and overseers in the stocks. Rebels burned boiling houses and brandished firearms, demanding that whites grant them "their right." Although 13,000 of the estimated 74,000 Demerara slaves participated in the revolt, the actions of the slaves were mostly nonviolent. The slaves "possessed themselves of fire arms & other destructive weapons, with which they paraded about the Coast in considerable bodies, resisting even the military, but we hear of only 3 whites being killed."[39] As the *Edinburgh Review* later described it, the rebellion was actually a "*slight disturbance* . . . occasioned by the Negroes . . . far more resembling a combination of European workmen to strike for wages for time or other indulgence than a rebellion of African slaves." Indeed, in a colony of seventy thousand slaves, over ten thousand of whom were insurgents, only two or three whites were killed. Whites, however, retaliated quickly. Nearly three hundred slaves were killed by the colonial militia, and those who escaped were hunted down by Amerindian slave catchers and shot. Those who went to trial, including Jack Gladstone, were hanged, their heads posted on metal stakes leading into Georgetown as warnings to other slaves. John Smith was arrested for his alleged involvement in the revolt and for failing to report the insurrection. Smith died of pneumonia in prison and became a "martyr" with whom thousands of British evangelicals identified.[40]

The Demerara revolt brought several important questions to the fore: what exactly was happening on colonial plantations? Why had the slaves revolted? What had become of amelioration in the West Indies? Naturally, John Gladstone was particularly interested in these questions, since no fewer than nineteen of the Success slaves participated in the insurrection.[41] But he was most concerned with the condition of his estate. Frederick Cort reported that "the Sugar Works & the Cane cultivation were for awhile at the mercy of the Negroes, yet they abstained from fire and depredation." The insurgents "might have opened the sluices to the sea, & destroyed the cultivation by salt water," but this "was not their plan." Cort believed that "there is scarcely a feature in the whole history of this insurrection that does not mark in the strongest manner the regulating hand of some individuals possessing plans of conduct that do not belong to the Negro character." Cort, like Gladstone and other planters, believed that slaves were below—or beyond the pale of—moral judgment. Slaves could not be culpable for a mass, orchestrated revolt if they were primitive, childlike beings. Rather, Cort and many other Demerara whites believed that "some religious fanatics of our own Colour have been at the bottom of the whole business."[42] In other words, John Smith.

John Smith became a liability for John Gladstone. As a West Indian planter, an MP, and a member of the West India Committee, he could not be seen as an ally of evangelical missionaries who incited slave revolts. After the 1823 rebellion, Cort told Gladstone that many colonial planters held the impression that "you stood remarkable for favouring the Missionary System, and that by your influence & encouragement it had been greatly helped," and that the "idea formed of your substantial circumstances attributed to the Missionary doctrines."[43] Of course, Gladstone had allowed Smith to preach to his slaves, believing that instruction in Christian precepts would "improve" the morals and habits of his workers.

The Demerara rebellion, and the death of Smith, became a catalyst for the antislavery movement back in Britain. Tens of thousands of petitions flooded into Parliament, the most since the 1814 campaign. The untimely death of a Christian Englishman and the clearly nonviolent labor protests of thousands of enslaved Africans resounded among Britons. Viewing African insurgents as laborers deprived of their just rights and Smith as a Christian brother helped to "domesticate" the issue of slavery as it never

Joshua Bryant, *Execution of Rebels on the Parade Ground in Cummingsburgh*, 1824. After the
Demerara slave revolt of 1823, forty-five slaves were sentenced to death for inciting rebellion.
(Courtesy of the John Carter Brown Library, Brown University)

Jas. Bryant Del et Sculp

had been before. Smith's death and the peaceful aims of the revolt differentiated it from other violent and chaotic Caribbean revolts in the British imagination. Relinquishing this "otherness" helped Britons identify the Demerara slaves not as insurgent "foreigners" but as freedom-loving Christians like themselves.[44]

PLANTATION PRACTICE

The Demerara rebellion called into question Gladstone's humanitarianism and ameliorative plantation practices. In 1824, he discovered that the London Missionary Society (LMS) was planning to publish and circulate Smith's Demerara journal. In that diary, Smith detailed that the Success slaves had "complained of hard and late work" ever since Gladstone had converted the plantation from cotton to sugar cultivation. Smith "told one of the Overseers on Success he thought they would work the people to death." Before such passages could be published in the LMS journal, Gladstone wrote a desperate "refutation of these slanders" to the LMS treasurer to remove "this stain upon my name." Gladstone charged that the "labour required from my people has always been moderate, without any complaint on their part." And the number of slaves had been more than doubled from 130 to 330 workers when "cultivation was changed from Cotton to Sugar," though no additional land was added to the plantation. Still, as labor became increasingly specialized on plantations, work became more rigorous; amelioration intensified work, rather than lessened it. Gladstone insisted that "my instructions have ever been to treat my people with kindness and attention to their wants of every description, and to grant them every reasonable and practicable indulgence." He was certain that "these instructions have been strictly adhered to by my Attorney & Manager." But as an absentee, rather than resident, planter, this was difficult to prove.[45]

In 1828, Gladstone decided to send his son, Robertson, to visit his estates in Demerara and Jamaica. Gladstone directed his son "to make yourself intimately acquainted with our two Estates" on Success and Vreeden Hoop, "how their respective Gangs can be turned to the best account, without being overworked, the extension of the cultivation, the construction of the Gangs, the state of the people, their comforts & arrangements for their general health & care." Gladstone was essentially most concerned that Robertson determine the means of maximizing production and profit from his landholdings. "I think it is much safer to prefer Sugar cultivation to Coffee," he directed, "but with so large a Gang at both Estates, if labour can be spared without interfering with making the most of Sugar, the labour should be given to Coffee."[46] Gladstone understood that more slaves on each plantation did not necessarily mean a greater crop yield.

Yet if Gladstone understood the value and efficiency of labor, his attorney did not. "I complain that Mr. Cort has neglected that which it is his bounded duty to attend to," Robertson reported to his father, "and for which alone he held the attorneyship, namely the protection and interests of the Estate. . . . Matters have not been conducted as they ought." Robertson believed that Cort "lacks judgment materially, and is too jealous of interference that he never will cooperate with any one . . . unless he is allowed to manage the whole according to his own discretion." Because Cort had no real "interest" in the estates, he proved a poor proxy for Gladstone and could not be considered a patriarch of an extended plantation family.[47]

Robertson further warned that Cort's poor management skills impeded the productivity of Success and Vreeden Hoop. The plantations were adjacent, and yet Cort did not share slaves and crop provisions, nor did he diversify cultivation. "It is very unfortunate for your own properties here, that Mr. Cort should draw a line of demarcation between the interests of Vreeden Hoop, and those of Success," Robertson wrote.[48] Cort apparently thought that increasing the number of slaves on Success would "produce 800 hhds. Sugar; but it is utterly impossible." Putting four hundred slaves on two hundred acres of cane field did not mean more sugar. Rather, Robertson suggested, gangs of slaves should be rotated between Vreeden Hoop and Success to facilitate sugar and coffee cultivation and maximize production. This would "increase the crop to 950 or 1000 hhds. of Sugar annually, besides Coffee."[49]

But what upset Robertson most was not Cort's mismanagement of the lands so much as his apparent neglect of the slaves. "In looking over the Success Journal for the greater part of last year," Robertson wrote, "I observed that nearly three fourths of the deaths upon the Estate were brought on and occasioned by dysentery." When he questioned Cort, "the circumstance . . . had not impressed him before," and "he did not relish my investigating the matter." When Robertson examined the water the "Negroes were in the habit of using," he discovered "that it was very thickly impregnated with earthy and vegetable matter, which must render it anything but wholesome, and no doubt, neither more nor less, the causes of so many cases of dysentery."[50]

Robertson was observing the very problem that abolitionists and evangelical missionaries had pointed out—that the amelioration of slaves and increased plantation production could not be effected if owners resided in Britain. Managers like Cort had little interest in protecting slaves or implementing agricultural reforms. Only self-interested resident owners could be concerned humanitarians who husbanded "improvement" in West Indian slave societies. Absentees could not create the plantation households and domestic realms that abolitionists believed constituted the key to an ameliorated slave regime. They could not be patriarchs who governed their own white dependent family as well as other dependent slave families. As Max Edelson has noted, the "fundamental, legitimizing action for any male head of household was not to provide, to scrutinize, or to discipline, but to be present to do so." Gladstone was not present on his plantations and therefore could not be considered the patriarch of a plantation household and could not effectively initiate his slaves' amelioration. Still, Robertson maintained that amelioration was taking place on the plantations, in spite of Cort's neglect. "Every comfort is theirs," Robertson wrote in his journal, and "slavery is to them a name without a meaning." Contrary to what the "meddlers" who "know little of the Negro and West Indies who suppose the people to be a wretched race," the slaves, particularly on the Gladstone plantations, were "what others are not, happy!"[51]

It was clear that managers functioned as poor protectors of slaves. The Office of Protector of Slaves, established in Berbice, Demerara, Trinidad, and St. Lucia (as well as in the Cape of Good Hope and Mauritius) in 1824, allowed slaves to lodge complaints against abusive managers or those who did not comply with the ameliorative laws. The role of the Protector was to exert a "firm conviction among them [slaves] that their rights will be strenuously defended, and their just complaints promptly addressed," so that they would become "accustomed to look to the Law for security" against grievances and "value the relation in which they stood to the State." In other words, these officials, as agents of the British state, would become conspicuous defenders of slaves' "rights." This move essentially amounted to the abolitionists' vote of no confidence in planters. Since managers did not care for slaves' welfare, then these new officials would offer protection instead.[52]

VIEWING AMERICA

Robertson Gladstone's claim that the Demerara slaves were "happy" was far from convincing. Planters could charge that "fanatical" missionaries incited their slaves to rebel. They could attribute the lack of slave births to the polygamy and heathenism of Africans. But these defenses fared badly when abolitionists repeated an indisputable fact: ever since the abolition of the slave trade, the West Indian slave population had been decreasing in nearly every Caribbean colony. After abolition in 1807, it became possible to compare national systems of slavery in the Atlantic world, including those of America, Cuba, and Brazil.[53]

It was the leader of the antislavery cohort James Stephen who emphasized Caribbean slave demography, derived from Malthusian population theory, throughout the 1820s. Stephen reframed the question of slavery and moved beyond images of individual dominion; he began to think of slavery as a social system based on economic oppression. For him, the moral and spiritual evils of West Indian slavery were all derivative. The central and invariable reality was that slaves were malnourished, overworked, and continually punished for not producing enough. Stephen was one of the few abolitionists whose arguments pushed beyond moral reform on a national level. He, like John Gladstone, was interested in measuring socioeconomic progress in the colonies through the lens of plantation slavery. He sought to measure West Indian slave societies' deficiencies—stasis or regression of sugar production and birthrates—so that the numbers, rather than moral arguments, could serve as the basis for emancipation.[54]

And Stephen had proof. West Indian slaves were dying off at alarming rates. It is an "indisputable fact," he wrote, "that among the field negroes, or common working-slaves, on sugar plantations, there has always been, and still is, a lamentable loss of life, such as the reproductive power of nature does not fully repair." Stephen charged that between 1818 and 1824, "the loss amounted to 3 percent" per year.[55] Indeed, in an official report made to the president of the Board of Trade in 1824, it was reported that between 1817 and 1821, the total slave population in all West Indian colonies dropped from 730,212 to 711,962. The only colony where the slave population had increased was Barbados, from 77,493 to 78,345.[56] Stephen attributed the "depopulating cause" not just to the system of slavery but to slave-grown sugar in particular. If population decline "occurs only in the sugar colonies, where forced labour is admittedly most severe, and there proportionate to the degrees in which sugar is raised," then West Indian slavery on sugar estates was the main cause for the "decrease." The fatal environment of the West Indies could be attributed to the "one peculiar cause": sugar cultivation.[57]

Stephen arrived at this conclusion after comparing West Indian slavery to American slavery—the only self-regenerating slave system in the world.

In America, Stephen wrote, "the increase in the slave population is from 2 to 2½ per cent per annum" even though "slavery, in point of law, and in practice too, the article of labour excepted, is not less severe than in our own sugar colonies" and "the climate is certainly much less favourable to African constitutions."[58] Stephen and his fellow abolitionists were certainly critical of American slavery, particularly of the Fugitive Slave Laws, which they deemed immoral. But British abolitionists had to admit that American slaveholders appeared to be what West Indian planters were not: humanitarian masters. American slave owners seemed to have successfully ameliorated their slave labor force—to such an extent that it was expanding across vast swathes of land in the cotton belt.

Like many other West Indian planters, John Gladstone reviewed the comparison of American and West Indian slavery in earnest. In 1823, William Myers sent Gladstone an "account of the white & slave population of the U. States." Myers reported that in the American South—Virginia, North Carolina, South Carolina, Georgia, Alabama, Mississippi, Louisiana, Tennessee, Kentucky and Missouri—between 1790 and 1820, the slave population increased from 545,401 to 1,413,780.[59] Myers believed that these numbers were artificially buoyed by the "notorious" fact that "Slaves were smuggled into the Mississippi until the last three years when the Am. Govt. employed force to stop it." The illegal slave trade suggested that American slavery might not be the exceptional, self-regenerating system that it appeared. Myers also enclosed an "account of the No. of male & female slaves," which "seems to be material, the proportion being so equal." Myers meant that the relatively equal gender ratio of slaves in America allowed them to create families and reproduce their numbers; in the West Indies, where male slaves were often a majority, population was declining.[60]

Yet Gladstone agreed with Stephen that American slavery, and American slaveholders, constituted a "peculiar" system. "In that republican government, so jealous of freedom, and of the rights of its citizens," he wrote, "with a people every where advocating humane and liberal principles, individually watching over their privileges," and "to whom the distinctions of rank and subordination are almost invidious," the system of "slavery is found to exist on a far more extended scale than with us!" In America, the equality of white citizens was premised upon the ownership of property in slaves. But there was another crucial difference between American and West Indian slavery. American slaveholders "live in the same land, where they have constant opportunities of observation, and therefore become intimately acquainted with the character and habits of the negro, the nature of his gratifications, and his ruling passions." Because American slavehold-ers lived in close proximity to their slaves, they "acquiesce in the existing state of things, as necessary and unavoidable, whilst they know that the comforts and wants of the slaves are cared for and attended to."[61] Of course, Gladstone was admitting that American slaveholders had created planta-tion households that constituted white patriarchs and extended "families" of white and black dependents. Absenteeism in the British world drove a wedge between masters and slaves, preventing owners like Gladstone from creating households that could "domesticate" slaves.[62]

Even if slavery took on different forms in the West Indies and the Amer-ican South, Gladstone still believed that slavery was an important force im-pelling civilization in the marchlands of the British Empire. In his view, the sugar islands relied on Britain as their model of civility—though the West Indies had not yet attained the level of British polite and commercial soci-ety, the islands were moving in that direction. And because of the unique climate of the colonies and their particular cash crop, slavery was neces-sary to promote colonization, especially in new settlements like Demerara, Essequibo, Berbice, and Trinidad. If abolitionists succeeded in their goal of emancipation, then rapid expansion—the underlying genius of the British Empire—would be thwarted. Gladstone never advocated slavery in Brit-ain. But he did advocate slavery in a particular part of the world because he believed that owning slaves and producing slave-grown sugar was the only *possible* path to civilization in the West Indies. It seemed obvious to him, who noted that "nature has given to the negroes, as to the other inhabitants of the tropics, peculiar constitutions, and the power of labouring beneath a vertical sun." White Europeans, by contrast, were "incapable of such la-bour, and, when so exposed, eventually sink under it."[63] Abolitionists be-lieved that a free trade, free labor model was the only path to modernity in the West Indies. Gladstone disagreed, believing that it was an untested model that went against centuries of British imperial expansion and colo-nization made possible by slave labor.

In an argument that was made highly problematic by his absenteeism, Gladstone asserted that the relationship fostered between master and slave in the West Indies could not be replicated in labor relationships *outside* of slavery. In his mind, slavery cultivated an interest among whites to care for bondsmen. At the same time, it cultivated slaves' interest to work and serve masters. So beneficial was slavery to slaves, Gladstone wrote, that even manumitted bondsmen sometimes returned to their masters, "desiring to be replaced in their service, that they might again enjoy the advantage of having all their wants provided for." Owners were obligated to ensure that "labour is moderate" and that all the slaves' "wants, whether in infancy or old age, in health or in sickness, are duly provided for." And, for their own safety and happiness, masters kept slaves within the confines of the plantation and slavery. Without slavery, slaves would not feel obliged to work; the "negroes will not work in the field from choice" and would "pass their time in idleness and dissipation." But within the system, "it is the duty of slaves to work in the field," for such is their "disposition and sense of that duty, that the labour is cheerfully performed, without injury to their health or comforts." Locked into these bonds of obligation, slavery was "shorn of all its chief evils."[64]

But Gladstone's preoccupation with the positive impacts of slavery in the abstract allowed him to forget a few things. The British West Indian model of slavery was no simple master-slave relationship. He had admitted as much when he compared British absentees with American planters. Many planters lived in England; it was attorneys and managers who oversaw and took care of slaves on plantations. On Gladstone's own Demerara estates, Frederick Cort had been responsible for repairing slave houses, making sure slaves received medical care, providing them with food and water, and treating them well. Unfortunately, Cort had neglected hundreds of slaves without Gladstone's knowledge. Cort's presence, and especially his neglect, challenged Gladstone's idealistic formulation of "domesticated" slavery.[65]

But resident proprietors—abolitionists' conception of the ideal West Indian patriarch—were not always successful either. Throughout the period of Parliament-imposed amelioration legislation, abolitionists repeatedly praised planters who resided on their West Indian plantations and took care of their slaves. They found models in the figures of Joshua Steele of Barbados and Mathew "Monk" Lewis of Jamaica. Steele, an avid agricultural improver and patron of the arts, moved from Britain to his Kendal plantation in Barbados, where he abolished the whip and paid his slaves for their work. Thomas Clarkson lauded Steele's efforts: "He advanced above three hundred debased field negroes, who had never moved without the whip, to a state nearly resembling that of contented, honest, and industrious servants."[66] Monk Lewis, a successful playwright in London, traveled to Jamaica after inheriting his father's plantations there. Lewis began residing on his plantations for long stretches of time, believing that his presence helped "protect the slaves." While in Jamaica, he made "many alterations in the system which he considered indispensably necessary for the comfort of the slaves, diminishing their labour & affording them many other advantages."[67] Many planters, however, countered that the efforts of these humanitarians only resulted in declining crop production and disciplinary problems on estates. Humanitarian impulses did not necessarily translate into better conditions for slaves and increased productivity of estates, West Indians thought.

These reductive debates about who amounted to a better paternalist, however, overshadowed what was really at stake in the master-slave relationship. The British Empire was a diffuse federal system wherein state power was vested in agents, or planters, in far-flung jurisdictions. The state offered protection to its agents in return for their loyalty. The plantation, at least in theory, mirrored this relationship. Masters offered protection to dependents, their slaves, in return for slaves' loyalty and work. During the slavery debates, abolitionists essentially charged that planters were not holding up their end of the deal; they abused their slaves rather than caring for them. Such an unnatural and inimical relationship—which implied stasis or regression—did not serve the interests of the British state, which relied on planters to be agents of expansion. Amelioration was thus a strategy by which the master-slave relationship could be both "improved" and repaired. Rather than a source of wastefulness and caprice, the relationship between masters and slaves could be transformed into a source of social improvement and productivity. In turn, plantations would become more progressive and profitable units of production in the empire.[68]

FACING EAST

Comparisons with American slavery allowed West Indian planters to define what Caribbean slavery was, and exactly how it differed from the system on the North American mainland. But other comparisons loomed, this time within the empire's limits. Beginning in 1823, after Parliament passed the slave amelioration measures, abolitionists and free traders turned their attentions east toward India. As a result of the Napoleonic Wars, Britain had acquired new holdings in India, and attention was focused especially around the port cities of Bombay, Madras, and Calcutta. With the East India Company monopoly dissolved in 1813, free traders in Britain were eager to exploit the Indian markets. In fact, British exports to India quadrupled between 1814 and 1832. Sugar appeared as one of the only goods that could be exported from India back to England profitably. British tariff legislation had banned India's exports of cotton goods to England

and made the Indian market safe for Lancashire goods. And India could not compete with American supplies of raw cotton. Thus, many East India traders chose sugar, an article to which William Pitt had turned his attention as early as 1790 in an effort to capture the European sugar market from France.[69]

Sugar, many contemporaries suggested, could be grown just as easily in southern India as in the West Indies. And the crop could be grown with free, rather than slave, labor. Essentially, a larger, pan-imperial issue was emerging from the antislavery debate. On one side, West Indian planters who supported slave labor favored the economic system of protectionism. In opposition, abolitionists and humanitarians favored free labor and free-trade principles. The issue was a critical one. It pointed to a division of labor systems and trade policies between the Atlantic and Eastern portions of the British Empire. And it showed that the two groups maintained radically different visions of how the empire should expand and maintain its position in the world.[70]

Thomas Clarkson was among the first to indict the West Indies while also heaping praise on India. Other abolitionists who owned stock in East Indian sugar, including Zachary Macaulay and James Cropper, soon followed suit. Sugar produced in the East Indies, Clarkson wrote in 1823, was not "stained with blood" because it was produced by free Indian peasants. It was a less expensive imperial project because free labor was inherently cheaper and because no costly standing militia was required to protect planters from slave insurrections, as was the case in the West Indies. Indian and Mauritian sugar, Clarkson reasoned, would benefit "Natives" and Britons alike; it was a colonial system separate from the "evils" of slavery. The East India Company, he wrote, distributed "an equal system of law and justice to all without respect of persons." The company dispelled "the clouds of ignorance, superstition, idolatry, and carry with them civilization and liberty wherever they go." In contrast, West Indian planters only "study to perpetuate ignorance and barbarism." In Clarkson's formulation, the West Indies were deviant colonies in the empire, while India represented a new model of British colonization.[71]

Of course, what Clarkson and other abolitionists did not know was that the line between West Indian slavery and East Indian peasantry was a fine one. Although most East Indian sugar was cultivated by free peasants, their condition was scarcely better than the hundreds of thousands of slaves who existed in British India. Abolitionists, however, did not clearly comprehend (and did not care to) the subtle differences between African chattel slavery and the peculiar nature of Indian bondage. Only one kind of enslavement—the West Indian kind—appeared to be the direct responsibility of the British nation.[72]

The West India Committee tried to head off the humanitarians with their own propaganda campaign. Planters produced tracts that advocated the sanctity of private property, the civilizing influence of slavery, and the geopolitical importance of the West Indies. Planters believed that they were "essentially British Land Owners, and cultivate[d] articles which the soil of the Mother Country cannot produce."[73] Because planters were British, they were not the "Orientals" to be found in India, a place where superstition, idolatry, ignorance, and "Mohammedan" white female slavery predominated. The reform of West Indian slavery and even the improved manners and religious tendencies of slaves made the Caribbean seem like an altogether more palatable, more civilized outpost of the British Empire. Take away slave labor and equalize sugar duties, planters protested, and British civilization would be thrown into chaos: the West Indies lost, and the "British" proprietors totally ruined. Furthermore, if emancipation resulted in the loss of the Caribbean, the whole empire could topple.[74]

Perhaps the most heated and explicit arguments over the East Indies and Caribbean sugar islands took place between John Gladstone and James Cropper. In the winter of 1824, Gladstone, writing under the pseudonym "Mercator," and Cropper exchanged no fewer than eighteen incensed letters, all of which were published in the *Liverpool Mercury*. Cropper was a Quaker and Liverpool merchant, not unknown to Gladstone as a colleague; he traded chiefly in American cotton. After becoming involved in the African Institution and the Antislavery Society at the turn of the century, Cropper ceased his importation of American slave-grown cotton. But before Cropper could withdraw from the trade, Gladstone charged that cotton crops were "the fruits of Slave labour" about which "not a word was said" by Cropper, for "it would not have accorded with his interest." Cropper soon became an outspoken proponent of British investment in East Indian sugar. Free trade with the subcontinent, he argued, would bring about West Indian slave emancipation and end outdated protectionism. Gladstone, on the other hand, saw Cropper's aims as more than transparent. "He lustily calls upon us only to use East Indian Sugar," Gladstone wrote, "which he will supply us cheap and good (an abominable lie for the price is high, the quality bad and the quantity small)."[75] Gladstone dismissed Cropper's purported humanity, arguing that his nemesis's free trade principles were actually inhumane.

What Cropper and Gladstone debated in their letters in 1824 centered on which economic theory would best expand the territory and wealth of the British Empire. And their departure point was not Adam Smith but David Ricardo. In two separate tracts, published in 1815 and 1817 respectively, Ricardo, like Smith, opposed protectionism for national economies, especially agricultural ones. Ricardo suggested repealing the Corn Laws, asserting that lifting protective tariffs on corn would distribute wealth to the most productive members of British society. Free trade would encourage the proliferation of industrial capitalists who would invest capital in diverse holdings and keep money away from feudal landlords (with whom West Indian planters could be identified), who invested only in luxuries. Ricardo's theory of comparative advantage showed that all nations could benefit from free trade, even if a country was less efficient at producing some goods than its trading partners.[76] Of course, Cropper agreed with many of Ricardo's theories. Gladstone dismissed them outright.

Cropper believed that the British Empire was a vastly pliable entity. Its capacity for change and progress was not yet realized. Cropper was confident that with the abolition of slavery, incalculable benefits could be brought to everyone. Emancipation would allow Britain to fulfill its imperial destiny in the east as well as in the west with a missionary-like zeal. Freeing West Indian slaves would wipe out the old protectionist regime that had hobbled Britain with its economically stagnant principles. Monopolies within the empire would crumble, allowing Britons to trade from India to Trinidad without hindrance. And Britain could trade freely with other nations, namely America. Cropper thought that the East Indies possessed an unlimited capacity for sugar production, and that Britain had an unlimited capacity to consume it. Cropper's supreme faith in the market allowed him to rationalize that free trade and competition would improve conditions in the colonies.[77]

Gladstone, on the other hand, believed that because the empire had succeeded under the existing protectionist, slaveholding regime for centuries, there was no need to abolish it. Free labor and free trade would constitute something akin to revolution and necessitate entanglements with the market, which Gladstone believed to be unpredictable and even dangerous. Unlike Cropper, Gladstone shied away from the market, which he could not control, and emphasized labor, which he could. In a protectionist economy, a buffer existed between planters and the market. They were then free to concentrate on the organization and productivity of their labor force. In short, control of labor meant control of crop production, which, in turn, meant control of profit. This was why Gladstone was so keen for his son Robertson to determine how best to use the gangs of slaves at Success and Vreeden Hoop in 1828. Gladstone also sought to introduce agricultural improvements, including crop rotation. He wholeheartedly endorsed the improvement of labor and agriculture but only within the existing protectionist framework.

Gladstone's apparently more conservative vision of the British Empire lacked Cropper's idealistic formulations and missionary zeal. But it was a pragmatic, not a static, one. Gladstone believed in a limited demand for sugar. If prices were lowered, Britain would find that she had destroyed her only certain supply of sugar, causing untold suffering to planters and their slaves.[78] Removing the protective duty on sugar would "put to imminent hazard the lives of both the planters and their slaves, with the destruction of the mass of interests interwoven with, and supported by our colonial system."[79] While Cropper believed that emancipation was the key to future imperial progress, Gladstone saw emancipation as the revolution that would destroy it. If slaves were freed, the cultivation of the West Indies would be "abandoned" because "free negroes cannot be induced to work in the field for hire." In other words, he thought emancipation would dismantle the authoritative relationship that made slavery so successful; it would destroy the labor system and produce on which Britain's empire depended. So too, Gladstone thought, would emancipation compel slaves to "rise generally in insurrection against their masters," and the consequences would "make the minds of all well-disposed persons shudder."[80]

If the sugar islands were lost, the sugar crop gone to rot, and the freed slaves dissipated and idle, Gladstone was not sure that the East Indies could supply Britain's demand for sugar, or that free-grown sugar would actually be cheaper than its slave-grown counterpart. The "immense consumption of sugar in the United Kingdom," he wrote to Robert Peel, could not be satisfied by "that proportion of the supply which is drawn from the East Indies, including Mauritius" because it "does not exceed one tenth the part of the whole." Rather, Britain would look to buy cheap sugar from the "Slave Colonies in Cuba & the Brazils."[81] Importation of sugar from these nations would result in "the direct encouragement of foreign slavery."[82] What then, Gladstone asked, was the point of slave emancipation, the equalization of sugar duties with the East Indies, and free trade with other nations? Gladstone wondered why abolitionists clamored to emancipate West Indian slaves if those same free-trade proponents were only going to support the importation of non-British, slave-grown sugar. Conversely, Gladstone thought it would simply be wiser to reform the present colonial system in the West Indies. Take, for instance, the example of his Demerara estates. He bought newer, faster packet ships to bring his sugar to British markets. He divided and redivided his estates, experimenting with new types of coffee and sugar cane plants. Gladstone sought to ameliorate West Indian slavery: to persuade his slaves to work efficiently, to go to church, to marry and have children. This, Gladstone thought, was progress, and the path to expansion and civilization in the West Indies.

A NEW REGIME

Gladstone's vision of the British Empire soon faded despite his vociferous protests. On the heels of the Reform Bill of 1832, the Emancipation Bill was approved in Parliament on August 1, 1833. The bill made slaves apprentices for four years until granted their full freedom in 1838. Planters in the West Indies were compensated £20,000,000 for their lost property by the British government. Yet Gladstone never abandoned his investments in the West Indies. For his West Indian slaves, Gladstone received approximately £70,000 in government compensation money.[83] What Gladstone needed, however, was a labor force. He was to become one of the first West Indian planters who turned his attention away from the newly liberated slaves to "obtaining people from other parts of the World."[84] Even Robertson asked his father, "What law is there, to prevent any individual sending his ship to the coast of Africa, taking over eight or ten trustworthy negroes, and bringing back with their own consent a number of blacks to Demerara" to serve as indentured servants on the Gladstone estates?[85] In 1837, one of Gladstone's managers in Demerara reported that there was "every prospect of immigration" of new servants "from Barbados."[86] But Gladstone turned his attention east, to India. He believed that in South Asian "coolies," as they were derogatively termed, he had found his new plantation laborers. Although the African slave trade had been prohibited for decades, Gladstone began importing laborers from southern Asia to augment his labor force.

Gladstone's importation of laborers from South Asia became an explosive issue in 1838. Wanting to make himself independent of the "negro population," Gladstone imported more than four hundred laborers from India. Abolitionists who got wind of the scheme protested that this kind of importation of indentured labor looked too much like the African slave trade. Abolitionists dubbed the practice the "Gladstone slave-trade," and their research showed that their hyperbolic language was not inaccurate. They found evidence of coerced ship-boarding practices, inhumane conditions aboard the ships, and high mortality rates once the servants reached Demerara. The scandal forced the British government to put an end to the recruitment of South Asian indentured labor for Caribbean plantations.[87]

But whatever the ironies of Gladstone's turning to India to facilitate his own prospects in the Caribbean, he had comprehended a vision of amelioration that few metropolitan humanitarians could match in the early nineteenth century. In his view, freedom was not the necessary outcome of slavery. He thought that the system of slave labor could be improved, mitigated, and reformed. He understood slavery to be a mechanism that assured West Indian planters' wealth and progress. In Gladstone's imagination, with the imperial marchlands of Demerara or Jamaica set at the center of his world, freedom figured little, if at all. Instead, there was expansion and the amelioration that undergirded it. Coffee and sugar crops improved. The morals of whites and blacks improved. Gladstone's profits improved. All of it was gradual, not sudden, ruptured, or unnatural. Slave labor, and all its attendant moral, religious, and financial progress, was the framework through which Gladstone imagined his plantation, his world, and the British Empire.

Gladstone's proslavery amelioration represented a legitimate vision of the modern world, one shared by many conservative politicians, planters, and merchants in the nineteenth-century British Atlantic. Although antislavery amelioration, with its emphasis on an ever-broadening sphere of "rights," seemed like the only vision of modernity in the era, this was not the case. Abolitionists' parochial arguments hamstrung the movement for decades in the nineteenth century. Emancipation was not inevitable in the West Indies, and the planters' arguments for "improvement" often resembled abolitionists' own schemes. While it had become clear that slavery, at least in its most violent and inhumane forms, had become incompatible with progress in the 1830s, it was by no means clear that ameliorated slavery was antithetical to progress. Gladstone argued for the truth of the latter, believing that an age of radical social revolution and its attendant failures had left the door open to his calls for moderate change.[88]

CONCLUSION

AMELIORATION AND EMPIRE, CA. 1845

In the mid-nineteenth century, southern planters and British anti-slavery exponents were empire-builders. They sought to create plantation empires that satisfied global demand for agricultural goods like sugar, cotton, coffee, spices, and tea. Their efforts to settle and colonize new lands in North America, the Caribbean, Africa, and South Asia were rooted in seemingly disparate imperial ideologies—an "empire of slavery" built with the labor of enslaved men and women or an "empire of liberty" constructed from the labor of free peasants. But the concept of amelioration undergirded both of these seemingly contrasting visions of colonization. For Anglo-American colonizers, amelioration was the process by which labor—whether free or enslaved—"improved" new territories and facilitated progress in provincial societies. In addition, amelioration was also the means by which labor itself was made more productive and "happy." The "improved" moral and physical condition of workers would then increase the rate and success of new settlements. As one southerner put it, "labor had been so directed" as to not only "allow a gradual and marked amelioration" of laborers but also "to convert hundreds of thousands of square miles of the wilderness into cultivated lands covered with prosperous people."[1]

Anglo-American colonization efforts rested on the amelioration of the laborer as the means to facilitate territorial expansion, thus "improving" frontier areas and including them under the aegis of the British Empire or the American federal union. In the British context, abolitionists, free traders, and imperial officials envisioned a plantation empire that would be created with free, if exploited, labor in the newer colonies of the "East." The colonies in the Caribbean, they reasoned, would be transformed into more productive spaces as a result of the transition to free labor. For these leaders, antislavery amelioration was the process by which free laborers on the margins became "improved" British subjects and new territories became civilized outposts of the empire. Even if violence and war characterized initial colonization efforts, these empire-builders reasoned that the protection and influence of British institutions—trade, manners, and government—would eventually ameliorate nonwhite "free" laborers while also improving the land that they worked. As historian David Brion Davis has noted, "the nation that called on the world for the universal emancipation of slaves was also the nineteenth century's archetype of progress and civilization."[2]

In the American context, southern slave owners and politicians prophesied that a slaveholding empire would eventually cover the entire North American continent and possibly the Caribbean. During the 1800s, antebellum southerners used slavery to settle and develop western lands that they colonized and eventually integrated into the federal union. For them, successful colonization efforts—particularly in light of territorial gains made as a result of wars with Mexico and southeastern Indian tribes—could only be realized through the use of slave labor. Southerners acknowledged that colonization, at least in its earliest stage, was a bloody and destructive process, especially for slaves and Indians. The presence of slave labor, however, would guarantee that new settlements could be "improved" and civilized by white property holders, they argued. And as whites settled and prospered in these new territories, slaves' condition would also be ameliorated, southerners predicted.[3]

By the 1840s, it appeared possible to measure the success of Anglo-American colonization efforts. Through the use of censuses and statistics, contemporary observers could quantify the so-called improvement of laborers as well as the progress of the lands they had settled. Not surprisingly, the most conspicuous example was a comparison of American slave society and the postemancipation British West Indies. In the nineteenth century, the criterion for modernity—and by implication, civilization—was self-reproducing populations and increasing economic output. In the United States, the slave population increased, despite the abolition of the transatlantic slave trade, from 654,121 in 1790 to 2,481,390 in 1840. Moreover, slave-grown cotton production increased exponentially in the 1820s and 1830s. But in the West Indies, the slave population declined 14 percent, from 775,000 to 665,000, between 1807 and provisional slave emancipation in 1834. The economic report was no better. By the time full freedom was granted to slaves in 1838, West Indian sugar production had declined significantly. Based on these statistics, it appeared that American slave society had embraced modernity and "improvement" as it expanded its territories and cotton production. But in the West Indies, amelioration seemed to have failed, with the economy declining and the population contracting.[4]

The argument over the state of colonization efforts and the societies they produced in the American South and British Caribbean was manifested in a heated debate between the British abolitionist Thomas Clarkson and the South Carolina slave owner and politician James Henry Hammond between 1840 and 1845. Clarkson, who had been a tireless campaigner for the end of the slave trade in the 1780s and 1790s, continued to be one of the most prominent opponents of slavery in the world in the nineteenth century. Hammond, on the other hand, was a shrewd South Carolina planter who owned hundreds of slaves; it was his business acumen that catapulted him to political office as a member of Congress, governor, and later U.S. senator in the antebellum years. Central to their dispute was the question whether slave or free labor better encouraged amelioration and expansion in plantation societies. The two men questioned whether the "condition" of laborers had been "improved" and whether, as a result, expansion and civilization were being realized. Both embraced stadial theory and agreed that amelioration was the process by which societies progressed from barbarism to enlightenment, but they differed over which labor system compelled progress through these stages of development.[5]

Clarkson seemingly enjoyed the advantage in the contest, especially after the abolition of slavery in 1838 established the liberal and progressive character of the British Empire. But Clarkson's treatise proved surprisingly weak, relying on biblical passages to stake out his moral superiority and deploying blatantly false statistics for the British West Indies that could not disguise the disappointing results of emancipation. In contrast, Hammond offered a more sophisticated approach to the "problem" of slavery in the modern world that outlined a moderate program for its progressive "improvement," albeit with tragic consequences. He understood that his argument for amelioration within the institution challenged Clarkson's faith in the prospects for amelioration outside of the system. Hammond astutely noted that Clarkson's greatest fear was that slavery might be capable of becoming an improvable, modernizing system, thus making calls for abolition unnecessary. Hammond declared that Clarkson was "exceedingly anxious for the immediate abolition" of slavery lest planters "mitigate its evils so as to destroy the force of your argument and facts." Indeed, if "improvement . . . has gone on steadily" in the American South, then Clarkson's calls for emancipation were moot.[6]

According to Hammond, American planters were overwhelmingly successful in ameliorating slavery and, consequently, in making the system modern. Slave owners used local knowledge and exploited the incredible power they garnered in the diffuse federal system of the antebellum United States. These "patriarchs" deployed this knowledge and power to deal with the "problem" of slavery in localized improvement plans that began on individual plantations but would ultimately encompass the entire South. Improving the material conditions of slaves and relinquishing the more violent features of the "peculiar institution" had tangible effects. Planters succeeded in ameliorating their slave system by creating "humane masters" and "happy" slaves, but this purported improvement in the master-slave relationship was not an end in itself, as studies of paternalism have suggested. Rather, the improved treatment of slaves and planters' newfound humanitarianism resulted in the expansion of territories, a rise in economic output, and a naturally self-reproducing slave labor population—all of which defined modernity in the nineteenth-century world, planters argued. While populations soared, especially in the burgeoning southwestern slave states, cotton production also doubled between 1826 and 1837. When the condition of laborers was "improved," then labor became more productive and efficient, and southern society garnered more wealth and progress, southerners rationalized.[7]

By 1834, when the British provisional emancipation bill was passed in Parliament, abolitionists had apparently succeeded in proving that West Indian planters' localized ameliorative efforts had failed—slave populations were declining and sugar production was in a tailspin. Abolitionists implemented their version of amelioration in the Caribbean, which entailed a gradual transition to freedom. The emancipation bill stipulated that West Indian slaves had to serve their masters as "apprentices" for another four to six years before achieving full freedom, in order to avoid rebellions and the destruction of property. By the 1840s, however, it appeared that abolitionists had also failed to implement a successful amelioration project in the postemancipation West Indies. By the end of the apprenticeship period in 1838, sugar production had fallen by 9 percent; by 1846, the output of sugar estates had declined 35 percent. Metropolitan abolitionists had used top-down imperial governance to find a radical solution to the problem of slavery in the West Indies: the transition to free labor. But the results were far from promising. A decline in sugar production and the size of the labor force, coupled with the coerced importation of Asian "coolie" labor, demonstrated that abolitionists had fallen short on amelioration, much as the West Indian planters had before them.[8]

Clarkson's main goal was to show that the condition of former slaves in the British sugar islands had much improved since emancipation. Through liberation, he argued, former slaves were "becoming useful members of society" as productive workers and members of "families." For him, the "change in the civil and moral conditions of the laborers, is . . . the most wonderful . . . of all the effects produced by the abolition of slavery." Freedmen became more productive workers in the cane fields; their incentive to work was wages rather than the lash. And liberated from work in the fields, female laborers established and kept households, while their children received education in new schools. Moreover, former slaves were attending religious services on Sundays and thousands of marriages were being "solemnized as a religious ceremony, in places of religious worship." Essentially, Clarkson argued that emancipation had enabled former slaves to establish households and form families—the development of domestic society that had previously been inhibited by the brutal slave regime. Sentimental ties and familial attachments were the necessary prerequisite for amelioration, he believed.[9]

Masters, on the other hand, were also being "improved" because, Clarkson decreed, "he sees under him a contented, industrious and happy people," which reinforced his own "happiness." There was a "better understanding between the master and the overseer, and his laborers," and the "harshness and contempt which formerly characterized their intercourse, are gradually subsiding." For Clarkson, slavery was a premodern system whose artificial perpetuation—through economic protectionism and whites' moral bankruptcy—had inhibited the amelioration of whites and blacks in the West Indies. Removing such an artifice, which had fomented "the very cruel inequality observable in the lots of men," as well as the "arbitrary rule" of masters over dependents, would restore order to society. There was "no law to restrain" a master, Clarkson wrote, from "doing as he pleases" and inflicting punishment on a "poor slave" with "the whip, the chain, the dungeon, the iron collar with its frightful spikes, or any instrument of torture that he may think proper even to invent." Thus, the abolition of slavery replaced the "arbitrary will" and wanton cruelty of masters with the rule of law and the "protection" of the crown.[10]

Once he had established that both masters and former slaves were improving as a result of emancipation, Clarkson attempted to show that the West Indian sugar enterprise was also progressing and expanding. The liberation of "eight hundred thousand persons, men, women, and children" had "stood the trial of two years and a half" and could thus be "held forth as an example." Each account from "that quarter of the world" indicated that West Indian society was "an improving one" with respect to the "good morals, industry, sobriety, and good behaviour of the newly emancipated slaves," as well as the "thriving and prosperous condition of the planters." Yet it was hard for Clarkson to make a convincing case for socioeconomic progress in the British West Indies given that the population was shrinking and production on sugar estates was in steep decline.[11]

Clarkson paid little attention to particulars or statistics because he believed that his view of antislavery amelioration was sanctioned by both God and the market. Adhering to the Enlightenment notion that slavery was incompatible with human progress, Clarkson's belief that modernization could only follow a transition to free labor and free trade remained unmoved despite the unfavorable reports of conditions in the sugar islands. His faith in the market allowed him to rationalize that "ONE EN-FRANCHISED NEGRO DOES THE WORK OF TWO SLAVES," that "profits are absolutely greater" than before 1838, and that the sugar "estates are rising in value" throughout the West Indies. Even if none of these things were true when Clarkson penned his letter in 1840, he trusted that all of them would be "realized in time" by the new free labor economy.[12] To him, the new system of free labor and free trade was "natural," while slavery was artificial and "archaic." But in reality, Clarkson's British West Indies seemed entirely unnatural. This was clear not only from the islands' economic stagnation and declining population, but also because of the importation of coerced Asian laborers in the 1840s and 1850s. The notion that abolitionists' emancipation plan had only resulted in shrinking populations, declining profits, and the forced migration of peoples demonstrated to American planters that the British West Indies were not modern at all. These artificial creations of British imperial policy were miserable and unproductive places.[13]

Clarkson continued to turn a deaf ear to reports of socioeconomic disaster in the postemancipation Caribbean not only because he thought freedom and, by implication, free labor made society more modern, but also because it dovetailed with new imperial policy. The transition from the so-called first British Empire, whose character was Atlantic, colonial, and commercial, to a "second" empire that was largely centered in Asia and imposed direct rule on thousands of nonwhite "subjects," had real implications for amelioration in the West Indies. In the 1800s, imperial governance became more bureaucratic, with the Colonial Office exerting top-down imperial control over colonies, which were given less and less autonomy within the British world. Antislavery amelioration—and the centralized, imperial policies that it spawned—was yet another way of asserting imperial oversight. The decision to ameliorate the empire would be made by civilized metropolitans who knew best how to reform uncivilized or regressive provincial societies.[14] Although Clarkson attempted to demonstrate that the conditions of laborers and plantation society had been ameliorated as a result of Parliament's emancipation bill, southerners dismissed the freedom "experiment" in the sugar islands as a socioeconomic disaster.[15]

Like Clarkson, Hammond's primary goal was to establish the improving condition of laborers in the American South. Most of Hammond's evidence was buttressed by demographic statistics. Citing the increasing population of slaves, Hammond charged that the "fact of their [slaves'] equal comparative increase and longevity," even after being "settled to our richest and least healthy lands," demonstrated slave owners' "leniency and providence of our management of them." In other words, owing to slaveholders' purportedly ameliorative plantation management schemes, slaves' numbers were fast increasing. Slaves' improvement, Hammond asserted, could also be linked to the fact that they had formed familial "connexions." There "are more families among our slaves," Hammond pronounced, "than have flourished in the same space of time and among the same number of civilized people in modern times." Slaves were also well-schooled in religious instruction; their adherence to church teachings improved their moral condition, he wrote. Hammond perversely decreed that such evidence demonstrated that, in the "absence of pain" and inculcated with Christian principles, "our slaves are the happiest three millions of human beings on whom the sun shines." By comparison, the white "poor and laboring classes" in Britain were "more miserable and degraded, morally and physically, than our slaves."[16]

Slaveholders' moral and physical conditions were also improved through the ownership of bondsmen, Hammond asserted. They understood the "obligations" to "treat humanely the fellow creatures whom God has trusted to my charge." This purported benevolence resulted in "kind masters" who were also "kind husbands, parents, and friends." But treating slaves "with proper kindness" was also, Hammond confessed, a necessity to "our deriving the greatest profit from them." "Bad masters," on the other hand, were men who "overworks his slaves, provides illy for them, or treats them with undue severity," thus inhibiting their own moral progress and minimizing the material gains that might be wrought from treating slaves well. Ameliorated slaves meant increased profits for planters—whether through their sale on the auction block or as a result of their efficient production of plantation staples. Treatment of slaves became a way to gauge whites' progress: their moral development as well as their ability to accumulate wealth. Indeed, the increased productivity of slave labor during the antebellum period—measured by the "ruling trinomial" of "bales to acre per hand"—demonstrated to Hammond and other slave owners the modernity of an exceptional American slave regime.[17]

Clarkson had suggested that the proliferation of domestic households in the postemancipation period had opened the door to socioeconomic progress in the West Indies. But Hammond asserted that the plantation household in the South—which contained both white *and* black families—was the social unit that allowed for the expansion of southern society. The key to Hammond's plan to "improve" slave society was also the result of amelioration: domesticity. Although an overwhelming majority of southerners continued to view slaves as a separate "people," they simultaneously viewed them as domesticated servants included within their households. Slaves were included in plantation "families" just as slavery was deeply embedded in the American nation. This "patriarchal domestic scheme" based on familial ties eluded British West Indian society, where slaves were still viewed as "foreign" Africans, and most planters were not proximate patriarchs but absentees living in Britain. Hammond claimed that the American slave system had created sympathetic "bonds" among millions of "human beings now peacefully and happily linked into our social system." According to him, "in this cold, calculating, ambitious world of ours, there are few ties more heartfelt, or of more benign influence than those which mutually bind the master and the slave." Masters' own feelings of sympathy—sentiments cultivated in the domestic sphere—were necessary for them to recognize slaves' suffering and wants, and then mitigate them. Hammond saw his plantations as sites of "domestication," not just by fathering mixed-race children by his enslaved women but also because his "Slaves of course live in families." Eschewing the division of families through the domestic slave trade, Hammond used his amelioration plans—including better housing, adequate food and clothing, sanitary drinking water, and regulated work hours—as a means to create a domesticated plantation household, the "cornerstone" of republican government in America.[18]

Hammond believed that the amelioration of slaves in the South enabled the colonization of new lands and the creation of new states in the federal union. Slavery, he noted, "is rapidly filling up our country with a hardy and healthy race, peculiarly adapted to our climate and conditions, and conferring signal political and social advantages on us as a people." Although "in the abstract" Hammond agreed with Clarkson's teleology of history—that liberty and free trade assured progress—he noted that the "exception" of the American slave system undercut this Enlightenment universalism. Hammond was "not an advocate of slavery in the abstract," and he also believed that, "as a general rule, free labor is cheaper than slave labor." But given the "increase" of a self-reproducing slave population and the fact that the United States contained too few inhabitants and too much land to transition to free labor, Hammond concluded that the presence of an ameliorated slave regime was necessary and legitimate in the American context. Since there was no "single moral truth universally acknowledged," he decreed, then it seemed possible to claim that the "domestic Slavery of these States" was "not only an inexorable necessity for the present, but a moral and humane institution, productive of the greatest political and social advantages."[19]

COLONIZATION AND "IMPROVEMENT"

Southerners' belief that an ameliorated slave regime ensured the survival of the federal union as well as its expansion was a powerful argument for the modernity of southern slavery in the antebellum period. Thus, proslavery amelioration undergirded the creation of new slaveholding states in the West as well as the "improvement" and progress of established states on the Atlantic coast. Slaves' "condition"—which whites interpreted as improving over time—was inextricably linked to the progressive condition of the union. Slaveholding also ensured that corporate equality would be preserved in the South: the equality of the slaveholding states in the union and the equality of white property owners. Planters in new western states sought to extend the cotton empire; their success in this endeavor, and their equality with other, established cotton states, depended on the existence of slavery. And the democratization of slave ownership allowed whites to improve themselves—through the accumulation of private wealth and influence—and embrace equality with other slave owners. As historian Walter Johnson has noted, "privilege"—which many slave owners conflated with "liberty"—"was defined by slaveholding even more than by race."[20]

In the western territories, slavery played a crucial role in the process of colonization. After wars incited by the United States against the Cherokee,

Choctaw, and Chickasaw nations resulted in their forced removal west of the Mississippi, politicians and planters finally had the "terra nullius" that they had imagined. Millions of acres of these newly "empty" lands were sold to profit-seeking speculators and settlers whose new investments were backed by British capital. Usually it was the slaves of these landowners who "settled" these new lands—they cut down forests, drained swamps, and created fields for cultivation. This "civilization" of the western landscape was a brutal task, but the forced migration of enslaved laborers through the domestic slave trade—nearly one million men, women, and children were sold to buyers in the Deep South—assured that new planters' insatiable demand for slave labor was never wanting. In Alabama, for example, the slave population increased more than fivefold from 47,449 in 1820 to 253,532 in 1840. Slaves were separated from their families and transported in coffles or aboard schooners from the Upper South to the Mississippi River Valley in order to pick cotton. This commodity became the mainstay of the antebellum South, and two-thirds of slave-grown cotton was shipped to Britain. "King Cotton" thus ultimately fueled Britain's industrialization, particularly textile production in bourgeoning Midlands cities. But slaves were not simply valued for their labor. In many cases, the slaves themselves were prized commodities; they were collateral in the boom-and-bust credit economy of the cotton empire.[21]

Slavery facilitated the expansion of the southern "empire" not only on the western frontier but also on the Atlantic coast. Urban slavery contributed to the rise of manufacturing in southern cities like Richmond. As with Britain and the northern states, the antebellum South experienced incredible urban growth. Moreover, southern slavery facilitated the development of the South's railroad and telegraph system in the antebellum era. By the 1840s and 1850s, southerners no longer believed that slavery was confined to an agricultural society—they began to envision a proto-industrial future predicated on slave labor. Of course, antislavery commentators rarely discussed the new industrial slavery that emerged in the southeastern states, where slaves laid railroad ties, worked in tobacco warehouses, labored in ironworks factories, or dug canals and built roads. This kind of slavery too closely resembled the wage labor and factory work of the urban North and Britain. Confining slavery to the plantation and agrarian life made slavery seem less modern, but the reality was that the "peculiar institution" was adapting to changing economic conditions in the South while also driving one of the world's leading economies in the antebellum period.[22]

Planters like Hammond proclaimed that the "increase" of the federal union—in territory and economic growth—was directly related to the increase of American slaves. And the self-reproduction of the enslaved population was, southern commentators agreed, a result of planters' ameliorative efforts. But so-called improvements in the material conditions of American slaves also masked a terrible truth: that brutality against bondsmen was both corporal and psychological. As Alexis de Tocqueville noted in his tour of antebellum America, slave owners had "spiritualized despotism and violence." He noted that, "in antiquity, one sought to prevent the slave from breaking his irons," while "in our day, one has undertaken to remove his desire for it."[23] The domestic slave trade and the unconscionable separation of slave families were the most horrific reminders of the psychological tortures exacted by the supposedly ameliorated slave regime. The purported "success" of southerners' amelioration project ultimately had devastating consequences: it legitimized the horrors committed against millions of African American men, women, and children. The scale of terror that southern slavery produced, through sexual and physical violence, the pain of families' separation on the auction block, and the denial of basic rights and personhood, were deeply embedded in southerners' proslavery amelioration but also rendered invisible by it. Because slave owners were able to use ameliorative schemes to contain and conceal slaves' suffering, masters made the ludicrous claim that their slaves were "happy."[24]

As much as proslavery amelioration came to exemplify southern civilization and expansionist aspirations, so too did antislavery amelioration exemplify British civilization and empire during the long nineteenth century. Isolated studies of the British Empire in the nineteenth century—confined to the Caribbean, Africa, and Asia—have obfuscated the reality that an entire empire was shaped and legitimized by abolitionism. Indeed, Britain's declaration of the illegality of the international slave trade in 1807 and the abolition of slavery in its imperial dominions in 1838 helped to define the British Empire as a liberal entity; its rule over its colonies, particularly in the case of India, was "cast as benign and progressive tutelage" by so-called British defenders of liberty. The "liberalism" of the nineteenth-century British Empire was thus forged in the crucible of abolition. As the antislavery imperialist Thomas Babington Macaulay wrote in 1835, Britons "have become the greatest and most highly civilised people that ever the world saw, have spread their dominion over every quarter of the globe," and "have been the acknowledged leaders of the human race in the career of political improvement."[25]

An empire without slaves, while seemingly laudable in humanitarian terms, proved problematic on a number of levels, particularly in Africa and the Caribbean. The vast plantation empire founded on free labor that abolitionists imagined in Africa and the West Indies was radical in a world where large-scale agricultural production was overwhelmingly executed by unfree laborers. Using emancipation as the departure point, the abolitionists invoked the creed of liberty when embarking on social experiments in imperial outposts. But rather than proving a humanitarian triumph, as abolitionists so confidently assumed would be the case, amelioration outside of the system of slavery was often plagued with social problems.[26]

In West Africa, abolitionists sought to effect "improvement" of Africans in the absence of the slave trade, and to replace the illegitimate "human traffic" with legitimate commerce. An expedition into the African interior on the Niger River, supported by the prominent parliamentary abolitionist Thomas Fowell Buxton, resulted in the death of most of the members of the expedition from malarial fevers. Those who did not perish used coerced labor to establish a short-lived experimental farm on the banks of the Niger. In the colony of Sierra Leone, considered a haven for former slaves, high mortality rates and atrocities abounded. The annual death rate of 160 per thousand in Sierra Leone exceeded that of any West Indian sugar island. Many of those settlers who did not die turned to the still-robust African slave trade as a means of economic survival. Thus, abolitionists' aims to "civilize" Africans outside of the confines of the slave trade met with poor results.[27]

Abolitionists' amelioration projects did not fare much better in the West Indies themselves after 1838. Population rates did not rise sufficiently on most sugar islands. Economic decline was apparent in the 1830s, and by the time of the repeal of the Corn Laws in 1846, West Indian planters were on the brink of total ruin. On the smaller islands, particularly Antigua, Barbados, and St. Kitts, the sugar industry survived in large part because sugar cultivation monopolized arable land, making alternative employment impossible. But on the larger, unsettled colonies of Trinidad, Jamaica, and Demerara, former slaves established their own communities and refused to work on sugar estates. This precipitated a labor shortage for planters in colonies that were already feeling the strain of competition with the sugar-producing slave regimes of Cuba and Brazil. The British government allowed planters in those colonies to import indentured laborers from East Asia and India, known as "coolies." The continued forced migration of "coolie" labor to the West Indies achieved a stunning result: more coerced laborers entered the West Indies after abolition than had before it.[28]

The new free-labor societies created after British emancipation seemed both artificial and regressive in the eyes of modernizing southerners. In order to deploy their project of amelioration in the British West Indies, abolitionists and imperial officials relied upon the incredible exertion of centralized power to effect emancipation and "unnatural" social experiments. But this use of state power in the implementation of radical social change often failed to result in substantial improvements for the colonies' white inhabitants or former slaves. The socioeconomic problems that continued to plague the British West Indies meant that abolitionists and government officials instead shifted their attention to an exception in the empire, the profitable free-labor experiment of British India.[29]

The amelioration projects of the nineteenth century are a reminder that there was not a single path toward modernity in the Anglo-American Atlantic world. Today, many believe that abolitionism and the liberal principles of the American Revolution—movements that introduced the radical idea of universal equality and liberty—opened up a singular path to modernity that is being most fully realized today in the form of global human rights. From a modern-day perspective, slavery was the primary obstacle to the realization of equal rights in the revolutionary age. But the emergence of antislavery and proslavery amelioration during the age of revolutions demonstrated that liberty and slavery actually shared the same genesis. Between the 1770s and the 1840s, it was plausible for contemporaries to argue that slavery could be "improved" toward its end, or, alternatively, that slavery could be ameliorated in order to strengthen and perpetuate the institution. In the nineteenth century, the British "empire of liberty" and the American "empire of slavery" were both sanctioned and legitimized by their supposed amelioration of enslaved African Americans and other nonwhite subjects and the "improvement" of undeveloped territories. British efforts to achieve amelioration on the margins through the use of free labor were often socioeconomic failures. But in the American South, planters' efforts at amelioration through the use of slave labor were more successful in economic terms; slave-grown cotton exports made the South one of the leading economies in the nineteenth century. Still, it is important to remember that, while slave owners were convinced that amelioration actually made slave labor more efficient and profitable, no amount of modernization or accumulation of wealth in the South could disguise the underlying fact that slavery was a moral "stain" in America, then and now.

NOTES

INTRODUCTION

1. Thomas Clarkson, *History of the Rise, Progress, and Accomplishment of the Abolition of the Slave Trade by the British Parliament,* 2 vols. (London: R. Taylor and Company, 1808).

2. On Clarkson's abolition map, see Dierksheide, "'Capable of Improvement'"; Wood, *Blind Memory,* 1–13; and Brown, *Moral Capital,* 1–8.

3. Morgan, "Ending the Slave Trade," 110.

4. Although she employs the term "gradualism" rather than "amelioration," Hannah Spahn offers the most sophisticated reading of slave owners' progressive vision for the gradual end to slavery: "It was essential to Jefferson's progressive thought . . . that he expected future generations to abolish slavery, because they would be . . . more morally refined than his own." *Thomas Jefferson, Time, and History,* 8–16, 9 (quotation).

5. Since I argue that "amelioration" lay at the heart of proslavery and antislavery ideas, I use the two terms "proslavery amelioration"—improvement toward slavery's perpetuation—and "antislavery amelioration"—improvement toward slavery's abolition—throughout this book.

On the other hand, Christopher Brown has argued for three distinct categories under the broader rubric of the antislavery campaign: "antislavery thought," "abolitionism," and the actual act of abolition or emancipation. Since this study is more focused on ideas than political action, however, I find "proslavery" and "antislavery" to be more useful, inclusive terms here. *Moral Capital,* 17–18.

6. See the definitions for "meliorate," "melioration," "ameliorate," and "amelioration" in *Oxford English Dictionary,* 2nd ed., 20 vols. (Oxford: Oxford University Press, 1989). In the later 1700s, "amelioration" was most commonly linked to the improvement of land. In 1767, Arthur Young advised farmers "to sow oats after a fallow of some ameliorating crop" in *The Farmer's Letters,* 112. But by the turn of the century, "amelioration" was more frequently linked to an improvement of the human condition. Thomas Macaulay noted in 1849 that "in every human being there is a wish to ameliorate his own condition." *The History of England, from the Accession of James II,* 5 vols. (London: J. M. Dent, 1907), 1:217.

7. Samuel Johnson, *A Dictionary of the English Language* (London: W. Strahan, 1773), s.v. "improvement"; Davis, *Slavery and Human Progress,* 132–33 (quotation); Spahn, *Thomas Jefferson, Time, and History,* 95–100; and *Encyclopedia Britannica,* 12:794–98.

8. Morgan, "Ending the Slave Trade," 121; Higman, "Slavery and the Development of Demographic Theory."

9. Davis, *The Problem of Slavery in the Age of Revolution,* 407–10; Davis, "The Emergence of Immediatism in British and American Antislavery Thought."

10. Relatively few historians have granted thorough attention to Malachy Postlethwayt's writings. See Brown, *Moral Capital,* 269–75; Miller, *Defining the Common Good,* 163–69; Gould, *Barbaric Traffic,* 21–24; Curtin, *The Image of Africa,* 70; and Drayton, *Nature's Government,* 63.

11. Postlethwayt, *The African Trade;* Postlethwayt, *The Importance of Effectually Supporting the Royal African Company of England.*

12. Quoted in Hochschild, *Bury the Chains,* 154–55.

13. Postlethwayt, *Universal Dictionary,* 1:24.

14. Drescher, *The Mighty Experiment,* 9–18; Onuf and Onuf, *Nations, Markets, and War,* 212–18; Smith, *Wealth of Nations,* 2:159, 432.

15. Burke, "A Letter to the Right Hon. Henry Dundas."

16. Ramsay, *An Essay on the Treatment and Conversion of African Slaves,* 31, 236.

17. Equiano, *The Interesting Narrative,* 211.

18. Gustavus Vassa (Olaudah Equiano), late commissary for the African settlement, to the Right Honorable Lord Hawkesbury, March 13, 1788, Equiano, *The Interesting Narrative,* 333–34.

19. See Gould, *Among the Powers of the Earth.*

20. Onuf, *Jefferson's Empire,* chap. 5; Hendrickson, *Peace Pact;* Nash, "Franklin and Slavery"; Nash, "Slaves and Slaveowners in Colonial Philadelphia"; Benjamin Franklin to John Waring, January 3, 1758, Van Horne, ed., *Religious Philanthropy and Colonial Slavery,* 124; Van Horne, "Collective Benevolence and the Common Good in Franklin's Philanthropy."

21. John Jay to Benjamin Rush, March 24, 1785; Jay to John Murray Jr., October 18, 1805; Jay to Egbert Benson, September 18, 1780, all in John Jay Papers.

22. Rush, "An Address to the Inhabitants of the British Settlements in America upon Slave-keeping."

23. Onuf, "Every Generation Is an 'Independent Nation.'"

24. Thomas Jefferson, "Jefferson's Notes from Condorcet on Slavery," Jefferson, *Papers,* 14:494–98; Condorcet, *Réflexions sur l'esclavage des nègres,* 26–33, 34 (quotation). See also the discussion of Condorcet and slavery in Ghatchem, *The Old Regime and the Haitian Revolution,* 224–25.

25. Fuente, "Slaves and the Creation of Legal Rights in Cuba"; Porteus, *The Civilization, Improvement, and Conversion of the Negro-Slaves,* 72.

26. Antillón, *Dissertacion sobre,* 34–61, 49 (quotation).

27. White, *Bosquejo del comercio de esclavos,* 173–84.

28. On this topic, see Berquist, "Early Anti-Slavery Sentiment."

29. "Immediatist" impulses, which included rashness, violence, and radical immediatism, came to be associated with despotic Old World regimes, while a "gradualist mentality" of future-oriented prudence characterized more enlightened thinkers. Spahn, *Thomas Jefferson, Time, and History,* 220; Brougham, *A Concise Statement Regarding the Abolition of the Slave Trade,* 60.

30. Both proslavery and antislavery forces used "amelioration" to claim that their views stemmed from the Enlightenment, thus legitimizing each strain of thought. As Hannah Spahn notes, "Within the usual paradoxes of the Enlightenment, it is also possible to claim that . . . slavery was the foundation of Enlightenment culture." *Thomas Jefferson, Time, and History,* 8n27.

31. Brown, "Empire without America," 84–100, 93 (quotation); Edelson, *Plantation Enterprise,* 267.

32. For the shift in American planters' views from the revolutionary period to the antebellum era, see Dierksheide and Onuf, "Slave-holding Nation, Slaveholding Civilization."

33. The best discussion of the amelioration of slavery is in Davis, *The Problem of Slavery in the Age of Revolution,* 412–20.

34. Condorcet and Tinsdale, *Outlines of a Historical View,* Tenth Epoch, "Future Progress of Mankind."

35. Davis, *Slavery and Human Progress,* 154–68; Davis, *The Problem of Slavery in Western Culture,* chap. 13.

36. On the "radicalism" of the French and Haitian revolutions, see Dubois, *Avengers of the*

New World; Nesbitt, *Universal Emancipation*; Popkin, "The French Revolution's Other Island"; and Hunt, "The French Revolution in Global Context."

37. Onuf, "Federalism, Democracy, and Liberty"; Harris, "Civil Society in Post-Revolutionary America"; Rozbicki, *Culture and Liberty in the Age of the American Revolution*, 172–76.

38. Morgan, *American Slavery, American Freedom*, 4–6, 369, 381.

39. Davis, *Slavery and Human Progress*, 195.

40. Jordan, *White over Black*, 368.

41. Rose, "The Domestication of Domestic Slavery"; Young, *Domesticating Slavery*, 123–60.

42. I use "patriarch" and "patriarchy" in this book to connote the early modern ideal of the hierarchical, extended family. Onuf, "Domesticating the Captive Nation"; McKeon, *The Secret History of Domesticity*, 14; Littlefield, *Rice and Slaves*, 62–63; Shammas, *A History of Household Government in America*, 34.

43. Drescher, *The Mighty Experiment*, 3, 6 (quotation), 34–53.

44. For a discussion of the voluminous antislavery debate, see Bender, ed., *The Antislavery Debate*; Holt, *The Problem of Freedom*; Davis, *Inhuman Bondage*, 231–49; and Brown, *Moral Capital*, 3–22.

45. Notable exceptions include O'Brien, *Conjectures of Order*; Rugemer, *The Problem of Emancipation*; and Mason, "A World Safe for Modernity."

46. Davis, *Slavery and Human Progress*, 159.

47. Mattes, *Citizens of a Common Intellectual Homeland*; Palmer, *The Age of Democratic Revolution*; Rozbicki, *Culture and Liberty in the Age of the American Revolution*.

48. Morgan, *Slave Counterpoint*, 258–61, 284–96; Walsh, "Plantation Management in the Chesapeake"; Stanton, "Thomas Jefferson: Planter and Farmer"; Roberts, *Slavery and the Enlightenment*.

49. Ward, *British West Indian Slavery*; Turner, "Planter Profits and Slave Rewards."

50. Fox-Genovese, *Within the Plantation Household*; Shammas, "Anglo-American Household Government."

51. Onuf, "Domesticating the Captive Nation"; Rose, "The Domestication of Domestic Slavery."

52. Edelson, *Plantation Enterprise*, 4; Tomlins, *Freedom Bound*, 1–17.

53. Newman, *A New World of Labor*, 219.

54. Walter Johnson emphasizes whites' brutality toward slaves in the "Cotton Kingdom"; this continued brutality was made possible by the high profit margins and fertile soil in these frontier areas. *River of Dark Dreams*, esp. 244–79.

55. Lipset, *The First New Nation*; Onuf and Onuf, *Nations, Markets and War*, 162–66, 225–39, 263–64.

56. Onuf, "Nations, Revolutions, and the End of History"; Gellner, *Nations and Nationalism*, 5–7.

57. Dierksheide and Onuf, "Slave-holding Nation, Slaveholding Civilization."

58. Johnson, "The Pedestal and the Veil"; Rugemer, *The Problem of Emancipation*, 17–41; Dierksheide, "Missionaries, Evangelical Identity."

59. Greene, *Peripheries and Center*; Onuf and Onuf, *Federal Union, Modern World*; Van Cleve, *A Slaveholders' Union*.

60. Watts, *The West Indies*, 219–23, 393–95; Jack P. Greene, "Colonial South Carolina and the Caribbean Connection," *South Carolina Historical Magazine* 88 (1987): 192–210.

61. Davis, *The Problem of Slavery in the Age of Revolution*, 326–29.

62. Emphasizing "resonance," Dror Wahrman seeks not to uncover "intellectual genealogies" but rather "patterns of broad cultural resonance." Similarly, I treat the planters in this book as representatives of distinct cultures rather than as figures in a teleological genealogy. Wahrman, *The Making of the Modern Self*, 292, xv.

63. Davis, *Slavery and Human Progress*, 154–68, 259–79; Dierksheide and Onuf, "Slave-holding Nation, Slaveholding Civilization."

1. "THE GREAT IMPROVEMENT AND CIVILIZATION OF THAT RACE"

1. Thomas Jefferson (hereafter TJ) to John Dickinson, March 6, 1801, Jefferson, *Writings*, 1084–85.

2. On the "captive nation" and "state of war," see Onuf, *Jefferson's Empire*, 147–88; TJ, *Notes on the State of Virginia*, Query XVIII, Jefferson, *Writings*, 288–89.

3. TJ to William Burwell, January 28, 1805, Jefferson Papers, Library of Congress (hereafter DLC); Gould, *Among the Powers of the Earth*; Van Cleve, *A Slaveholders' Union*; Dierksheide, "'The Great Improvement and Civilization of That Race.'"

4. Patrick Henry, Speech to the Virginia House of Burgesses, January 18, 1773, Granville Sharp Papers, reel 1.

5. Fairfax, "Plan for Liberating the Negroes."

6. Tucker, *A Dissertation on Slavery*, 7.

7. Taylor, *Arator*, 74.

8. Sadosky et al., eds., *Old World, New World*, 1–13; Hendrickson, *Peace Pact*; Onuf and Onuf, *Federal Union, Modern World*, 108–13.

9. TJ to John Adams, September 4, 1823, Jefferson Papers, DLC; TJ to James Monroe, June 11, 1823, Jefferson, *The Writings of Thomas Jefferson*, ed. Lipscomb and Bergh, 15:435–39. On Jefferson's attitude toward the international system, see Onuf and Onuf, *Nations, Markets, and War*, 247–77.

10. Onuf, "American Exceptionalism and National Identity"; Onuf, "Domesticating the Captive Nation"; TJ, *Notes on the State of Virginia*, Query VIII, Jefferson, *Writings*, 214.

11. Davis, *Slavery and Human Progress*; Onuf, "Domesticating the Captive Nation"; Onuf, "Every Generation Is an 'Independent Nation.'"

12. Onuf, "American Exceptionalism and National Identity"; Onuf, *Jefferson's Empire*, 153–57.

13. TJ, *Summary View of the Rights of British America* (1774), Jefferson, *Writings*, 106–7. On the eagerness with which Virginia colonists purchased slaves, see Coombs, "The Phases of Conversion," and Horn, "Transformations of Virginia."

14. Quoted in Shore, *Southern Capitalists*, 4–5.

15. TJ, *Summary View of the Rights of British America*, Jefferson, *Writings*, 106.

16. TJ, Declaration of Independence (rough draft), ibid., 22.

17. Quoted in Pybus, *Epic Journeys*, 8–9.

18. TJ to William Gordon, July 16, 1788, Jefferson, *Papers*, 13:362–65; Pybus, "Jefferson's Faulty Math."

19. Furstenberg, "Beyond Freedom and Slavery"; Taylor, *The Internal Enemy*, 441–42.

20. TJ, *Notes on the State of Virginia*, Query XVIII, Jefferson, *Writings*, 288–89.

21. Ibid.; Taylor, *The Internal Enemy*, 6, 43–46; Holly Brewer, "Entailing Aristocracy in Colo-

nial Virginia: 'Ancient Feudal Restraints' and Revolutionary Reform," *William and Mary Quarterly*, 3rd. ser., 54 (April 1997): 307–46.

22. TJ, *Notes on the State of Virginia*, Query VIII, Jefferson, *Writings*, 214. Matthew Mason argues that "most Northerners trusted that slavery would effortlessly disappear once they abolished the slave trade and hoped it would keep to itself in the meantime." *Slavery and Politics in the Early American Republic*, 9–28, 28 (quotation).

23. On Locke's classic definition, see John Locke, *Two Treatises of Government*, ed. Peter Laslett, rev. ed. (Cambridge: Cambridge University Press, 1963), Second Treatise, chap. 4 ("Of slavery"), 324–26; Onuf, *Jefferson's Empire*, 149; TJ, *Notes on the State of Virginia*, Query XIV, Jefferson, *Writings*, 264–65, 270.

24. TJ marginalia, quoted in Sowerby, comp., *Catalogue of the Library of Thomas Jefferson*, 2:11–12; Helo and Onuf, "Jefferson, Morality, and the Problem of Slavery."

25. Konig, "Antislavery in Jefferson's Virginia"; Onuf, "Domesticating the Captive Nation."

26. TJ to Edward Bancroft, January 26, 1788, Jefferson, *Papers*, 14:492.

27. TJ to Edward Coles, August 25, 1814, Jefferson, *Writings*, 1344–46.

28. Onuf, "Domesticating the Captive Nation."

29. Van Cleve, *A Slaveholder's Union*; TJ, *Summary View of the Rights of British America*, Jefferson, *Writings*, 115–16.

30. Dierksheide and Onuf, "Slave-holding Nation, Slaveholding Civilization."

31. TJ, "Sixth Annual Message," December 2, 1806, Jefferson, *The Writings of Thomas Jefferson*, ed. Ford, 7:492.

32. TJ, *Notes on the State of Virginia*, Query VIII, Jefferson, *Writings*, 211–12; Onuf, *Jefferson's Empire*, 156–69. The best study of Jefferson's relationship with Sally Hemings—and of the reality of interracial relationships in Jefferson's Virginia—is Gordon-Reed, *The Hemingses of Monticello*.

33. TJ, *Notes on the State of Virginia*, Query XIV, Jefferson, *Writings*, 264, 270.

34. Jefferson, *Summary View of the Rights of British America*, ibid., 106.

35. TJ, First Inaugural Address, March 4, 1801, Jefferson, *Papers*, 33:145; TJ, *Notes on the State of Virginia*, Query XIX, Jefferson, *Writings*, 290–91; Peter S. Onuf, "The Empire of Liberty: Land of the Free and Home of the Slave," unpublished paper, 2013.

36. Onuf, "Every Generation Is an 'Independent Nation.'"

37. TJ, *Notes on the State of Virginia*, Query XIV, Jefferson, *Writings*, 264.

38. TJ to John Lynch, January 21, 1811, ibid., 1239–41.

39. TJ to James Monroe, November 24, 1801, ibid., 1096–99.

40. Quoted in Morgan, *Slave Counterpoint*, 667. My understanding of the Prosser Conspiracy is indebted to Sidbury, *Ploughshares into Swords*.

41. Mosby Sheppard to James Monroe, August 30, 1800, Virginia Senate, *Journal*, 26. Pharaoh and Tom were emancipated as a result of their demonstration of loyalty; they also adopted the name "Sheppard." Household, 1794–1812, 39, Account Book, Box 668, Mosby Sheppard Papers.

42. James Monroe to TJ, September 15, 1800, Monroe, *The Writings of James Monroe*, 3:208–9.

43. Box 115 ("persons obnoxious"), Executive Papers; *Acts Passed at the General Assembly of the Commonwealth . . . Begun and Held . . . on Monday the 1st Day of December 1800* (Richmond: M. Jones, 1801), 19–39. Other than deportation of insurgent slaves, the provisions of these laws included the creation of a guard to protect public property in Richmond, the provision of arms to town militias in time of emergency, prohibition of slaves hiring themselves out, requirements

that free blacks register with local court clerks in resident localities, and the authorization of slave testimony against free blacks in criminal trials.

44. TJ to James Monroe, November 24, 1801, Jefferson, *Writings*, 1096–99.

45. TJ to Rufus King, July 13, 1802, Jefferson Papers, DLC.

46. Rufus King to Henry Thornton, April 30, 1803, ibid.

47. Rufus King to William Wilberforce, January 8, 1803, ibid.

48. For more on the importance of Africa to Anglo-Americans, see Dierksheide, "'Capable of Improvement'"; Stern, "'Rescuing the Age from a Charge of Ignorance.'"

49. Onuf, *Jefferson's Empire*, 178–82.

50. TJ to Jared Sparks, February 4, 1824, Jefferson, *Writings*, 1484–87.

51. Ibid.

52. TJ, First Inaugural Address, March 4, 1801, ibid., 492–96.

53. U.S. Census, 1790, 1800; McCoy, *Last of the Fathers*, 269.

54. TJ to Edward Coles, August 25, 1814, Jefferson, *Writings*, 1345–46.

55. *Annals of Congress*, 42 vols. (Washington: Gales and Seaton, 1834–56), 5th Cong., 2nd sess., 8:1306–10; Rothman, *Slave Country*, 22–27, 213.

56. Hughes, *Thirty Years a Slave*, 11.

57. Giese, *Tobacco Cultivation in Virginia*, 3–7, 75–121; Herndon, "A History of Tobacco in Virginia."

58. TJ to Albert Gallatin, December 26, 1820, Jefferson, *Writings*, 1447–50.

59. TJ to Charles Pinckney, September 30, 1820, Jefferson Papers, DLC.

60. The idea of diffusion—of linking population, welfare, and a fixed geographic space—owes much to Thomas Malthus, whose work Jefferson labeled "one of the ablest I have ever seen." See TJ to Joseph Priestley, January 29, 1804, Jefferson, *Writings*, 1141–42; TJ to Jean Baptiste Say, February 1, 1804, ibid., 1143–44.

61. TJ to Albert Gallatin, December 26, 1820, ibid., 1447–50.

62. Lafayette obtained books on the slave trade and slavery from Granville Sharp through John Adams, American minister in London. Kennedy, *Lafayette and Slavery*; Gottschalk, *Lafayette between the American and French Revolutions*.

63. TJ to Lafayette, December 26, 1820; Lafayette to TJ, July 1, 1821; Lafayette to TJ, June 1, 1822, all in Jefferson and Lafayette, *Letters*, 402, 407, 409.

64. Spencer Roane to James Monroe, February 16, 1820, Roane, "Letters of Spencer Roane," 174–75.

65. TJ to Albert Gallatin, December 26, 1820, Jefferson, *Writings*, 1447–50.

66. TJ to James Monroe, November 24, 1801, ibid., 1097.

67. TJ, *Notes on the State of Virginia*, Query XIX, ibid., 290–91; TJ to Jean Baptiste Say, February 4, 1801, ibid., 1143–44.

68. TJ, *Notes on the State of Virginia*, Query XIX, ibid., 290–91; TJ, "Rough Notes of a Journey through Champagne, Burgundy, Beaujolois," March 3, 1787, Jefferson, *Papers*, 11:464; Lewis, "The Problem of Slavery in Southern Discourse."

69. The "improvement" project on Jefferson's plantations is deftly discussed in Stanton, "Thomas Jefferson: Planter and Farmer," and "Perfecting Slavery: Rational Plantation Management at Monticello," 71–89, in *"Those Who Labor."*

70. Lewis, "'The Blessings of Domestic Society'"; Lewis, *The Pursuit of Happiness*; TJ to Angelica Schuyler Church, November 27, 1793, Jefferson, *Writings*, 1013.

71. Taylor, *The Internal Enemy*, 17–19; Kulikoff, *Tobacco and Slaves*, 131, 141–53; Newman, *A New World of Labor*, 217–19.

72. TJ, *Notes on the State of Virginia*, Query XX, Jefferson, *Writings*, 293.

73. Jefferson, *Thomas Jefferson's Farm Book*, 258; TJ to Alexander Donald, August 29, 1790, Jefferson Papers, DLC.

74. TJ to George Washington, 28 June 1793, Jefferson, *Papers*, 26:396–97.

75. As a general rule, West Indian planters imported nearly all of their goods from the North American colonies before the revolution. On islands where nearly every square acre was devoted to sugar, coffee, or indigo, there was room for little else. Consequently, planters imported livestock, lumber, corn, wheat, and salted cod to feed their slave laborers. For a contemporary account, see Edwards, *Thoughts on the Late Proceedings*.

76. TJ to Francis Willis, July 15, 1796, Jefferson, *Papers*, 29:153.

77. TJ to John Harvie, July 25, 1790, ibid., 17:210; TJ to Jonathan Williams, July 3, 1796, ibid., 29:140; Stanton, "Thomas Jefferson: Planter and Farmer," 260; TJ to Joel Yancey, January 17, 1819, Jefferson, *Thomas Jefferson's Farm Book*, 43.

78. McCoy, *The Elusive Republic*, 230; Stanton, "Thomas Jefferson: Planter and Farmer," 265–66.

79. TJ to James Lyle, July 10, 1795, Jefferson, *Papers*, 28:405; TJ to James Maury, June 16, 1815, Jefferson, *Thomas Jefferson's Farm Book*, 490. See also Stanton, *"Those Who Labor,"* 71–89.

80. TJ to Charles Willson Peale, April 17, 1813, Jefferson, *Papers*, 6:69; TJ to Thomas Mann Randolph, April 19, 1792, ibid., 23:435–36.

81. TJ to Thomas Mann Randolph, February 18, 1793, Jefferson Papers, DLC; James Oldham to TJ, November 26, 1804, Jefferson Papers, Massachusetts Historical Society.

82. TJ to James Dinsmore, December 1, 1802, Jefferson Papers, University of Virginia; TJ to Thomas Mann Randolph, January 23, 1801, Jefferson, *Papers*, 32:499–500, Stanton, *"Those Who Labor,"* 71–89.

83. Thomas Mann Randolph and Martha Jefferson Randolph to TJ, January 31, 1801, Jefferson, *Papers*, 32:526–28.

84. Thomas Mann Randolph to TJ, June 3, 1797, Jefferson, *Papers*, 30:385–86. On George Granger Sr.'s tenure as the only African American overseer at Monticello, see Stanton, *"Those Who Labor,"* 120–23.

85. Neiman, "The Lost World of Monticello."

86. TJ to John Wayles Eppes, June 30, 1820, Jefferson Papers, University of Virginia.

87. Jefferson, *Jefferson's Memorandum Books*, 1:263.

88. Ibid., 1:758; TJ to William Fitzhugh, July 21, 1790, Jefferson, *Papers*, 17:241–43.

89. Jefferson, *Jefferson's Memorandum Books*, 2:968, 1265.

90. TJ, *Notes on the State of Virginia*, Query XVIII, Jefferson, *Writings*, 288; Thomas Mann Randolph to TJ, March 5, 1802, Jefferson Papers, Massachusetts Historical Society.

91. TJ to Thomas Mann Randolph, June 8, 1803, Jefferson Papers, DLC; Thomas Mann Randolph to TJ, May 30, 1803, ibid.

92. On the enslaved families of Monticello, see Stanton, *"Those Who Labor,"* 105–211. On the Hemingses in particular, see Gordon-Reed, *The Hemingses of Monticello*.

93. Onuf, *Jefferson's Empire*, 149; TJ to John Dickinson, March 6, 1801, Jefferson, *Writings*, 1084–85; TJ to John Holmes, April 22, 1820, ibid., 1434; TJ to William Short, September 8, 1823, Jefferson, *The Writings of Thomas Jefferson*, ed. Lipscomb and Bergh, 16:469.

94. Davis, *Slavery and Human Progress*; U.S. Census, 1790, 1830; TJ to James Heaton, May 20, 1826, Jefferson, *Writings*, 1516.

2. "THE DESIDERATUM IS TO DIMINISH THE BLACKS AND INCREASE THE WHITES"

1. Thomas Jefferson to William Ludlow, September 6, 1824, Jefferson, *Writings*, 1496–97.

2. Dew, *Review of the Debate in the Virginia Legislature*, 5. On Cocke and slavery, see Taylor, *The Internal Enemy*, 63–64.

3. On John Hartwell Cocke's colonization schemes, see Coyner, "John Hartwell Cocke of Bremo," and Gudmestad, *A Troublesome Commerce*, 118–22. On Thomas Dew and the "positive good" proslavery thesis, see Genovese, *The Slaveholders' Dilemma*, and O'Brien, *Conjectures of Order*, 2:941–47.

Although I am not labeling Dew "antislavery," his vision of a free, proto-industrial Virginia was the true aim of his supposedly proslavery theory. On this more sophisticated reading of Dew, see Ford, *Deliver Us from Evil*, 378–82, 389.

4. *Richmond Constitutional Whig*, September 3, 1831.

5. French, *The Rebellious Slave*; Aptheker, *Nat Turner's Slave Rebellion*; Greenberg, *Nat Turner*.

6. Jesse Burton Harrison to Richard Randolph Gurley, October 13, 1832, American Colonization Society Papers.

7. Oakes, "'Whom Have I Oppressed.'"

8. For previous studies of the Virginia slave debates that have focused on the rift between antislavery and proslavery ideas, see Freehling, *Drift toward Dissolution*; Robert, *The Road from Monticello*; Shade, *Democratizing the Old Dominion*; Wolf, *Race and Liberty in the New Nation*, 235–36; O'Brien, *Conjectures of Order*, 2:798–816; and Freehling, *Road to Disunion*, 178–96.

9. Hughes, *Thirty Years a Slave*, 11.

10. In 1830, there were 47,348 free persons of color and 469,757 slaves in Virginia. By comparison, in 1820, there were 36,889 free blacks and 425,153 slaves. U.S. Census, 1820, 1830.

11. Brodnax, *The Speech of William H. Brodnax*, 26–35.

12. Huston, "Theory's Failure"; McCoy, *The Elusive Republic*, 185–93; Spengler, "Population Doctrine US-I"; Spengler, "Population Doctrine US-II"; Spengler, "Population Theory in the Antebellum South"; Gibson, *Americans versus Malthus*.

13. Jane Hollins Randolph to Sarah E. Nicholas, 1831, Edgehill-Randolph Papers.

14. Thomas Jefferson Randolph to Jane Hollins Randolph, January 29, 1832, ibid.

15. Cornelia Jefferson Randolph to Ellen Wayles Randolph, August 28, 1831, Ellen Wayles Randolph Coolidge Papers.

16. Onuf, *Jefferson's Empire*, 147–88.

17. Mary Jefferson Randolph to Ellen Wayles Randolph Coolidge, September 25, 1831, Ellen Wayles Randolph Coolidge Papers.

18. Martha Jefferson Randolph to Joseph Coolidge, October 27, 1831, ibid.

19. Thomas Jefferson Randolph to Jane Hollins Randolph, January 29, 1832, Edgehill-Randolph Papers.

20. The petitions are analyzed in Wolf, *Race and Liberty in the New Nation*, 242–47

21. Edward Coles to Thomas Jefferson Randolph, December 29, 1831, Coles and Jefferson, "Letters of Edward Coles to Thomas Jefferson," 105.

22. Randolph, *The Speech of Thomas J. Randolph*.

23. Brodnax, *The Speech of William H. Brodnax.*

24. Berry, *The Speech of Henry Berry*; Faulkner, *The Speech of Charles Faulkner.*

25. Rugemer, *The Problem of Emancipation*, 3.

26. Virginia House of Delegates, *Journal*, 109–10.

27. Wolf, *Race and Liberty in the New Nation*, 232–33.

28. An excellent study of the transition from tobacco to wheat in Virginia can be found in Neiman, "The Lost World of Monticello."

29. Martha Jefferson Randolph to Joseph Coolidge, October 27, 1831, Ellen Wayles Randolph Coolidge Papers.

30. Most of the congregants in Cocke's slave chapel were women; enslaved men felt that adherence to white evangelical Christianity undermined their masculinity. See Irons, *The Origins of Proslavery Christianity*, 161.

31. John Hartwell Cocke, "Negroes Not Chattel," n.d., Cocke Family Papers.

32. John Hartwell Cocke to Joseph C. Cabell, January 31, 1832, Joseph C. Cabell Papers.

33. Moore, "Gen. John Hartwell Cocke of Bremo."

34. Coyner, "John Hartwell Cocke of Bremo."

35. John Hartwell Cocke to Henry Smith, October 1, 1833, Cocke Family Papers.

36. Freehling, *Drift toward Dissolution*, 122–58; John Hartwell Cocke, "Fragment on Slavery," n.d., ibid.

37. John Hartwell Cocke to unknown, September 23, 1831, ibid.

38. Ibid.

39. Ibid. On soil exhaustion and debt, see Kulikoff, *Tobacco and Slaves*, and Craven, "Soil Exhaustion as a Factor."

40. John Hartwell Cocke to unknown, September 23, 1831, Cocke Family Papers. For an excellent study on slave hiring in the Chesapeake, see Schermerhorn, *Money over Mastery*, 136–57.

41. John Hartwell Cocke to unknown, September 23, 1831, Cocke Family Papers. On the "domesticity" of slaves, see Rose, "The Domestication of Domestic Slavery." Alan Taylor has suggested that in the early 1800s, masters "thought of blacks in two radically different ways," as the "internal enemy" on a collective level and as "secure with . . . slaves well known to them." *The Internal Enemy*, 7.

42. John Hartwell Cocke to unknown, September 23, 1831, Cocke Family Papers.

43. John Hartwell Cocke to Smith, October 1, 1833, ibid.

44. John Hartwell Cocke, "Standing Rules for the Government of Slaves on a Virginia Plantation," n.d., ibid.

45. John Hartwell Cocke to Smith, October 1, 1833, ibid.

46. "Schedule of Genl. Cocke's Servants & Those at Bremo Recess," n.d., ibid.

47. John Hartwell Cocke to unknown, December 1833, ibid.; Irons, *The Origins of Proslavery Christianity*, 146–49, 161–71.

48. Rose, *A Documentary History of Slavery in North America*, 446–47; Miller, ed., *"Dear Master,"* 138–263; Coyner, "John Hartwell Cocke of Bremo," 372–409.

49. "Certificate of Emancipation of Peyton Skipwith," October 1833, Cocke Family Papers.

50. Peyton Skipwith to John Hartwell Cocke, April 22, 1840, ibid.

51. Matilda Lomax to John Hartwell Cocke, June 20, 1854, ibid.

52. John Hartwell Cocke to Charles Cocke, December 26, 1836, ibid.

53. Miller, ed., *"Dear Master,"* 138–52.

54. James Madison to Richard Randolph Gurley, February 19, 1833, American Colonization Society Papers.

55. "Circular, Virginia Colonization Society," July 17, 1833, ibid.

56. Jesse Burton Harrison to Richard Randolph Gurley, July 28, 1833, ibid.

57. John Hartwell Cocke to John Hartwell Cocke Jr., December 31, 1832, ibid.

58. John Hartwell Cocke to Richard Randolph Gurley, January 14, 1833, American Colonization Society Papers.

59. Richard Randolph Gurley to John Hartwell Cocke, February 15, 1833, Cocke Family Papers.

60. John Hartwell Cocke to Sally F. Cocke, March 4, 1831, ibid.

61. Dew, *Review of the Debate in the Virginia Legislature*, 12, 35.

62. Brownlee and Carlander, "Antebellum Political Economists and the Problem of Slavery"; O'Brien, *Conjectures of Order*, 2:943–46.

63. Dew, *Review of the Debate in the Virginia Legislature*, 106.

64. O'Brien, *Conjectures of Order*, 2:943–46.

65. Dew to James Madison, January 15, 1833, James Madison Papers.

66. James Madison to Thomas R. Dew, February 23, 1833, ibid.

67. Dew, *Review of the Debate in the Virginia Legislature*, 8, 5; O'Brien, *Conjectures of Order*, 2:944.

68. Dew, *Review of the Debate in the Virginia Legislature*, 53, 86–93, 118.

69. Ibid., 119–20.

70. Ibid., 49, 54–55; John Hartwell Cocke to Richard Randolph Gurley, March 31, 1833, American Colonization Society Papers.

71. Ford, *Deliver Us from Evil*, 379–81, 389.

72. Dew, *Review of the Debate in the Virginia Legislature*, 6, 66, 113.

73. Ibid., 113, 114, 125.

74. Ibid., 108–10.

75. Ibid., 36–37.

76. Crowley, *The Invention of Comfort*, 141–70; Dew, *Review of the Debate in the Virginia Legislature*, 111–12.

77. Ibid., 28.

78. Ibid., 123–24.

79. Ibid., 122–24.

80. Ibid.

81. Ibid., 130.

82. Schoen, *The Fragile Fabric of Union*; Ford, *Deliver Us from Evil*, 379–81, 389.

83. Deyle, *Carry Me Back*, 4–5, 48 (quotation), 59.

84. Dew, *Review of the Debate in the Virginia Legislature*, 49, 54–55.

85. Miller, ed., *"Dear Master*," 37–135.

3. "RISING GRADATIONS TO UNLIMITED FREEDOM"

1. Although Henry Laurens purchased Mepkin Plantation in 1762, it passed through a variety of owners after his death in 1792. In 1936, it was bought by the philanthropist and Time, Inc., co-founder Henry R. Luce; in 1949, the Luce family donated over a thousand acres to the Abbey of Gethsemani to establish a monastery there.

2. The most recent treatment of Laurens and slavery is Rakove, *Revolutionaries*, 198–214. Rakove links Laurens's antislavery leanings to the *Somerset* decision in 1772 in London. For a sophisticated reading of Laurens's plantation endeavors, see Edelson, *Plantation Enterprise*, 200–254. See also Stockdale, *'Tis Treason My Good Man!* 77–94; Kelly, "Henry Laurens"; Olwell, *Masters, Slaves and Subjects*; Rediker, *The Slave Ship*, 35–37; and Kirschke and Sensenig, "Steps toward Nationhood."

3. Henry Laurens (hereafter HL) to John Laurens, August 14, 1776, Laurens, *Papers*, 11: 224–25.

4. On Laurens's attitudes toward slavery, with a particular focus on paternalism, see Morgan, "Three Planters and Their Slaves"; Olwell, "'A Reckoning of Accounts'"; and Young, "Domesticating Slavery," 38–54. On his limited antislavery, see Massey, "The Limits of Antislavery Thought."

5. Edelson, *Plantation Enterprise*, 220–29; Hancock, *Citizens of the World*, 279–380; Chaplin, *An Anxious Pursuit*, chap. 1; Drayton, *Nature's Government*.

6. HL to Edward Bridgen, January 8, 1787, Laurens, *Papers*, 16:689. The relationship between a nation's legitimacy "among the powers of the Earth" and slavery has been neglected. The exception is Gould, "The Laws of War and Peace."

7. For civilization as a protean idea during the age of revolutions, see Dierksheide and Onuf, "Slave-holding Nation, Slaveholding Civilization."

8. Chaplin, *An Anxious Pursuit*, 23–65; Edelson, *Plantation Enterprise*, 255–68.

9. On the supposed genealogy of proslavery thinking in America, see Tise, *Proslavery*, and Young, *Proslavery and Sectional Thought*.

10. Thomas, *The Slave Trade*, 440, 444, 486.

11. Littlefield, *Rice and Slaves*, chap. 1; Berlin and Morgan, eds., *Cultivation and Culture*, 12–14; Coclanis, *The Shadow of a Dream*, 82–83; Peter McCandless, *Slavery, Disease, and Suffering in the Southern Lowcountry* (Cambridge: Cambridge University Press, 2011), 125–48.

12. McDonough, *Christopher Gadsden and Henry Laurens*, 22 (quotation); Donnan, "The Slave Trade into South Carolina before the Revolution."

13. HL to Smith & Clifton, May 26, 1755, Laurens, *Papers*, 1:254–57.

14. HL to Wells, Wharton & Doran, May 27, 1755, ibid., 1:257–59.

15. HL to Devonshire, Reeve & Lloyd, June 24, 1755; ibid., 1:267–69; HL to Wells, Wharton & Doran, July 17, 1755, ibid., 1:293–94.

16. HL to Devonshire, Reeve & Lloyd, June 24, 1755, ibid., 1:267–69.

17. HL to Smith & Clifton, July 17, 1755, ibid., 1:294–95; HL to Augustus, John Boyd & Co., September 23, 1755, ibid., 1:340–41.

18. HL to Thomas Easton & Co., June 23, 1755, ibid., 1:266–67; HL to Richard Prankhead & Co., July 5, 1755, ibid., 1:287–88.

19. McDonough, *Christopher Gadsden and Henry Laurens*, 23.

20. HL to John Holman, September 8, 1770, Laurens, *Papers*, 6:149.

21. McDonough, *Christopher Gadsden and Henry Laurens*, 22–26, 24 (quotation).

22. "Appendix to the Extracts from the Proceedings of the High Court of Vice-Admiralty in Charlestown, South-Carolina," 1769, Laurens, *Papers*, 7:99–100. On the rising costs associated with the African slave trade, including insurance, see Klein, *The Atlantic Save Trade*, 99–101, and Coughtry, *The Notorious Triangle*, 90–102.

23. HL to James Grant, January 30, 1767, Laurens, *Papers*, 5:226.

24. HL to Devonshire & Reeve, September 12, 1764, ibid., 5:419; HL to Mathew Robinson, May 30, 1764, ibid., 5:295–96; Young, *Domesticating Slavery,* 41; HL to Richard Oswald, July 7, 1764, Laurens, *Papers,* 5:332.

25. HL to John McCullough, December, 16, 1771, ibid., 8:98–99. Laurens was disappointed by the civility and manners he encountered in England. He implied that provincials like himself were actually more worldly and, as a result, more eager to improve, while metropolitans, so assured of their civility, neglected their improvement.

26. HL to Lloyd & Borton, December 24, 1764, ibid., 10:557–58; HL to Elias Ball, April 1, 1765, ibid., 10:595–97.

27. HL to Joseph Clay, September 22, 1772, ibid., 8:468; *London Chronicle,* June 20, 1772; HL to George Appleby, February 28, 1774, Laurens, *Papers,* 9:317; Gould, "Zones of Law, Zones of Violence"; Van Cleve, "Somerset's Case and Its Antecedents in Imperial Perspective."

28. Alan Taylor has argued, "because class mattered as much as race to British leaders, they could consider blacks as potentially equals of common whites in a society" that could only be ruled by legitimate aristocrats. *The Internal Enemy,* 140.

29. Joyce Chaplin has argued that planters evinced "anxiety" about their status as slaveholders and that slavery jeopardized their claims to civility. *An Anxious Pursuit,* 23–65.

30. HL to Richard Oswald, April 27, 1768, Laurens, *Papers,* 5:669; McDonough, *Christopher Gadsden and Henry Laurens,* chap. 5.

31. HL to Johann Randolph von Valltravers, May 22, 1775, Laurens, *Papers,* 10:134; HL to Richard Oswald, September 10, 1770, ibid., 7:344.

32. HL to George Grenville, February 24, 1769, ibid., 6:386–87; Eliga H. Gould, "The Making of an Atlantic Slave System: Britain and the United States, 1795–1825," in Julie Flavell and Stephen Conway, eds., *Britain and America Go to War: The Impact of War and Warfare in Anglo-America, 1754–1815* (Gainesville: University Press of Florida, 2004), 241–65.

33. For a detailed discussion of the battle of Charleston, see O'Shaughnessy, *The Men Who Lost America,* 223–32; James Custer to HL, June 1780, Laurens, *Papers,* 15:301–4.

34. HL to Richard Price, February 1, 1785, ibid., 16:532–35.

35. *South Carolina Gazette and Country Journal,* April 4, 1769.

36. HL to Richard Price, February 1, 1785, Laurens, *Papers,* 16:533–34; HL to Edward Bridgen, February 13, 1786, Laurens Papers, South Carolina Historical Society.

37. Pierce Butler to John Mygies, August 5, 1792, Pierce Butler Letterbook, vol. 2.

38. HL to Alexander Hamilton, April 19, 1785, Laurens Papers, University of South Carolina.

39. HL to James Bourdieu, May 6, 1785, Laurens, *Papers,* 16:559. On the importance of treaty-worthiness in the postrevolutionary period, see Gould, *Among the Powers of the Earth,* chap 1.

40. McDonough, *Christopher Gadsden and Henry Laurens,* 263–64, 271; William Henry Drayton to Thomas Jefferson, November 27, 1787, William Henry Drayton Papers; Ralph Izard to Thomas Jefferson, April 3, 1789, Ralph Izard Papers.

41. Edelson, *Plantation Enterprise,* 251; Ralph Izard to Gabriel Manigault, June 9, 1789, Ralph Izard Papers; Jacob Read to Adam Tunno, May 19, 1787, Jacob Read Papers; William Read to Jacob Read, February 26, 1796, ibid.

42. Newman, *A New World of Labor,* 217–19.

43. *South Carolina Gazette and Public Advertiser,* August 27, 1785; William Henry Drayton to Thomas Jefferson, May 22, 1787, William Henry Drayton Papers; HL to Bridgen & Waller, January 7, 1786, Laurens Papers, University of South Carolina.

44. David Ramsay, Fourth of July Oration, 1778, Ramsay, "David Ramsay, a Selection of His Writings."

45. HL to William Henry Drayton, February 15, 1783, Laurens, *Papers*, 16:146; HL to Drayton, February 23, 1783, ibid., 16:156–57.

46. HL to Richard Price, February 1, 1785, ibid., 16:534; Thomas Jefferson to James Heaton, May 20, 1826, Jefferson, *Writings*, 1516.

47. HL to William Henry Drayton, February 23, 1783, Laurens, *Papers*, 16:155–56.

48. The Regulator Movement was an uprising staged by British Americans in the Carolina backcountry against royal officials who imposed heavy taxes. See Kars, *Breaking Loose Together*.

49. HL to William Henry Drayton, February 23, 1783, Laurens, *Papers*, 16:156. On Jefferson and race war, see Onuf, *Jefferson's Empire*, 147–88.

50. HL to Richard Price, February 1, 1785, Laurens, *Papers*, 16:534; HL to Alexander Hamilton, April 19, 1785, ibid., 16:555.

51. HL to William Henry Drayton, February 23, 1783, ibid., 16:155–56; Rogers, *Evolution of a Federalist*, 136–37.

52. Max Edelson suggests that the "colonial plantation enterprise began with ... expansion into new lands. With every extension, planters continually worked to bring plantations back into connection with established points of order." *Plantation Enterprise*, 267. See also Christopher Tomlins's definition of colonization as a replication of jurisdictions in *Freedom Bound*, 184–94.

53. Edelson, *Plantation Enterprise*, 210–18.

54. Ibid., 201; HL to John Lewis Gervais, January 29, 1766, Laurens, *Papers*, 5:55.

55. Edelson, *Plantation Enterprise*, 210–18.

56. HL to John Smith, May 9, 1766, Laurens, *Papers*, 5:125; HL to James Habersham, October 1, 1770, ibid., 7:376; Edelson, *Plantation Enterprise*, 237–39.

57. Ibid., 202–3.

58. HL to Bridgen & Waller, May 19, 1786, Laurens, *Papers*, 16:658; HL to Michael Hillegas, April 14, 1786, ibid., 16:646; HL to James Woodmason, July 13, 1787, ibid., 16:726–27.

59. On Laurens's portrait, see McInnis, *In Pursuit of Refinement*, 123–24.

60. HL to Richard Price, February 1, 1785, Laurens, *Papers*, 16:535; HL to Alexander Hamilton, April 19, 1785, ibid., 16:554–55.

61. HL to Bridgen & Waller, January 7, 1786, ibid., 16:628; HL to Alexander Hamilton, April 19, 1785, ibid., 16:554–55.

62. HL to Richard Oswald, August 16, 1783, ibid., 16:267; HL to James Bourdieu, February 6, 1783, ibid., 16:144; Taylor, *The Internal Enemy*, 6.

63. Samuel Massey to HL, June 12, 1780, ibid., 15:304–7.

64. HL to Alexander Hamilton, April 19, 1785, ibid., 16:554–55; HL to Jacob Read, July 16, 1785, ibid., 16:579–80; HL to Jacob Read, September 15, 1785, ibid., 16:596–97; Taylor, *The Internal Enemy*, 7.

65. HL to James Bourdieu, February 6, 1783, Laurens, *Papers*, 16:144.

66. Laurens's political-economic vision of South Carolina before cotton conveys the contingency of the postrevolutionary era. For more on "deep contingency," see Ayers, *What Caused the Civil War?*, 134–35.

67. Joseph Manigault to Gabriel Manigault, December 17, 1805, Manigault Family Papers; Henry William DeSaussure to Ezekiel Pickens, December 1, 1805, Henry William DeSaussure Papers; John Drayton, *A View of South Carolina, as Respects Her Natural and Civil Con-*

cerns (Charleston: W. P. Young, 1802), 103; Message of Governor Paul Hamilton to the Senate, November 25, 1805, Governors' Messages, Papers of the General Assembly of South Carolina, South Carolina Department of Archives and History; Henry William DeSaussure to Ezekiel Pickens, September 10, 1805, Henry William DeSaussure Papers.

Those who wanted tighter credit also wanted an end to the slave trade. Alexander Gillon, a state legislator, hoped to abolish the foreign slave trade so that "negroes would rise in value, and the debtor who sold slaves had a better chance of satisfying his creditors." *Charleston Morning Post,* March 23, 1787.

68. Klein, *Unification of a Slave State,* 251–52; Elliot, ed., *Debates in the Several State Conventions,* 4:285; Joyner, *Down by the Riverside,* 19; Dusinberre, *Them Dark Days,* 388–96; Edelson, *Plantation Enterprise,* 255–68.

4. "THE ENORMOUS EVIL THAT HAS HAUNTED THE IMAGINATIONS OF MEN"

1. Harper, *Anniversary Oration,* 3, 7.

2. Ibid., 10, 8.

3. There have been many recent studies of modernizing, proslavery South Carolinians in the antebellum period. For further reading, see O'Brien, *Conjectures of Order;* Ford, *Deliver Us from Evil;* Young, *Domesticating Slavery;* and Wyatt-Brown, "Modernizing Southern Slavery."

4. Johnson, "On Agency"; Margaret Abruzzo, *Polemical Pain: Slavery, Cruelty, and the Rise of Humanitarianism* (Baltimore: Johns Hopkins University Press, 2011), 159–89.

5. On the cosmopolitan thinking that dovetailed with southerners' burgeoning nationalism, see O'Brien, *Conjectures of Order,* 1:1–24, and Harper, "Memoir on Slavery," 82.

6. Gould, "American Independence and Britain's Counter-Revolution"; Colley, *Britons,* 321–63; Evans, *Britain before the Reform Act.*

7. Klein, *Unification of a Slave State,* 203–37; Pamela Pilbeam, "The Growth of Liberalism and the Crisis of the Bourbon Restoration, 1827–1830," *The Historical Journal* 25, no. 2 (1982): 351–66.

8. Dubois, *Avengers of the New World;* Davis, *Challenging the Boundaries of Slavery,* 81–86; Drescher, *The Mighty Experiment;* Wilkins, "Window on Freedom"; Rugemer, *The Problem of Emancipation.*

9. Peter S. Onuf, "A Declaration of Independence for Diplomatic Historians," in Onuf, *The Mind of Thomas Jefferson,* 65–81; Armitage, *The Declaration of Independence;* Matson and Onuf, *A Union of Interests.*

10. Harper, *Anniversary Oration,* 9–10.

11. Hugh Swinton Legaré to J. E. Holmes, October 2, 1833, Hugh Swinton Legaré Papers.

12. Hugh Swinton Legaré to unidentified sister, June 16, 1833, ibid.

13. Harper, *Anniversary Oration,* 8.

14. Lipset, *The First New Nation;* Onuf and Onuf, *Nations, Markets, and War,* 263–64.

15. Harper, "Memoir on Slavery," 4.

16. On proslavery free traders, see Schoen, *The Fragile Fabric of Union;* Brownlee and Carlander, "Antebellum Political Economists and the Problem of Slavery."

17. Hugh Swinton Legaré to J. E. Holmes, October 2, 1833, Hugh Swinton Legaré Papers.

18. Cooper, "Slavery."

19. Harper, "Memoir on Slavery," 11–12, 28. On slavery and positive law, see Van Cleve, *A Slaveholders' Union,* 17, 31–36.

20. Harper, "Memoir on Slavery," 7. On the meaning of "liberty" and "equality" as the enjoy-

ment of "privileges"—such as slaveholding or the accumulation of private property—within a fundamentally hierarchical and unequal society, see Rozbicki, *Culture and Liberty in the Age of the American Revolution*, 172–76.

21. Hugh Swinton Legaré to J. E. Holmes, October 2, 1833, Hugh Swinton Legaré Papers.

22. Egerton, *He Shall Go out Free*; Lofton, *Insurrection in South Carolina*; Scott, "The Common Wind."

23. Johnson, "Denmark Vesey and His Co-Conspirators."

24. Rugemer, *The Problem of Emancipation*, 78–80; Killens, ed., *The Trial Record of Denmark Vesey*.

25. Furstenberg, "Beyond Freedom and Slavery."

26. *Southern Intelligencer*, November 16, 1822, p. 183; November 23, 1822, p. 188; Holland, *A Refutation of the Calumnies*, 82–87; Benjamin M. Palmer to Robert R. Gurley, April 8, 1827, American Colonization Society Papers.

27. *Southern Intelligencer*, November 16, 1822, p. 183; November 23, 1822, p. 188; Holland, *A Refutation of the Calumnies*, 82–87; Benjamin M. Palmer to Robert R. Gurley, April 8, 1827, American Colonization Society Papers.

28. "Speech of Robert Y. Hayne," *Register of Debates in Congress*, Senate, 19th Cong., 2nd sess., 290–95, American Memory, Library of Congress, memory.loc.gov; Turnbull, *The Crisis*, 7, 126–38; Seabrook, *A Concise View of the Critical Situation*, 13–14; Pinckney, *An Address Delivered in Charleston*, 1–24.

29. Clay, *Speech of the Hon. Henry Clay*, 326, 318.

30. Ibid., 326; Harper, "Colonization Society," 2, 3.

31. *David Walker's Appeal*, ed. Sean Wilentz (New York: Hill and Wang, 1995), 25; *Charleston City Gazette*, March 3, 1830; Peter Hinks, *To Awaken My Afflicted Brethren: David Walker and the Problem of Antebellum Slave Resistance* (University Park: Pennsylvania State University Press, 1997), 30–40.

32. For an overview of the southern reaction to the abolitionist mail campaign, see Wyly-Jones, "The 1835 Anti-Abolition Meetings in the South," and Ford, *Deliver Us from Evil*, 484–503.

33. Garrison, "To the Public."

34. Garrison, "On the Constitution and the Union."

35. Garrison, "On Walker's Appeal."

36. "An Act for the Better Regulation of Government of Free Negroes and Persons of Color"; *House Journal*, 1834, Records of the General Assembly, 59–107, South Carolina Department of Archives and History.

37. January, "The South Carolina Association."

38. On "radicalism" and "states' rights" in antebellum South Carolina, see Sinha, *The Counterrevolution of Slavery*, and Ford, *Origins of Southern Radicalism*.

39. Alexis de Tocqueville, *Democracy in America*, trans. Arthur Goldhammer (New York: Library of America, 2004), 719; Onuf, "Antebellum Southerners and the National Idea"; Read, *Majority Rule versus Consensus*; Knupfer, *The Union as It Is*; Schoen, *The Fragile Fabric of Union*, chap. 3.

40. Slave Population, 1830. On corporate identity, see Greene, *Imperatives, Behaviors, and Identities*, 14–15, 113–14.

41. Harper, "Memoir on Slavery," 14–15, 23, 29; Onuf, "Domesticating the Captive Nation," 34–60.

42. Harper, "Memoir on Slavery," 11–12.

43. Ibid., 29.

44. Ibid., 47

45. Ibid., 13, 5, 133.

46. Ibid., 76–77, 88–89. For the argument that slaves who did not rebel did not desire their freedom, see Furstenberg, "Beyond Freedom and Slavery." On the domestication of the "captive nation," see Onuf, "Domesticating the Captive Nation."

47. Harper, "Memoir on Slavery," 83, 19–20.

48. Ibid., 14, 61, 64–65.

49. Ibid., 31, 32, 34.

50. Ibid., 35–37.

51. Irons, *The Origins of Proslavery Christianity*, 169–209; Cornelius, *Slave Missions and the Black Church in the Antebellum South*; Webber, *Deep Like the Rivers*.

52. Ian Beamish, "Saving the South: Printing Agricultural Improvement in the American South, 1820–1870" (Ph.D. dissertation, Johns Hopkins University, forthcoming); Taylor, *The Internal Enemy*, 102.

53. Charles Cotesworth Pinckney, *An Address Delivered in Charleston*; Dierksheide, "Missionaries, Evangelical Identity"; Cornelius, *Slave Missions and the Black Church in the Antebellum South*; Irons, *The Origins of Proslavery Christianity*; Dalcho, *Practical Considerations Founded on the Scriptures*, 3–10.

54. Clay, *Detail of a Plan*; Ford, *Deliver Us from Evil*, 474.

55. Bowen, *A Pastoral Letter*, 6–8.

56. Ibid., 19.

57. Ibid., 9; Clay, *Detail of a Plan*.

58. Rosengarten, "The Southern Agriculturist in an Age of Reform"; Newman, *A New World of Labor*, 217–19.

59. Johnson, *Nugae Georgicae*, 35–38.

60. Legaré, "Account of an Agricultural Excursion," 359. For other examinations of the Couper family and Hopeton, see Clifton, "Hopeton," and Bagwell, *Rice Gold*.

61. Legaré, "Account of an Agricultural Excursion," 359.

62. Ibid., 571–72.

63. Ibid., 572.

64. Ibid., 576; Clifton, "Hopeton."

65. "Tabby" was a building material commonly used in the Lowcountry and composed of water, crushed oyster shells, lime, and sand.

66. Legaré, "Account of an Agricultural Excursion," 573–74; Clifton, "Hopeton."

67. Ferguson, *The John Couper Family at Cannon's Point*, 108–9.

68. Harper, "Memoir on Slavery," 22; Tomlins, *Freedom Bound*; *The National Era*, October 6, 1853.

5. "WE MAY ALLEVIATE, THOUGH WE CANNOT CURE"

1. "The Sable Venus: An Ode" in Edwards, *The History, Civil and Commercial*, 2:32–38.

2. "The Voyage of the Sable Venus from Angola to the West Indies," in Edwards, *List of Maps and Plates*, plate 12. On interpretations of the "Ode," see Wood, *Blind Memory*, 21–23.

3. Brown, "The Politics of Slavery"; Greene, *Peripheries and Center*. Bryan Edwards's argument is in line with Thomas Haskell's theory that an increasingly strong humanitarian sentiment

stimulated the rise of the abolitionist movement in Britain. Edwards charged that the notion of an ameliorated slave trade emerged from West Indians' and merchants' own humanitarianism. Haskell, "Capitalism and the Origins of the Humanitarian Sensibility."

4. Davis, *Slavery and Human Progress*, 154–68; Tomlins, *Freedom Bound*; Greene, *The Constitutional Origins of the American Revolution*; Greene, *Peripheries and Center*.

5. Sidbury, *Becoming African in America*; Gould, *Barbaric Traffic*; Davis, "The Emergence of Immediatism in British and American Antislavery Thought," 209–30.

6. Most of the abolition literature focuses on the success of the abolitionists and the decline of the sugar industry and the planter class. See Blackburn, *The Overthrow of Colonial Slavery*; Drescher, *Econocide*; Ragatz, *The Fall of the Planter Class*; Anstey, *The Atlantic Slave Trade and British Abolition*; Craton, *Testing the Chains*; Klingberg, *The Anti-Slavery Movement in England*; Drescher, "The Decline Thesis"; and Ward, "The Profitability of Sugar Planting in the British West Indies." Scholars who view abolition through the lens of "improvement" rather than "decline" are few and far between. Philip D. Morgan has recently stated that, "if economic decline is not the relevant theme for linking the Caribbean to abolition, then arguably the alternative— improvement—is." See Morgan, "Ending the Slave Trade," 101–28, 105 (quotation), and Lambert, *White Creole Culture*, 41–72. On abolitionists' vision of a modern empire without slaves, see Brown, "Empire without Slaves."

7. Ramsay, *An Essay on the Treatment and Conversion of African Slaves*, 276, 280.

8. Brown, "The Politics of Slavery," 220; Morgan, "Ending the Slave Trade," 109.

9. Roscoe, *A General View of the African Slave-Trade*, 26, 29–31; Wilberforce, *The Speech, of William Wilberforce*, 11–12.

10. Dundas, *Substance of the Argument*, 2, 18, 26.

11. Long, *History of Jamaica*, 1:433–34; Ward, "The Profitability of Sugar Planting in the British West Indies"; Mason, "The Battle of Slave-Holding Liberators"; Dubois, *A Colony of Citizens*.

12. Venault de Charmilly, *Answer, by Way of Letter, to Bryan Edwards*, 36.

13. Edwards, *An Historical Survey of the French Colony in the Island of St Domingo*; Rugemer, *The Problem of Emancipation*, chap. 2.

14. Burke, "A Letter to the Right Hon. Henry Dundas"; Stephen Fuller to Bryan Edwards, March 3, 1790, Stephen Fuller Letterbook 1.

15. Morgan, "Ending the Slave Trade," 107–8; Sheridan, *Doctors and Slaves*; Newman, *A New World of Labor*, 217–19; Higman, "Slavery and the Development of Demographic Theory."

16. Cundall, "Bryan Castle"; Davis, *The Problem of Slavery in the Age of Revolution*, 184–95; Olwyn M. Blouet, "Bryan Edwards"; Higman, *Jamaica Surveyed*, 253.

17. Edwards, *The History, Civil and Commercial*, 2:179; Tim Fulford and Debbie Lee, "Mental Travelers: Joseph Banks, Mungo Park, and the Romantic Imagination," *Nineteenth-Century Contexts* 24, no. 2 (2002): 117–37; Hallett, *The Penetration of Africa*, 321–24.

18. Hochschild, *Bury the Chains*, 155–56, 308; Wood, *Blind Memory*, 35–39.

19. Evidence of John Mathews, Sierra Leone Coast, March 4, 1788, Collections Relating to the Slave Trade, ff. 17–19.

20. Evidence of James Renny, March 6, 1788, Collections Relating to the Slave Trade, f. 32.

21. Report of the House of Assembly in Jamaica, October 16, 1788, Colonial Office Papers (hereafter CO) 137/88, f. 268.

22. Examination of Captain William Sherwood, Joint Committee on the Slave Trade, December 1, 1789, CO 187/88, f. 307.

23. Memorandum of Slaves Consigned to, and Sold by, Alexander Lindo, from January 9, 1786 to August 19, 1788, CO 187/88, f. 293.

24. Edwards, *A Speech Delivered at a Free Conference*, 24–25.

25. Anstey, *The Atlantic Slave Trade and British Abolition*, 419–20; "Certificate of Slaves on Board the Ship Express," Records of the House of Lords, HL/PO/JO/10/7/982A, Parliamentary Archives, London.

26. Wilberforce, *The Speech, of William Wilberforce*, 6.

27. Clarkson, *An Essay on the Comparative Efficiency of Regulation or Abolition*, 67.

28. Clarkson, *Letters on the Slave-Trade*, 2:80, 1:iv.

29. Edwards, *A Speech Delivered at a Free Conference*, 57–58.

30. Council of Jamaica to Adam Williamson, November 25, 1791, CO 137/90, ff. 49–50.

31. "Short Reasons against the Abolition of the Slave Trade," annotated by Edward Long, Long MSS.

32. Stern, "'Rescuing the Age from a Charge of Ignorance'"; Drayton, *Nature's Government*, 111–15; Hallett, *The Penetration of Africa*, 193–285.

33. Hallett, ed., *Records of the African Association*, 163.

34. Bryan Edwards to Joseph Banks, October 22, 1798, quoted in Anthony Saltin, *The Gates of Africa: Death, Discovery, and the Search for Timbuktu* (New York: Macmillan, 2003), 179.

35. Whishaw, *The Journal of a Mission*, 20.

36. Ibid., 3.

37. Park, *Travels in the Interior Districts of Africa*, 288–89; Thornton, *Africa and Africans*.

38. Park, *Travels in the Interior Districts of Africa*, 297–98.

39. A Jamaican Planter, *Notes on the Two Reports*, iv.

40. Ibid., 7. On West Indians' backward provincialism, see Ragatz, *The Fall of the Planter Class*.

41. Long, *History of Jamaica*, 2:353, 376–77.

42. Bryan Edwards, "Notes on Long's History of Jamaica," John Carter Brown Library.

43. Edwards, *The History, Civil and Commercial*, 2:70–119.

44. Ibid., 2:70–72.

45. Ibid., 2:80.

46. Ibid., 2:90–95.

47. Ibid., 2:180–85; Philip D. Morgan, "Task and Gang Systems: The Organization of Labor on New World Plantations," in Stephen Innes, ed., *Work and Labor in Early America* (Chapel Hill: University of North Carolina Press, 1988), 189–220; Mintz, *Caribbean Transformations*, chap. 7.

48. Edwards, *The History, Civil and Commercial*, 2:178–79.

49. Edwards, *An Historical Survey of the French Colony in the Island of St. Domingo*, 194.

50. Edwards, *A Speech Delivered at a Free Conference*, 58.

51. Edwards, *The History, Civil and Commercial*, 2:5.

52. Ibid., 2:7, 15–16.

53. Consolidation of the Slave Code, Jamaica, December 22, 1787, CO 137/87, ff. 86–108.

54. Consolidation of the Slave Code, Jamaica, 1788, CO 137/87, f. 167.

55. Edwards, *A Speech Delivered at a Free Conference*, 53, 58.

56. Martin, *Essay upon Plantership*; Schaw, *Journal of a Lady of Quality*, 103–6; Lascelles et al., *Instructions for the Management*, 2.

57. "Plan of Improved Sugar Mill by Edwards Woolery Esq. of Jamaica," in Edwards, *List of Maps and Plates*, plate 14; John Dovaston, "Agricultura Americana; or, Improvements in West-India Husbandry Used in England," 1774, Codex Eng. 60, vol. 2, John Carter Brown Library, Brown University, Providence, R.I.; Watts, *The West Indies*, 382–447; Newman, *A New World of Labor*, 217–19; Roberts, "Working between the Lines"; Morgan, "Task and Gang Systems," 189–220.

58. Mulcahy, *Hurricanes and Society*.

59. Edwards, *The History, Civil and Commercial*, 1:314–15, 248–49, 306.

60. Newton, *Thoughts upon the African Slave Trade*, 6.

61. Roscoe, *A General View of the African Slave-Trade*, 26.

62. Clarkson, *An Essay on the Comparative Efficiency of Regulation or Abolition*, 76.

63. Notes on the Slave Trade, [Anonymous MP], April 18–19, 1791, John Carter Brown Library.

64. Edwards, *A Speech Delivered at a Free Conference*, 57.

65. Hochschild, *Bury the Chains*, 299–308.

6. "A MATTER OF PORTENTOUS MAGNITUDE, AND STILL MORE PORTENTOUS DIFFICULTY"

1. John Gladstone took great care in establishing himself as a gentleman of importance at Seaforth, located just outside of Liverpool. He was constantly expanding and improving his house and gardens, and filling the house with expensive furnishings and paintings. By 1833, the Seaforth house alone was worth £40,000, the capital in the house was £60,000, and the "furniture, plate, pictures" were valued at £8,000. "Memorandum Relating to Sir J. Gladstone's Affairs," September 8, 1850, Glynne-Gladstone Correspondence, MSS 1139.

In 1822, Christie's of London catalogued all "pictures at Seaforth" including Benjamin West's *The Deposition*. In all, Gladstone possessed 206 paintings at Seaforth. "Mr. Christie's Catalogue of My Pictures at Seaforth Taken in the Autumn of 1822," Glynne-Gladstone Correspondence, MSS 2418.

2. Comparatively few works have dealt with John Gladstone, Demerara, and slavery. On this understudied topic, see Davis, *Slavery and Human Progress*, 182–91; Seymour Drescher, *Abolition: A History of Slavery and Antislavery* (Cambridge: Cambridge University Press, 2009), 255–59; and Davis, "James Cropper and British Antislavery Movement, 1821–1823." See also Davis, "James Cropper and British Antislavery Movement, 1823–1833."

3. Checkland, *The Gladstones*; Davis, *Slavery and Human Progress*, 182.

4. Memorandum Relating to Sir J. Gladstone's Affairs, September 8, 1850, Glynne-Gladstone Correspondence, MSS 1139.

5. Davis, *Slavery and Human Progress*, 231–72; Davis, "James Cropper and British Antislavery Movement, 1821–1823." See also Davis, "James Cropper and British Antislavery Movement, 1823–1833."

6. Lambert, *White Creole Culture*; Ward, *British West Indian Slavery*.

7. Davis, *Slavery and Human Progress*, 182, 191; Temperley, *British Antislavery*, 93–110, 153–83; Drescher, *The Mighty Experiment*, 54–72.

8. Robert Jenkisson to Baron Bexly, 1823, Liverpool Papers, f. 102.

9. On the actual economic "decline" in the West Indies, see Ryden, "Does Decline Make Sense?" I am suggesting that *perceived* West Indian decline also accounted for why Britain's political economic policies came under scrutiny—in concert with the slavery question—in the 1820s.

10. Historians' interpretation of British slave-trade abolition have generally fallen into two camps: those who see abolition as causing the "decline" of the West Indies and the beginning of free-trade ideology, and those who view abolition as the consequence of an already-existing "decline." For the former camp, see Drescher, *Econocide,* and "The Decline Thesis." For the latter camp, see Williams, *Capitalism and Slavery;* Carrington, *The British West Indies during the American Revolution;* Minchinton, "Williams and Drescher"; and Ragatz, *The Fall of the Planter Class.* The most sophisticated recent reading of the debate is David Beck Ryden, whose analysis undermines Drescher's work; see "Does Decline Make Sense?"

11. Mitchell, *British Historical Statistics;* Malthus, *An Essay on the Principle of Population;* Drescher, *The Mighty Experiment,* 34–53.

12. Brown, "Empire without Slaves"; Greene, *Peripheries and Center;* Ward, *British West Indian Slavery.*

13. Marshall, "Amelioration and Emancipation"; Watson, *The Civilised Island;* Cateau, "Conservatism and Change Implementation"; Galloway, *The Sugar Cane Industry;* Ward, "The Profitability of Sugar Planting in the British West Indies."

14. For the definition of the plantation as a tool of colonization in the British world, see Edelson, *Plantation Enterprise,* 4. For abolitionists' accounts of a free labor plantation empire in Africa in particular, see Wadström, *An Essay on Colonization;* Sharp, *A Short Sketch of Temporary Regulations;* and Thornton, "General Outlines of a Settlement."

15. On "household governance," see Shammas, *A History of Household Government in America.* On patriarchy in slave societies, see Littlefield, *Rice and Slaves,* 62–63. On the importance of domesticity in early modern Britain, see McKeon, *The Secret History of Domesticity.*

16. Drescher, *The Mighty Experiment,* 34–53; Higman, *Slave Populations of the British Caribbean,* 6–37.

17. Walvin, "The Public Campaign in England."

18. Davis, *Slavery and Human Progress,* 176–77.

19. George Home to Thomas Hankey, May 20, 1816, George Home of Paxton Letterbook, GD 267/5/38.

20. Costa, *Crowns of Glory,* 52.

21. Lambert, *White Creole Culture,* 10–40; Brown, *Moral Capital.*

22. Lambert, *White Creole Culture,* 114–15; Dierksheide, "Missionaries, Evangelical Identity."

23. Quoted in Davis, *Slavery and Human Progress,* 168.

24. House of Commons, May 15, 1823, *Hansard Parliamentary Debates,* 2nd series, 20 vols. (London: T. C. Hansard, 1820–29), 9:255–360.

25. Scott, "The Common Wind."

26. William Huskisson to John Gladstone, November 2, 1823, Glynne-Gladstone Correspondence, MSS 353.

27. George Canning, *The Speech of the Rt. Hon. George Canning.*

28. The strength of the absentee West India interest in Parliament, even in the 1820s, should not be underestimated. Between 1821 and 1833, absentees held between thirty-nine and fifty-six seats in the House of Commons. O'Shaughnessy, "The Formation of a Commercial Lobby"; Higman, "The West India 'Interest' in Parliament."

29. Declaration by the Agents for the West India Colonies to Earl Bathurst, March 9, 1824, MSS 726, National Library of Jamaica.

30. Memorandum from the Agents for the West Indies Regarding Proposed Laws for Ameliorating the Condition of the Slaves, n.d. (1829?), MSS 722, National Library of Jamaica.

31. Frederick Cort to John Gladstone, March 1823, Glynne-Gladstone Correspondence, MSS 2757.

32. Davis, *Slavery and Human Progress*, 192–94; Lambert, *White Creole Culture*, 146–47; Murray, *The West Indies and the Development of Colonial Government*.

33. William Huskisson to John Gladstone, November 2, 1823, Glynne-Gladstone Correspondence, MSS 353.

34. Sheridan, *Doctors and Slaves*.

35. William Hillhouse, "Account of British Guiana, c. 1830–5, with Two Coloured Maps, Together with a Journal of an Expedition up the River Cuyuni," William Hillhouse MSS.

36. Thompson, "Enslaved Children in Berbice"; *Berbice Gazette,* September 30, 1815, April 12, 1820; Higman, *Slave Populations of the British Caribbean,* 415.

37. William Hilhouse, "Map of British Guiana, with Remarks and Observations Illustrative of Hillhouse's General Chart of British Guiana, etc." (London: n.p., 1836), map 84010.(1.), British Library.

38. Costa, *Crowns of Glory,* 180; Frederick Cort to John Gladstone, 1822, Glynne-Gladstone Correspondence, MSS 2757.

39. Costa, *Crowns of Glory,* 191–92; Frederick Cort to John Gladstone, August 29, 1823, Glynne-Gladstone Correspondence, MSS 2757.

40. Quoted in Matthews, *Caribbean Slave Revolts,* 75–76, 83.

41. List of Prisoners Belonging to Success in Custody at the Jail in George Town, September 30, 1823, Glynne-Gladstone Correspondence, MSS 2804–9.

42. Frederick Cort to John Gladstone, August 29, 1823, Glynne-Gladstone Correspondence, MSS 2804–9.

43. Frederick Cort to John Gladstone, April 22, 1824, Glynne-Gladstone Correspondence, MSS 2804–9.

44. Drescher, *Abolition,* 255–59; Drescher, "People and Parliament."

45. John Gladstone to William Hankey, December 21, 1824, Glynne-Gladstone Correspondence, MSS 2804–9.

46. John Gladstone to Robertson Gladstone, October 20, 1828, Glynne-Gladstone Correspondence, MSS 543.

47. Robertson Gladstone to John Gladstone, January 11, 1829, Glynne-Gladstone Correspondence, MSS 136.

48. Ibid.

49. Robertson Gladstone to John Gladstone, January 12, 1829, Glynne-Gladstone Correspondence, MSS 136.

50. Ibid.

51. Edelson, *Plantation Enterprise,* 219; Robertson Gladston quoted in Checkland, *The Gladstones,* 199–200.

52. Viscount Goderich to Benjamin D'Urban, February 17, 1832, CO 112/16.

53. Higman, *Slave Populations of the British Caribbean,* 72–89; Drescher, *The Mighty Experiment,* 34–53.

54. Davis, *Slavery and Human Progress,* 171.

55. Stephen, *Slavery in the British West India Colonies,* 2:76.

56. Yates, *Colonial Slavery.*

57. Stephen, *Slavery in the British West India Colonies,* 2:77.

58. Ibid., 2:78.

59. In 1790, the actual slave population was 694,207 and in 1820, it was 1,529,012. U.S. Census.

60. William Myers to John Gladstone, 1823, Glynne-Gladstone Correspondence, MSS 2855–58.

61. Gladstone, *Facts, Relating to Slavery,* 22–23.

62. Craton, "Reluctant Creoles."

63. Gladstone, *Facts, Relating to Slavery,* 6–7.

64. Ibid., 6–7.

65. For studies on the effects of attorneys' plantation management, see Higman, *Plantation Jamaica,* and Burnard, *Mastery, Tyranny, and Desire.*

66. Thomas Clarkson, "Mr. Steele's Plan for the Manumission of Slaves," 1815, Clarkson Correspondence, Add. MSS 41,267A, ff. 76–78.

67. Henry Lushington to Thomas Clarkson, August 11, 1828, Clarkson Correspondence, Add. MSS 41,266, ff. 272–75.

68. My thinking has been shaped by Tomlins, *Freedom Bound.* On the federative identity of the British Empire, see Greene, *Peripheries and Center.*

69. Williams, "Laissez Faire, Sugar and Slavery"; Travers, *Ideology and Empire in Eighteenth-Century India.*

70. Lambert, *White Creole Culture,* 144–45; Sheller, *Consuming the Caribbean;* Sussman, *Consuming Anxieties;* Colley, *Captives.*

71. Clarkson, *Thoughts on the Necessity,* 48–50, 60. On the East India Company, see Travers, "Contested Despotism."

72. Adam, *The Law and Custom of Slavery,* 6, 11, 14–15, 82, 104–38.

73. Petition by the West India Planters and Merchants on the Subject of the Sugar Duties, 1826, MSS 745, National Library of Jamaica.

74. M'Queen, *The West India Colonies;* Said, *Orientalism.*

75. John Gladstone to William Cobbett, October 28, 1823, quoted in Checkland, *The Gladstones,* 192–93.

76. Ricardo, *Essay on the Influence;* Ricardo, *Principles of Political Economy and Taxation;* Semmel, *The Rise of Free Trade Imperialism.*

77. Cropper and Gladstone, *Correspondence;* Davis, "James Cropper and British Antislavery Movement, 1821–1823." See also Davis, "James Cropper and British Antislavery Movement, 1823–1833."

78. Cropper and Gladstone, *Correspondence.*

79. Gladstone, *Mercator's Reply to Mr. Booth's Pamphlet on Free Trade,* 8.

80. John Gladstone to Robert Peel, April 7, 1831, Glynne-Gladstone Correspondence, MSS 303.

81. John Gladstone to Robert Peel, n.d., Glynne-Gladstone Correspondence, MSS 303.

82. John Gladstone to Robert Peel, April 7, 1831, Glynne-Gladstone Correspondence, MSS 303.

83. Memorandum Relating to Sir J. Gladstone's Affairs, September 8, 1850, Glynne-Gladstone Correspondence, MSS 1139.

84. James Stuart (in Demerara) to John Gladstone, n.d., MSS 809, National Library of Jamaica.

85. Robertson Gladstone to John Gladstone, August 11, 1833, quoted in Checkland, *The Gladstones,* 276.

86. James Stuart (in Demerara) to John Gladstone, n.d., MSS 809, National Library of Jamaica.

87. Drescher, *The Mighty Experiment,* 156.

88. Davis, *Slavery and Human Progress,* 259–79.

CONCLUSION

1. Tomlins, *Freedom Bound,* 509–70; "Thomas Jefferson and the Expanding Union" and "The Louisiana Purchase and American Federalism" in Onuf, *The Mind of Thomas Jefferson,* 109–36; McCoy, *The Elusive Republic;* Davis, "Message of Jefferson Davis."

2. Huzzey, *Freedom Burning,* 40–74; Davis, *Slavery and Human Progress,* 231–79, 231 (quotation).

3. Matthew Pratt Guterl, *American Mediterranean: Southern Slaveholders in the Age of Emancipation* (Cambridge, Mass.: Harvard University Press, 2008), 12–45; Dierksheide and Onuf, "Slave-holding Nation, Slaveholding Civilization."

4. Drescher, *The Mighty Experiment,* chap. 8; Engerman, "Economic Adjustments to Emancipation."

5. For biographical information on the two men, see Wilson, *Thomas Clarkson,* and Faust, *James Henry Hammond and the Old South.*

6. Hammond, *Gov. Hammond's Letters on Southern Slavery,* 12.

7. On paternalism, see Genovese, *Roll, Jordan, Roll,* and Engerman and Fogel, *Without Consent or Contract,* 30.

8. Drescher, *The Mighty Experiment,* chap. 8; Engerman, "Economic Adjustments to Emancipation."

9. Clarkson, *A Letter to the Clergy of Various Denominations,* 54–58.

10. Ibid., 54–55, 50, 18, 21.

11. Ibid., 54–55.

12. Ibid., 54–57.

13. On southern planters' perception of the British West Indies, see Rugemer, *The Problem of Emancipation,* 180–221.

14. Clarkson, *A Letter to the Clergy of Various Denominations,* 53; Jasanoff, *Liberty's Exiles,* 12–13; Marshall, *The Making and Unmaking of Empires,* chap. 6; Bayly, *Imperial Meridian.*

15. Rugemer, *The Problem of Emancipation,* 260–76.

16. Hammond, *Gov. Hammond's Letters on Southern Slavery,* 15–16.

17. Ibid., 12; Johnson, *River of Dark Dreams,* 246–47.

18. Hammond, *Gov. Hammond's Letters on Southern Slavery,* 27; Rose, "The Domestication of Domestic Slavery"; Young, *Domesticating Slavery.*

19. Hammond, *Gov. Hammond's Letters on Southern Slavery,* 1, 3, 5, 10–11.

20. Onuf, "Federalism, Democracy, and Liberty"; Harris, "Civil Society in Post-Revolutionary America"; Johnson, *River of Dark Dreams,* 72.

21. Walter Johnson, "King Cotton's Long Shadow," *New York Times,* March 31, 2013, p. SR12; Slave Population, 1820, 1840; Deyle, *Carry Me Back;* Gudmestad, *A Troublesome Com-*

merce; Martin, *Divided Mastery*; Schermerhorn, *Money over Mastery*; Schoen, *The Fragile Fabric of Union*.

22. Frank Towers, *The Urban South and the Coming of the Civil War* (Charlottesville: University of Virginia Press, 2004), chap. 2; William G. Thomas, *The Iron Way: Railroads, the Civil War, and the Making of Modern America* (New Haven, Conn.: Yale University Press, 2011), 17–36; Charles B. Dew, *Ironmaker to the Confederacy: Joseph R. Anderson and the Tredegar Iron Works* (New Haven, Conn.: Yale University Press, 1966).

23. Alexis de Tocqueville, *Democracy in America*, trans. Arthur Goldhammer (New York: Library of America, 2004), 417.

24. On the psychological horrors wrought by slave auctions, see Johnson, *Soul by Soul*.

25. On this point, see especially Huzzey, *Freedom Burning*. See also Drescher, "Emperors of the World"; Armitage, *Ideological Origins of the British Empire*, 197; Colley, *Britons*, 359–60; and Blackburn, *The Overthrow of Colonial Slavery*, 436–59. Thomas Babington Macaulay, 1835, quoted in John Clive, *Macaulay: The Shaping of the Historian* (New York: Vintage Books, 1975), 481–82.

26. Drescher, "Emperors of the World."

27. Howard, "Nineteenth-Century Coastal Slave-Trading"; Temperley, *White Dreams, Black Africa*, chaps. 6–7; Braidwood, *Black Poor and White Philanthropists*, 7–12; Schwartz, "Commerce, Civilization, and Christianity."

28. Engerman, "Economic Adjustments to Emancipation"; Drescher, *The Mighty Experiment*, chaps. 10–11.

29. Drescher, "Emperors of the World."

BIBLIOGRAPHY

MANUSCRIPT SOURCES

American Colonization Society Papers. Library of Congress, Washington, D.C.

Pierce Butler Letterbook. South Caroliniana Library, University of South Carolina, Columbia.

Joseph C. Cabell Papers. MSS 13923. Albert and Shirley Small Special Collections Library, University of Virginia, Charlottesville

Clarkson Correspondence. British Library, London.

Cocke Family Papers. MSS 640. Albert and Shirley Small Special Collections Library, University of Virginia, Charlottesville.

Collections Relating to the Slave Trade, Consisting of Evidence from Merchants Given in the Years 1775–1788. Add. MSS 18,272. British Library, London.

Colonial Office Papers. National Archives, Kew, London.

Ellen Wayles Randolph Coolidge Papers. MSS 9090. Albert and Shirley Small Special Collections Library, University of Virginia, Charlottesville.

Council for World Mission Collection. School of Oriental and African Studies, Special Collections Library, University College London.

Henry William DeSaussure Papers. South Caroliniana Library, University of South Carolina, Columbia.

William Henry Drayton Papers. South Caroliniana Library, University of South Carolina, Columbia.

Edgehill-Randolph Papers. MSS 1397. Albert and Shirley Small Special Collections Library, University of Virginia, Charlottesville.

Bryan Edwards. "Notes on Long's History of Jamaica." John Carter Brown Library, Brown University, Providence, R.I.

Executive Papers. Library of Virginia, Richmond.

Stephen Fuller Letterbook 1. William R. Perkins Library, Duke University, Durham, N.C.

Glynne-Gladstone Correspondence. Flintshire Record Office, Hawarden, Wales.

William Hillhouse Manuscripts. Add. MSS 37,057. British Library, London.

George Home of Paxton Letterbook. National Archives of Scotland, Edinburgh.

Ralph Izard Papers. South Caroliniana Library, University of South Carolina, Columbia.

John Jay Papers. Rare Book and Manuscript Division, Butler Library, Columbia University Libraries, New York.

Thomas Jefferson Papers. Albert and Shirley Small Special Collections Library, University of Virginia, Charlottesville.

Thomas Jefferson Papers. Library of Congress, Washington, D.C.

Thomas Jefferson Papers. Massachusetts Historical Society, Boston.

Henry Laurens Papers. South Carolina Historical Society, Charleston.

Henry Laurens Papers. University of South Carolina, Columbia.

Hugh Swinton Legaré Papers. South Caroliniana Library, University of South Carolina, Columbia.

Liverpool Papers. Add. MSS 38,295. British Library, London.
Edward Long Manuscripts. Add. MSS 12,431. British Library, London.
James Madison Papers. Library of Congress, Washington, D.C.
Manigault Family Papers. South Caroliniana Library, University of South Carolina, Columbia.
Notes on the Slave Trade. John Carter Brown Library, Brown University, Providence, R.I.
Jacob Read Papers. South Caroliniana Library, University of South Carolina, Columbia.
Granville Sharp Papers. New-York Historical Society.
Mosby Sheppard Papers. Henrico County Human Services Office, Henrico, Virginia.
James Stuart to John Gladstone, n.d. MSS 809. National Library of Jamaica, Kingston.

PERIODICALS

Berbice Gazette	*Richmond Constitutional Whig*
Charleston City Gazette	*South Carolina Gazette and Country Journal*
Charleston Morning Post	*South Carolina Gazette and Public Advertiser*
London Chronicle	*Southern Intelligencer*
The National Era	

PUBLISHED SOURCES

"An Act for the Better Regulation of Government of Free Negroes and Persons of Color; and for Other Purposes." In *South Carolina Statutes at Large,* 10 vols., edited by Thomas Cooper and David J. McCord, 7:461–62. Columbia, S.C.: A. H. Johnston, 1836–41.

Adam, William. *The Law and Custom of Slavery in British India.* Boston: Weeks, Jordan, and Company, 1840.

Anstey, Roger. *The Atlantic Slave Trade and British Abolition, 1760–1810.* Atlantic Highlands, N.J.: Humanities Press, 1975.

Antillón, Isidoro. *Dissertacion sobre el origen de la esclavitud de los negros, motivos que a han perpetuado, ventajas que se le atribuyen y medios que podrían adoptarse para hacer prosperer sin ella nuestras colinias.* Mallorca, Spain: Imprenta de Miguel Domingo, 1811.

Aptheker, Herbert. *Nat Turner's Slave Rebellion.* New York: Humanities Press, 1966.

Armitage, David. *The Declaration of Independence: A Global History.* Cambridge, Mass.: Harvard University Press, 2007.

———. *Ideological Origins of the British Empire.* Cambridge: Cambridge University Press, 2000.

Armitage, David, and Sanjay Subrahmanyam. *The Age of Revolutions in Global Context, c. 1760–1840.* Basingstoke, Eng.: Palgrave Macmillan, 2010.

Ayers, Edward L. *What Caused the Civil War? Reflections on the South and Southern History.* New York: Norton, 2005.

Bagwell, James E. *Rice Gold: James Hamilton Couper and Plantation Life on the Georgia Coast.* Macon, Ga.: Mercer University Press, 2000.

Bayly, C. A. *Imperial Meridian: The British Empire and the World, 1780–1830.* London: Longman, 1989.

Bender, Thomas, ed. *The Antislavery Debate: Capitalism and Abolitionism as a Problem in Historical Interpretation.* Berkeley: University of California Press, 1992.

Berlin, Ira, and Philip D. Morgan, eds. *Cultivation and Culture: Labor and the Shaping of Slave Life in the Americas.* Charlottesville: University Press of Virginia, 1993.

Berquist, Emily. "Early Anti-Slavery Sentiment in the Spanish Atlantic World, 1765–1817." *Slavery and Abolition* 31, no. 2 (June 2010): 181–205.

Berry, Henry. *The Speech of Henry Berry (of Jefferson), in the House of Delegates of Virginia, on the Policy of the State in Relation to Her Colored Population: Delivered on the 11th and 25th of January, 1832.* Richmond: T. W. White, 1832.

Blackburn, Robin. *The Overthrow of Colonial Slavery, 1776–1848.* London: Verso, 1988.

Blouet, Olwyn M. "Bryan Edwards, F.R.S., 1743–1800." *Notes and Records of the Royal Society of London* 54, no. 2 (May 2000): 215–22.

Bowen, Nathaniel. *A Pastoral Letter, on the Religious Instruction of the Slaves of Members of the Protestant Episcopal Church in the State of South Carolina.* Charleston: A. E. Miller, 1835.

Braidwood, Stephen. *Black Poor and White Philanthropists: London's Blacks and the Foundation of the Sierra Leone Settlement, 1786–1791.* Liverpool: Liverpool University Press, 1994.

Brodnax, William H. *The Speech of William H. Brodnax on the Policy of the State with Respect to Its Colored Population, Delivered January 19, 1832.* Richmond: T. W. White, 1832.

Brougham, Henry. *A Concise Statement Regarding the Abolition of the Slave Trade.* London: J. Hatchard, 1804.

Brown, Christopher L. "Empire without America: British Plans for Africa." In *Abolitionism and Imperialism in Britain, Africa, and the Atlantic,* edited by Derek R. Peterson, 84–100. Athens: Ohio University Press, 2010.

———. "Empire without Slaves: British Concepts of Emancipation in the Age of the American Revolution." *William and Mary Quarterly,* 3rd ser., 56, no. 2 (April 1999): 273–306.

———. *Moral Capital: Foundations of British Abolitionism.* Chapel Hill: University of North Carolina Press, 2006.

———. "The Politics of Slavery." In *The British Atlantic World, 1500–1800,* edited by David Armitage and Michael Braddick, 214–32. New York: Palgrave Macmillan, 2002.

Brownlee, W. Elliot, and Jay R. Carlander. "Antebellum Political Economists and the Problem of Slavery." *American Nineteenth Century History* 7, no. 3 (September 2006): 389–416.

Burke, Edmund. "A Letter to the Right Hon. Henry Dundas, One of His Majesty's Principal Secretaries of State, with the Sketch of the Negro Code." In *Select Works of Edmund Burke,* 4 vols., edited by F. J. Payne. Indianapolis: Liberty Fund, 1999. http://oll.libertyfund.org /title/659/20406.

Burnard, Trevor. *Mastery, Tyranny, and Desire: Thomas Thistlewood and His Slaves in the Anglo-Jamaican World.* Chapel Hill: University of North Carolina Press, 2004.

Canning, George. *The Speech of the Rt. Hon. George Canning, in the House of Commons, on the 16th Day of March 1823, on Laying before the House the Papers in Explanation of the Measures Adopted by His Majesty's Government, for the Amelioration of the Condition of the Slave Population in His Majesty's Dominions in the West Indies.* London: Maurice, 1830.

Carrington, Selwyn H. H. *The British West Indies during the American Revolution.* Providence, R.I.: Foris Publications, 1988.

Cateau, H. "Conservatism and Change Implementation in the British West Indian Sugar Industry, 1750–1810." *Journal of Caribbean History* 29 (1995): 1–36.

Chaplin, Joyce E. *An Anxious Pursuit: Agricultural Innovation and Modernity in the Lower South, 1730–1815.* Chapel Hill: University of North Carolina Press, 1993.

Charmilly, Venault de. *Answer, by Way of Letter, to Bryan Edwards, Esq., M.P., F.R.S., Planter of*

Jamaica, &c. Containing a Refutation of His Historical Survey on the French Colony of St. Domingo, etc. etc. London: Baylis, 1797.

Checkland, S. G. *The Gladstones: A Family Biography, 1764–1851.* Cambridge: Cambridge University Press, 1971.

Clarkson, Thomas. *An Essay on the Comparative Efficiency of Regulation or Abolition, as Applied to the Slave Trade.* London: J. Phillips, 1789.

———. *Letters on the Slave-Trade, and the State of the Native in Those Parts of Africa, Which Are Contiguous to Fort St. Louis and Goree, Written at Paris in December 1789, and January 1790.* 2 vols. London: J. Phillips, 1790.

———. *A Letter to the Clergy of Various Denominations, and to the Slaveholding Planters, in the Southern Parts of the United States of America.* London: Johnston and Barrett, 1841.

———. *Thoughts on the Necessity of Improving the Slaves in the British Colonies, with a View to Their Ultimate Emancipation.* London: Richard Taylor, 1823.

Clay, Henry. *Speech of the Hon. Henry Clay, before the American Colonization Society: In the Hall of the House of Representatives, January 20, 1827.* Washington, D.C.: Columbian Office, 1827.

Clay, Thomas S. *Detail of a Plan for the Moral Improvement of Negroes on Plantations, Read before the Georgia Presbytery.* N.p.: Georgia Presbytery, 1833.

Clifton, James M. "Hopeton, Model Plantation of the Antebellum South." *Georgia Historical Quarterly* 66, no. 4 (1982): 428–49.

Coclanis, Peter A. *The Shadow of a Dream: Economic Life and Death in the South Carolina Low Country, 1670–1920.* New York: Oxford University Press, 1991.

Coles, Edward, and Thomas Jefferson. "Letters of Edward Coles to Thomas Jefferson." *William and Mary Quarterly,* 2nd ser., 7, no. 2 (April 1927): 97–113.

Colley, Linda. *Britons: Forging the Nation 1707–1837.* New Haven, Conn.: Yale University Press, 1992.

———. *Captives: Britain, Empire and the World.* New York: Pantheon Books, 2002.

Condorcet, Jean-Antoine-Nicolas de Caritat. *Réflexions sur l'esclavage des nègres.* Neuchatel, Switzerland: La Societé Typographique, 1781.

Condorcet, Jean-Antoine-Nicolas de Caritat, and Elkhanah Tinsdale. *Outlines of a Historical View of the Progress of the Human Mind, Being a Posthumous Work of the Late M. de Condorcet.* Philadelphia: Land and Ustick, 1796.

Coombs, John C. "The Phases of Conversion: A New Chronology for the Rise of Slavery in Early Virginia." *William and Mary Quarterly,* 3rd ser., 68, no. 3 (July 2011): 332–60.

Cooper, Thomas. "Slavery." *Southern Literary Journal and Magazine of Arts,* November 1835, 188–93.

Cornelius, Janet Duitsman. *Slave Missions and the Black Church in the Antebellum South.* Columbia: University of South Carolina Press, 1991.

Costa, Emilia Da. *Crowns of Glory, Tears of Blood: The Demerara Slave Rebellion of 1823.* New York: Oxford University Press, 1994.

Coughtry, Jay. *The Notorious Triangle: Rhode Island and the African Slave Trade, 1700–1807.* Philadelphia: Temple University Press, 1981.

Coyner, Martin Boyd, Jr. "John Hartwell Cocke of Bremo: Agriculture and Slavery in the Ante-bellum South." PhD diss., University of Virginia, 1961.

Craton, Michael. "Reluctant Creoles: The Planters' World in the British West Indies." In *Strangers within the Realm: Cultural Margins of the First British Empire,* edited by Bernard

Bailyn and Philip D. Morgan, 314–62. Chapel Hill: University of North Carolina Press, 1991.

———. *Testing the Chains: Resistance to Slavery in the British West Indies.* Ithaca, N.Y.: Cornell University Press, 1982.

Craven, Avery Odell. "Soil Exhaustion as a Factor in the Agricultural History of Virginia and Maryland, 1606–1860." *University of Illinois Studies in the Social Sciences* 13, no. 1 (1925): 9–172.

Cropper, James, and John Gladstone. *The Correspondence between John Gladstone, Esq., M.P., and James Cropper, Esq.* Liverpool: West India Association, 1824.

Crowley, John E. *The Invention of Comfort: Sensibilities and Design in Early Modern Britain and Early America.* Baltimore: Johns Hopkins University Press, 2000.

Cundall, Frank. "Bryan Castle." *The West India Committee Circular* (1911): 363–65.

Curtin, Philip D. *The Image of Africa: British Ideas and Action, 1780–1850.* Madison: University of Wisconsin Press, 1964.

Dalcho, Frederick. *Practical Considerations Founded on the Scriptures, Relative to the Slave Population of South Carolina.* Charleston: A. E. Miller, 1823.

Davis, David Brion. "Capitalism, Abolitionism and Hegemony." In *British Capitalism and Caribbean Slavery: The Legacy of Eric Williams,* edited by Barbara L. Solow and Stanley L. Engerman, 209–27. Cambridge: Cambridge University Press, 1987.

———. *Challenging the Boundaries of Slavery.* Cambridge, Mass.: Harvard University Press, 2003.

———. "The Emergence of Immediatism in British and American Antislavery Thought." *Mississippi Valley Historical Review* 49, no. 2 (1962): 209–30.

———. *Inhuman Bondage: The Rise and Fall of Slavery in the New World.* Oxford: Oxford University Press, 2006.

———. "James Cropper and British Antislavery Movement, 1821–1823." *Journal of Negro History* 45, no. 4 (October 1960): 241–68.

———. "James Cropper and British Antislavery Movement, 1823–1833." *Journal of Negro History* 46, no. 3 (April 1961): 154–73.

———. *The Problem of Slavery in the Age of Revolution, 1770–1823.* New York: Oxford University Press, 1999.

———. *The Problem of Slavery in Western Culture.* 1966. Reprint New York: Oxford University Press, 1988.

———. *Slavery and Human Progress.* New York: Oxford University Press, 1984.

Davis, Jefferson. "Message of Jefferson Davis to the Confederate Congress, April 29, 1861." In *The Rebellion Record: A Diary of American Events,* 11 vols., edited by Frank Moore, 1:169. New York: G. P. Putnam and Van Nostrand, 1861–68.

Dew, Thomas R. *Review of the Debate in the Virginia Legislature of 1831 and 1832.* Richmond: T. W. White, 1832.

Deyle, Steven. *Carry Me Back: The Domestic Slave Trade in American Life.* New York: Oxford University Press, 2005.

Dierksheide, Christa. "'Capable of Improvement': Commerce, Christianity, and the Idea of an Independent Africa, ca. 1740–1810." International Seminar on the History of the Atlantic World, Harvard University, August 2006.

———. "'The Great Improvement and Civilization of That Race': Jefferson and the

'Amelioration' of Slavery, ca. 1770–1826." *Early American Studies* 6, no. 1 (Spring 2008): 165–97.

———. "Missionaries, Evangelical Identity, and the Religious Ecology of Early Nineteenth Century South Carolina and the British Caribbean." *American Nineteenth Century History* 7, no. 1 (2006): 63–88.

Dierksheide, Christa, and Peter S. Onuf. "Slave-holding Nation, Slaveholding Civilization." In *In the Cause of Liberty: How the Civil War Redefined American Ideals*, edited by William J. Cooper Jr. and John M. McCardell Jr., 9–24. Baton Rouge: Louisiana State University Press, 2009.

Donnan, Elizabeth. "The Slave Trade into South Carolina before the Revolution." *American Historical Review* 33, no. 4 (July 1928): 810.

Drayton, Richard. *Nature's Government: Science, Imperial Britain, and the "Improvement" of the World*. New Haven, Conn.: Yale University Press, 2000.

Drescher, Seymour. "The Decline Thesis of British Slavery since *Econocide*." *Slavery and Abolition* 7, no. 1 (1986): 3–24.

———. *Econocide: British Slavery in the Age of Abolition*. Pittsburgh: University of Pittsburgh Press, 1977.

———. "Emperors of the World: British Abolitionism and Imperialism." In *Abolitionism and Imperialism in Britain, Africa, and the Atlantic*, edited by Derek R. Peterson, 129–49. Athens: Ohio University Press, 2010.

———. *The Mighty Experiment: Free Labor versus Slavery in British Emancipation*. New York: Oxford University Press, 2002.

———. "People and Parliament: The Rhetoric of the British Slave Trade." *Journal of Interdisciplinary History* 20 (1990): 561–63.

Dubois, Laurent. *Avengers of the New World: The Story of the Haitian Revolution*. Cambridge, Mass.: Belknap Press of Harvard University Press, 2004.

———. *A Colony of Citizens: Revolution and Slave Emancipation in the French Caribbean, 1787–1804*. Chapel Hill: University of North Carolina Press, 2004.

Dundas, Henry. *Substance of the Argument of the Right Honourable Henry Dundas, on the Slave Trade, April 23, 1792*. London: n.p., 1792.

Dusinberre, William. *Them Dark Days: Slavery in the American Rice Swamps*. New York: Oxford University Press, 1996.

Edelson, S. Max. *Plantation Enterprise in Colonial South Carolina*. Cambridge, Mass.: Harvard University Press, 2006.

Edwards, Bryan. *An Historical Survey of the French Colony in the Island of St. Domingo: Comprehending a Short Account of Its Ancient Government, Political State, Population, Productions, and Exports; a Narrative of the Calamities Which Have Desolated the Country Ever Since the Year 1789*. London: J. Stockdale, 1797.

———. *The History, Civil and Commercial, of the British Colonies in the West Indies*. 3 vols. London: J. Stockdale, 1807.

———. *List of Maps and Plates for the History, Civil and Commercial, of the British Colonies in the West Indies*. London: J. Stockdale, 1794.

———. *A Speech Delivered at a Free Conference between the Council and Assembly of Jamaica . . . on the Subject of Mr. Wilberforce's Propositions in the House of Commons, Concerning the Slave Trade*. London: J. Debrett, 1790.

———. *Thoughts on the Late Proceedings of Government Respecting the Trade of the West India Islands with the United States of North America*. London: J. Stockdale, 1784.

Egerton, Douglas R. *He Shall Go out Free: The Lives of Denmark Vesey*. Madison, Wis.: Madison House, 1999.

Elliot, Jonathan, ed. *The Debates in the Several State Conventions on the Adoption of the Federal Constitution*. 5 vols. Philadelphia: J. B. Lippincott and Company, 1876.

Encyclopedia Britannica: Of a Dictionary of Arts, Sciences and Miscellaneous Literature. 3rd edition. 10 vols. Edinburgh: A. Bell and C. MacFarquar, 1797–1801.

Engerman, Stanley L. "Economic Adjustments to Emancipation in the United States and the British West Indies." *Journal of Interdisciplinary History* 13 (Autumn 1982): 191–220.

Engerman Stanley L., and Robert William Fogel. *Without Consent or Contract: The Rise and Fall of American Slavery*. New York: Norton, 1992.

Equiano, Olaudah. *The Interesting Narrative and Other Writings*. Edited by Vincent Caretta. New York: Penguin Books, 1995.

Evans, Eric J. *Britain before the Reform Act: Politics and Society, 1815–32*. London: Longman, 1989.

Fairfax, Ferdinando. "Plan for Liberating the Negroes within the United States." *American Museum*, December 1790, 285–87.

Faulkner, Charles. *The Speech of Charles Faulkner (of Berkeley) in the House of Delegates of Virginia, on the Policy of the State with Respect to Her Slave Population. Delivered January 20, 1832*. Richmond: T. W. White, 1832.

Faust, Drew Gilpin. *James Henry Hammond and the Old South: A Design for Mastery*. Baton Rouge: Louisiana State University Press, 1982.

Ferguson, T. Reed. *The John Couper Family at Cannon's Point*. Macon, Ga.: Mercer University Press, 1994.

Fiering, Norman, and David Patrick Geggus. *The World of the Haitian Revolution*. Bloomington: Indiana University Press, 2009.

Ford, Lacy K. *Deliver Us from Evil: The Slavery Question in the Old South*. New York: Oxford University Press, 2009.

———. *Origins of Southern Radicalism: The South Carolina Upcountry, 1800–1860*. New York: Oxford University Press, 1991.

Fox-Genovese, Elizabeth. *Within the Plantation Household: Black and White Women of the Old South*. Chapel Hill: University of North Carolina Press, 1988.

Freehling, Alison Goodyear. *Drift toward Dissolution: The Virginia Slave Debate of 1831–1832*. Baton Rouge: Louisiana State University Press, 1982.

Freehling, William W. *The Road to Disunion, vol. 1, Secessionists at Bay*. Oxford: Oxford University Press, 1991.

French, Scot A. *The Rebellious Slave: Nat Turner in American Memory*. New York: Houghton Mifflin, 2004.

Fuente, Alejandro de la. "Slaves and the Creation of Legal Rights in Cuba: Coartación and Papel." *Hispanic American Historical Review* 87, no. 4 (November 2007): 659–92.

Furstenberg, François. "Beyond Freedom and Slavery: Autonomy, Virtue, and Resistance in Early American Political Discourse." *Journal of American History* 89, no. 4 (March 2003): 1295–1330.

Galloway, J. H. *The Sugar Cane Industry: An Historical Geography from Its Origins to 1914*. Cambridge: Cambridge University Press, 1989.

Garrison, William Lloyd. "On the Constitution and the Union." *The Liberator,* December 29, 1832.

———. "On Walker's Appeal." *The Liberator,* January 8, 1831.

———. "To the Public." *The Liberator,* January 1, 1831.

Gellner, Ernest. *Nations and Nationalism.* Ithaca, N.Y.: Cornell University Press, 1983.

Genovese, Eugene D. *Roll, Jordan, Roll: The World the Slaves Made.* New York: Pantheon Books, 1974.

———. *The Slaveholders' Dilemma: Freedom and Progress in Southern Conservative Thought, 1820–1860.* Columbia: University of South Carolina Press, 1992.

Ghatchem, Malick W. *The Old Regime and the Haitian Revolution.* Cambridge: Cambridge University Press, 2012.

Gibson, James R., Jr. *Americans versus Malthus: The Population Debate in the Early Republic, 1790–1840.* New York: Garland, 1989.

Giese, Ronald L. *Tobacco Cultivation in Virginia, 1610–1863, and Patterns of Thought Related to Thomas Jefferson.* Middleton, Wis.: R. L. Giese, 2003.

Gladstone, John. *Facts, Relating to Slavery in the West Indies and America, Contained in a Letter Addressed to the Right Hon. Robert Peel, Bart.* London: Baldwin and Cradock, 1830.

———. *Mercator's Reply to Mr. Booth's Pamphlet on Free Trade, as Published in the Liverpool Standard: To Which Are Added Two Letters on the Currency Question, and One on Taxation.* Liverpool: S. Franceys, 1833.

Gordon-Reed, Annette. *The Hemingses of Monticello: An American Family.* New York: Norton, 2008.

Gottschalk, Louis. *Lafayette between the American and French Revolutions.* Chicago: University of Chicago Press, 1950.

Gould, Eliga H. "American Independence and Britain's Counter-Revolution." *Past and Present* 154, no. 1 (February 1997): 107–14.

———. *Among the Powers of the Earth: The American Revolution and the Making of a New World Empire.* Cambridge, Mass.: Harvard University Press, 2012.

———. "The Laws of War and Peace: Legitimating Slavery in the Age of the American Revolution." In *State and Citizen: British America and the Early United States,* edited by Peter Thompson and Peter S. Onuf, 52–76. Charlottesville: University of Virginia Press, 2013.

———. "Zones of Law, Zones of Violence: The Legal Geography of the British Atlantic, ca. 1772." *William and Mary Quarterly,* 3rd ser., 60, no. 3 (July 2003): 471–510.

Gould, Philip. *Barbaric Traffic: Commerce and Antislavery in the Eighteenth-Century Atlantic World.* Cambridge, Mass.: Harvard University Press, 2003.

Greenberg, Kenneth S. *Nat Turner: A Slave Rebellion in History and Memory.* Oxford: Oxford University Press, 2003.

Greene, Jack P. *The Constitutional Origins of the American Revolution.* New York: Cambridge University Press, 2011.

———. *Imperatives, Behaviors, and Identities: Essays in Early American Cultural History.* Charlottesville: University Press of Virginia, 1992.

———. *Peripheries and Center: Constitutional Development in the Extended Polities of the British Empire and the United States, 1607–1788.* Athens: University of Georgia Press, 1986.

Gudmestad, Robert H. *A Troublesome Commerce: The Transformation of the Interstate Slave Trade.* Baton Rouge: Louisiana State University Press, 2004.

Hallett, Robin. *The Penetration of Africa: European Enterprise and Exploration Principally in Northern and Western Africa up to 1830.* London: Routledge and Kegan Paul, 1965.

————, ed. *Records of the African Association, 1788–1831.* New York: T. Nelson, 1962.

Hammond, James Henry. *Gov. Hammond's Letters on Southern Slavery: Addressed to Thomas Clarkson, the English Abolitionist.* Charleston: Walker and Burke, 1845.

Hancock, David. *Citizens of the World: London Merchants and the Integration of the British Atlantic Community.* Cambridge: Cambridge University Press, 1995.

Harper, William. *Anniversary Oration; Delivered by the Hon. William Harper, in the Representative Hall, Columbia, S.C., Dec. 9, 1835.* Washington, D.C.: Duff Green, 1836.

————. "Colonization Society." *Southern Review* 1 (February 1828): 233.

———— "Memoir on Slavery." In *The Pro-Slavery Argument; As Maintained by the Most Distinguished Writers of the Southern States, Containing the Several Essays, on the Subject, of Chancellor Harper, Governor Hammond, Dr. Simms, and Professor Dew.* Charleston: Walker, Richards, and Company, 1852.

Harris, Mark. "Civil Society in Post-Revolutionary America." In *Empire and Nation: The American Revolution in the Atlantic World,* edited by Eliga H. Gould and Peter S. Onuf, 197–216. Baltimore: Johns Hopkins University Press, 2005.

Haskell, Thomas L. "Capitalism and the Origins of the Humanitarian Sensibility." *American Historical Review* 90–91 (April–June 1985): 339–62, 547–67.

Helo, Ari, and Peter S. Onuf. "Jefferson, Morality, and the Problem of Slavery." *William and Mary Quarterly,* 3rd ser., 60, no. 3 (July 2003): 583–614.

Hendrickson, David C. *Peace Pact: The Lost World of the American Founding.* Lawrence: University of Kansas Press, 2006.

Herndon, G. Melvin. "A History of Tobacco in Virginia, 1613–1860." MS thesis, University of Virginia, 1956.

Higman, B. W. *Jamaica Surveyed: Plantation Maps and Plans of the Eighteenth and Nineteenth Centuries.* Kingston: Institute of Jamaica Publications, 1988.

————. *Plantation Jamaica 1750–1850: Capital and Control in a Colonial Economy.* Kingston: University of the West Indies Press, 2005.

————. *Slave Populations of the British Caribbean, 1807–1834.* Baltimore: Johns Hopkins University Press, 1984.

————. "Slavery and the Development of Demographic Theory in the Age of the Industrial Revolution." In *Slavery and British Society, 1776–1846,* edited by James Walvin, 164–94. Baton Rouge: Louisiana State University Press, 1982.

————. "The West India 'Interest' in Parliament, 1807–1833." *Historical Studies* 13, no. 49 (October 1967): 1–19.

Hochschild, Adam. *Bury the Chains: Prophets and Rebels in the Fight to Free an Empire's Slaves.* New York: Houghton Mifflin, 2005.

Holland, Edwin Clifford. *A Refutation of the Calumnies Circulated against the Southern & Western States.* Charleston: A. E. Miller, 1822.

Holt, Thomas C. *The Problem of Freedom: Race, Labor, and Politics in Jamaica and Britain, 1832–1938.* Baltimore: Johns Hopkins University Press.

Horn, James. "Transformations of Virginia: Tobacco, Slavery, and Empire." *William and Mary Quarterly,* 3rd ser., 68, no. 3 (July 2011): 327–31.

Horn, James, Jan Ellen Lewis, and Peter S. Onuf, eds. *The Revolution of 1800: Democracy, Race, and the New Republic.* Charlottesville: University of Virginia Press, 2002.

Howard, Allen M. "Nineteenth-Century Coastal Slave-Trading and the British Abolition Campaign in Sierra Leone." *Slavery and Abolition* 27, no. 1 (2006): 23–49.

Hugh, Thomas. *The Slave Trade: The Story of the Atlantic Slave Trade, 1440–1870.* New York: Simon and Schuster, 1997.

Hughes, Louis. *Thirty Years a Slave: From Bondage to Freedom.* Milwaukee: South Side, 1897.

Hunt, Lynn. "The French Revolution in Global Context." In *The Age of Revolutions in Global Context, c. 1760–1840,* edited by David Armitage and Sanjay Subrahmanyam, 20–36. Basingstoke, Eng.: Palgrave Macmillan, 2010.

Huston, James L. "Theory's Failure: Malthusian Population Theory and the Projected Demise of Slavery." *Civil War History* 55, no. 3 (2009): 354–81.

Huzzey, Richard. *Freedom Burning: Anti-Slavery and Empire in Victorian Britain.* Ithaca, N.Y.: Cornell University Press, 2012.

Irons, Charles F. *The Origins of Proslavery Christianity: White and Black Evangelicals in Colonial and Antebellum Virginia.* Chapel Hill: University of North Carolina Press, 2008.

A Jamaican Planter. *Notes on the Two Reports from the Committees of the Honorable House of Assembly of Jamaica.* London: J. Phillips, 1789.

January, Alan F. "The South Carolina Association: An Agency for Race Control in Antebellum Charleston." *South Carolina Historical Magazine* 78 (1977): 191–201.

Jasanoff, Maya. *Edge of Empire: Lives, Culture, and Conquest in the East.* New York: Knopf, 2005.

———. *Liberty's Exiles: American Loyalists in the Revolutionary World.* New York: Knopf, 2011.

Jefferson, Thomas. *Jefferson's Memorandum Books: Accounts, with Legal Records and Miscellany, 1767–1826.* Edited by James A. Bear and Lucia C. Stanton. 2 vols. Princeton, N.J.: Princeton University Press, 1997.

———. *The Papers of Thomas Jefferson.* Edited by Julian P. Boyd, Charles T. Cullen, John Catanzariti, Barbara B. Oberg, et al. 39 vols. to date. Princeton, N.J.: Princeton University Press, 1950–.

———. *Thomas Jefferson's Farm Book: With Commentary and Relevant Extracts from Other Writings.* Edited by Edwin M. Betts. Princeton, N.J.: Princeton University Press, 1953.

———. *Writings.* Edited by Merrill D. Peterson. New York: Library of America, 1984.

———. *The Writings of Thomas Jefferson.* Edited by Paul Leicester Ford. 10 vols. New York: G. P. Putnam's Sons, 1892–99.

———. *The Writings of Thomas Jefferson.* Edited by Andrew A. Lipscomb and Albert A. Bergh. 20 vols. Washington, D.C.: Thomas Jefferson Memorial Association, 1903–7.

Jefferson, Thomas, and Marie Joseph Paul Yves Roch Gilbert Du Motier de Lafayette. *Letters of Lafayette and Jefferson.* Edited by Gilbert Chinard. Baltimore: Johns Hopkins University Press, 1929.

Johnson, Michael D. "Denmark Vesey and His Co-Conspirators." *William and Mary Quarterly,* 3rd ser., 58, no. 4 (October 2001): 915–76.

Johnson, Walter. "On Agency." *Journal of Social History* 37, no. 1 (2003): 113–24.

———. "The Pedestal and the Veil: Rethinking the Capitalism/Slavery Question." *Journal of the Early Republic* 24 (Summer 2004): 301–10.

———. "Planters and Patriarchy: Charleston, 1800–1860." *Journal of Southern History* 46 (1980): 45–72.

————. *River of Dark Dreams: Slavery and Empire in the Cotton Kingdom.* Cambridge, Mass.: Belknap Press of Harvard University Press, 2013.

————. *Soul by Soul: Life Inside the Antebellum Slave Market.* Cambridge, Mass.: Harvard University Press, 1999.

Johnson, William. *Nugae Georgicae: An Essay Delivered to the Literary and Philosophical Society of Charleston, South Carolina.* Charleston: J. Hoff, 1815.

Jordan, Winthrop. *White over Black: American Attitudes toward the Negro, 1550–1812.* Baltimore: Pelican Books, 1969.

Joyner, Charles W. *Down by the Riverside: A South Carolina Slave Community.* Urbana: University of Illinois Press, 1984.

Kars, Marjoleine. *Breaking Loose Together: The Regulator Rebellion in Pre-Revolutionary North Carolina.* Chapel Hill: University of North Carolina Press, 2002.

Kelly, Joseph P. "Henry Laurens: The Southern Man of Conscience in History." *South Carolina Historical Magazine* 107, no. 2 (April 2006): 82–123.

Kennedy, Melvin D. *Lafayette and Slavery, from His Letters to Thomas Clarkson and Granville Sharp.* Easton, Penn.: American Friends of Lafayette, 1950.

Keyes, Sarah. "'Like a Roaring Lion': The Overland Trail as a Sonic Conquest." *Journal of American History* 96, no. 1 (June 2009): 19–43.

Killens, John Oliver, ed. *The Trial Record of Denmark Vesey.* Boston: Beacon Press, 1970.

Kirschke, James J., and Victor J. Sensenig. "Steps toward Nationhood: Henry Laurens and the American Revolution in the South." *Historical Research* 78, no. 200 (May 2005): 180–92.

Klein, Herbert S. *The Atlantic Slave Trade.* Cambridge: Cambridge University Press, 1999.

Klein, Rachel N. *Unification of a Slave State: The Rise of the Planter Class in the South Carolina Backcountry, 1760–1808.* Chapel Hill: University of North Carolina Press, 1990.

Klingberg, Frank J. *The Anti-Slavery Movement in England: A Study in English Humanitarianism.* London: Yale University Press, 1926.

Knupfer, Peter B. *The Union as It Is: Constitutional Unionism and Sectional Compromise, 1787–1861.* Chapel Hill: University of North Carolina Press, 1991.

Konig, David Thomas. "Antislavery in Jefferson's Virginia: The Incremental Attack on an Entrenched Institution." Unpublished paper, 2006.

Kulikoff, Allan. *Tobacco and Slaves: The Development of Southern Cultures in the Chesapeake, 1680–1800.* Chapel Hill: University of North Carolina Press, 1986.

Lambert, David. *White Creole Culture, Politics, and Identity during the Age of Abolition.* Cambridge: Cambridge University Press, 2005.

Lascelles, Edwin, et al. *Instructions for the Management of Plantation in Barbados, and for the Treatment of Negroes &c.* London: n.p., 1786.

Laurens, Henry. *The Papers of Henry Laurens.* Edited by Philip Hamer, George C. Rogers, David R. Chesnutt, C. James Taylor, et al. 16 vols. Columbia: University of South Carolina Press, 1968–2003.

Legaré, John D. "Account of an Agricultural Excursion Made into the South of Georgia in 1832; by the Editor." *Southern Agriculturist and Register of Rural Affairs* 6 (April 1833): 157–78; (May 1833): 243, 249–53; (June 1833): 281–87; (July 1833): 358–63; (November 1833): 571–74, 576–77.

Lewis, Jan. "'The Blessings of Domestic Society': Thomas Jefferson's Family and the Transformation of American Politics." In *Jeffersonian Legacies,* edited by Peter S. Onuf, 109–46. Charlottesville: University Press of Virginia, 1993.

————. "The Problem of Slavery in Southern Discourse." In *Devising Liberty: Preserving and Creating Freedom in the New American Republic,* edited by David T. Konig, 265–97. Palo Alto: Stanford University Press, 1995.

————. *The Pursuit of Happiness: Family and Values in Jefferson's Virginia.* Cambridge: Cambridge University Press, 1983.

Lipset, Seymour Martin. *The First New Nation: The United States in Historical and Comparative Perspective.* New York: Basic Books, 1963.

Littlefield, Daniel C. *Rice and Slaves: Ethnicity and the Slave Trade in Colonial South Carolina.* Baton Rouge: Louisiana State University Press, 1981.

Lofton, John. *Insurrection in South Carolina: The Turbulent World of Denmark Vesey.* Yellow Springs, Ohio: Antioch Press, 1964.

Long, Edward. *History of Jamaica; or, General Survey of the Antient and Modern State of That Island: With Reflections on Its Situation, Settlements, Inhabitants.* 3 vols. London: T. Lowndes, 1774.

McCoy, Drew R. *The Elusive Republic: Political Economy in Jeffersonian America.* Chapel Hill: University of North Carolina Press, 1980.

————. *Last of the Fathers: James Madison and the Republican Legacy.* New York: Cambridge University Press, 1989.

McDonald, Roderick A., and Richard B. Sheridan. *West Indies Accounts: Essays on the History of the British Caribbean and the Atlantic Economy in Honour of Richard Sheridan.* Kingston, Jamaica: University of the West Indies Press, 1996.

McDonough, Daniel J. *Christopher Gadsden and Henry Laurens: The Parallel Lives of Two American Patriots.* Sellinsgrove, Penn.: Susquehanna University Press, 2000.

McInnis, Maurie D. *In Pursuit of Refinement: Charlestonians Abroad, 1740–1860.* Columbia: University of South Carolina Press, 1999.

McKeon, Michael. *The Secret History of Domesticity: Public, Private, and the Division of Knowledge.* Baltimore: Johns Hopkins University Press, 2005.

Major, Andrea. *Slavery, Abolitionism, and Empire in India, 1772–1843.* Liverpool: Liverpool University Press, 2012.

Malthus, Thomas. *An Essay on the Principle of Population.* London: J. Johnson, 1798.

Marshall, P. J. *The Making and Unmaking of Empires: Britain, India and America c. 1750–1783.* Oxford: Oxford University Press, 2005.

Marshall, Woodville. "Amelioration and Emancipation (with Special Reference to Barbados)." In *Emancipation I: A Series of Lectures to Commemorate the 150th Anniversary of Emancipation,* edited by Alvin O. Thompson, 72–87. Bridgetown, Barbados: Cedar Press, 1984.

Martin, Jonathan D. *Divided Mastery: Slave Hiring in the Antebellum South.* Cambridge, Mass.: Harvard University Press, 2004.

Martin, Samuel. *Essay upon Plantership, Humbly Inscrib'd to All the Planters of the British Sugar-Colonies in America.* Antigua: T. Smith, 1750.

Mason, Matthew. "The Battle of Slave-Holding Liberators: Great Britain, the United States, and Slavery in the Early Nineteenth Century." *William and Mary Quarterly,* 3rd ser., 59, no. 3 (July 2002): 665–96.

————. *Slavery and Politics in the Early American Republic.* Chapel Hill: University of North Carolina Press, 2006.

————. "A World Safe for Modernity: Antebellum Southern Intellectuals Confront Great

Britain." In *The Old South's Modern Worlds: Slavery, Region, and Nation in the Age of Progress*, edited by L. Diane Barnes, Brian Schoen, and Frank Towers, 47–65. New York: Oxford University Press, 2011.

Massey, Gregory D. "The Limits of Antislavery Thought in the Revolutionary Lower South: John Laurens and Henry Laurens." *Journal of Southern History* 63, no. 3 (August 1997): 495–530.

Matson, Cathy D., and Peter S. Onuf. *A Union of Interests: Political and Economic Thought in Revolutionary America*. Lawrence: University Press of Kansas, 1990.

Mattes, Armin. *Citizens of a Common Intellectual Homeland: The Transatlantic Context of the Origins of American Democracy and Nationhood, 1775–1840*. Charlottesville: University of Virginia Press, forthcoming.

Matthews, Gelien. *Caribbean Slave Revolts and the British Abolitionist Movement*. Baton Rouge: Louisiana State University Press, 2006.

Miller, Peter N. *Defining the Common Good: Empire, Religion, and Philosophy in Eighteenth-Century Britain*. Cambridge: Cambridge University Press, 1994.

Miller, Randall M., ed. *"Dear Master": Letters of a Slave Family*. Ithaca, N.Y.: Cornell University Press, 1978.

Minchinton, Walter E. "Williams and Drescher: Abolition and Emancipation." *Slavery and Abolition* 4 (1983): 79–105.

Mintz, Sidney W. *Caribbean Transformations*. New York: Columbia University Press, 1989.

Mitchell, B. R. *British Historical Statistics*. Cambridge: Cambridge University Press, 1988.

Monroe, James. *The Writings of James Monroe*. Edited by Stanislaus Murray Hamilton. 7 vols. New York and London: G. P. Putnam's Sons, 1898–1903.

Moore, William Cabell. "Gen. John Hartwell Cocke of Bremo: A Brief Biography and Genealogical Review with a Short History of Old Bremo." *William and Mary Quarterly*, 2nd ser., 13, no. 3 (July 1933): 143–54.

Morgan, Edmund. *American Slavery, American Freedom: The Ordeal of Colonial Virginia*. New York: Norton, 1975.

Morgan, Philip D. "Ending the Slave Trade: A Caribbean and Atlantic Context." In *Abolitionism and Imperialism in Britain, Africa, and the Atlantic*, edited by Derek R. Peterson, 101–28. Athens: Ohio University Press, 2010.

———. *Slave Counterpoint: Black Culture in the Eighteenth Century Chesapeake and Lowcountry*. Chapel Hill: University of North Carolina Press, 1998.

———. "Three Planters and Their Slaves: Perspectives on Slavery in Virginia, South Carolina, and Jamaica." In *Race and Family in the Colonial South*, edited by Winthrop Jordan and Sheila Skemp, 54–68. Jackson: University Press of Mississippi, 1987.

M'Queen, James. *The West India Colonies: The Calumnies and Misrepresentations Circulated against Them by the Edinburgh Review, Mr. Clarkson, Mr. Cropper, etc. etc.* London: Baldwin, Craddock, Joy, 1824.

Mulcahy, Matthew. *Hurricanes and Society in the British Greater Caribbean, 1624–1783*. Baltimore: Johns Hopkins University Press, 2006.

Murray, D. J. *The West Indies and the Development of Colonial Government, 1801–1834*. Oxford: Oxford University Press, 1965.

Nash, Gary B. "Franklin and Slavery." *Proceedings of the American Antiquarian Society* 150, no. 4 (December 2006): 618–35.

————. "Slaves and Slaveowners in Colonial Philadelphia." *William and Mary Quarterly*, 3rd ser., 30, no. 2 (April 1973): 223–56.

Neiman, Fraser D. "The Lost World of Monticello: An Evolutionary Perspective." *Journal of Anthropological Research* 64 (Summer 2008): 161–93.

Nesbitt, Nick. *Universal Emancipation: The Haitian Revolution and the Radical Enlightenment.* Charlottesville: University of Virginia Press, 2008.

Newman, Simon P. *A New World of Labor: The Development of Plantation Slavery in the British Atlantic.* Philadelphia: University of Pennsylvania Press, 2013.

Newton, John. *Thoughts upon the African Slave Trade.* London: J. Buckland and J. Johnson, 1788.

Oakes, James. "'I Own My Slaves, but They Also Own Me': Property and Paternalism in the Slave South." *Reviews in American History* 38, no. 4 (December 2010): 587–94.

————. *The Ruling Race: A History of American Slaveholders.* New York: Norton, 1998.

————. "'Whom Have I Oppressed': The Pursuit of Happiness and the Happy Slave." In *The Revolution of 1800: Democracy, Race, and the New Republic,* edited by James Horn et al., 220–39. Charlottesville: University Press of Virginia, 2003.

O'Brien, Michael. *Conjectures of Order: Intellectual Life and the American South, 1810–1860.* 2 vols. Chapel Hill: University of North Carolina Press, 2004.

Olwell, Robert. *Masters, Slaves and Subjects: The Culture of Power in the South Carolina Low Country, 1740–1790.* Ithaca, N.Y.: Cornell University Press, 1998.

————. "'A Reckoning of Accounts': Patriarchy, Market Relations, and Control on Henry Laurens's Lowcountry Plantations, 1762–1785." In *Working toward Freedom: Slave Society and Domestic Economy in the American South,* edited by Larry Hudson Jr., 33–52. Rochester, N.Y.: University of Rochester Press, 1994.

Onuf, Nicholas, and Peter Onuf. *Federal Union, Modern World: The Law of Nations in an Age of Revolution, 1776–1814.* Madison, Wis.: Madison House, 1990.

————. *Nations, Markets, and War: Modern History and the American Civil War.* Charlottesville: University of Virginia Press, 2006.

Onuf, Peter S. "American Exceptionalism and National Identity." *American Political Thought* 1 (2012): 77–100.

————. "Antebellum Southerners and the National Idea." In *The Old South's Modern Worlds: Slavery, Region, and Nation in the Age of Progress,* edited by L. Diane Barnes, Brian Schoen, and Frank Towers, 25–46. New York: Oxford University Press, 2011.

————. "Domesticating the Captive Nation: Thomas Jefferson and the Problem of Slavery." In *Jefferson, Lincoln, and Wilson: The American Dilemma of Race and Democracy,* edited by Thomas J. Knock and John Milton Cooper Jr., 34–60. Charlottesville: University of Virginia Press, 2010.

————. "Every Generation Is an 'Independent Nation': Colonization, Miscegenation, and the Fate of Jefferson's Children." *William and Mary Quarterly,* 3rd ser., 57, no. 1 (January 2000): 153–70.

————. "Federalism, Democracy, and Liberty in the New American Nation." In *Exclusionary Empire: English Liberty Overseas, 1600–1900,* edited by Jack P. Greene, 132–59. Cambridge: Cambridge University Press, 2010.

————. *Jefferson's Empire: The Language of American Nationhood.* Charlottesville: University Press of Virginia, 2000.

————. *The Mind of Thomas Jefferson.* Charlottesville: University Press of Virginia, 2007.

————. "Nations, Revolutions, and the End of History." In *Revolutionary Currents: Nation Building in the Transatlantic World,* edited by Michael A. Morrison and Melinda Zook, 173–88. New York: Rowman and Littlefield, 2004.

O'Shaughnessy, Andrew. "The Formation of a Commercial Lobby: The West India Interest, British Colonial Policy, and the American Revolution." *Historical Journal* 40, no. 1 (1997): 71–95.

————. *The Men Who Lost America: British Leadership, the American Revolution, and the Fate of the Empire.* New Haven, Conn.: Yale University Press, 2013

Palmer, R. R. *The Age of Democratic Revolution.* 2 vols. Princeton, N.J.: Princeton University Press, 1959–64.

Park, Mungo. *Travels in the Interior Districts of Africa: Performed under the Direction and Patronage of the African Association, in the Years 1795, 1796, and 1797.* London: W. Bulmer, 1799.

Peterson, Derek R., ed. *Abolitionism and Imperialism in Britain, Africa, and the Atlantic.* Athens: Ohio University Press, 2010.

Pinckney, Charles Cotesworth. *An Address Delivered in Charleston before the Agricultural Society of South Carolina at Its Anniversary Meeting.* Charleston: A. E. Miller, 1829.

Pocock, J. G. A. "States, Republics, and Empires: The American Founding in Early Modern Perspective." In *Conceptual Change and the Constitution,* edited by Terence Ball and J. G. A Pocock, 55–77. Lawrence: University Press of Kansas, 1988.

Popkin, Jeremy D. "The French Revolution's Other Island." In *The World of the Haitian Revolution,* edited by David Patrick Geggus and Norman Fiering, 199–222. Bloomington: Indiana University Press, 2009.

Porteus, Bielby. *The Civilization, Improvement, and Conversion of the Negro-Slaves in the British Islands: By the Right Revered Bielby Porteus, D.D. Bishop of Chester.* Dublin: John Exshaw, 1784.

Postlethwayt, Malachy. *The African Trade, the Great Pillar and Support of British Plantation Trade in America.* London: J. Robinson, 1745.

————. *The Importance of Effectually Supporting the Royal African Company of England.* London: M. Cooper, 1745.

————. *The Universal Dictionary of Trade and Commerce.* 2 vols. London: J. and P. Knapton, 1751–55.

Pybus, Cassandra. *Epic Journeys of Freedom: Runaway Slaves of the American Revolution and Their Global Quest for Liberty.* Boston: Beacon Press, 2006.

————. "Jefferson's Faulty Math: The Question of Slave Defections in the American Revolution." *William and Mary Quarterly,* 3rd ser., 62, no. 2 (April 2005): 243–64.

Ragatz, Lowell J. *The Fall of the Planter Class in the British Caribbean.* New York: Century and Company, 1928.

Rakove, Jack. *Revolutionaries: A New History of the Invention of America.* New York: Houghton Mifflin, 2010.

Ramsay, David. "David Ramsay, a Selection of His Writings." Edited by Robert L. Brunhouse. *Transactions of the American Philosophical Society* 55 (1965): 185–88.

Ramsay, James. *An Essay on the Treatment and Conversion of African Slaves in the British Sugar Colonies.* London: J. Phillips, 1784.

Randolph, Thomas Jefferson. *The Speech of Thomas J. Randolph (of Albemarle) in the House of Delegates of Virginia, on the Abolition of Slavery: Delivered Saturday, January 21, 1832.* Richmond: T. W. White, 1832.

Read, James H. *Majority Rule versus Consensus: The Political Thought of John C. Calhoun.* Lawrence: University Press of Kansas, 2009.

Rediker, Marcus. *The Slave Ship: A Human History.* New York: Viking Penguin, 2007.

Ricardo, David. *Essay on the Influence of the Low Price of Corn on the Profits of Stock.* London: John Murray, 1815.

———. *Principles of Political Economy and Taxation.* London: John Murray, 1817.

Roane, Spencer. "Letters of Spencer Roane, 1788–1822." *Bulletin of the New York Public Library* 10 (1906): 167–80.

Robert, Joseph Clarke. *The Road from Monticello: A Study of the Virginia Slavery Debate of 1832.* Durham, N.C.: Duke University Press, 1941.

Roberts, Justin. *Slavery and the Enlightenment in the British Atlantic, 1750–1807.* New York: Cambridge University Press, 2013.

———. "Working between the Lines: Labor and Agriculture on Two Barbadian Slave Plantations, 1796–1797." *William and Mary Quarterly,* 3rd ser., 63, no. 3 (July 2006): 551–86.

Rogers, George C. *Evolution of a Federalist: William Loughton Smith of Charleston, 1758–1812.* Columbia: University of South Carolina Press, 1962.

Roscoe, William. *A General View of the African Slave-Trade, Demonstrating Its Injustice and Impolicy: With Hints towards a Bill for Its Abolition.* London: R. Faulder, 1788.

Rose, Willie Lee, ed. *A Documentary History of Slavery in North America.* Athens: University of Georgia Press, 1976.

———. "The Domestication of Domestic Slavery." In *Slavery and Freedom,* edited by William W. Freehling, 18–36. New York: Oxford University Press, 1982.

Rosengarten, Theodore. "The *Southern Agriculturist* in an Age of Reform." In *Intellectual Life in Antebellum Charleston,* edited by Michael O'Brien and David Moltke-Hansen, 279–94. Knoxville: University of Tennessee Press, 1986.

Rothman, Adam. *Slave Country: American Expansion and the Origins of the Deep South.* Cambridge, Mass.: Harvard University Press, 2005.

Rozbicki, Michal Jan. *Culture and Liberty in the Age of the American Revolution.* Charlottesville: University of Virginia Press, 2011.

Rugemer, Edward Bartlett. *The Problem of Emancipation: The Caribbean Roots of the American Civil War.* Baton Rouge: Louisiana State University Press, 2008.

Rush, Benjamin. "An Address to the Inhabitants of the British Settlements in America upon Slavekeeping." In *American Political Writing during the Founding Era: 1760–1805,* 2 vols., edited by Charles S. Hyneman and Donald Lutz, 1:217–30. Indianapolis: Liberty Fund, 1983.

———. *Letters of Benjamin Rush.* Edited by L. H. Butterfield. 2 vols. Princeton, N.J.: Princeton University Press, 1951.

Ryden, David Beck. "Does Decline Make Sense? The West Indian Economy and the Abolition of the British Slave Trade." *Journal of Interdisciplinary History* 31, no. 3 (2001): 347–74.

Sadosky, Leonard J., Peter Nicolaisen, Peter S. Onuf, and Andrew J. O'Shaughnessy, eds. *Old World, New World: Europe and America in the Age of Jefferson.* Charlottesville: University of Virginia Press, 2010.

Said, Edward. *Orientalism.* New York: Pantheon Books, 1978.

Schaw, Janet. *Journal of a Lady of Quality: Being the Narrative of a Journey from Scotland to the*

West Indies, North Carolina, and Portugal, in the Years 1774 to 1776. Edited by Evangeline W. Andrews and Charles M. Andrews. New Haven, Conn.: Yale University Press, 1921.

Schermerhorn, Calvin. *Money over Mastery, Family over Freedom: Slavery in the Antebellum Upper South.* Baltimore: Johns Hopkins University Press, 2011.

Schoen, Brian. *The Fragile Fabric of Union: Cotton, Federal Politics, and the Global Origins of the Civil War.* Baltimore: Johns Hopkins University Press, 2009.

Schwartz, Suzanne. "Commerce, Civilization, and Christianity: The Development of the Sierra Leone Company." In *Liverpool and Transatlantic Slavery,* edited by David Richardson, Suzanne Schwartz, and Anthony Tibbles, 252–76. Liverpool: Liverpool University Press, 2007.

Scott, Julius S. "The Common Wind: Currents of Afro-American Communication in the Era of the Haitian Revolution." PhD diss., Duke University, 1986.

Seabrook, Whitemarsh. *A Concise View of the Critical Situation and Future Prospects of the Slaveholding States.* Charleston: A. E. Miller, 1825.

Semmel, Bernard. *The Rise of Free Trade Imperialism: Classical Political Economy, the Empire of Free Trade and Imperialism 1750–1850.* Cambridge: Cambridge University Press, 1970.

Shade, William G. *Democratizing the Old Dominion: Virginia and the Second Party System, 1824–1861.* Charlottesville: University Press of Virginia, 1996.

Shammas, Carole. "Anglo-American Household Government in Comparative Perspective." *William and Mary Quarterly,* 3rd ser., 52, no. 1 (January 1995): 104–44.

———. *A History of Household Government in America.* Charlottesville: University of Virginia Press, 2002.

Sharp, Granville. *A Short Sketch of Temporary Regulations (until Better Shall Be Proposed) for the Intended Settlement on the Grain Coast of Africa, near Sierra Leone.* London: H. Baldwin, 1786.

Sheller, Mimi. *Consuming the Caribbean: From Arawaks to Zombies.* London: Routledge, 2003.

Sheridan, Richard B. *Doctors and Slaves: A Medical and Demographic History of Slavery in the British West Indies, 1680–1834.* Cambridge: Cambridge University Press, 1985.

Shore, Laurence. *Southern Capitalists: The Ideological Leadership of an Elite, 1832–1885.* Chapel Hill: University of North Carolina Press, 1986.

Sidbury, James. *Becoming African in America: Race and Nation in the Early Black Atlantic.* Oxford: Oxford University Press, 2007.

———. *Ploughshares into Swords: Race, Rebellion, and Identity in Gabriel's Virginia, 1730–1810.* New York: Cambridge University Press, 1997.

Sinha, Manisha. *The Counterrevolution of Slavery: Politics and Ideology in Antebellum South Carolina.* Chapel Hill: University of North Carolina Press, 2000.

Slave Population, 1820–1840. Historical Census Browser, University of Virginia Geospatial and Statistical Data Center.

Smith, Adam. *An Inquiry into the Nature and Causes of the Wealth of Nations.* 2 vols. London: W. Strahan, 1778.

Sowerby, E. Millicent, comp. *Catalogue of the Library of Thomas Jefferson.* 5 vols. Washington, D.C.: Library of Congress, 1952–59.

Spahn, Hannah. *Thomas Jefferson, Time, and History.* Charlottesville: University of Virginia Press, 2011.

Spengler, Joseph A. "Population Doctrine US-I: Anti-Malthus." *Journal of Political History* 41 (August 1933): 433–67.

———. "Population Doctrine US-II: Malthusians." *Journal of Political Economy* 41 (October 1933): 639–72.

———. "Population Theory in the Antebellum South." *Journal of Southern History* 2 (August 1936): 360–89.

Stanton, Lucia C. "Thomas Jefferson: Planter and Farmer." In *A Companion to Thomas Jefferson,* edited by Francis D. Cogliano, 253–70. Malden, Mass.: Wiley-Blackwell, 2012.

———. *"Those Who Labor for My Happiness": Slavery at Thomas Jefferson's Monticello.* Charlottesville: University of Virginia Press, 2012.

Stephen, James. *Slavery in the British West India Colonies Delineated, as It Exists in Both Law and Practice, and Compared with the Slavery of Other Countries, Antient and Modern.* 2 vols. London: Saunders and Benning, 1830.

Stern, Philip. "'Rescuing the Age from a Charge of Ignorance': Gentility, Knowledge, and the British Exploration of Africa in the Later Eighteenth Century." In *A New Imperial History: Culture, Identity and Modernity in Britain and the Empire, 1660–1840,* edited by Kathleen Wilson, 115–35. Cambridge: Cambridge University Press, 2004.

Stockdale, Eric. *'Tis Treason My Good Man! Four Revolutionary Presidents and a Piccadilly Bookshop.* New Castle, Del.: Oak Knoll Press, 2005.

Sussman, Charlotte. *Consuming Anxieties: Consumer Protest, Gender and British Slavery, 1713–1833.* Stanford, Cal.: Stanford University Press, 2000.

Taylor, Alan. *The Internal Enemy: Slavery and War in Virginia, 1772–1832.* New York: Norton, 2013.

———. *William Cooper's Town: Power and Persuasion on the Frontier of the Early American Republic.* New York: Knopf, 1996.

Taylor, John. *Arator: Being a Series of Agricultural Essays, Practical and Political.* Edited by M. E. Bradford. 1818. Reprint Indianapolis: Liberty Fund, 1977.

Temperley, Howard. *British Antislavery, 1833–1870.* Columbia: University of South Carolina Press, 1972.

———. *White Dreams, Black Africa: The Antislavery Expedition to the River Niger, 1841–1842.* New Haven, Conn.: Yale University Press, 1991.

Thomas, Hugh. *The Slave Trade: The Story of the Atlantic Slave Trade, 1440–1870.* New York: Simon and Schuster, 1997.

Thompson, Alvin O. "Enslaved Children in Berbice, with Special Reference to the Government Slaves, 1803–31." In *In the Shadow of the Plantation: Caribbean History and Legacy,* edited by Alvin O. Thompson, 163–94. Kingston, Jamaica: Jan Randle Publishers, 2002.

Thornton, Henry. "General Outlines of a Settlement on the Tooth or Ivory Coast of Africa." In *The Papers of William Thornton,* edited by C. M. Harris, 38–41. Charlottesville: University Press of Virginia, 1995.

Thornton, John K. *Africa and Africans in the Making of the Atlantic World, 1400–1800.* Cambridge: Cambridge University Press, 1992.

Tise, Larry. *Proslavery: A History of the Defense of Slavery in America, 1701–1840.* Athens: University of Georgia Press, 1987.

Tomlins, Christopher L. *Freedom Bound: Law, Labor, and Civic Identity in Colonizing English America, 1580–1865.* New York: Cambridge University Press, 2010.

Travers, Robert. "Contested Despotism: Problems of Liberty in British India." In *Exclusionary Empire: English Liberty Overseas 1600–1900,* edited by Jack P. Greene, 191–219. Cambridge: Cambridge University Press, 2009.

————. *Ideology and Empire in Eighteenth-Century India: The British in Bengal.* Cambridge: Cambridge University Press, 2007.

Troutman, Phillip D. "Slave Trade and Sentiment in Antebellum Virginia." PhD diss., University of Virginia, 2000.

Tucker, St. George. *A Dissertation on Slavery: With a Proposal for the Gradual Abolition of It, in the State of Virginia.* Philadelphia: M. Carey, 1796.

Turnbull, Robert J. *The Crisis; or, Essay of the Usurpations of the Federal Government, by Brutus.* Charleston: A. E. Miller, 1827.

Turner, Mary. "Planter Profits and Slave Rewards: Amelioration Reconsidered." In *West Indies Accounts: Essays on the History of the British Caribbean and Atlantic Economy in Honor of Richard Sheridan,* edited by Richard B. Sheridan and Roderick A. McDonald, 232–52. Kingston, Jamaica: University of the West Indies Press, 1996.

U.S. Census, 1790–1830. Historical Census Browser, University of Virginia Geospatial and Statistical Data Center.

Van Cleve, George. *A Slaveholders' Union: Slavery, Politics, and the Constitution in the Early American Republic.* Chicago: University of Chicago Press, 2010.

————. "Somerset's Case and Its Antecedents in Imperial Perspective." *Law and History Review* 24, no. 3 (Fall 2006): 601–46.

Van Horne, John C. "Collective Benevolence and the Common Good in Franklin's Philanthropy." In *Reappraising Franklin: A Bicentennial Perspective,* edited by J. A. Leo Lamay, 434–35. Newark: University of Delaware Press, 1993.

————, ed. *Religious Philanthropy and Colonial Slavery.* Urbana: University of Illinois Press, 1985.

Virginia General Assembly. *Journal of the Senate of the Commonwealth of Virginia.* Richmond: Thomas Nicolson, 1801.

Virginia House of Delegates. *Journal of the House of Delegates of the Commonwealth of Virginia, Begun and Held at the Capitol, in the City of Richmond, on Monday, the Fifth Day of December, One Thousand Eight Hundred and Thirty-One.* Richmond: Thomas Ritchie, 1832.

Wadström, C. B. *An Essay on Colonization, Particularly Applied to the Western Coast of Africa.* London: Darton and Harvey, 1794.

Wahrman, Dror. *The Making of the Modern Self: Identity and Culture in Eighteenth Century England.* New Haven, Conn.: Yale University Press, 2005.

Walsh, Lorena S. "Plantation Management in the Chesapeake, 1620–1820." *Journal of Economic History* 49, no. 2 (1989): 393–406.

Walvin, James. "The Public Campaign in England against Slavery, 1787–1834." In *The Abolition of the Atlantic Slave Trade: Origins and Effects in Europe, Africa, and the Americas,* edited by David Eltis and James Walvin, 63–79. Madison: University of Wisconsin Press, 1981.

Ward, J. R. *British West Indian Slavery, 1750–1834: The Process of Amelioration.* Oxford: Clarendon Press, 1988.

————. "The Profitability of Sugar Planting in the British West Indies, 1650–1834." *Economic History Review* 31, no. 2 (1978): 197–213.

Watson, Karl. *The Civilised Island, Barbados: A Social History.* Bridgetown, Barbados: Graphic Printer, 1970.

Watts, David. *The West Indies: Patterns of Development, Culture and Environmental Change since 1492.* Cambridge: Cambridge University Press, 1987.

Webber, Thomas L. *Deep Like the Rivers: Education in the Slave Quarter Community, 1831–1865*. New York: Norton, 1978.

Whishaw, John. *The Journal of a Mission to the Interior of Africa, in the Year 1805. By Mungo Park. Together with Other Documents, Official and Private, Relating to the Same Mission. To Which Is Prefixed an Account of the Life of Mr. Park*. Philadelphia: Edward Earle, 1815.

White, José Maria Blanco. *Bosquejo del comercio de esclavos y reflexiones sobre este tráfico considerado moral, política y cristianamente*. Seville, Spain: Alfar, 1999.

Wilberforce, William. *The Speech, of William Wilberforce, Esq. Representative of the County of York, on Wednesday, the 13th Day of May, 1789, on the Question of the Abolition of the Slave Trade*. London: Logographic Press, 1789.

Wilkins, Joe Bassette, Jr. "Window on Freedom: The South's Response to the Emancipation of Slaves in the British West Indies, 1833–1861." PhD diss., University of South Carolina, 1977.

Williams, Eric. *Capitalism and Slavery*. 1944. Reprint London: Andre Deutsch, 1964.

———. "Laissez Faire, Sugar and Slavery." *Political Science Quarterly* 58, no. 1 (March 1943): 67–85.

Wilson, Ellen Gibson. *Thomas Clarkson: A Biography*. New York: St. Martin's Press, 1990.

Wolf, Eva Sheppard. *Race and Liberty in the New Nation: Emancipation in Virginia from the Revolution to Nat Turner's Rebellion*. Baton Rouge: Louisiana State University Press, 2006.

Wood, Marcus. *Blind Memory: Visual Representations of Slavery in England and America, 1780–1865*. Manchester: Manchester University Press, 2000.

Wood, Peter H. *Black Majority: Negroes in Colonial South Carolina from 1670 through the Stono Rebellion*. New York: Knopf, 1974.

Wyatt-Brown, Bertram. "Modernizing Southern Slavery: The Proslavery Argument Reinterpreted." In *Region, Race, and Reconstruction: Essays in Honor of C. Vann Woodward*, edited by J. Morgan Kousser and James M. McPherson, 27–49. New York: Oxford University Press, 1982.

Wyly-Jones, Susan. "The 1835 Anti-Abolition Meetings in the South: A New Look at the Controversy over the Abolition Postal Campaign." *Civil War History* 47 (December 2001): 289–309.

Yates, John Ashton. *Colonial Slavery: Letters to the Rt. Hon. William Huskisson (Pres. of the Board of Trade)*. Reprint edition. Whitefish, Mont.: Kessinger Publishing, 2010.

Young, Arthur. *The Farmer's Letters to the People of England: Containing the Sentiments of a Practical Husbandman*. London: W. Nicoll, 1778.

Young, Jeffry Robert. "Domesticating Slavery: The Ideological Formation of the Master Class in the Deep South, from Colonization to 1837." PhD diss., Emory University, 1996.

———. *Domesticating Slavery: The Master Class in Georgia and South Carolina, 1670–1837*. Chapel Hill: University of North Carolina Press, 1999.

———, ed. *Proslavery and Sectional Thought in the Early South, 1740–1829: An Anthology*. Chapel Hill: University of North Carolina Press, 2006.

INDEX

Italicized page numbers refer to illustrations.

coartación, 8. *See also* manumission

Cocke, John Hartwell: amelioration and, 65–66, 70–72; Bremo, 58, 65, 67, 70–71, 72–74; colonization ideas, 60, 67–69, 70, 232n3; Dew and, 58–59, 60, 75–76, 77–80, 85–87; emancipation, 67–69, 70–74; Hopewell, 58, 74; Jefferson and, 58, 66, 85; New Hope, 58, 74, 99, 113, 114; progress, 58, 67, 74, 87; religion, 65–66, 71–72; summary of views, 58–59

coerced labor, 216, 222

Coles, Edward, 34, 35, 63

Colonial Office, 187, 216

colonies: Dutch, 191; French, 127, 161–62, 179; French and British, comparison of, 161–62; Spanish, 8

colonization: antislavery amelioration and, 12, 23, 26–27, 65–66, 72–74; cost of, 39, 67, 73, 78–80, 85; debates over, 59, 64, 135; emancipation and, 65–66, 72–74; ex post nati scheme, 39, 42, 44, 46; formative experience (*see under* settlement); frontier areas and, 76, 95, 108, 112, 121; Jefferson and, 7, 26–27, 29, 35, 37–42; Liberia, 71, 72–74, 78, 85, 87; nationhood and, 17, 43, 47; obstacles to, 12, 68, 77–79, 135; slave response to, 73–74, 135

commerce, 49, 112, 203, 231n75; civilization and, 108, 112–15, 120–21, 157, 167; Laurens and, 99, 101–3, 108, 119–20

Condorcet, Marquis de, 7–8, 11, 226n24

Congress, 36, 44, 78, 136, 213

conspiracies, slave, 144–45; Prosser, 40, 42, 229n40; Vesey, 132–33, 136. *See also* rebellions, slave

Constitution (U.S.), 35, 138

constitutional rights, 26, 33, 35, 78, 134–35, 138

coolies, 208, 214, 222

Cooper River, 91, 93, 99, 115

Cooper, Thomas, 76, 128, 130

Copley, John Singleton, *Henry Laurens*, 116, 117

corn, 231n75; agricultural improvement and, 49, 64, 108, 116; slaves and, 50, 72, 149

Corn Laws, 126, 185, 206, 222

Cornwallis, Charles (Lord Cornwallis), 31–32

corporal punishment, 52, 114–15, 148–49, 215

Cort, Frederick, 190, 193, 197, 198, 202

cotton: colonization and, 73–74, 85; culture, 89, 121, 137; economics of, 94, 146, 147, 203–4, 220; Sea Island, 147; slaves and, 85–86, 137, 212–13

Couper, James Hamilton, 147–50, 240n60; Hopeton Plantation, 147–50, 240n60

Court of Policy, 192

crop diversification, 49, 108, 112, 147, 176

Cropper, James, 180, 183, 204–7

crop prices: amelioration and, 49, 163, 176; cotton, 85–86; grain, 49; sugar, 148, 163, 183, 205, 207; tobacco, 68–69

Cuba, 183, 185, 199, 207, 222

customs, British, 102, 166

debt, 107, 233n39, 237n67; to British, 49, 69, 89, 93, 106

Declaration of Independence, 16, 30, 130

Demerara, 187; absenteeism, effects of, 196–98, 202; amelioration and, 186, 190–91, 208–9

Demerara revolt, 44, 162, 180, 191–96, 194–95

demographics, 15, 18–19, 184, 199, 217

deportation, 40–43, 54–55, 63, 77–78, 115; cost of, 63–64

DeSaussure, Henry, 120, 121

despotism. *See* British "tyranny"

Dessalines, Jean-Jacques, 127

Dew, Thomas: amelioration and, 21, 58, 75, 80–81, 87; Cocke compared to, 20–21, 58, 76, 85, 87; colonization, 58, 75–76, 78–80, 85; diffusion, 58, 79–80, 84–85, 87; influence, 77, 87; modernity, 32, 76; "positive good" thesis, 57, 232n3; progress, 75–76, 81–83; responses to, 75, 77, 78; slavery, 58–59, 75–76, 82–84, 87

diaspora, African, 39, 73

diffusion, 32, 45–47, 89, 131, 230n60; Alabama, 72, 74; Jefferson and, 29, 46; market forces and, 21, 85; population control through, 44–45; western U.S., 21, 39; western Virginia, 78 disease, 95; slave deaths from, 31, 97–98, 166, 187, 197

divided sovereignty, 19; federative systems, 17, 19, 105, 185, 203, 246n68; states' rights, 137–38, 239n38

Dolben Act of 1788, 167, 179

Drayton, William, 106–7, 108, 112, 115

Dundas, Henry, 161, 162

Dutch, 103, 106, 170, 191

duties, 148, 160, 182, 185, 205, 207

East India Company, 181, 203, 204

East Indies: free labor in, 184–85, 204, 207; sugar market, 184, 204–7

economy: abolition and, 4, 183, 212–15, 222–23, 241n6; amelioration and, 17–18, 48, 163, 176; development in the South, 220; depression, 126, 146; duties, 148, 160, 182, 185, 205, 207; economic oppression, 79, 103–4, 199; protectionism, 83, 180–81, 182–86, 188, 204–7; slavery and, 69, 94, 106, 220–21; South Carolina, 89, 107, 146, 147, 237n66; tariffs, 79, 137–38, 148, 203–4, 206; Virginia, 48–49, 64, 68–69, 85–86, 220; West Indies, 22, 110, 177, 212–16, 222, 243n9. See also free trade

Edgehill Plantation, 61–62, 64

education, 6, 7, 27, 143, 145, 215; literacy, 7, 137, 144–45, 189

Edwards, Bryan, 21, 155, 163–64; abolition and, 162, 163, 166, 179; Africans, civilization of, 21, 155, 158, 164, 167–70, 172–73; commonality with Laurens, 157, 182; emancipation, 174–75; ethnography of slaves, 164, 172–73; history of West Indies, 155, 162–63; Long, response to, 171–72; proslavery amelioration, 21, 157, 162, 163, 173–77; reform of trade, 163, 166, 178, 180; slavery, 21, 155, 157–58, 164

elites, 49, 69, 70; amelioration and, 26, 58, 66, 89, 94

emancipation: colonization and, 39, 42, 65–66, 72–74; compensation to slave owners, 35, 43, 63–64, 78, 208; constitutionality and, 26, 35–36; effect on empire, 127, 208–9, 214–16; gaining of, 70–74; happiness and,

43, 82, 116; immediatism, 2–3, 7–9, 11, 160–61, 226n29; manumission, 4–5, 6–7, 71–74, 91, 119; planters in favor of, 26–27, 29, 67–69, 91–92, 118; planters' rejection of, 22, 174–75, 181–82, 207; progress and, 26–27, 87, 207–8; violence and, 174, 192.

Emancipation Proclamation (U.S.), 16

emigration, 34, 38, 79, 83, 110, 133

English Poor Laws, 128, 129

Enlightenment, 2, 8, 11, 16, 78; abolition and, 75, 182, 216; antislavery amelioration and, 65, 68, 226n30; proslavery amelioration and, 56, 226n30; rejection of, 75, 78, 176

entail, 32, 69, 118, 120, 131

equality, 12–13, 236n28; corporate, 16, 32, 56, 103–4, 130, 219; Enlightenment idea of, 65, 78, 130–31, 182, 238n20

Equiano, Olaudah, 5–6

Essequibo, 181, 191

ethnographies, slave, 164, 172–73

exceptionalism (U.S.), 11, 28

Execution of Rebels on the Parade Ground in Cummingsburgh, 194–95

exile, 40–41, 42, 55, 115. *See also* deportation

expansion, 121, 206; abolition and, 163–64, 201; amelioration and, 17–18, 73, 209, 211; debates about, 181, 184–85, 213; proslavery amelioration and, 124, 151, 177; slavery as facilitator of, 56, 105, 121, 157–58, 186; slavery as impediment to, 59, 74, 85, 87, 188; U.S., 38, 47–48, 57–58, 76, 220

Fairfax, Ferdinando, 27

families, 215; happiness and, 100, 116, 118; organization of slaves into, 52–53, 71, 149, 217; separation at auction, 100, 111, 118, 221; slaves as part of, 48, 142, 218. *See also* plantation households

farmers, 38, 47–49, 55–56, 94, 109

farms, small-scale, 47, 54, 84, 94

Faulkner, Charles, 63

federal government, 78, 83, 134–35, 137–38; role in abolition and slave trade, 26, 33, 35–36, 45

federative systems, 17, 19, 105, 185, 203,

246n68; U.S. Federalists, 25, 45–46. *See also* government

Foreign Slave Trade Act, 179

Franklin, Benjamin, 1, 6, 7, 106

free blacks, autonomy of, 137, 174

free trade: abolition and, 167, 183–84, 216, 244n10; modernity and, 22, 76, 84, 87, 180–81, 201; proslavery views of, 182–84, 203–8, 238n16

French Republicanism, 28

French Revolution, 12, 28, 126–28, 130

French Terror. *See* French Revolution

Fugitive Slave Laws, 200

Gabriel's Rebellion. *See* Prosser conspiracy

Garrison, William Lloyd, 136

George III, 29–32, 35, 92, 102, 104

Gibbon, Edward, 168

Gibson, Gideon, 110–11

Giles, William, 44–45

Gladstone, John, 180–81, 243n1; absentee planter, 186, 196–97, 198, 201–2; Cropper, argument with, 180–81, 205–7; Demerara plantation, 191, 193, 196, 243n2; emancipation, 181–82, 207; "Gladstone slave-trade," 208; politician, 180, 181, 183, 189; progress, views on, 182, 207–8, 209; progressive planter, 180, 182, 185, 186, 190–91; proslavery amelioration, 182–83, 189–90, 196, 201, 208–9; protectionism, 180, 182, 183, 207–8; religion, 22, 190–91, 193

Gladstone, Robertson, 196–98

government: colonial, 162; constitution, 35, 138; divided sovereignty, 19; provincial, 102, 162, 175, 185, 187–90; Regulator movement, 111, 237n48; South Carolina, 102, 134, 137–38; Virginia, 40, 47, 60, 61–63, 77; West Indies, 175, 185. *See also* federative systems; Parliament

gradualism, 5, 7–9, 26, 68; Burkean, 4, 123; definition of, 1–2, 4, 225n4. *See also* immediatism

Granger, George Sr., 52, 231n84

Gurley, Richard Randolph, 75

Gwynn, Charles, 96–98

Haiti, 132, 162, 182. *See also* Saint Domingue

Haitian revolution, 127, 162, 226n36

Hamilton, James, Jr., 132

Hamilton, Paul, 121

Hammond, James Henry, 213–14, 217–19, 221, 247n5

happiness, 10, 43, 82–83, 140; amelioration and, 15, 48, 111, 138–42, 162, 202; families and, 100, 116, 118; population and, 55, 61; protection and, 116, 131–32, 138–42; religion and, 65–66, 145–46

Harper, William: progress, views on, 123, 126–27, 142; proslavery amelioration, 21, 123, 124, 138–43; response to revolution, 123, 125–28; scientific racism, 124–25

Harrison, Jesse Burton, 59, 75

Hartford Convention, 138

Hayne, Senator Robert Y., 134

Hemings, James, 52, 231n92

Hemings, Martin, 53, 231n92

Hemings, Robert, 53, 231n92

Hemings, Sally, 37, 229n32, 231n92

Hemingses, 55, 231n92

Hemmings, John, 53

Henry, Patrick, 26–27

Henry Laurens, 117

heterogeneity, 37, 78; incorporation, 15, 27, 36, 37, 101, 110; interracial relationships, 37, 110, 218, 229n32

homogeneity, 29, 37–39, 42–43, 47–48, 78

Hopeton Plantation, 147–50, 240n60

Hopewell, 58, 74

households. *See* plantation households

House of Assembly (Virginia), 60, 61, 63, 77

House of Commons, 126, 160, 165

housing, plantation, 51, 149; building materials, 53, 71, 149, 240n65; organization into family units, 52–53, 71, 149, 217

humane treatment, 48, 52, 148–49, 175–77, 217

humanitarianism, 14, 123, 158–59, 188, 196; abolition and, 203, 204, 240n3; resident planters and, 198, 200; self-interest and, 53, 98, 150, 163, 176, 214; West Indies and, 203, 204, 205, 222

human rights, 11, 36, 136, 158, 223

immediatism, 2–3, 7–9, 11, 160–61, 226n29

imperial crisis, 23, 30, 89, 102–3, 105

imperial policy: expansion, 180–85, 204–9, 213–17; protectionism, 180, 181, 182–86, 188, 204–7. See also British "tyranny"

imperial systems, reform of, 105, 153, 160, 181, 185

incentives, 52, 71, 116, 147–49, 176, 215

incorporation, 15, 27, 36, 37, 101, 110; heterogeneity, 37, 78; interracial relationships, 37, 110, 218, 229n32

indentured servitude, 7, 208, 209

India: colonization, new model of, 184, 204–5, 221; free labor, source of, 183, 184, 204, 208–9; indentured labor, source of, 208–9, 222; sugar market, 183, 184, 203, 204

indigo, 97–98, 107

inferiority of races, 33, 124–25, 130, 193

infrastructure, improvements to, 83–84

insurgency. See rebellions, slave

insurgents, deportation of, 40–42, 63

insurrection. See rebellions, slave

International states system. See Atlantic family of nations

interracial relationships, 37, 110, 218, 229n32; heterogeneity, 37, 78; incorporation, 15, 27, 36, 37, 101, 110

Izard, Ralph, 94, 106–7

Jamaica, 161, 155, 157, 222; abolition bill, response to, 170–71; amelioration in, 176; economy, 176–77; slave trade and, 97–98, 166, 172

James River, 52, 65, 67

James River and Kanawha Canal project, 66, 83

Jay, John, 6, 7, 106

Jefferson, Thomas: abolition, constitutionality of, 26, 33, 35–36; Africans as separate nation, 33, 35, 38, 55; amelioration, 20, 26, 28, 48–56; Declaration of Independence, 30–31; "ex post nati" scheme, 39, 42, 44, 46; incorporation, 36, 37, 55; international system, 28, 228n9;

nationhood, 27–28, 36, 38, 43; Notes on the State of Virginia, 37, 42, 81; progress, views on, 26–27, 29, 37, 55–56, 57; repatriation, 26, 27, 29, 37–40, 43–44; slavery as Old World, 25–29, 30, 32, 35, 46. See also Monticello

July Revolution of 1830, 126

Kanawha Company, 66, 83

King, Rufus, 41, 133

labor, Asian, 188, 208–9, 214, 216, 222

labor, free, 78–79, 84–85, 159, 188, 244n14; economics of, 4, 129–30, 182–85, 206, 216; expansion, role in, 185–86, 211, 213, 214; free trade and, 22, 182–83, 203–7, 216; modernity and, 76, 84, 201, 216; slavery, similarities to, 185, 204–5, 208–9; southerners' attitudes toward, 76, 109, 129–30, 139–40, 223

labor, slave: efficiency, 49–50, 100, 147–49, 176–77, 196–97; task system, 89, 95, 148, 173–74

Lafayette, Marquis de, 46, 230n62

Laurens, Henry, 91, 103–4, 116, 117, 236n25; amelioration and, 94, 100, 110, 116; commerce and, 99, 101–3, 108, 119–20; emancipation and, 91–92, 118; Jefferson and, 92, 110, 111; Mepkin Plantation, 91, 116, 118–19, 120, 234n1; nationhood, 92, 93–94, 103–6; plantations, 99–100, 115, 120, 235n2; progress, 92–94, 103, 105, 157; Rattray Green, 93, 113–14; slavery, attitude toward, 21, 91–92, 99, 232n2; slave trade, 92, 95, 98–99, 106; Success, 180, 191–93, 196–97

laws: free blacks, 64, 137; slave, 137, 175, 187–88, 198, 200; slave trade, 160, 164–67

Legaré, Hugh Swinton, 128, 130, 151

Legaré, John D., 146–48, 150

Lewis, Mathew "Monk," 202

Liberia, 71, 72–74, 78, 85, 87

liberty, 10, 82, 131, 211, 219; definitions of, 82, 128, 140, 219, 238n20; Jefferson and, 27–28, 38, 47, 55; slave, 34–35, 40, 158

Lindo, Alexander, 166

literacy, 7, 137, 144–45, 189

Locke, John, 11, 33, 34, 229n23, 232n2

London Missionary Society, 192, 196

Long, Edward, 161, 171, 172

Macaulay, Thomas Babington, 221, 225n6, 248n25

Macaulay, Zachary, 41, 204

Madison, James, 68, 74, 77–78

Malthus, Thomas, 61, 78, 184, 199, 230n6

manufacturing, 50, 108, 147, 155, 220

manumission, 4–5, 6–7, 71–74, 91, 119; *coartación*, 8. *See also* emancipation

martial law, 192

Martin, Samuel, 176

Massey, Samuel, 118–19

master-slave relationship, 32, 202–3, 240n46; amelioration and, 17, 203; tyranny of, 81–82, 111, 115

Mathews, John, 165

Mauritius, 184, 198, 207

melioration. *See* amelioration

Mepkin Abbey, 91, 234n1

Mepkin Plantation, 91, 116, 118–19, 120, 234n1

Middle Passage, 38, 39, 164, 172, 173

Miller, Lewis, "Slave Trader, Sold to Tennessee," 86

missionaries, 71, 143, 145, 185, 186, 190; rebellion and, 192, 193, 196, 198

Missouri Compromise, 138

Missouri crisis of 1819, 45, 47

modernity, 16, 105, 124, 157, 159; slavery and, 20, 28, 87, 182, 238n3

monarchy: slavery as vestige of, 29, 30, 92, 94, 104; tyranny of, 30, 92, 126, 130

Monroe, James, 40, 68

Monticello, 50, *51*; agriculture, 49–50, 230n69, 233n28; Mulberry Row, 50, *51*, 52, 55; slaves, 52–53, 54–55, 229n32, 231n84, 231n92

morals: slave, 14, 70–72, 110, 142–44, 193; slave owner, 13, 17, 81–82, 141–44, 188

Morgan, Edmund, 13

mortality, slave, 134, 165–67, 197, 199, 222

Murray, John (Lord Dunmore), 31–32, 192

Murray, William (Chief Justice Lord Mansfield), 101, 131

Napoleonic Wars, 28, 179, 188, 191, 203

nation, definitions of, 12, 37

nationhood, American, 18, 27–28, 38, 48, 129; experiment in, 12, 19–20, 36–38, 135; Jefferson and, 27–28, 36, 38, 43; slavery and, 92–95, 106, 135–36, 151, 235n6

Nat Turner rebellion. *See* Turner rebellion

Negro Laws, 110, 116

Negro Seaman's Act, 137

New Hope, 58, 74, 99, 113, 114

Newton, John, 158, 177–78, 179

Nicholas, John, 44–45

Niger River, 164, 168–69, 222

nonimportation resolutions, 102

Notes on the State of Virginia, 37, 42, 81

Nullification Crisis, 138

obeah, 144

"Ode," 155

Office of Protector of Slaves, 198. *See also* ameliorative laws, enforcement of

Official Report of the Vesey Conspiracy, 132–33

Old World–New World binary, 29, 36, 104–5

Oswald, Richard, 95, 96, 99, 102, 118

overseers, 187, 192, 197, 246n65; African American, 5–6, 52, 118–19, 150, 231n84; Frederick Cort, 190, 193, 197, 198, 202; problems with, 52, 130, 196–98, 202; relationship to planters, 52, 113. *See also* planters, absentee; planters, resident

Panic of 1819, 45, 146

Park, Mungo, 164, 168, 169

Parliament, 104; oppressive policies of, 30, 102–3, 126; planters as MPs, 21, 164, 179, 183, 193; provincial legislatures and, 30, 35, 162, 185, 187–90; reform, 126, 166–67, 187–88; regulation by, 21, 160, 164–65, 167; resistance to, 163, 190. *See also* British Emancipation Bill paternalism, 139, 176, 214, 235n4, 247n7

patriarchs, 15, 17, 227n42, 244n15; Cocke, 70–72; Dew, 81–82; ideal of, 53–54, 81–82; Jefferson, 48, 53–55; Laurens, 113–16, 120; resident, 186, 197–98, 218; responsibilities of, 81–82, 113–18. *See also* paternalism; plantation households

peasant labor. *See* labor, free

Peterloo Massacre of 1819, 126

Philadelphia, 6, 52

Pinckney, Charles, 45, 94

Pinckney, Charles Cotesworth, 121, 134, 144

Pinckney, Thomas, 1

Pitt, William, 165

plantation households, 17, 139, 218, 244n15; dependents, 17, 48, 81–82, 113, 131, 203. *See also* patriarchs

plantations: civilization and, 114, 150, 185–86, 237n52; frontier, 18, 76, 95, 108, 114–15, 227n54; model, 176, 185–86; networks, 112, 113, 131; rational management, 54, 146–50, 230n69; sexual impropriety, 74, 114

planters, absentee, 22–23, 113, 187, 190; amelioration and, 54, 189, 196, 198, 202, 218; Parliament and, 189, 244n28; problems with, 74, 196–98, 201, 202

planters, resident, 54, 200–202; absentee planters, contrast with, 186, 196, 198; amelioration and, 114–15, 120, 186, 198, 202–3

Pleasants, Robert, 34–35

political economics, 61, 76, 140, 184, 188, 237n66; slavery and, 183–84, 188

Poor Laws, 128, 129

population: happiness and, 55, 61; modernity and, 28, 212, 214; progress and, 61, 76, 184; self-reproducing, 33, 61, 184, 212, 214

population, slave, 56, 229n43, 246n59; Alabama, 220; comparisons, 212; control of, 44, 79, 85; decline in, 199, 216; discrepancy between white and black populations, 60, 62, 96, 191; increase in, 78, 96, 121, 176, 200; proslavery amelioration and, 140, 176, 221; South Carolina, 89, 121; Virginia, 44, 60, 62, 85, 232n10

Porteus, Beilby, 8

"positive good" thesis, 57, 232n3. *See also* Dew, Thomas

postemancipation, 110, 212–18

Postlethwayt, Malachy, 1, 3, 4, 6, 225n10

postrevolution America, 26, 94, 104, 236n39; economy, 108, 237n66

Price, Richard, 104, 105, 116

primogeniture, 32, 69, 118, 131. *See also* entail

Prioleau, John, 132

Prioleau, Peter, 132

progress, 57, 124–25; ameliorated slavery and, 26, 123, 142, 182, 209; definitions of, 19–20, 127; emancipation and, 26–27, 87, 207–8; freedom and, 126–27; homogeneity and, 37; planters' conceptions of, 6, 9–10, 13, 19–20, 151 (*see also individual planters*); shifting ideas of, 93, 103, 105; slavery antithetical to, 11–12, 19–20, 25–27, 29, 58–59, 93–94; slavery as facilitator of, 56, 75–76, 81–83, 92–93, 157. *See also* Enlightenment; stadial theory

property, private: amelioration and, 162, 188; government and, 26, 35–36, 135, 188; rights, 12–13, 103, 131; sanctity of, 19, 33, 35–36; slaves as, 7–8, 45, 139, 141

Prosser conspiracy, 40, 42, 229n40

Prosser, Gabriel, 40

protectionism, 83, 180–81, 182–86, 188, 204–7. *See also* free trade; tariffs

provincial governments, 162, 175, 185, 187–90

provincialism, 171, 242n40

provision-ground system, 174, 175

punishment, slave: corporal, 52, 114–15, 148–49, 215; mitigation of, 116, 120, 147, 149, 176–77, 189; violence or running away, 54–55, 114–15, 119, 149. *See also* incentives

Quakers, 1, 5, 34, 205

race ratios, 60, 62, 96, 191

races, mixing of: heterogeneity, 37, 78; incorporation, 15, 27, 36, 37, 101, 110; interracial relationships, 37, 110, 218, 229n32

race war, 31, 37, 85, 133; amelioration and, 80–81, 111; fears of, 59, 61–62, 80, 132, 136–37

radicalism, 137–38, 226n36, 226n38

slavery, domestication of, 14–15, 144–46, 150–51, 218–19, 233n41, 240n46; resident planters and, 52–56, 70–72, 80–82, 113–20, 139–42, 186

slaves: brutality toward, 221, 227n54, 248n24; "captive nation," 26, 33, 55, 81, 228n2; classes of, 53–55, 70, 118–19, 233n40; commodity, 64–65, 69, 79, 85, 233n40; common identity of, 38–39, 173; compensation for loss of, 35, 43, 63–64, 78, 208; disease, 31, 95, 97–98, 166, 187, 197; gender ratios, 149, 166, 167, 200; happiness of, 82, 131–32, 140; homeland of, 39–40, 42, 73–74, 78; hospitals, 149, 163, 191; loyalty, 40, 53–55, 118–19, 150, 229n41; material needs, 71, 113, 115, 149; medical care, 149, 163, 175, 188, 191, 202; memories of Africa, 164, 172–74; nationhood and, 47, 48; organization into families, 52–53, 71, 149, 217; population (*see* population, slave); property (*see under* property, private); protection of, 81, 116, 139–42, 144–45, 175, 179; recruitment by British, 31, 115, 119; religious instruction of (*see under* religion); value of, 69, 78, 97–98, 233n40; Virginia's biggest export, 45, 60, 64–65, 86–87

slave ships, 96–98, 136, 165–67, 177; conditions, 97, 165, 209; reform, 166–67

slave trade, 30, *86*, 155, *156*; abolition, 33, 112, 120–21, 153, 159; civilization and, 98, 155, 157; commercial importance, 3, 155, 157; expansion and, 3, 163; extent of, 155, 157; illegal, 187; origins of, 168–70; profits, 79, 96, 98, 99; quarantine, 97–98; regulation of, 21, 160, 164–65, 167; risks, 96–99, 235n22. *See also* slave ships

slave trade, domestic, 79, 80, 85–86, 89; population regulator, 60, 79, 80, 85, 220; profits of, 60, 79, 80, 85; rise of, 23, 45. *See also* diffusion

slave trade, transatlantic, 120–21, 155–57, 167–68, 183–84, 212; abolition of, 6, 8–9; British system, 32, 35, 94, 104, 106; civilization and, 20

Smith, Adam, 1, 3–4, 84, 182, 206

Smith, John, 192–93, 196

Society for Effecting the Abolition of the Slave Trade, 158

Society of West India Merchants and Planters, 189

Somerset v. Stewart, 101, 131, 235n2

Southampton County, 59, 72, 77. *See also* Turner rebellion

South Carolina: economy, 89, 102, 107, 146, 147, 237n66; legislation, 137; Lowcountry, 95, 108, 112, 137, 240n65; Lowcountry colonization, 133–34; Lowcountry economy, 89, 94, 97–98, 106–7; population, 96, 121, 125, 138; slaves and, 120–21, 144–45; Upcountry, 92, 108–9, 121, 133, 137

South Carolina Agricultural Society, 108

South Carolina Association, 137

Southern Agriculturist, 146

Southern Review, 128

sovereignty, provincial, 138, 162, 185. *See also* federative systems

stadial theory, 108, 112–15, 213; agriculture, 82–84, 141; commerce, 105, 127. *See also* Enlightenment

"state of war," 11, 17, 111, 228n2; Dew on, 75, 77, 80–81, 85, 87; Jefferson on, 26–27, 33–34

states' rights, 137–38, 239n38

statistics: civilization and, 184, 212; slavery debate and, 15, 19, 61, 199

St. Domingo. *See* Saint Domingue

Steele, Joshua, 202

Stephen, James, 179, 199

St. Kitts, 158, 159, 163, 191, 222

Stothard, Thomas, *Voyage of the Sable Venus*, 155, *156*

Success (plantation), 180, 191–93, 196–97

sugar: economics, 19, 148, 153, 185, 203, 207, 212; industry, 161, 214, 216, 222; labor and, 183, 184, 199, 204

Suli-bul-Ali, 150

Summary View of the Rights of British America, 30, 35

tariffs, 79, 137–38, 148, 203–4, 206. *See also* protectionism task system, 89, 95, 148, 173–74

taxes: British, 103, 104, 237n48; colonization and, 63, 67; Corn Laws, 126, 185; free blacks, 131

Taylor, John, 27, 266

Teale, Isaac, "Ode," 155

temperance, 71–72, 73, 74, 176

tenant farmers, 34–35

Thornton, Henry, 41

Tidewater region, 31, 63, 68, 69

tobacco, 49, 68–69, 233n28

Tories, 128, 181, 183, 189

trade with Britain, 50, 100, 179

treaties, 36, 44, 106, 107, 187

treatment, slave: families, separation of, 100, 111, 118, 221; hospitals, 149, 163, 191; material needs, 71, 113, 115, 149; medical care, 149, 163, 175, 188, 191, 202; rations, 149. *See also* housing, plantation; punishment, slave

Treaty of Paris, 106, 187

Turner rebellion, 59, 77; aberration, 59–60, 80; portent of race war, 61, 80; response to, 59–60, 71, 137, 143–44. *See also* Southampton County

Vassa, Gustavus. *See* Equiano, Olaudah

Vesey conspiracy, 132–34, 137, 143–44

Vesey, Denmark, 132

violence: between slaves, 54–55, 192; master-slave relationship, 32, 33, 55, 228n2, 240n46; toward slaves, 52, 114–16, 147, 149, 175, 189, 215

Virginia: economy, 48, 68, 69; government, 40, 47, 60, 61–63, 77; Legislature, 40, 47, 60, 62–63, 77; "mother of slavery," 45, 60, 64–65, 86–87; politics, 62–63, 64, 66, 232n8; slave trade in, 80, 228n13

Voyage of the Sable Venus, 155, 156

wages, 69, 116, 174, 215

Walker, David, 125, 136

War of 1812, 31, 77

Washington, George, 40, 49

western U.S.: colonization to, 39–40, 47, 78; diffusion to, 44–45; expansion into, 38, 47–48, 57–58, 76, 220

West India Committee, 189, 193, 205

West Indies: colonization to, 7, 26, 39–41; economy, 22, 110, 177, 212–16, 222, 243n9; government, 175, 185; Office of Protector of Slaves, 198; postemancipation conditions in, 127, 208, 214–16

wheat, 49–50, 53, 64, 72, 231n75

Whigs, 189

White, José Blanco, 8

Wilberforce, William, 158, 160–61, 174, 187

Recent Books in the JEFFERSONIAN AMERICA SERIES